1988
17th EDITION
THE COMPLETE HANDBOOK OF
PRO HOCKEY

D1475009

EXCITING SPORTS ACTION

1988
17th EDITION
THE COMPLETE HANDBOOK OF
PRO HOCKEY

EDITED BY ZANDER HOLLANDER

A SIGNET BOOK
NEW AMERICAN LIBRARY

ACKNOWLEDGMENTS

Ron Hextall evoked memories of Hextalls past when he excited the hockey world as a Flyer rookie last season. But he broke with family tradition when he became the first Hextall goaltender in the NHL and almost brought Philadelphia the Stanley Cup. Here's to all the Hextalls!

Marking the 17th edition of *The Complete Handbook of Pro Hockey*, we acknowledge contributing editor Eric Compton, the writers listed on the contents page and Mark Ruskie, Steve Wisniewski, Richard Rossiter, Stu Hackel, Belinda Lerner, the NHL team publicity directors, Dot Gordineer and Beri Greenwald of Libra Graphics and the people at Westchester Book Composition.

Zander Hollander

PHOTO CREDITS: Cover—Paul Bereswell; back cover—Bruce Bennett. Inside photos—Bruce Bennett, Robert Shaver, Wide World and the NHL team photographers.

SIGNET TRADEMARK REG. U.S. PAT. OFF. AND FOREIGN COUNTRIES REGISTERED TRADEMARK—MARCA REGISTRADA
HECHO EN CHICAGO, U.S.A.

SIGNET, SIGNET CLASSIC, MENTOR, ONYX, PLUME, MERIDIAN AND NAL BOOKS are published by NAL PENGUIN, 1633 Broadway, New York, New York 10019

First Printing, November 1987

1 2 3 4 5 6 7 8 9

PRINTED IN THE UNITED STATES OF AMERICA

CONTENTS

Editor's Note: The material herein includes trades and rosters up to final printing deadline.

THE HEXTALL LEGACY

By RAY DIDINGER

For the Hextalls and the Philadelphia Flyers, it wasn't exactly love at first sight.

"The Hextalls?" said Bill Barber, the former Flyer winger, now assistant coach. "I hated the S.O.B.s."

"I don't think there's one of them [Flyers] that I didn't fight," Bryan Hextall said. "I fought three of 'em in one night."

"The Hextalls were tough and nasty," said Hall of Famer Bobby Clarke, now the Flyers' general manager. "A real pain in the butt to play against."

"That Clarke," Dennis Hextall said. "He was always starting a lot of crap on the ice. He liked to whack you behind the knees with his stick."

"The first time I played against Dennis," Clarke said, "he tried to take my head off."

"I was playing in Oakland then," Hextall recalled. "Yeah, I cranked Clarke pretty good."

"Dennis broke Terry Crisp's jaw one night in Minnesota," Barber said. "Caught him with an elbow right in front of our bench."

"I swear, I don't remember," Hextall said.

"The game wound up in a riot," Barber said.

"I fought [Don] Saleski, [Moose] Dupont and [Bob] Kelly one night," Bryan Hextall said. "[Dave] Schultz? Yeah, I fought him, too."

It was in this friendly atmosphere that Ron Hextall, Bryan's son and Dennis' nephew, was raised. Needless to say, the Flyers weren't his favorite NHL team.

Ray Didinger, a sports columnist at the Philadelphia Daily News, *is covering his second generation of Hextalls in the NHL.*

Ron Hextall's notorious slash of Kent Nilsson.

"How would you feel about a bunch of guys who bounced your father around all the time?" Ron Hextall asked. "I went to the games with my mother and brother. I'd sit and watch. I didn't like the Flyers at all. I didn't like Bobby Clarke at all. My father didn't play on tough teams. He was usually the only one who'd stand up to them. It made for some long nights.

"My brother and I knew better than to say the word 'Flyers' around the house. Dad would shoot us a look. Now here I am playing for the Flyers. It's funny how things work out."

It's funny, all right. Last season, the Flyers laughed all the

Bryan Hextall Jr., Ron's dad, as a Penguin in 1971-72.

way to the Stanley Cup finals with 23-year-old rookie Ron Hextall in goal. And now Bryan and Dennis Hextall are rabid Flyer fans.

Crazy game, hockey.

Bryan Hextall was in the Philadelphia locker room after the final game, congratulating his son on winning the Conn Smythe Trophy as Most Valuable Player in the playoffs. The kid played brilliantly, posting a 2.76 goals-against average in 26 postseason starts. The Flyers came up just short in the finals, losing Game 7 in Edmonton, 3-1, but the 6-3, 185-pound Hextall was a tower of strength in goal, turning aside 40 Oiler shots.

"He may be the best goalie I've ever played against," Wayne Gretzky said.

Bryan Hextall traveled from his Brandon, Manitoba, home for the final game. He sat in the upper deck at the Northlands Coliseum with wife Fay and they sweated every time the Oilers brought the puck across the blue line.

Afterward, Hextall was in the locker room, commiserating with a dozen ex-Flyers who had flown in for Game 7. These were the same Broad Street Bullies that Bryan Hextall fought a decade ago.

"That's quite a son you have there, Bryan," Dave Schultz said.

"Thanks, Davey," the elder Hextall said. "We're really proud of him."

"Where did he get all that talent?" asked Orest Kindrachuk, the former Flyer center. "Must be his mother's side of the family."

Bryan laughed. "No," he said. "Ronald plays like a Hextall."

*   *   *

It would be hard to pick the First Family of hockey. The Howes—Gordie, Mark and Marty—are the most distinguished. The Sutters—six brothers in the NHL—are the most abundant.

There were numerous father-son combinations: Ace Bailey and son Garnet; Syl Apps Sr. and Syl Jr.; Ab DeMarco Sr. and Ab Jr. There were all-star-brothers: the Espositos, the Hulls, the Richards and the Mahovlichs. But the Hextalls have a special distinction: They are a three-generation NHL family. Only the Patricks—Lester, Lynn and Craig—can make a similar claim.

The Hextalls' professional hockey roots can be found in the Hall of Fame: the late Bryan Sr., was a three-time NHL all-star, a New York Ranger winger who won the league scoring title in 1941-42. Bryan Sr. scored 20 or more goals in seven of his 12 NHL seasons. "A 20-goal season back then was the equivalent of a 40-goal season today," Dennis Hextall said. "It was a different game. If you scored 20 then, you were a helluva player."

Bryan Sr. is best remembered as the man who helped bring the last Stanley Cup to New York. On April 13, 1940, Hextall scored in overtime to lift the Rangers to a 3-2 win over Toronto in Game 6 of the Cup final. His name is still legend in Madison Square Garden.

"Our father never talked about his career," said Dennis, now a manufacturers representative in Detroit. "He was a modest guy. If he had pushed himself [in the press] he could have been an NHL coach. But it wasn't his nature. Bryan and I would ask about his career and he'd pass it off. The only time we'd hear things was when other players from that era would drop by our house. We lived in Poplar Point, which was on the main highway through Manitoba.

"All the kids in the neighborhood would gather around. These were legendary figures like Sid Abel. They'd tell stories and our eyes would be this wide. I remember them talking about my father's goal in the Stanley Cup.

"Phil Watson got the puck behind the net and passed it out front. My father put it in with his backhand. The goalie was Turk Broda, another Hall of Famer. I played it back in my mind a thousand times, imagining what it must have looked like."

At 5-10, 195 pounds, Bryan Hextall Sr., was a bull who could skate through an enemy defenseman without breaking stride. He played tough, but seldom fought. He didn't feel a man had to drop his gloves to prove himself on the ice. Another Hall of Famer, James Dunn, wrote of Bryan Hextall: "He is a very clean-living individual and an excellent ambassador for professional hockey." So what happened with Bryan Jr., and Dennis? They were known as "chippy" players. That's hockeyspeak for "dirty little buggers."

Bryan played nine NHL seasons with five teams; Dennis played 13 seasons with six teams. Bryan retired in 1976 with 99 goals in 549 games. Dennis bowed out in 1980 with 153 goals in 681 games. Between them, the brothers Hextall had 2,136 penalty minutes.

"We weren't superstars but nobody outworked us," said Bryan Jr., now a sales representative for the Molson Brewery.

"Our father came to our junior games," Dennis said, "and he cursed us out if we fought. I had 20 goals and 20 majors [fighting penalties] one season. My father said, 'You'd have 30 [goals] if you didn't spend so much time in the box.'

"I told him, 'Dad, if something happens out there, I'm not gonna back away.' He understood. He just didn't like the cheap

Wayne Gretzky congratulates Hextall, Stanley Cup MVP.

penalties. He said there was a difference between being tough and being dumb."

What advice do you think Bryan Sr., gave young Ronald when he started playing? You guessed it.

"He told me to quit taking dumb penalties," the youngest Hextall said. "He told me to leave the fighting to the other players. I had a pretty short temper back then."

Hextall's temper hasn't improved much, if at all, since his peewee days. Last season, the rookie had 104 penalty minutes, most ever for an NHL goaltender. And he received an eight-game suspension, to be served at the start of this season, for chopping Kent Nilsson with a two-handed slash across the Achilles tendon in the Stanley Cup finals.

Hextall was angered when Glenn Anderson whacked him across the left arm, trying to knock the puck from his grasp. That

Uncle Dennis Hextall as a Red Wing in 1976-77.

slash, on top of the frustration of a 4-1 Oiler lead in Game 4, set the goalie off. Hextall took a full, Samurai swing at the next Oiler to skate into view. That turned out to be Nilsson, one of the NHL's most passive players. He went down like he was struck with an axe. Hextall was referred to as "Hackstall" in the Edmonton papers the next day.

"Ronald took a lot of [media] criticism," his father said. "And I don't think it was fair. Nothing was said about Anderson's slash on him and everyone knows Anderson is one of the worst stickmen in the league. It burned me to read some of those comments."

Many players, even veterans, would have unraveled in the face of such pressure. The Edmonton fans taunted him, waving hostile banners ("A Class Axe") in his face. The press kept asking and writing about his "dark side." And, of course, there were the Oilers, the NHL's most potent offensive machine, storming the gates.

The Oilers took a three-games-to-one lead in the final and were hungry to clinch at home in Game 5. Hextall held them off, 4-3, and frustrated them again in Game 6, 3-2, even though the Oilers had a 32-23 edge in shots. Hextall's final stand in Game 7 was so compelling that the same media types who crucified him for the Nilsson incident voted him the Conn Smythe. It marked the fourth time a player from a losing team won the award. Reggie Leach of the Flyers was the last in 1976.

Hextall also became the second consecutive rookie goalie to win the Smythe, following Montreal's Patrick Roy.

"I'd trade this [trophy] in a second for the Stanley Cup," a tearful Hextall said after the game. "I've never been so disappointed in my life."

"We're a family of competitors," Bryan Hextall said. "We hate to lose at anything. You play this game for one thing, to win the Stanley Cup. When you get to this point, that's all you think about. If you lose, even if you give a hell of an effort, it's still a loss. As an athlete, that's tough to swallow.

"When Ronald came off the ice I hugged him and told him no goalie could have played better than he did tonight. He said, 'But it wasn't good enough.' That's the way he is."

*   *   *

Bryan Hextall Sr., was an NHL forward. So were Bryan Jr., and Dennis. Everyone thought it ran in the family. Then Ronald came along and changed everything.

"I think Ronald wanted to be a goalie the day he was born," Fay Hextall said. "That's all he talked about. When he was 3, he'd stand in the goal when the neighborhood kids played street hockey. I'd tell him to come away from there. The minute I'd turn my back, he was in goal again.

"He wanted to play goal when he signed up for youth hockey, but Bryan wouldn't let him. He felt it was better for Ronald to play another position so he could develop his skating. He played defense and did well, but it was obvious where his heart was. One day our goalie didn't show up. Ronald said, 'This is my big chance.' He played [in goal] and won. He's been a goalie ever since."

"I never seriously tried to talk him out of it," Bryan said. "Once he got in there, it was obvious that's where his interest was. He'd come to my practices and sit behind the goalies. He'd watch how they moved, how they played the shooters. I played with Eddie Giacomin in Detroit and Ron watched Eddie come out of the net and handle the puck. That's where he picked up that [roaming] style.

"Dan Bouchard worked with Ronald in Atlanta. The kids played after our practices and Dan would stand behind Ronald with his hands on his shoulders. He'd move him side-to-side, he'd show him how to play the angles. That's why Ronald's fundamentals are so good."

But Bryan Hextall spent enough time around professional hockey to understand the odds against a kid making it. He didn't allow himself to get excited about his son's NHL chances until he was deep into his teens, playing junior hockey in Manitoba.

"The first time I can honestly say I saw that [NHL] potential in Ronald was when he was 16," Bryan said. "He helped the Brandon midgets win the province championship. He was like [Ken] Dryden, a big kid with a quick glove. The other thing was he really wanted it [a pro career]. It was his dream to play in the NHL and he was willing to work to make it come true. That desire can carry you a long way."

Hextall played for a weak Brandon junior team, which accounts for his bloated goals-against average (5.33 in three seasons), but Flyer scout Jerry Melnyk saw enough of the youngster to recommend him for the 1982 draft.

The Flyers selected Hextall in the sixth round, No. 119 overall. "The name had something to do with it," Flyer vice-president Keith Allen said. "The Hextalls have always been hard-working, winner types. It's like the Sutters. You can't go wrong with kids like that."

Hextall's first professional stop was Kalamazoo in the International League (1984-85). He was promoted to the Flyers' American Hockey League affiliate in Hershey later that season. Hextall won 30 games and posted five shutouts in 1985-86 as he led the Bears to the Calder Cup final. He was named AHL Rookie of the Year. Next stop, Philadelphia.

"Ron came along faster than I expected," said Bernie Parent, the Hall-of-Fame goalie, now a Flyer assistant coach. "When I first saw him [1984] he was a raw talent. You think he leaves the net now? You should have seen him then. He was all over the place. I didn't try to change him. You change a goalie's style, you throw him off. All I did was teach Ron our system and fit

Grandpa Bryan Hextall Sr. as a Ranger in early '40s.

him into it. I gave him a few basics to remember, then turned him loose.

"His greatest strength is here," Parent added, tapping his head. "He can allow a bad goal or have a bad period and put it out of his mind. He's on an even keel. A goalie has to be like that or he won't last."

For awhile, it was hard to see just where Hextall fit into the Flyers' plans. They had Pelle Lindbergh, who won the Vezina Trophy and took the team to the Stanley Cup finals in 1985. Behind him they had Bob Froese, who led all active NHL goalies in winning percentage prior to last season.

Lindbergh and Froese were both young guys with bright futures. There didn't seem to be a whole lot of room in Philadelphia for another goaltender. But Lindbergh was fatally injured in an automobile accident in November 1985, and the dominoes began to fall.

The Flyers' management resisted the urge to recall Hextall, feeling he could learn more playing regularly in the AHL than he could backing up Froese in Philadelphia. Darren Jensen came up from Hershey instead and played in just 29 games.

"Staying down [in the minors] was the best thing that could have happened to me," Hextall said. "The minor-league life wasn't the greatest. Three games in three nights, traveling by bus. It was rough, I hated it, but I learned a lot. When I came to camp [last summer] I was ready to compete for a regular job. I didn't worry about the odds, competing against Froese and Chico [Resch], I just went out every day to do my best. The decision was in the coaches' hands anyway.

"At first I was a little reluctant to play my [roaming] game. Mike Keenan pulled me aside one day and said, 'What are you doing? Get aggressive.' That gave me a lift. I realized they believed in me."

Hextall was unbeaten in the preseason and Keenan felt the kid earned the right to start against the Oilers on opening night. He won that game, 2-1, and never looked back.

By November, the rookie was clearly the Flyers' No. 1 goalie. An angry Froese asked to be traded. In December, Clarke shipped Froese to the New York Rangers for Swedish-born defenseman Kjell Samuelsson. Some people called it a gamble, wondering how the Flyers could be so sure that Hextall wasn't a flash in the pan. What happened if the kid went bust in the second half of the season? Didn't it make sense to keep Froese around as insurance?

"We never worried about Hextall," Clarke said. "We felt quite sure he could do the job and do it over the long haul. As it turned out, he played beyond all our expectations. He actually carried us most of the season."

Hextall played in 92 games, counting playoffs, the most ever by an NHL goalie. He beat out Hartford's Mike Liut and Edmonton's Grant Fuhr for the Vezina Trophy. He led the league in regular-season wins (37) and save percentage (.902) and his 3.00 goals-against average was third behind Montreal's Brian Hayward and Patrick Roy.

Hextall befuddled opposing teams with his ability to leave the crease, control the puck and fire it down the ice as well as any defenseman. His mobility and stick-handling added a whole new dimension to the Flyers' penalty-killing unit.

"He's better with the stick than I was," said Giacomin, the Hall of Famer the young Hextall studied in Detroit. "He moves the puck better than any goalie I ever saw."

Resch, the 13-year NHL veteran who retired after the 1987 Cup finals, watched the kid up close all season. He calls Hextall "the most graceful goaltender in the game, ever. It's like watching Nureyev out there. I'm keeping the tapes just so if I ever coach young goalies, I'll say, 'This is the standard you'd like to attain. You probably won't, but this is the goal.'

"Ronnie is today—and he will be five years from now, probably ten years from now—the best goalie in the league."

Will all this acclaim prove to be the undoing of Ron Hextall? Will he let the success go to his head? The people who know him best say no.

"Ronald is 23 going on 35," his father said. "He was mature at 16."

"I'm basically a quiet person," said Hextall, who is married to a former Canadian national figure skater [Diane] and the father of a one-year-old daughter [Kristin]. "Bright lights and glamor, you can keep all that. My idea of a good time is staying home and playing with the baby. I sit for hours, talking to her, making her laugh. To me, that's the most exciting thing in the world.

"Of course, when I come to the rink, that's like a different world. I keep things pretty much in perspective. I don't want to be a one-year player. I want to stick around the league awhile. I enjoy the game. My father played a long time and when he retired, I could see how he missed the life. I want to last, I want to make my mark. What I've done so far is a good start, but that's all it is, a start. I've still got a long way to go."

And how far can he go?

"My father always wanted to see another Hextall carry the Stanley Cup around the ice," Bryan Jr., said. "I never did, but I know one of these days Ronald will get his chance."

KEEPING UP WITH THE GREAT GRETZKY

By DICK CHUBEY

Nothing Wayne Gretzky does should come as a complete surprise any more.

On and off the ice, despite his lofty roost as hockey's nonpareil performer, the 26-year-old Gretzky has increasingly recognized the contributions of his teammates and friends.

This was especially apparent on the night of May 31, following the Edmonton Oilers' seventh-game, Stanley Cup-winning triumph over the Philadelphia Flyers. Right after Gretzky had been given the Cup by NHL president John Ziegler, the Oiler captain pumped it into the air and then sought out a teammate to hoist the ancient urn at the Northlands Coliseum.

The fact that he gave the trophy to Steve Smith was no coincidence. Thirteen months earlier, Smith was the rookie defenseman who inadvertently knocked the puck into his own net during the Calgary Flames' 3-2 victory in Game 7 of the Stanley Cup quarterfinals. That goal cost the defending champion Oilers an opportunity to make it three straight postseason championships. The date was April 30, 1986—Smith's 23rd birthday, of all things.

Just as swiftly as he made his considerate handoff to Smith, Gretzky wasted little time getting on with his private life after the grueling 1986-87 season. After meeting team, civic and social obligations over the next few days, he was on a plane to Los Angeles and the National Basketball Association championship series between the L.A. Lakers and the Boston Celtics. "I'm looking forward to just sitting back and watching somebody else

As hockey writer for the Edmonton Sun, *Dick Chubey has witnessed the exploits of Wayne Gretzky from his WHA beginnings nine years ago.*

Vikki Moss joins Wayne Gretzky at 1985 awards ceremony.

sweating in a pressure situation," he said.

There was a more pressing reason for the world's worst flier to board another long flight. Her name is Vikki Moss, the woman in Gretzky's life. She has been living in Los Angeles, taking singing and acting lessons in the hope of a show-business career. And Gretzky obviously had his fill of reaching out and touching someone by phone.

"We talk every day, sometimes twice a day," Vikki was saying from her apartment in Hollywood. "Sometimes I have to console him."

The Great Gretzky needs consolation? It all traces back to his early days; when he was 10 and already a prodigy, he was intro-

*Gretzky visited M*A*S*H cast in Hollywood in 1982.*

duced to the pressure that would dog him throughout his hockey days.

"It was our 70th game of the year and I had an awful game—just horrid," said Gretzky of a novice tournament in Kingston, Ont., where a sellout crowd had come to see the young phenom.

Afterwards he told his father, Walter, that it was just another game—that there would be another game the next day. And the day after. His dad admonished: "You can't play a bad game. People are going to judge you on how you perform every night. Never forget that!"

The heat's been on ever since. And the Oiler center has responded in legendary fashion, shattering or equaling 41 NHL records. Only Gordie Howe (1,850), Marcel Dionne (1,683) and Phil Esposito (1,590) have accumulated more points than this scrawny 6-foot, 170-pounder, whose 1,520 points have come in only eight NHL seasons.

Yet, despite Gretzky's incredible accomplishments—including winning the MVP award all eight seasons—he has to contend with a growing battery of critics.

"For some reason, even to this day, some people question my ability and what I've done," he said. "When I first came into the league, I came under a lot of heat for my early success. It seemed they wanted to protect the guys who held the old records . . . They would say, 'He's doing fine, but he doesn't play on a good team.' Then, 'Sure, but he hasn't won a Stanley Cup.' Now that we've won three, it seems they want someone else to take over.

"It's probably beneficial to me that I have to prove myself every night. My attitude has always been to prove them wrong. But it gets me mad."

There's a character named Wayne Mook from Lethbridge, Albeta, who has even organized the Anti-Gretzky Fan Club. "He thinks he's God on ice," said Mook. "You can't touch him . . . But it wouldn't be so bad if he'd just shut his mouth and stop whining. And he's too damn pretty. He doesn't even look like a hockey player. Maybe if somebody knocked out a couple of front teeth . . ."

While No. 99 said he cannot control what people think, his girl is more vehement. "They say he's too perfect," Vikki said. "What is he supposed to do? Fail on purpose? There are a lot of jerks out there. He can't please everyone."

Vikki, 24, met Wayne in Edmonton when she was 17. Gretzky and teammate Kevin Lowe walked into a lounge, where she was on stage. "He asked me if I wanted a drink," she recalled. "I was too young, so we had a cup of coffee."

She has witnessed the anti-Gretzky movement and said that she wouldn't doubt "if he gets sick of it real soon. I know he wants to get out when he's on top."

Nonetheless, during the offseason Gretzky signed a contract that will keep him in Oiler blue for the next five years.

The latest heir apparent to Gretzky is Pittsburgh's Mario Lemieux. The Penguins' center, not Gretzky, was the people's choice during fan voting for Rendez-Vous '87, the two-game all-star series against the Soviet Nationals last February in Quebec City. Gretzky was named Most Valuable Player. "That's pretty incredulous," Vikki laughed. "But I want to stress Wayne has no animosity towards Mario. If anything, he's sympathetic. He knows this puts tremendous pressure on Mario."

Vikki and Wayne would seem to be the Barbie and Ken of the NHL. But things aren't always as idyllic as they seem. "Wayne gets hate mail, but you should see mine," she said. "Girls in wedding dresses send photos to him. They say, 'I'm waiting for you, Wayne.'"

Mugging with Goldie Hawn and Burt Reynolds.

Like any affair, of course, this one could conclude at any time. But they have talked marriage. And they have discussed children. Gretzky does dream of the day when he can take a son skating. "I don't know if I'll still be playing when I have kids," he said. "But what Gordie Howe was able to do with his kids was something special."

Whenever his playing career ends, Gretzky figures to stay in Edmonton. "Edmonton is now home for me and that's where I'd like to be," said Gretzky, a native of Brantford, Ont., a community of 75,000 south of Toronto. "Edmonton is a nice city with a small-town atmosphere. I have a lot of opportunities here. They've always treated me first-class. I see no reason to go anywhere else."

Earning $1 million annually from hockey and twice that amount from endorsements, Gretzky is, indeed, financially secure. He has a 20-year personal services contract with Oiler owner Peter Pocklington that extends through 2002.

When will he hang up his skates? "There are some very special athletes—like Reggie Jackson—who play for a very long time," he said. "I'm not sure I'm one of those athletes."

He spoke about Bjorn Borg, the Swede who conquered the tennis world and retired in 1982 at age 26. "I know what Borg felt like when he was 26. I know why he retired at 26," said the 26-year-old Gretzky.

Wayne celebrates winning of Stanley Cup in 1987.

DOUG JARVIS: INCREDIBLE IRON MAN

By HUGH DELANO

The year is 1975.

Remember?

Heavyweight champion Muhammad Ali knocks out Joe Frazier in a fight known as the "Thrilla in Manila"... The Captain and Tennille are singing *Love Will Keep Us Together*... Yankees' catcher Thurman Munson says he'd like to own an airplane someday... Disco music is in... so is a dance called the Hustle ... A young tennis player named Martina Navratilova defects from Czechoslovakia to the United States... "Welcome Back Kotter" is a TV sitcom hit... Crowds are lining up to watch *Jaws*... A New Jersey singer named Bruce Springsteen is starting to make a name for himself... And in hockey Doug Jarvis starts his NHL career by playing in every game for the Montreal Canadiens.

Now all that has changed... except that Doug Jarvis still is playing in every game, every season.

Jarvis is hockey's Iron Man. Lou Gehrig on ice. Never has he missed playing in a regular-season game. Not in 12 physically punishing NHL seasons. Never has he been unable to play because of injury or illness. Never has he been benched and missed a game.

Incredible!

Consider this: Despite improved protective equipment, training methods and medical treatment, there is an increase in NHL players who are injured and unable to play. Players are bigger, stronger, younger, more aggressive. Hockey is faster. There is

Like Doug Jarvis, Hugh Delano of the New York Post *is an iron man who hasn't missed a game assignment in 18 years on the hockey beat.*

Doug Jarvis aims at 1,000 straight games this season.

greater body contact. Pucks shot at race-car speed break players' jaws and ankles. Razor-sharp skate blades and sticks often used as weapons cause cuts and broken bones. Players are knocked to the ice or crash into the boards. Flu strikes down dozens of players each season.

Of the 683 men who played in the NHL last season, only 46 survived for all 80 games. Jarvis, playing for the Hartford Whalers, is one of the six percent who played every game.

And he's been doing it for 962 consecutive games.

Twelve years without missing a game. Twelve years of withstanding jarring body checks in a contact sport of controlled and sometimes uncontrolled violence, with injury risk as high as

Manhattan's World Trade Center. Not only is hockey physically dangerous, it is mentally tiring. The season extends from September training camp to Stanley Cup playoffs continuing almost until June.

No player in NHL history has done what Jarvis has done. Hartford's red-haired, 32-year-old center and defensive specialist broke Garry Unger's consecutive-game mark on Dec. 23, 1986, when he played in his 915th straight game. By season's end, Jarvis had extended it to 962, so he enters the 1987-88 season needing only 38 more in a row for 1,000 consecutive games.

Barring injury or illness, he should reach this milestone during the first week of 1988.

Records, as they say, are made to be broken, but Jarvis' nonstop mark—as the game gets tougher—will be increasingly hard to eclipse.

Making it more remarkable, Jarvis is not a big man physically. He is 5-9, 170.

"A most amazing thing . . . to never have missed a game for so long a time," Jean Beliveau said. "Hockey has always been a tough game, and now it's played by men bigger and taller in size. All the physical play and risk of injury and Doug still has not missed a game. I admire and respect what he has done."

Beliveau is a hockey legend, one of the greatest players in the history of the game, the heart and soul of the Montreal Canadiens during a glorious 18-year NHL career. He now is senior vice president of corporate affairs for the Canadiens.

"The record should last a long time," Beliveau said. "I don't know if it is a record that will be broken. A coach doesn't ever have to worry about a player like Doug; he knows he comes to play every game, will do his utmost to help his team, always give 100 percent. Doug is a team player."

Jarvis started his NHL career with Montreal in 1975-76 as a 20-year-old rookie who was born in Brantford, Ont., and played in the Ontario Junior League for the Peterborough Petes. His skill as a defensive forward helped the Canadiens win four consecutive Stanley Cup championships in 1976, 1977, 1978 and 1979.

"Doug didn't always get a lot of recognition but he was very valuable when we won those Stanley Cups," said Beliveau. "He doesn't have a flashy style but he's always been steady, each game, each season as a defense-minded player."

"When I was growing up, I didn't have a lot of so-called sports idols," said Jarvis. "But the one player I admired and respected the most was Jean Beliveau . . . the captain of the Montreal Canadiens."

A quiet, soft-spoken man, Jarvis seems at a loss of words to

Garry Unger held the mark at 914 before Jarvis.

explain his record of never having missed playing in a game.

"It's something that just happened, just sneaked up on me," he said. "It's not something you can plan or set your sights on. It's something I never consciously thought about. Certainly not in my early years in the league. Certainly not until I read stories in the newspapers about it. Even then I never dwelled on it. I always took one game at a time. I still do."

Don't get the impression Jarvis does not take pride in his record. He does. But like all dedicated athletes, the team comes first, not the individual.

"I think I'll look at the record when my career is over and it will mean more to me then," he said.

The Iron Man's consecutive game streak began Oct. 8, 1975, at the Montreal Forum. The Canadiens whipped the Los Angeles Kings, 9-0, on opening night. Jarvis had one assist in his first NHL game. He played on a checking line with Bob Gainey and veteran Jimmy Roberts. He was a typical rookie in his first NHL game, thrilled by it all, especially because he was playing in the famous Montreal Forum, but a trifle nervous. He had no idea what the future held for him.

Jarvis didn't know if he'd play in the next game. The Canadiens always had a large roster, brought rookies along slowly and often rotated players. You play one game, not play the next. Jarvis, however, was never taken out of the lineup as a rookie.

Luck has something to do with it.

"Of course," said Jarvis. "I've been very fortunate. I don't know why some players seem to get hurt and others don't. All those practices, all the games, all those years, all the bumps and bruises. I've never been hurt badly enough that I couldn't play. I've never had the flu, been sick and couldn't play."

But it has to be more than luck.

Jarvis' ability and style of play have a lot to do with his record. Jarvis, a role player of the highest form, is probably the best all-around defensive forward in the NHL. He and his linemates are on ice to check the opposition's best offensive line. Jarvis excels as a forechecker and backchecker and is a dynamic penalty-killer. He is one of the best faceoff centers in the NHL. In a game against the New Jersey Devils three years ago, he won a remarkable 27 of 32 faceoffs, 15 in a row in pressure-packed late-game defensive situations.

Jarvis' calm, mild-mannered office personality belies the fact that he is a fiercely intense competitor. His game seldom varies. He is consistently effective. Although not flashy or spectacular, he does his job well, game in, game out. Seldom does he play a bad game. He is consistently steady. Although his role is primarily that of defender, he has the quick, slick moves to score or set up goals.

"He's the kind of player you need in the lineup every game," said Beliveau.

Jarvis must have been one of those rare kids who had a perfect attendance record, never missed a day of school.

The Whalers' forward laughed. "Not really," he said. "I had the chicken pox like most kids did but if I was able to go to school, my parents made me go."

Once, three or four years ago, Jarvis came close to missing a game. He was playing for the Washington Capitals.

HOCKEY IRON MEN
Most Consecutive Games Played

	Years	G
Doug Jarvis, Montreal, Washington, Hartford	1975-1987	962
Garry Unger, Toronto, Detroit, St. Louis, Atlanta . . .	1968-1979	914
Craig Ramsay, Buffalo	1973-1983	776
Andy Hebenton, N.Y. Rangers, Boston	1955-1964	630
Johnny Wilson, Detroit, Chicago, Toronto.	1952-1960	580
Billy Harris, N.Y. Islanders	1972-1979	576
Alex Delvecchio, Detroit	1956-1964	548
John Marks, Chicago	1973-1980	508
Murray Murdoch, N.Y. Rangers.	1926-1937	508

Most Consecutive Games by a Goalie

Glenn Hall, Detroit, Chicago	1955-1962	503

Most Consecutive Games by a Defenseman

Tim Horton, Toronto	1961-1968	486

"I got knocked unconscious near the end of a game," he said. "Got hit by a pretty hard check in center ice, went down and hit my head on the ice. They put me in a hospital for observation overnight. The next morning a doctor checked me and said he saw no reason why I couldn't play the next game. That's the closest I came to missing a game."

What is the magic that helps him stay free from injury and illness?

"Conditioning and keeping in shape is very important to me but I don't do any more than the average player does," he said. "I try to keep myself in good condition during the offseason. I do some running, ride the stationary bike, do some light weight-lifting."

Has Jarvis ever missed a game?

"I missed a game in junior hockey when I was 18 because of a concussion," he said.

That was during the 1974-75 season, when Jarvis set Peterborough scoring records with 88 assists and 133 points. Jarvis was a high scorer in junior hockey but also was a good defensive player.

Although some people are not aware of it, Jarvis did miss four games during the 1979 Stanley Cup playoffs. Playoff games do not count in compiling regular-season consecutive game streaks.

"I hurt a knee in practice and couldn't play," Jarvis said of the only injury which prevented him from playing.

"I don't like missing games," he said. "I think it's natural for hockey players to play with a certain amount of normal bumps and bruises or sickness."

Jack (Tex) Evans, Hartford's successful coach, readily acknowledges Jarvis' streak, and for special reason. Evans once missed only five games in eight years during his career as a hard-rock NHL defenseman with the New York Rangers and Chicago Blackhawks from 1948 to 1963.

"Some players are always hanging around the trainer's room . . . you never see Doug Jarvis there," said Evans.

Emile (The Cat) Francis has the same high regard for Jarvis. Hartford's team president and general manager is a former NHL goalie and coach. He once played despite a separated shoulder.

"Doug Jarvis has the perfect work ethic," said Francis. "It's amazing that he's never missed a game, especially when you consider the type of player he is. He goes out and plays in the toughest situations, goes up against the best lines in the league and kills penalties. All those pucks being shot around him and he's never been hurt. He's not a big guy but it doesn't make him shy about getting into the thick of the battle. He works as hard in practice as he does in games."

Jarvis has never played for a losing team in the NHL. The three teams for which he's played—Montreal, Hartford, Washington—have a combined record of 587-243-132 with Jarvis in their lineup.

He was voted 1987 winner of the Bill Masterton Memorial Trophy, awarded by the Professional Hockey Writers Association to the player who best exemplifies the qualities of perseverance, sportsmanship, dedication. In 1984 with Washington, he won the Frank Selke Trophy as the NHL's best defensive forward.

Jarvis was drafted by the Toronto Maple Leafs in 1975. A few days later, Sam Pollack, then the Canadiens' general manager, acquired Jarvis from Toronto in a trade for defenseman Greg Hubick, who played only 77 NHL games in two seasons for Toronto and Vancouver, then dropped out of the NHL.

On Sept. 8, 1982, Jarvis was involved in a big trade. Washington traded forward Ryan Walter and defenseman Rick Green to Montreal for Jarvis, defensemen Rod Langway and Brian

MAJOR LEAGUE BASEBALL IRON MEN
Most Consecutive Games Played

	Years	G
Lou Gehrig, N.Y. Yankees	1925-1939	2,130
Everett Scott, Boston Red Sox, N.Y. Yankees	1919-1924	1,307
Steve Garvey, L.A. Dodgers, San Diego	1974-1986	1,207
Billy Williams, Chicago Cubs	1962-1974	1,117
Joe Sewell, Cleveland Indians	1921-1930	1,103

Engblom and forward Craig Laughlin. Jarvis' defensive skill helped Washington become a championship contender. Jarvis was traded on Dec. 6, 1985, to Hartford for Swedish forward Jorgen Pettersson. The Whalers wanted Jarvis for his defensive ability; Washington believed Pettersson would give them greater scoring firepower. Pettersson didn't last long in Washington; Jarvis has played a vital role in Hartford's rise from pushover to power.

"Dougie didn't always get the recognition he deserved, because he was a defensive player, not a big goal-scorer, but he was a big part of our winning four Stanley Cups," said Montreal defenseman Larry Robinson.

Jarvis has an impressive plus-minus record of +122 for his NHL career. Only twice in 12 years has he been minus (on ice for more goals-against than goals scored by his team). His career scoring totals are commendable for a player assigned mainly to defensive duties: 139 goals, 264 assists, 403 points. He plays hard but he plays a clean game.

Until last December, the record for playing in the most consecutive NHL games belonged to Garry Unger. He played in 914 consecutive games from 1968 to 1979 with Toronto, the Detroit Red Wings, St. Louis Blues and Atlanta Flames. Jarvis tied Unger's record when Hartford beat the Boston Bruins, 2-0, on Dec. 23, 1986. Fittingly, the record-tying game was played in Hartford and Jarvis assisted on the Whalers' second goal, a short-handed shot by Dave Tippett. Jarvis made it 915 three days later at Hartford when the Whalers tied Montreal, 1-1.

Unger's style of play and image were different from those of Jarvis. A high-scoring center with long blond hair, Unger often received more attention because of his eligible-bachelor status and for dating 1970 Miss America Pam Eldred. Unger was more than a pretty face. He was a flashy but hard-working center who loved the outdoors and riding horses. He once injured his back

Craig Ramsay achieved his record as a Sabre.

falling off a horse in the offseason but kept his streak alive by
playing several games despite torn rib muscles. He said his
younger sister, Carol Ann, was his inspiration for never missing a
game.

"She's my motivation to keep going," said Unger. "She's
crippled by polio and can't walk. How could I say, 'My God! I'm
hurt . . . I can't play.'"

Unger's streak ended in controversy on Dec. 21, 1979. He had
played several games with an injured shoulder and his play had
suffered. He was on the bench for a game in St. Louis but Atlanta
coach Al MacNeil, a former NHL player, did not put him into the

PRO FOOTBALL IRON MEN (NFL)
Most Consecutive Games Played

	Years	G
Jim Marshall, Cleveland, Minnesota	1960-1979	282
Mick Tinglehoff, Minnesota....................	1962-1978	240
Jim Bakken, St. Louis	1962-1978	234

game, not even for a token appearance to sustain his record streak.

"I had taken him along as far as I could in my mind," said MacNeil, now Calgary Flames' assistant general manager. "It wasn't tough for me to not put him in the game. He had gotten to the point where he couldn't function physically."

Unger, now a player-coach in England, said, "It wasn't a classy thing to do."

When Jarvis broke his record, Unger called to congratulate him.

Craig Ramsay played in 776 consecutive games for the Buffalo Sabres from 1973 to 1983. Like Jarvis, he starred as a defensive forward and physically was not a big player. He now scouts for Buffalo. Ramsay's non-stop playing streak once was threatened by an allergy which made his eyes swollen and watery, blurring his vision. He used folk medicine to keep himself in the lineup; he laid down on his hotel bed and placed teabags on his eyes. It cured his allergy. It kept his streak alive. Teabags could not help when he was struck in the ankle by a puck shot by a teammate during a game.

"I knew right away it was broken," said Ramsay . . . meaning a bone in his foot as well as his streak.

You don't talk about Iron Men without mentioning Andy Hebenton. He played in every game of his nine-year, 70-game-season career with the Boston Bruins and New York Rangers from 1955 to 1964. His 630 consecutive games was a record until Unger broke it. The right wing's mark ended when he was sold by Boston to Portland of the Western League. Hebenton never had missed a game in the minor leagues before reaching the NHL. It was several years after he returned to the minor leagues that he finally missed a game . . . because his father died. Hebenton was 45 when he finally retired after a 26-year pro career.

"Doug Jarvis plays hockey the way Andy Hebenton did," said

Jarvis' streak began with the Canadiens in 1975.

PRO BASKETBALL IRON MEN (NBA)
Most Consecutive Games Played

	Years	G
Randy Smith, Buffalo, San Diego, Cleveland, N.Y. Knicks, Atlanta..............................	1972-1983	906
Johnny Kerr, Syracuse, Philadelphia, Baltimore	1954-1965	844
Dolph Schayes, Syracuse	1952-1961	706

(Ron Boone played in 1,041 consecutive games from 1968-1981 with Dallas, Utah, St. Louis of ABA and Kansas City, Los Angeles of NBA).

Tom McVie, the colorful character who coached against Jarvis in the NHL and played on a line with Hebenton in the minor leagues.

"Doug doesn't play it safe by staying in the center-ice lanes. He isn't a guy who won't gallop into the corners and go after his man or the puck. Sometimes the guys who are too careful, avoid contact, stay away from the corners and the walls are the ones who get hurt and miss games."

If any hockey record is unbreakable, it could be Jarvis'. No active player is close to it. Chicago's Steve Larmer has played in 400 consecutive games, Winnipeg's Dale Hawerchuk in 369 consecutive games.

"They can tear up the record book now . . . no one's even going to come close to Doug's record," predicted Hartford's Torrie Robertson.

"That's one record they can carve in stone," said the Whalers' Ray Ferraro.

They could be right. At this time it seems unlikely anyone will ever play in as many consecutive games as Doug Jarvis, hockey's Incredible Iron Man.

Red Wings' Steve Yzerman is the youngest NHL captain.

Steve Yzerman Leads Revolution In Detroit

By VARTAN KUPELIAN

For Steve Yzerman, it was the season he went from prodigy to professional; from just another promising youngster to polished performer. And with the 22-year-old center on his journey to NHL stardom went the Detroit Red Wings.

The 1986-87 season was special in many ways for the Red Wings and their long-suffering followers, not the least of which was the coming of age of Yzerman.

It marked the arrival of a new coach, Jacques Demers, and a transformation. Once a NHL power, the Red Wings had fallen on lean times. The drought lasted an agonizingly long time until Demers, the NHL's Coach of the Year, orchestrated a reversal so stunning that even he expressed surprise at how quickly and completely it all came together.

If Demers' was the off-ice symbol of the renaissance, Yzerman was the on-ice catalyst as the Red Wings enjoyed their best season in almost 20 years.

Together, they spearheaded a return to respectability and turned on a city. The Red Wings led the NHL in attendance. Every crowd was capacity. Every hockey night in Detroit meant audiences of 19,000-plus. The Red Wings were back, and so were their once-again adoring fans.

There was plenty of reason for the excitement. The Wings, after narrowly missing first place in the Norris Division on the final night of the regular season with an overtime loss to the St. Louis Blues, forced the Stanley Cup champion Edmonton Oilers to play their best hockey in the Campbell Conference finals.

Vartan Kupelian has been the hockey writer at the Detroit News *since 1973.*

The Oilers needed five solid performances to win the series. As he had all season, Yzerman starred in the playoffs and, against the Oilers in particular, his performance reached new levels. Yzerman led the Wings in playoff scoring with 18 points in 16 games.

The fun is just beginning.

"I'm proud to be a Red Wing again," said Yzerman, who flourished in the role of team captain.

Pride, indeed. That's a long-lost ingredient in Red Wings' hockey and if there is one player who personifies pride and triumph and hope, it is Steve Yzerman.

He's the leader of the new breed of Red Wings. The cornerstone. The star. The player with skills so breathtakingly special that teammates and opponents alike stand in awe.

Yzerman—his nickname is Silk because of his effortless, smooth skating style—posted 31 goals and 59 assists for a career-high 90 points. But his contributions went far beyond that, further than anybody could have imagined.

The Wings hoped for all those things when GM Jimmy Devellano made him the club's No. 1 pick, fourth overall, in the 1983 entry draft. But hoping and happening are two different things where the NHL's draft is concerned. A draft of teenagers offers only slightly better odds than a national lottery. At best, it's a chancy proposition.

The Class of '83 was star-studded. Brian Lawton, Sylvain Turgeon and Pat LaFontaine went 1-2-3. Yzerman, a star in the Ontario Hockey League with the Peterborough Petes, was limited to 56 games in his draft year because of a leg injury. Obviously, by his No. 4 pick, his draft rating didn't fall far, just far enough for the Wings to grab the young man who was born in Cranbrook, B.C., and began playing hockey at age five.

"My dad signed me up," Yzerman said. "My brother, Mike, who is 13 months older, started playing the year before and my dad would take me to watch him. I enjoyed it and I got interested."

There are five children in the Yzerman family—four boys and a girl. Steve's father is employed in the social services branch of the Canadian government and was assigned to duties in British Columbia when Steve, the second son, was attracted to the game.

The family moved to Ottawa when Steve was nine and that's when the dream began for hockey's newest star.

"I played for the Nepean Raiders," Yzerman said, recalling his Ottawa roots.

When the Peterborough Petes of the Ontario Hockey League selected Yzerman in the 1981 midget draft, it marked the begin-

Jacques Demers stands tall as 1986-87 Coach of the Year.

ning of an interesting coincidence.

"They drafted me fourth overall, same as Detroit," Yzerman said.

Dave Dryden, the former goaltender, was Peterborough's GM/coach at the time. Dryden is now an assistant coach with the Wings.

"My first year in junior was the first time I'd been away from home," Yzerman said. "The hockey was good. It was fun. I didn't have a great season, or anything. I only had 20 goals or something [21 goals]. It was an experience."

Yzerman's offensive statistics were accelerated in his second junior season at Peterborough. Despite a knee injury which limited him to 56 games, Yzerman scored 42 goals and 49 assists for 91 points.

The Wings, guaranteed a high pick in the 1983 Entry Draft, watched Yzerman closely. They were impressed by his ability to beat defensemen one-on-one, by his skating skills and his playmaking.

While LaFontaine, who grew up in the Detroit area, would have been an ideal addition for a team in search of a drawing card, he was gone by the time the Wings' turn came around. The New York Islanders selected him just ahead, at third overall.

That left Yzerman, and what a consolation prize he has been!

Yzerman's first two NHL seasons were outstanding. As a rookie, he scored 39 goals and added 48 assists for 87 points in 1983-84 and, barely 18, he became the youngest player ever to skate in the NHL All-Star Game.

The second season was no less impressive. He totaled 89 points, including 59 assists, and only two players in Wings' history ever had as many—Marcel Dionne with a club-record 74 and the incomparable Gordie Howe with 59.

Then it happened. Steve Yzerman fell on hard times. He started slowly in his third professional season—1985-86. "I'd signed a new contract [seven-year], big things were expected of me—and I expected big things from myself," he said. "I felt great coming to camp and I thought I had a pretty good exhibition season. But right from the first game against Minnesota, I played terribly. No excuses. I was just in a rut."

Steve had never missed a game, but on Jan. 31, 1986, he suffered a broken right-collarbone in a collision with St. Louis' Lee Norwood. He was out for the season, missing the final 29 games.

His winter of discontent faded into a summer of reflection. It was an emotional labyrinth so overpowering that this most promising of prospects admitted on the eve of the 1986-87 season, "I feel kind of run-of-the-mill right now."

Steve Yzerman run-of-the-mill?

Never.

Too much talent, too much potential, too much at stake and too many people counting on him to deliver a woebegone hockey franchise to the promised land.

Enter Demers, freshly arrived after an impressive three-year stint at St. Louis and embarking on a five-year contract as coach of the Red Wings. "I want to win a Stanley Cup with Steve Yzerman," Demers announced prior to training camp last year. "And that says how I feel about him as a player."

Yzerman so appealed to Demers that he named Steve the Wings' captain.

"He questioned it," Demers said. "He said, 'Why me?' Because my No. 1 priority was to pick someone with class. There was never a doubt in my mind."

Yzerman approached the season with heightened resolve, and the results speak for themselves. He seldom had a bad shift or a bad period, never mind a bad game. He was the Red Wings' leader on the ice, figuratively and literally.

Yzerman had some spectacular games, some incredible personal spurts, as the Wings went from 21st and last the season before to within a point of finishing first in the Norris Division in 1986-87.

Fittingly, he scored the game-winning goal in the Wings' first victory of the season in the home opener on Oct. 11 against Chicago. In the second victory, in the fifth game, he set up the game-winning goal in addition to scoring himself. Less than two weeks into the season, the trend had been set.

But his best waited until December when Yzerman went on a scoring spree against Norris Division opponents. He set up three goals against Chicago, had a goal and five assists in back-to-back games against Toronto and a pair of goals, including the winner, against Minnesota to start the New Year—all in a span of six games. Yzerman had two other four-point games and a five-point game against Quebec to cap his personal midseason tear.

"I learned to take better care of myself," he said. "It paid off at the end of the season. I grew up a bit. I felt comfortable around the guys speaking my mind. You don't have to have a dominant personality to be a leader."

"Steve can lead this team anywhere," said Dave Lewis, a 14-year NHL defenseman who joined Detroit last season. "He's very mature. He has a mind of his own and doesn't necessarily follow the traditional route. He listens to the older guys, of course, but sometimes he'll say, 'We're going to do it this way.'

"A lot of people look to the captain on the ice to get the points, the goals, to provide the leadership, and they look to him in the dressing room. He provided all of that. I can't think of any reason why he would have a problem being captain of the Red Wings for as long as he plays here."

Don McAdams, who was added to the Wings' coaching staff last season, said: "Steve is 22, and being a captain at that age is one thing. Handling it the way he has, so admirably, is another. He's intense on the ice, first-class off."

Darren Veitch, the defenseman who was given a second NHL life by Demers in Detroit, added: "Stevie anticipates the play so well, gets into the open and creates so much. When he gets the

The captain says he and the Wings still have a way to go.

puck, he's always looking for someone. If nobody is there, he holds on until somebody comes free. And he can put it in the net himself."

Fittingly, Yzerman and Veitch shared *The Hockey News'* Comeback Player of the Year award, Yzerman as the comeback forward, Veitch as the defensive counterpart.

"I've got to be the youngest guy ever to make a comeback," Yzerman quipped.

The Red Wing leader is basically quiet, almost shy. His lifestyle is contemporary. He dresses in trendy fashions, and he adores his Porsche. At the same time, he cherishes his privacy. His closest friend on the team is Gerard Gallant, an alternate captain and star in his own right.

Just as they have grown as professional athletes, so has a mutual respect between the two men.

Despite his enormous gains, Yzerman doesn't put himself among the upper echelon of NHL's centers—not yet, anyway.

"I don't know if I belong there," he said. "Hopefully, one day I will. When I play against those guys—the Dale Hawerchuks and Bryan Trottiers and Peter Stastnys and Mark Messiers and Wayne Gretzkys—I still feel I've got a lot to learn. There are so many little things they do so well, things they do day after day, shift after shift. I don't consider myself in that category. I feel I've made important strides but I'm still improving. Trying to, anyway."

So are the Red Wings.

"I'd like to be captain for a long time. I want to win the Stanley Cup one day," said Yzerman.

INSIDE THE NHL

By REYN DAVIS, RICH CHERE and TIM MORIARTY

PREDICTED ORDER OF FINISH

Adams	Patrick	Norris	Smythe
Montreal	Philadelphia	Detroit	Edmonton
Hartford	N.Y. Rangers	St. Louis	Winnipeg
Quebec	Washington	Toronto	Calgary
Buffalo	N.Y. Islanders	Minnesota	Los Angeles
Boston	New Jersey	Chicago	Vancouver
	Pittsburgh		

Stanley Cup: Philadelphia

There are the lingering questions that cross one's mind long after the Edmonton Oilers have won their third Stanley Cup: Did the best team win? Would the Philadelphia Flyers have won if they'd been healthy, if they'd had the services of 58-goal scorer Tim Kerr and broken-ribs Dave Poulin?

In any event, one wonders if we have seen the beginning of the end of the Edmonton era and the arrival of the Flyers as champions-elect.

Success is spoiling the Oilers. Thirteen members of the team played out their options in pursuit of new contracts or different residences while Wayne Gretzky demanded—and received—revisions in his personal services contract with owner Peter Pocklington.

Gretzky continues to be the NHL's most dominating force but the pressures and the pace involved in staying on top may be taking a toll. If anyone in hockey deserves a year off, he does. But his pride won't let him stop until he's ready to retire—

Tim Moriarty wrote the Patrick division, Rich Chere of the Newark Star-Ledger *did the Adams and Reyn Davis of the* Winnipeg Free Press *covered the Smythe and Norris divisions. Davis wrote the introduction after a faceoff with Moriarty and Chere.*

probably within three years. It is impossible to imagine Gretzky playing beyond his 30th birthday or in the wake of a serious injury or after he's been supplanted as the NHL scoring champion by Mario Lemieux or Dale Hawerchuk or Pierre Turgeon.

But the fascination with the 1987-88 season extends far beyond Gretzky and the Oilers or the Flyers and Ron Hextall, their bombastic goaltender.

No fewer than six teams start the season with new coaches.

Surely, anything is possible after "Trader Phil" Esposito and the New York Rangers enticed the excitable Michel Bergeron out of Quebec to be their coach.

Out west, the Canucks are trying to recover their lost credibility in Vancouver under new management and the same owners. With suits pending, the previously-suspended Pat Quinn assumes his functions as president and general manager with an old Philadelphia friend, Bob McCammon, hired as coach.

The Pittsburgh Penguins have the city tingling, thanks to Mario Lemieux, a new coach (Pierre Creamer) and others. This is Lemieux' fourth year and he has never played a playoff game. He's had everybody but Mutt and Jeff for linemates. If nothing else, the Penguins have given him a bodyguard, Jimmy Mann, an old adversary who once received a nine-game suspension for breaking Paul Gardner's jaw.

Terry Crisp, a Fred Shero clone, succeeds Badger Bob Johnson as coach of Calgary Flames, the NHL's third-best team in 1986-87. Johnson takes over as executive director of the Amateur Hockey Association of the U.S.

A Calgary assistant, Bob Murdoch, has surfaced as the coach of Chicago Blackhawks, taking some of the heat off general manager Bob Pulford, while the struggling North Stars put their fate in the hands of Minnesota native son Herb Brooks.

At the bottom of the spectrum, Ted Sator and the Buffalo Sabres enter the post-Scotty Bowman years on a high note after taking Pierre Turgeon first overall in the entry draft. He is the living prize for finishing dead last.

A team on the move is the Los Angeles Kings, strengthened through trades and intelligent drafting that has produced Luc Robitaille, Jimmy Carson and Steve Duschene, half the members of the NHL's All-Rookie team.

Buckle up the chin strap, take a deep breath and drop the puck. It's a brand new season. Who'll take home the Cup? The pick from here is Philadelphia.

BOSTON BRUINS

TEAM DIRECTORY: Pres.: William D. Hassett Jr.; GM: Harry Sinden; Asst. GM: Tom Johnson; Dir. Pub. Rel.: Nate Greenberg; Coach: Terry O'Reilly. Home ice: Boston Garden (14,451; 195' x 83'). Colors: Gold, black and white. Training camp: Wilmington, Mass.

SCOUTING REPORT

OFFENSE: The lack of offensive speed was never more evident —and costly—for the Bruins than in the playoffs against the Montreal Canadiens. It is a sad commentary when either of Boston's 1986-87 coaches, Terry O'Reilly or Butch Goring, could've returned to the ice and improved the team speed.

Just as alarming was the drop in production of the power-play unit, falling from eighth-best two years ago to 15th in the NHL last season. Keith Crowder fell from 20 to 4 power-play goals in one season while Ray Bourque (11 to 6) and Charlie Simmer (14 to 11) also dropped. Bourque and Simmer remain the key to Boston's power play, which must return to form for the Bruins to remain competitive.

No longer do opposing clubs say, "Stop Bourque and the Bruins are beatable." The emergence of Cam Neely has seen to that. "Beyond Ray, Cam Neely was our other major concern," said Montreal's Chris Nilan. While Bourque led Boston in scoring with 95 points and is still the heart of the offense, Neely topped the team with 36 goals. Perhaps Harry Sinden's biggest fear should be a severe drop in that department from Neely.

DEFENSE: Injuries have turned Boston's defense into a nightmare, and advancing age will not make it any stronger this season. Gord Kluzak was out all of last season and had missed two of the last three years with knee problems that threaten his career, while the most reliable defenseman after Bourque—Reed Larson —is 31.

Even the goaltending combination of Bill Ranford and Doug Keans, who compiled the seventh-best stats in the league, has not thrilled Sinden. "Between Keans and Ranford," said the Boston GM, "it's not the type of goaltending that can win the Stanley Cup."

Once the Big Bad Bruins, they may not be tough enough any longer to prevent other clubs from walking all over them. Keans and Ranford were both roughed-up by Montreal in the playoffs. O'Reilly, beginning his first full season as coach, will certainly change that side of Boston's game. He cannot, however, do much about his players' birth certificates or medical reports.

OUTLOOK: In his postseason review of the 1986-87 Bruins, Sinden had positive feelings only about one position—right wing. That is where Neely, Rick Middleton, Tom McCarthy and Keith Crowder provided all the accompaniment for Bourque. Of

Ray Bourque and Charlie Simmer make the Bruins dangerous.

BRUIN ROSTER

No.	Player	Pos.	Ht.	Wt.	Born	1986—87	G	A	Pts.	PIM
3	John Blum	D	6-3	205	10-8-55/Detroit, Mich.	Washington	2	8	10	133
7	Raymond Bourque	D	5-11	205	12-28-60/Montreal, Que.	Boston	23	72	95	36
12	Randy Burridge	LW	5-9	178	1-7-66/Ridgeway, Ont.	Moncton	26	41	67	139
						Boston	1	4	5	16
33	Lyndon Byers	RW	6-1	190	2-29-64/Nipawin, Sask.	Boston	2	3	5	53
						Moncton	5	5	10	63
	Wade Campbell	D	6-4	220	2-1-61/Peace River, Alta.	Boston	0	3	3	34
						Moncton	12	23	35	34
32	John Carter	LW	5-10	165	5-3-63/Winchester, Mass.	Moncton	25	30	55	60
						Boston	0	1	1	0
40	Alain Cote	D	6-0	200	4-4-67/Montmagny, Que.	Boston	0	0	0	0
14	Geoff Courtnall	LW	5-11	165	6-18/62/Victoria, B.C.	Boston	13	23	36	117
18	Keith Crowder	RW	6-0	195	1-6-59/Windsor, Ont.	Boston	22	30	52	106
20	Dwight Foster	C-RW	5-10	175	4-2-57/Toronto, Ont.	Boston	4	12	16	37
10	Thomas Gradin	C	5-11	175	2-18-56/Selleftea, Swe.	Boston	12	31	43	18
39	Greg Johnston	RW	6-1	200	1-14-65/Barrie, Ont.	Boston	12	15	27	79
11	Steve Kasper	LW	5-8	175	9-28-61/Montreal, Que.	Boston	20	30	50	51
6	Gord Kluzak	D	6-4	210	3-6-64/Climax, Sask.	Injured—Did Not Play				
	Doug Kostynski	C	6-1	170	2-23-63/Castlegar, B.C.	Moncton	21	45	66	22
28	Reed Larson	D	6-0	195	7-30-56/Minneapolis, Minn.	Boston	12	24	36	95
13	Ken Linseman	C	5-9	168	8-11-58/Kingston, Ont.	Boston	15	34	49	126
17	Nevin Markwart	LW	5-10	170	12-9-64/Toronto, Ont.	Boston	10	9	19	225
						Moncton	3	3	6	11
19	Tom McCarthy	LW	6-2	200	7-31-60/Toronto, Ont.	Boston	30	29	59	31
						Moncton	0	1	1	0
16	Rick Middleton	RW	5-11	175	12-4-53/Toronto, Ont.	Boston	31	37	68	6
29	Jay Miller	LW	6-2	205	7-16-60/Wellesley, Mass.	Boston	1	4	5	208
8	Cam Neely	RW	6-1	205	6-6-65/Maple Ridge, B.C.	Boston	36	36	72	143
38	Kraig Nienhuis	LW	6-2	205	5-9-61/Sarina, Ont.	Boston	4	2	6	2
						Moncton	10	17	27	44
37	Dave Pasin	RW	6-1	186	7-8-66/Edmonton, Alta.	Moncton	27	25	41	47
41	Al Pederson	D	6-3	180	1-13-65/Edmonton, Alta.	Boston	1	11	12	71
	Ray Podloski	C	6-2	190	1-5-66/Edmonton, Alta.	Moncton	23	27	50	12
	Stephane Quintal	D	6-3	220		Granby	13	41	54	178
36	Dave Reid	LW	6-1	210	5-5-64/Toronto, Ont.	Boston	3	3	6	0
						Moncton	12	22	34	23
23	Charlie Simmer	LW	6-3	210	3-20-54/Terrace Bay, Ont.	Boston	29	40	69	59
21	Frank Simonetti	D	6-1	190	9-1-62/Melrose, Man.	Boston	1	0	1	17
						Moncton	0	1	1	6
25	Louis Sleigher	RW	5-11	195	10-23-58/Nouvelle, Que.	Injured—Did Not Play				
	Bob Sweeney	C	6-3	210	1-25-64/Concord, Mass.	Boston	2	4	6	21
						Moncton	29	26	55	81
22	Michael Thelvin	D	5-11	180	1-7-61/Sweden	Boston	5	15	20	18
27	Mats Thelin	D	5-10	180	3-30-61/Sweden	Boston	1	3	4	69
	Glen Wesley	D	6-1	192	10-2-68/Red Deer, Alta.	Portland	16	46	62	72

No.	Player	Pos.	Ht.	Wt.	Born	1986—87	GP	GA	SO	Avg.
35	Cleon Daskalakis	G	5-9	175	9-29-62/Boston, Mass.	Boston	2	7	0	4.33
						Moncton	27	118	0	4.88
31	Doug Keans	G	5-7	185	1-7-58/Pembroke, Ont.	Boston	36	108	0	3.34
30	Bill Ranford	G	5-10	170	12-14-66/Brandon, Man.	Boston	41	124	3	3.33
						Moncton	3	6	0	2.00
1	Roberto Romano	G	5-6	170	10-11-62/Montreal, Que.	Pitt.-Bos.	26	93	0	3.48
						Balt.-Moncton	6	21	0	3.72

course, can Sinden possibly expect another 36-goal season from Neely and a 30-goal campaign from McCarthy?

It figures to be a winter of struggle for the Bruins unless 23-year-old center Bob Sweeney, a 6-3, 210-pound prospect from Boston College, and 21-year-old left wing Randy Burridge mature fast enough to take some of the work load off the backs of veterans such as Middleton, Simmer and Bourque.

BRUIN PROFILES

CAM NEELY 22 6-1 205   Right Wing

Another Harry Sinden steal who turned out to be the most pleasant surprise of the season for Boston... His plus-23 rating was second only to Ray Bourque on club... In his first season as a Bruin after being acquired June 6, 1986, from Vancouver for Barry Pederson, he shattered his career-high totals in goals (36), assists (36) and points (72)... Added to All-Star team when Mike Bossy couldn't play with bad back... Scored hat trick in second playoff game April 9... Became close friends with actor Michael J. Fox four years ago... Battled private pressures as both parents fought cancer... Won Seventh Player Award given to Bruin whose play furthest exceeds expectations... Born June 6, 1965, in Comox, Sask.

Year	Club	GP	G	A	Pts.
1983-84	Vancouver.........	56	16	15	31
1984-85	Vancouver.........	72	21	18	39
1985-86	Vancouver.........	73	14	20	34
1986-87	Boston	75	36	36	72
	Totals	276	87	89	176

TOM McCARTHY 27 6-2 200   Right Wing

Revitalized in Boston after spending seven stormy seasons with North Stars... Traded to Bruins for a third-round 1986 pick and finished fourth in NHL shooting percentage (24.8)... Called playing in Boston his childhood dream... 30-goal season was his best since scoring 39 in 1983-84... Failed to live up to reviews in Minnesota, ending with nightmare 1985-86 season in which he played in only 25 games (12 goals)... Underwent chemical dependency rehab in summer of '85... Bell's Palsy, flu, knee and wrist injuries, separated shoulder and broken thumb cut his playing time two years ago . . . Born July 31, 1960, in Toronto.

Year	Club	GP	G	A	Pts.
1979-80	Minnesota.........	68	16	20	36
1980-81	Minnesota.........	62	23	25	48
1981-82	Minnesota.........	40	12	30	42
1982-83	Minnesota.........	80	28	48	76
1983-84	Minnesota.........	66	39	31	70
1984-85	Minnesota.........	44	16	21	37
1985-86	Minnesota.........	25	12	12	24
1986-87	Boston	68	30	29	59
	Totals	453	176	216	392

RAY BOURQUE 26 5-11 205   Defenseman

Simply the franchise for the Bruins . . . Named to first or second All-Star team every year of pro career . . . A power-play terror . . . Led league's defensemen in scoring with 95 points and was second in the NHL to Gretzky in assists (72) . . . Four years remaining on a six-year contract . . . Co-captain with Rick Middleton . . . Played at RendezVous '87 despite a bad groin pull . . . Has always been a workhorse, playing over 30 minutes a game in emergency situations. Now he rarely plays less than 35 minutes a game . . . Most shots in NHL (334 in 78 games) . . . Plus-44 rating . . . Born Dec. 28, 1960, in Montreal . . . Named 1986-87 winner of Norris Trophy as top defenseman.

Year	Club	GP	G	A	Pts.
1979-80	Boston	80	17	48	65
1980-81	Boston	67	27	29	56
1981-82	Boston	65	17	49	66
1982-83	Boston	65	22	51	73
1983-84	Boston	78	31	65	96
1984-85	Boston	73	20	66	86
1985-86	Boston	74	19	57	76
1986-87	Boston	78	23	72	95
	Totals	580	176	437	613

RICK MIDDLETON 33 5-11 175   Right Wing

Injuries and age have begun to catch up with him, yet the Bruins are not the same team without their veteran co-captain . . . First began wearing a helmet after suffering a severe head injury two seasons ago . . . Tops current Bruins in longevity with 11 seasons . . . Played in 900th career game Dec. 20 at Chicago . . . Scored goals in six straight games Mar. 5-17 . . . Conked on head in Montreal and missed one game with a slight concussion . . . After going scoreless in first two games back, he went on a tear and became "Nifty" of old... Recorded 500th career assist Jan. 15 and reached 900-point mark early in season... Born Dec. 4, 1953, in Toronto.

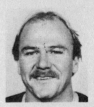

Year	Club	GP	G	A	Pts.
1974-75	New York R........	47	22	18	40
1975-76	New York R........	77	24	26	50
1976-77	Boston	72	20	22	42
1977-78	Boston	79	25	35	60
1978-79	Boston	71	38	48	86
1979-80	Boston	80	40	52	92
1980-81	Boston	80	44	59	103
1981-82	Boston	75	51	43	94
1982-83	Boston	80	49	47	96
1983-84	Boston	80	47	58	105
1984-85	Boston	80	30	46	76
1985-86	Boston	49	14	30	44
1986-87	Boston	76	31	37	68
	Totals	946	435	521	956

BILL RANFORD 20 5-10 170   Goaltender

As a 20-year-old rookie he topped the Bruins with 41 games played and a 3.33 GAA... Save percentage of .891 ranked fifth in NHL and second behind Ron Hextall among rookies... Three shutouts were second-high behind Mike Liut... Did not have a shutout in 118 Western League games with New Westminster but stopped 45 shots to shut out Minnesota, 1-0, on Feb. 21, 1987 ... Also blanked Calgary and Philly with 43 saves in each game ... Relies on quickness... Beat Canadiens in Forum the night before his 20th birthday... Started season as Bruins' No. 1 goalie but was sent to minors after eight games with 2-5-1 record and 4.09 GAA... Born Dec. 12, 1966, in Brandon, Man.

Year	Club	GP	GA	SO	Avg.
1985-86	Boston	4	10	0	2.50
1986-87	Boston	41	124	3	3.33
	Totals	45	134	3	3.25

KEITH CROWDER 28 6-0 195   Right Wing

Bruins' assistant captain may lack the recognition of his teammates but when he was sidelined for 11 games early in the season because of a separated shoulder, Bruins went 2-6-3... Returned Nov. 22... Scored points in 12 straight games Nov. 22 to Dec. 18... Skated on a line with Ken Linseman and Charlie

Simmer . . . Required offseason surgery on his right wrist . . . Led Bruins in scoring two seasons ago but injuries cut his goal total from 38 to 22 last year . . . Second to Tom McCarthy (6) with five game-winning goals . . . Born Jan. 6, 1959, in Windsor, Ont.

Year	Club	GP	G	A	Pts.
1978-79	Birmingham (WHA) .	5	1	0	1
1980-81	Boston	47	13	12	25
1981-82	Boston	71	23	21	44
1982-83	Boston	74	35	39	74
1983-84	Boston	63	24	28	52
1984-85	Boston	79	32	38	70
1985-86	Boston	78	38	46	84
1986-87	Boston	58	22	30	52
	NHL Totals	470	187	214	401
	WHA Totals........	5	1	0	1

CHARLIE SIMMER 33 6-3 210   **Left Wing**

Only Bruin to play in all 80 regular-season games . . . Missed opening playoff game against Montreal with a dislocated thumb and sprained wrist . . . Played in 600th NHL game Nov. 17 at Montreal . . . Tallied Boston franchise's 13,000th goal, a power-play score against the Rangers . . . Strong forward who can throw his weight around in the corners . . . His goal-scoring production fell off. After scoring 36 goals in 55 games in 1985-86, he netted 29 last year . . . Led Bruins with 11 power-play goals. No one else was in double figures . . . Born Mar. 20, 1954, in Terrace Bay, Ont.

Year	Club	GP	G	A	Pts.
1974-75	California	35	8	13	21
1975-76	California	21	1	1	2
1976-77	Cleveland	24	2	0	2
1977-78	Los Angeles	3	0	0	0
1978-79	Los Angeles	38	21	27	48
1979-80	Los Angeles	64	56	45	101
1980-81	Los Angeles	65	56	49	105
1981-82	Los Angeles	50	15	24	39
1982-83	Los Angeles	80	29	51	80
1983-84	Los Angeles	79	44	48	92
1984-85	LA-Bos	68	34	30	64
1985-86	Boston	55	36	23	59
1986-87	Boston	80	29	40	69
	Totals	662	331	351	682

REED LARSON 31 6-0 195   **Defenseman**

Became fifth defenseman in history to score his 200th career goal on Jan. 15 against Hartford . . . Obtained on Mar. 10, 1986, from

Detroit in exchange for Mike O'Connell ... Strong slap shot made him perfect on the point with Ray Bourque ... Missed first four games of the season with a shoulder separation suffered in training camp ... With his hard shot, he is the highest-scoring U.S.-born player in NHL history with 203 goals, 410 assists and 613 points ... Teamed with Bourque, they may be NHL's top 1-2 blue-line punch ... Born July 30, 1956, in Minneapolis.

Year	Club	GP	G	A	Pts.
1976-77	Detroit	14	0	1	1
1977-78	Detroit	75	19	41	60
1978-79	Detroit	79	18	49	67
1979-80	Detroit	80	22	44	66
1980-81	Detroit	78	27	31	58
1981-82	Detroit	80	21	39	60
1982-83	Detroit	80	22	52	74
1983-84	Detroit	78	23	39	62
1984-85	Detroit	77	17	45	62
1985-86	Det-Bos	80	22	45	67
1986-87	Boston	66	12	24	36
	Totals	787	203	410	613

STEVE KASPER 26 5-8 175   **Center**
One of the few players to hold Wayne Gretzky scoreless in a game last season, he ranks as one of the top two or three defensive forwards in hockey ... Close friends with Ray Bourque, who was his junior teammate at Verdun ... Scored 20 goals for the first time in five seasons and the third time in his career ... Finished one goal shy of his personal high, set in rookie campaign ... Ability to stay with opposing forwards stride for stride earned him nickname "The Shadow." ... Born Sept. 28, 1961, in Montreal.

Year	Club	GP	G	A	Pts.
1980-81	Boston	76	21	35	56
1981-82	Boston	73	20	31	51
1982-83	Boston	24	2	6	8
1983-84	Boston	27	3	11	14
1984-85	Boston	77	16	24	40
1985-86	Boston	80	17	23	40
1986-87	Boston	79	20	30	50
	Totals	434	99	160	259

GORD KLUZAK 23 6-4 210   **Defenseman**
Deja vu for Boston fans who watched injuries cut short Bobby Orr's career as a Bruin defenseman ... Two of his five NHL seasons have been injury-jinxed ... A return this season could make

the Bruins serious contenders. His absence means trouble... Planned to go to Sweden during the offseason for off-ice training program which includes six weeks of dry-land training... Still remains doubtful for 1987-88 season since undergoing three arthroscopic procedures on left knee in nine months... He missed the entire 1986-87 season with knee trouble but is tough enough to give it another go... Born Mar. 4, 1964, in Climax, Sask.

Year	Club	GP	G	A	Pts.
1982-83	Boston	70	1	6	7
1983-84	Boston	80	10	27	37
1984-85	Boston	Did Not Play			
1985-86	Boston	70	8	31	39
1986-87	Boston	Did Not Play			
	Totals	220	19	64	83

COACH TERRY O'REILLY: Agreed to return as Bruins' coach for 1987-88 season in May, but only after giving it a great deal of thought... Succeeded Butch Goring as Boston coach on Nov. 7, two days after Goring's dismissal with a 5-7-1 record... Bruins went 34-27-6 under local favorite and finished third... Once anchored tough-guy line of O'Reilly, John Wensink and Stan Jonathan... Retired as a player after 1984-85 campaign... Popular with fans, media and his players... Down-to-earth type who worked as a delivery boy on a milk truck as a kid and bought a '71 Olds Cutlass Supreme with his first hockey bonus... Has two sons, Conor (7) and Evan (3)... Holds Bruin record for penalty minutes with 2,095 ... Turned down four-year scholarship at St. Louis University to pursue NHL dream... Will have tough days ahead with aging, injury-plagued squad... Born June 7, 1951, in Niagara Falls, Ont.

GREATEST COACH

There are coaches in Bruins' history with better winning percentages (Tom Johnson at .738 and Don Cherry at .658). There are also Boston coaches who guided better teams (Harry Sinden's clubs in the 1960s) and were better-loved by the fans (Milt Schmidt). But there has never been a Bruins' coach to compare with Art Ross.

A true hockey legend, Ross is the only coach in the team's 63-year history to win two Stanley Cups (1929 and 1939), while winning 361 games in four separate terms behind the bench. It was Ross, whose longtime feud with Toronto's Conn Smythe is part of hockey lore, who was named the Bruins' first coach and GM by owner Charles F. Adams when the NHL granted Boston the first American franchise in 1924. Ross did not qualify for the playoffs his first two seasons, keeping terrible teams respectable, but took the Bruins to the finals in 1927. Just five years after the franchise was formed he won his first Stanley Cup with a club featuring Eddie Shore.

Ross retired to the front office after his fourth stint as coach in 1945. His record of 361-277-90 (.558), not to mention his playing days as a defenseman, got him elected to the Hall of Fame that same year.

ALL-TIME BRUIN LEADERS

GOALS: Phil Esposito, 76, 1970-71
ASSISTS: Bobby Orr, 102, 1970-71
POINTS: Phil Esposito, 152, 1970-71
SHUTOUTS: Hal Winkler, 15, 1927-28

BUFFALO SABRES

TEAM DIRECTORY: Chairman: Seymour H. Knox III; Pres.: Northrup R. Knox; GM: Gerry Meehan; Dir. Pub. Rel.: John Gurtler; Coach: Ted Sator. Home ice: Memorial Auditorium (16,433; 196' x 85'). Colors: Blue, white and gold. Training camp: North Tonawanda, N.Y.

SCOUTING REPORT

OFFENSE: If the Sabres could magically bring back a 20-year-old Gilbert Perreault, their offense would look much more formidable. As it is, they won't even have a 36-year-old Perreault, who has finally retired for good. That is why it is so vital that No. 1 draft choice Pierre Turgeon becomes a franchise player resembling the junior superstar who scored 69 goals and 85 assists in 58 games for Granby of the Quebec League.

Like Scotty Bowman, coach Ted Sator concentrates on a defensive style. While 23-year-old Finnish center Christian Ruuttu (22 goals as a rookie) may be the player to watch, the line of Dave Andreychuk (25-48-73), John Tucker (17-34-51) and Mike Foligno (30-29-59) is Buffalo's most reliable scoring unit.

The Sabres finished dead last in the Adams Division for the second straight season, and lack of offense is a major reason. Not one Buffalo player was among the league's top 20 scorers and only one player (Foligno) reached the 30-goal plateau. Big seasons from Ruuttu, Turgeon and newcomer Jan Ludvig would help, but Sator needs some support from the rear by the No. 2 line of Paul Cyr (if he's healthy), Doug Smith and Scott Arniel.

DEFENSE: Sator has a solid defensive foundation, beginning with a top offensive-minded defenseman (Phil Housley) and a quality defensive-minded back-liner (Mike Ramsey). Those two players have become the backbone of the club and figure to play an even greater role this season. Housley, Buffalo's centerpiece at this point, is solid on defense and raised his offensive production from fourth on the club two seasons ago to second. Ramsey remains one of the most reliable defensemen in the game.

If the Sabres plan to fight their way out of the Adams basement, second-year men Joe Reekie and Shawn Anderson must continue to improve. Both players thrived when Sator arrived, although Anderson's season was cut to 41 games because of shoulder injuries.

During the offseason, Buffalo traded physical veteran Jim Korn to the Devils. Korn did not play for Sator, who wanted to look at his younger players, but the move was surprising in that the Sabres desperately need some size and experience on defense, not to mention a full, return-to-form season from goaltender Tom Barrasso.

OUTLOOK: After setting the franchise record for most losses in a season (36) and most goals-against (308) during a dismal

Phil Housley ranked fifth among NHL defensemen in scoring.

SABRE ROSTER

No.	Player	Pos.	Ht.	Wt.	Born	1986–87	G	A	Pts.	PIM
	Mikael Andersson	C	5-9	185	5-10-66/Sweden	Buffalo	0	3	3	0
						Rochester	6	20	26	14
37	Shawn Anderson	D	6-1	191	2-7-68/Montreal, Que.	Buffalo	2	11	13	23
						Rochester	2	5	7	11
25	Dave Andreychuk	C	6-3	200	9-29-63/Hamilton, Ont.	Buffalo	25	48	73	46
9	Scott Arniel	LW	6-1	172	9-17-62/Kingston, Ont.	Buffalo	11	14	25	59
	Greg Brown	D	6-1	185	3-7-68/Hartford, Conn.					
	Paul Brydges	C	5-11	175	6-21-65/Guelph, Ont.	Rochester	13	17	30	54
38	Adam Creighton	C	6-5	205	6-2-65/Burlington, Ont.	Buffalo	18	22	40	26
18	Paul Cyr	LW	5-10	185	10-31-63/Pt. Alberoni, B.C.	Buffalo	11	16	27	122
3	Richie Dunn	D	6-0	192	5-12-57/Boston, Mass.	Buffalo	0	1	1	179
						Rochester	6	26	32	47
42	Steve Dykstra	D	6-2	190	2-3-62/Edmonton, Alta.	Buffalo	0	1	1	179
						Rochester	6	26	32	47
8	Dave Fenyves	D	5-11	188	4-19-60/Dunnville, Ont.	Rochester	6	16	22	57
						Buffalo	1	0	1	0
33	Lee Fogolin	D	6-0	204	2-7-55/Chicago, Ill.	Edm.-Buff.	1	5	6	25
17	Mike Foligno	RW	6-3	195	1-29-59/Sudbury, Ont.	Buffalo	30	29	59	176
12	Jody Gage	RW	5-11	182	11-29-59/Toronto, Ont.	Rochester	26	39	65	60
39	Clark Gillies	LW	6-3	215	4-4-54/Moose Jaw, Sask.	Buffalo	10	17	27	81
	Keith Gretzky	C	5-8	156	2-16-67/Brantford, Ont.	Bell.-Hamilton	35	66	101	18
3	Richard Hajdu	LW	6-1	185	5-10-65/Victoria, B.C.	Buffalo	0	0	0	0
						Rochester	7	15	22	90
19	Bob Halkidis	D	5-11	196	3-5-66/Toronto, Ont.	Buffalo	1	1	2	19
						Rochester	1	8	9	144
	Jim Hofford	D	6-0	188	10-4-64/Sudbury, Ont.	Buffalo	0	0	0	40
						Rochester	1	8	9	204
6	Phil Housley	D	5-10	180	5-9-64/St. Paul, Minn.	Buffalo	21	46	67	57
40	Uwe Krupp	D				Buffalo	1	4	5	23
						Rochester	3	19	22	50
26	Bob Logan	RW	6-0	180	2-22-64/Montreal, Que.	Rochester	30	14	44	27
						Buffalo	7	3	10	0
	Jan Ludwig	RW	5-10	187	9-17-61/Liberec, Czechoslovakia	New Jersey	7	9	16	98
						Maine	6	4	10	46
65	Mark Napier	RW	5-10	185	1-28-57/Toronto, Ont.	Edm.Buff.	13	18	31	2
23	Gates Orlando	C	5-8	175	11-16-62/Montreal, Que.	Buffalo	2	8	10	16
						Rochester	22	42	64	42
29	Jeff Parker	C	6-3	175	9-7-64/St. Paul, Minn.	Buffalo	3	3	6	7
						Rochester	14	8	22	75
12	Ken Priestlay	C	5-11	180	8-24-67/Richmond, B.C.	Buffalo	11	6	17	8
						Victoria	43	39	82	37
5	Mike Ramsey	D	6-3	190	12-3-60/Minneapolis, Minn.	Buffalo	8	31	39	109
31	Joe Reckie	D	6-3	195	2-22-63/Petawawa, Ont.	Buffalo	1	8	9	82
						Rochester	0	6	6	52
22	Lindy Ruff	D-LW	6-2	190	2-17-60/Warburg, Alta.	Buffalo	6	14	20	74
21	Christian Ruuttu	C	5-11	180	2-20-64/Finland	Buffalo	22	43	65	62
	Ray Sheppard	RW	6-1	186	5-27-66/Ottawa, Ont.	Rochester	18	13	31	11
15	Doug Smith	C	5-11	180	5-17-63/Ottawa, Ont.	Buffalo	16	24	40	106
						Rochester	5	6	11	35
19	Doug Trapp	LW	6-0	182	11-28-65/Belcarres, Sask.	Buffalo	0	0	0	0
						Rochester	27	35	62	80
7	John Tucker	C	6-0	185	9-29-64/Windsor, Ont.	Buffalo	17	34	51	21
	Pierre Turgeon	C	6-3	205	/Noranda, Que.	Granby	69	85	154	8
	Claude Verret	C	5-10	164	4-20-63/Lachine, Que.	Rochester	13	12	25	2

No.		Pos.	Ht.	Wt.	Born		GP	GA	SO	Avg.
30	Tom Barrasso	G	6-3	205	3-31-65/Boston, Mass.	Buffalo	46	152	2	3.65
1	Jacques Cloutier	G	5-7	155	1-5-60/Noranda, Que.	Buffalo	40	137	0	3.79
	Mike Craig	G	6-0	165	11-1-62/Calgary, Alta.	Rochester	23	82	0	4.13
						Flint	2	5	0	2.50
35	Daren Puppa	G	6-3	195	3-23-65/Kirkland Lake, Ont.	Buffalo	3	13	0	4.22
						Rochester	57	146	1	2.80

1986-87 campaign, it is doubtful that the Sabres can be any worse this season. Buffalo's 64 points was the third-lowest in franchise history and was only one point better than the original 1970 expansion Sabres.

Sator rejuvinated the club upon his arrival on Dec. 22, but his iron-fisted style will be put to the test right from training camp this year. His two biggest projects will be Barrasso and Cyr, who had just 27 points last season. If Barrasso does not respond, Sator will have to turn to young goalie Daren Puppa.

Buffalo fans are hoping Turgeon can do for the Sabres what Mario Lemieux did for the Pittsburgh Penguins. If he can't, it may be a long winter in Buffalo.

SABRE PROFILES

CHRISTIAN RUUTTU 23 5-11 180   **Center**
Brightest spot in a rather dismal season in Buffalo . . . Drafted in the seventh round of the 1983 NHL entry draft (134th overall) from Finland . . . Improved as season went on, scoring 23 points in first half and 42 in second half . . . Tallied first NHL goal on Oct. 9 in Winnipeg . . . His 22 goals tied Peter McNab and John Tucker for fourth-highest rookie total in club history . . . 42 assists was second highest total in Sabres' history . . . Played in World Championships in Vienna on a line with Petri Skriko and Raimo Summanen . . . Brought to Buffalo by Scotty Bowman after he scored 56 points in 36 games for Team IFK in Helsinki during 1985-86 . . . Born Feb. 20, 1964, in Lappeenranta, Finland.

Year	Club	GP	G	A	Pts.
1986-87	Buffalo	76	22	43	65

TOM BARRASSO 22 6-3 205   **Goaltender**
Benched early in the season when the Sabres fell to 5-20-4 . . . On Dec. 17, his record was 1-9-2 with a 4.21 GAA after a 7-0 loss in Quebec . . . Sought advice from Northeastern University assistant coach Bill Berglund, who coached him as a 6-to-14-year-old . . .

Could reach full potential under Ted Sator... Seemed relieved when Scotty Bowman was fired. It was Bowman who sent goalie back to the minors for a week as punishment early in his second season... Earns in excess of $250,000 a season and said he wanted to be the "Wayne Gretzky of goalies."... Tied for second on Sabres' all-time shutout list (11)... Needs three victories for 100... Married wife, Meaghen, in summer of '86... Born March 31, 1965, in Boston.

Year	Club	GP	GA	SO	Avg.
1983-84	Buffalo	42	117	2	2.84
1984-85	Buffalo	54	144	5	2.66
1985-86	Buffalo	60	214	2	3.61
1986-87	Buffalo	46	152	2	3.65
	Totals	202	627	11	3.19

DAVE ANDREYCHUK 24 6-3 200   Left Wing

A master at going to the net and using his size... Led Sabres in scoring (73 points) for the second straight season and seems to be he heir to Gil Perreault in that department... Anchored No. 1 ine with John Tucker and Mike Foligno... Declined a spot on RendezVous '87 roster... Scored points in 11 consecutive games between Oct. 24 and Nov. 19... Tallied 300th career point on Jan. 18 against Edmonton... Played in 300th NHL game Dec. 31... Missed most of preseason with a bruised knee cap ... Lacks speed but is a menace in front of the net... Born Sept. 29, 1963, in Hamilton, Ont.

Year	Club	GP	G	A	Pts.
1982-83	Buffalo	43	14	23	37
1983-84	Buffalo	78	38	42	80
1984-85	Buffalo	64	31	30	61
1985-86	Buffalo	80	36	51	87
1986-87	Buffalo	77	25	48	73
	Totals	342	144	194	338

MIKE FOLIGNO 28 6-3 195   Right Wing

Topped Sabres in goals (30) and was second to Steve Dykstra in penalty minutes (176)... Topped club with a plus-13 rating... Alternate captain... Bruised kidney suffered against New Jersey sidelined him from Dec. 9 to Dec. 17... Tallied 300th point as a Sabre Oct. 12 against Flames... Scored 500th NHL point on

Feb. 22 during back-to-back, three-point nights . . . Has scored 20 or more goals in each of his eight seasons . . . He finished season with 30 goals, reaching that plateau for the fifth time . . . Played in 600th game Mar. 17 at Calgary . . . Born Jan. 29, 1959, in Sudbury, Ont.

Year	Club	GP	G	A	Pts.
1979-80	Detroit	80	36	35	71
1980-81	Detroit	80	28	35	63
1981-82	Det-Buf	82	33	44	77
1982-83	Buffalo	66	22	25	47
1983-84	Buffalo	70	32	31	63
1984-85	Buffalo	77	27	29	56
1985-86	Buffalo	79	41	39	80
1986-87	Buffalo	75	30	29	59
	Totals	609	249	267	516

PAUL CYR 24 5-10 185   Left Wing

A major disappointment in his fifth NHL season and now his status is uncertain following injuries suffered in a shooting incident last May in the Dominican Republic . . . Finished with 27 points, matching his rookie-season totals of 1982-83. That year he played in just 36 games. Last season he played in 73 . . . Skated on second line with Scott Arniel and Doug Smith . . . Benched in late November, ending a streak of 64 straight games played . . . Drafted in the first round of '82 entry draft (ninth overall) . . . Offensive totals had improved in each season until last season . . . It is becoming clear that he is not living up to his No. 1 billing . . . Has failed to take advantage of substantial speed and a hard shot . . . Born Oct. 31, 1963, in Port Alberni, B.C.

Year	Club	GP	G	A	Pts.
1982-83	Buffalo	36	15	12	27
1983-84	Buffalo	71	16	27	43
1984-85	Buffalo	71	22	24	46
1985-86	Buffalo	71	20	31	51
1986-87	Buffalo	73	11	16	27
	Totals	322	84	110	194

PHIL HOUSLEY 23 5-10 180   Defenseman

On another club, he would be regarded as a superstar . . . Fifth in scoring among league defensemen with 67 points . . . Will pass Jerry Korab this season for the team assist record for backliners . . . Declined to play for Team USA in World Championships in

Vienna . . . Tallied 300th point on Dec. 14 against Whalers . . . Scored 100th goal on Mar. 26 against Kings . . . Collected 200th assist Nov. 5 against Bruins . . . Considered team's MVP by several teammates . . . Paired on defense with Steve Dykstra . . . Born March 9, 1964, in St. Paul, Minn.

Year	Club	GP	G	A	Pts.
1982-83	Buffalo	77	19	47	66
1983-84	Buffalo	75	31	46	77
1984-85	Buffalo	73	16	53	69
1985-86	Buffalo	79	15	47	62
1986-87	Buffalo	78	21	46	67
	Totals	382	102	239	341

SCOTT ARNIEL 25 6-0 172   Right Wing

Traded from Winnipeg to Buffalo on June 21, 1986, for Gilles Hamel . . . A 52-goal scorer in juniors for Cornwall but he has never found that touch in the NHL . . . Played with Dale Hawerchuk for current N.J. coach Doug Carpenter's 1979-80 Memorial Cup champion Cornwall Royals . . . After tallying four points before Ted Sator's arrival, he scored 21 points in his final 40 games under the new coach. Better days may be ahead for the former No. 2 draft choice . . . Awarded Buffalo Booster Club's unsung player award . . . Born July 17, 1962, in Cornwall, Ont.

Year	Club	GP	G	A	Pts.
1981-82	Winnipeg	17	1	8	9
1982-83	Winnipeg	75	13	5	18
1983-84	Winnipeg	80	21	35	56
1984-85	Winnipeg	79	22	22	44
1985-86	Winnipeg	80	18	25	43
1986-87	Buffalo	63	11	24	35
	Totals	394	86	119	205

ADAM CREIGHTON 22 6-5 205   Center

Another Sabre who came to life when Ted Sator arrived in Buffalo . . . Although he is big, the gangly youngster fails to use his size to his advantage . . . Collected only 26 minutes in penalties . . . Finished on positive note with 39 points in final 45 games after scoring one point in first 11 contests . . . Helped revive veteran Mike Ramsey . . . Led Ottawa to Memorial Cup in 1984 . . . His father, Dave, played 10 seasons in the NHL for four clubs . . . This could be a pivotal season in deciding whether

he has a future with Sabres or he becomes trade bait . . . Born
June 2, 1965, in Burlington, Ont.

Year	Club	GP	G	A	Pts.
1983-84	Buffalo	7	2	2	4
1984-85	Buffalo	30	2	8	10
1985-86	Buffalo	19	1	1	2
1986-87	Buffalo	56	18	22	40
	Totals	112	23	33	56

Tom Barrasso's goal is a return to full-time status.

Mike Ramsey is a powerhouse at his end of the ice.

COACH TED SATOR: From villain in New York to savior in Buffalo in a little over one month . . . Fired as coach of the Rangers on Nov. 21 after a stormy tenure under GM Phil Esposito . . . Nicknamed Darth Sator and Teddy Robot by the New York media . . . Hired by the Sabres on Dec. 22 . . . Guided Buffalo to a 21-22-4 record after the team went 7-22-4 under Scotty Bowman and Craig Ramsay . . . After serving as a scout and assistant coach for the Flyers, he was hired as

Rangers' coach June 19, 1985, and piloted club to 1986 Stanley Cup semifinals... Blamed for loss of Mark Pavelich, Reijo Ruotsalainen and Barry Beck... Graduated magna cum laude from Bowling Green University. Returned for master's degree in phys. ed... First American to be invited to Czechoslovakia National Team symposium... Coached for over five years in Sweden to learn European style... Speaks fluid Swedish and married a Swedish girl... Born Nov. 18, 1949, in Utica, N.Y..

GREATEST COACH

When Floyd Smith went behind the Buffalo Sabres' bench to make his NHL coaching debut during the 1971-72 season it could've been another Wally Pipp/Lou Gehrig scenario. Pipp was the New York Yankees' first baseman who was taken ill on June 1, 1925. Gehrig filled in for Pipp that afternoon and remained at first base for the next 2,130 games.

Smith was filling in for the ill Punch Imlach, but his story did not parallel Gehrig's. After coaching a 2-1 loss to the Maple Leafs, Smith found himself coaching the Sabres' AHL farm club in Cincinnati. It wasn't until May of 1974, two seasons later, that the former NHL forward for 11 seasons (Boston, Rangers, Detroit, Toronto and Buffalo) returned as coach of the Sabres for good. He lasted three seasons as Buffalo coach, compiling a 143-62-36 record (.668) and guiding the Sabres into the playoffs all three seasons.

Under Smith, Buffalo became a power which reached the 1975 Stanley Cup finals before losing to the Flyers in six games. The Sabres bowed out in the quarterfinals the next two seasons before Smith was replaced by Marcel Pronovost in May of 1977.

ALL-TIME SABRE LEADERS

GOALS: Danny Gare, 56, 1979-80
ASSISTS: Gil Perreault, 69, 1975-76
POINTS: Gil Perreault, 113, 1975-76
SHUTOUTS: Don Edwards, 5, 1977-78
　　　　　　　Tom Barrasso, 5, 1984-85

HARTFORD WHALERS

TEAM DIRECTORY: Chairman/Managing Gen. Partner: Howard Baldwin; Pres.-GM: Emile Francis; Dir. Pub. Rel.: Phil Langan; Coach: Jack Evans. Home ice: Hartford Civic Center (15,126; 200' x 85'). Colors: Green, blue and white. Training camp: Hartford, Ct.

SCOUTING REPORT

OFFENSE: What a disappointment! After completing an inspiring regular season, the Whalers were eliminated by the Quebec Nordiques in the opening round of the playoffs. After winning the first two games, Hartford's offense lacked the toughness to hit Quebec with the knockout punch. In games 3 and 4, the Whalers were held to one goal.

Sorely missed was left winger Torrie Robertson, who missed the final 60 games of the regular season and all of the playoffs with a badly broken left leg. The Whalers were hoping for 20 goals from Robertson, who finished with just one goal in his 20 games.

They may not have size, but the Whalers still boast two of the most talented scoring lines in the NHL. The top line consists of leading goal-scorer Kevin Dineen at right wing (40 goals), Ron Francis at center (93 points) and 22-goal scorer Paul Lawless on the left side. They are complemented by Dean Evason, Stewart Gavin and Sylvain Turgeon, all 20-goal scorers.

DEFENSE: Only Montreal and Philadelphia gave up fewer goals as a team than the Whalers. Coach Jack Evans, a former NHL defenseman, has the same cast, in addition to a healthy Joel Quenneville, back this season.

Ulf Samuelsson and Dana Murzyn have developed into all-star calibre defensemen, with Samuelsson leading the club with a plus-28 rating and Murzyn finishing plus-17. Although Scot Kleinendorst has not become the player the Whalers had hoped for when they got him from the Rangers in 1984, Samuelsson has exceeded all expectations and Murzyn has turned his 6-2, 200-pound frame into a weapon. Quenneville, a steady, stay-at-home veteran, will be back to add more stability after missing three months (43 games) with a broken right shoulder.

The jewels in Hartford's defense, of course, remain goalie Mike Liut and forward Doug Jarvis. Beginning his ninth NHL season and third full year in Hartford, Liut, the team's acknowledged MVP, only gets better. Steve Weeks is a capable backup

Mike Liut has won more than any goalie in Whaler history.

but a serious injury to Liut would create panic in Hartford. Even at age 32, Jarvis remains one of the league's most reliable and efficient defensive forwards.

OUTLOOK: Emile Francis, who became president and GM of the Whalers on May 2, 1983, has authored a living textbook on how to build a franchise. He has taken the Whalers step-by-step from a respectable club to a competitive team and now to a unit which could challenge for the Stanley Cup. The next step, of

WHALER ROSTER

No.	Player	Pos.	Ht.	Wt.	Born	1986—87	G	A	Pts.	PIM
20	John Anderson	RW	5-11	180	3-28-57/Toronto, Ont.	Hartford	31	44	75	19
44	Dave Babych	D	6-2	215	5-23-61/Edmonton, Alta.	Hartford	8	33	41	44
17	Wayne Babych	RW	5-11	191	6-6-58/Edmonton, Alta.	Hartford	0	0	0	4
						Binghamton	2	5	7	6
34	Adam Burt	D	6-2	186	1-15-69/Detroit, Mich.	North Bay	4	27	31	138
22	Shane Churla	RW	6-1	200	6-24-65/Fernie, B.C.	Hartford	0	1	1	78
						Binghamton	1	5	6	249
21	Sylvain Cote	D	6-0	175	1-19-66/Quebec City, Que.	Hartford	2	8	10	20
						Binghamton	2	4	6	0
	Yves Courteau	RW	6-0	193	4-25-64/Montreal, Que.	Hartford	0	0	0	0
						Binghamton	15	28	43	8
11	Kevin Dineen	LW	5-10	180	10-28-63/Quebec City, Que.	Hartford	40	39	79	110
12	Dean Evason	C	5-9	172	8-22-64/Flin Flon, Man.	Hartford	22	37	59	67
26	Ray Ferraro	C	5-10	165	8-23-64/Trail, B.C.	Hartford	27	32	59	42
10	Ron Francis	C	6-2	200	3-1-63/Sault Ste. Marie, Ont.	Hartford	30	63	93	45
14	Bill Gardner	C	5-10	170	3-19-60/Toronto, Ont.	Hartford	0	1	1	2
						Binghamton	17	44	61	18
	Dallas Gaume	C	5-11	180	8-27-63/Innisfal, Alta.	Binghamton	18	39	57	31
7	Stewart Gavin	LW	6-0	180	3-15-60/Ottawa, Ont.	Hartford	20	21	41	28
	Mike Hoffman	LW	5-11	186	2-26-63/Cambridge, Ont.	Binghamton	9	32	41	120
24	Pat Hughes	RW	6-1	180	3-25-55/Calgary, Alta.	St. L-Hart.	1	5	6	28
	Jody Hull	RW	6-0	188	2-2-69/Cambridge, Ont.	Peterborough	18	34	52	22
27	Doug Jarvis	C	5-9	175	3-24-55/Brantford, Ont.	Hartford	9	13	22	20
18	Scot Kleinendorst	D	6-3	205	1-16-60/Grand Rapids, Minn.	Hartford	3	9	12	130
29	Randy Ladouceur	D	6-3	200	6-30-60/Brockville, Ont.	Det.-Hart.	5	9	14	121
28	Paul Lawless	LW	5-11	185	7-2-64/Scarborough, Ont.	Hartford	22	32	54	14
23	Paul MacDermid	RW	6-1	209	4-14-63/Chesley, Ont.	Hartford	7	11	18	202
4	Dana Murzyn	D	6-3	200	12-9-66/Calgary, Alta.	Hartford	9	19	28	95
8	Mike Millar	RW	5-10	170	4-28-65/St. Catharines, Ont.	Hartford	2	2	4	0
						Binghamton	45	32	77	38
3	Joel Quenneville	D	6-0	180	9-15-58/Windsor, Ont.	Hartford	3	7	10	24
32	Torrie Robertson	LW	5-11	184	8-2-61/Victoria, B.C.	Hartford	1	0	1	98
5	Ulf Samuelsson	D	6-1	195	3-26-64/Leksand, Swe.	Hartford	2	31	33	166
72	Dave Semenko	LW	6-3	215	7-12-57/Winnipeg, Man.	Edm.-Hart.	4	8	12	87
33	Brad Shaw	D	5-10	169	4-28-64/Kitchener, Ont.	Hartford	0	0	0	0
						Binghamton	9	30	39	43
36	Gord Sherven	C	6-0	185	8-21-63/Gravelbourg, Sask.	Hartford	0	0	0	0
15	Dave Tippett	C	5-10	180	8-25-61/Moosonin, Sask.	Hartford	9	22	31	42
16	Sylvain Turgeon	C	6-0	195	1-17-65/Noranada, Que.	Hartford	23	13	36	45

No.	Player	Pos.	Ht.	Wt.	Born	1986—87	GP	GA	SO	Avg.
1	Mike Liut	G	6-2	195	1-7-56/Weston, Ont.	Hartford	59	187	4	3.23
	Pete Sidorkiewicz	G	5-9	165	6-29-63/Poland	Binghamton	57	161	4	2.92
31	Steve Weeks	G	5-11	165	6-30-58/Scarborough, Ont.	Hartford	25	78	1	3.42
	Kay Whitmore	G	5-11	165	4-10-67/Sudbury, Ont.	Peterborough	36	118	1	3.28

course, is the biggest step of all. The Whalers need to learn how to win in postseason play.

Hartford was a better team than Quebec last season, yet the Nords won the playoff series in six games. Hartford and Montreal will be the class of the Adams Division this season. The question remains: can the Whalers learn what the Canadiens have known for decades—how to win in the Stanley Cup playoffs?

WHALER PROFILES

MIKE LIUT 31 6-2 195   Goaltender

At $450,000, he is the eighth highest-paid player in the NHL... Recorded most shutouts (4) of his eight-season career... Passed Greg Millen as Whalers' all-time shutout leader (7) and victory leader (63)... Excluded from RendezVous '87, which many feel was a reflection on his 8-1 loss to the Soviet National Team in 1981 Canada Cup final in Montreal... Named MVP by team-mates, booster club and writers... Posted five-game winning streak February 23 to March 7... Second to Ron Hextall with 31 wins... Fifth among active NHL goalies with 16 career shutouts... Born Jan. 7, 1956, in Weston, Ont.

Year	Club	GP	GA	SO	Avg.
1977-78	Cincinnati (WHA) ..	27	86	0	4.25
1978-79	Cincinnati (WHA) ..	54	184	3	3.47
1979-80	St. Louis	64	194	2	3.18
1980-81	St. Louis	61	199	1	3.34
1981-82	St. Louis	64	250	2	4.06
1982-83	St. Louis	68	235	1	3.72
1983-84	St. Louis	58	197	3	3.45
1984-85	St L-Hart	44	156	2	3.60
1985-86	Hartford	57	198	2	3.62
1986-87	Hartford	59	187	4	3.23
	NHL Totals	475	1616	17	3.52
	WHA Totals.......	81	270	3	3.69

ULF SAMUELSSON 23 6-1 195   Defenseman

Physical defenseman who has become a key in Hartford... Named to NHL All-Star team for RendezVous '87... Led Whalers with a plus-28 rating... Swede is known for his zany antics as much as his skating ability. After throwing a puck into the net with his hands he raised his arms in celebration. Also tried to prevent Anton Stastny from scoring a breakaway empty-net goal by throwing his stick and gloves at him... Suspended for

five games for making obscene gestures at Quebec coach Michel
Bergeron during playoffs ... Shares hometown of Fagur, Sweden, with the Rangers' Tomas Sandstrom ... Did not skate until
the age of nine ... Born March 26, 1964, in Leksands, Sweden.

Year	Club	GP	G	A	Pts.
1984-85	Hartford	41	2	6	8
1985-86	Hartford	80	5	19	24
1986-87	Hartford	78	2	31	33
	Totals	199	9	56	65

PAUL LAWLESS 23 5-11 185   **Left Wing**
Plays with a reckless style ... May be reaching potential which
made him Whalers' first-round draft pick in 1982 as an underage
junior ... Played under ex-Rangers coach Tom Webster in Salt
Lake City, where he was voted Mr. Hustle Award ... Missed 18
games with strained left knee ligaments after being slashed in St.
Louis Jan. 7 ... Three days earlier, he had set a club record by
scoring six points against Toronto ... Suffered a broken right
hand when slashed in Montreal by Claude Lemieux April 1 ...
Led Whalers' forwards with plus-24 rating ... Born July 2, 1964,
in Scarborough, Ont.

Year	Club	GP	G	A	Pts.
1982-83	Hartford	47	6	9	15
1983-84	Hartford	6	0	3	3
1985-86	Hartford	64	17	21	38
1986-87	Hartford	60	22	32	54
	Totals	177	45	65	110

RON FRANCIS 24 6-2 200   **Center**
Backbone of the Whalers ... Injured left shoulder, suffered
March 10 in Quebec, probably cost him his first 100-point
season ... Quebec Colisee has been bad luck for Whaler captain.
He broke his left ankle there when hit by Mike Eagles in January
of 1986 ... Scored 400th point of his career on opening night and
played in his 400th game later in the season ... Tallied 300th
career assist and 150th career goal ... Voted MVP in three of last
four seasons by teammates ... First player to represent Whalers

in two All-Star Games . . . Drafted fourth overall when Hartford lost shot at Bobby Carpenter in 1981 . . . Born March 1, 1963, in Sault Ste. Marie, Ont.

Year	Club	GP	G	A	Pts.
1981-82	Hartford	59	25	43	68
1982-83	Hartford	79	31	59	90
1983-84	Hartford	72	23	60	83
1984-85	Hartford	80	24	57	81
1985-86	Hartford	53	24	53	77
1986-87	Hartford	75	30	63	93
	Totals	418	157	335	492

DOUG JARVIS 32 5-9 175 Center

Established NHL record of 915 consecutive games played when he skated against his first NHL club, the Montreal Canadiens, on Dec. 26 . . . Broke Garry Unger's record of 914 and has currently played in 962 straight games. Going for 1,000 this season . . . Excellent face-off man . . . Scored 400th career point on March 7, 1987, against the Flyers . . . Point total of 22 was the lowest of his 12-year career . . . Has not missed a game in all 12 campaigns . . . Because of size, he stays away from physical game . . . Although he is modest about his streak, old pro's keys are luck and a high tolerance for pain . . . Born March 24, 1955, in Brantford, Ont.

Year	Club	GP	G	A	Pts.
1975-76	Montreal..........	80	5	30	35
1976-77	Montreal..........	80	16	22	38
1977-78	Montreal..........	80	11	28	39
1978-79	Montreal..........	80	10	13	23
1979-80	Montreal..........	80	13	11	24
1980-81	Montreal..........	80	16	22	38
1981-82	Montreal..........	80	20	28	48
1982-83	Washington	80	8	22	30
1983-84	Washington	80	13	29	42
1984-85	Washington	80	9	28	37
1985-86	Wash-Hart	82	9	18	27
1986-87	Hartford	80	9	13	22
	Totals	962	139	264	403

SYLVAIN TURGEON 22 6-0 195 Left Wing

Hurt severely by eight-month layoff caused by mysterious abdominal problem which baffled doctors for seven months. Problem was eventually corrected by surgery Nov. 14 . . . Returned to action Jan. 9 after missing 40 games—39 last season and the seventh game of Hartford's 1986 playoff series with Montreal

. . . Three days after returning he scored his first of 23 goals, on a power play against the Devils . . . Power-play specialist since his NHL career began in 1983 . . . Linemates are Stewart Gavin and Dean Evason . . . Nicknamed "Sly" . . . Tallied 100th career assist on Jan. 15 at Boston . . . Born Jan. 17, 1965, in Noranda, Que.

Year	Club	GP	G	A	Pts.
1983-84	Hartford	76	40	32	72
1984-85	Hartford	64	31	31	62
1985-86	Hartford	76	45	34	79
1986-87	Hartford	41	23	13	36
	Totals	257	139	110	249

DAVE BABYCH 26 6-2 215   Defenseman
Inspiration to teammates . . . Played the seventh game of the 1986 Adams Division finals with an injured groin and a pulled hip muscle . . . Both injuries carried into last season . . . Acquisition from Winnipeg in November of 1985 for Ray Neufeld stands as Emile Francis' finest deal in Hartford . . . Despite his size, he is an unassuming, gentle person . . . Played in 500th NHL game last season . . . Scored 400th career point . . . His minus-18 rating was the worst on the club . . . Born May 23, 1961, in Edmonton.

Year	Club	GP	G	A	Pts.
1980-81	Winnipeg	69	6	38	44
1981-82	Winnipeg	79	19	49	68
1982-83	Winnipeg	79	13	61	74
1983-84	Winnipeg	66	18	39	57
1984-85	Winnipeg	78	13	49	62
1985-86	Winn-Hart.........	81	14	55	69
1986-87	Hartford	66	8	33	41
	Totals	518	91	324	415

KEVIN DINEEN 24 5-10 180   Right Wing
Represented the Whalers and scored a goal against the Soviets in RendezVous '87 . . . Tireless worker who never stops skating . . . Let Whalers down by going scoreless in first five playoff games against Montreal . . . Needs two goals for No. 100 of his career . . . Voted favorite Whaler by Hartford fans . . . Perhaps the best in the NHL at obstructing opposing goalie . . . Son of former Whalers' coach and head scout Bill Dineen . . . Brother, Gord, is an Islander defenseman . . . Second to Ron Francis in Whalers'

scoring but led club with 40 goals... Born Oct. 28, 1963, in Quebec.

Year	Club	GP	G	A	Pts.
1984-85	Hartford	57	25	16	41
1985-86	Hartford	57	33	35	68
1986-87	Hartford	78	40	39	79
	Totals	192	98	90	188

JOHN ANDERSON 30 5-11 180   Right Wing

Consistency is his biggest asset, having scored 30 or more goals in five of the last six seasons... His 31 goals were second to Kevin Dineen's 40... Scored 500th career point at New Jersey on Jan. 12 with a pair of assists... A big pickup by Emile Francis on March 8, 1986, for Risto Siltanen... Boasts good speed as well as better-than-average defensive skills... Maple Leafs drafted him No. 1 in 1977, ahead of such players as Mike Bossy, Ron Duguay, Rod Langway and John Tonelli... Collected six points in a 1986 playoff game. Only Wayne Gretzky has scored more... Born March 28, 1957, in Toronto.

Year	Club	GP	G	A	Pts.
1977-78	Toronto	17	1	2	3
1978-79	Toronto	71	15	11	26
1979-80	Toronto	74	25	28	53
1980-81	Toronto	75	17	26	43
1981-82	Toronto	69	31	26	57
1982-83	Toronto	80	31	49	80
1983-84	Toronto	73	37	31	68
1984-85	Toronto	75	32	31	63
1985-86	Que-Hart	79	25	49	74
1986-87	Hartford	76	31	44	75
	Totals	698	245	297	542

DAVE TIPPETT 26 5-10 180   Left Wing

An iron man in his own right. He has played in 257 consecutive games... Whalers' best all-around player in 1987 playoffs... Outstanding checker who comprised fourth line with Doug Jarvis and Paul MacDermid... Failed to match goal total and point total of previous season... Like Jarvis, he has never missed a game in his NHL career... Captained Team Canada in 1984 Olympics as a center... Member of the 1982 NCAA championship North Dakota hockey squad...Strong penalty-killer...Born Aug. 25, 1961, in Moosomin, Sask.

Year	Club	GP	G	A	Pts.
1983-84	Hartford	17	4	2	6
1984-85	Hartford	80	7	12	19
1985-86	Hartford	80	14	20	34
1986-87	Hartford	80	9	22	31
	Totals	257	34	56	90

COACH JACK EVANS: Only NHL coach to lose his team bus when it was stolen from a New Jersey hotel parking lot...Won 200th game as an NHL coach with a 5-2 victory at Washington on Feb. 6...Completed fourth season as Whalers' coach with a 43-30-7 record and the first Adams Division first-place finish in club history...Nicknamed "Tex" during his playing days with the Rangers. One night during a card game he sang a cowboy song and the tag stuck...Shaky relationship with Hartford fans and media over the years. Booing became so bad at Civic Center during team's 2-13-1 streak Jan. 27-March 1, 1986, that the PA announcer stopped announcing his name before games...NHL defenseman for 14 seasons... Born April 21, 1928, in Morriston, South Wales.

GREATEST COACH

Jack Evans has never won a popularity contest in Hartford. He has had run-ins with the media, including an incident with one writer which turned into a lawsuit, and he has been booed by the Civic Center crowd unmercifully. Yet Evans, who turned 59 last April, has stuck to his principles and has given the Whalers the leadership the team so badly needed. In four seasons he has taken the team from 20th overall in the standings to fourth.

Evans has posted a 215-278-67 record as Hartford coach, a

.444 winning percentage which is best in the club's NHL history. Although they suffered a disappointing loss to Quebec in the 1987 playoffs, the Whalers finished first in the Adams Division for the first time ever last season. It was also Evans who guided the Whalers to the playoffs in 1986 for the first time in six years, upsetting the Nordiques in the playoffs before losing to the Stanley Cup-bound Montreal Canadiens.

Formerly coach of the California Golden Seals and Cleveland Barons, Evans was hired in Hartford in 1983 by longtime friend Emile Francis. He had coached the Blues' Salt Lake farm team for five seasons.

ALL-TIME WHALER LEADERS

GOALS: Blaine Stoughton, 56, 1979-80
ASSISTS: Mark Howe, 65, 1978-79
　　　　　Mike Rogers, 65, 1980-81
POINTS: Mark Howe, 107, 1978-79
SHUTOUTS: Mike Liut, 4, 1986-87

MONTREAL CANADIENS

TEAM DIRECTORY: Pres.: Ronald Corey; Managing Dir.: Serge Savard; Dir. Scouting: Andre Boudrias; Dir. Hockey Personnel: Jacques Lemaire; Dir. Press Rel.: Michele Lapointe; Dir. Pub. Rel.: Claude Mouton; Coach: Jean Perron. Home ice: Montreal Forum (16,074; 200′ x 85′). Training camp: Montreal.

SCOUTING REPORT

OFFENSE: With a 40- or 50-goal sniper in the lineup, the Canadiens undoubtedly would've been able to defeat the Flyers in the Wales Conference finals, assuring them a second straight trip to the Stanley Cup finals. However, not only do the Canadiens not boast a scorer of that quality; they did not have a single 30-goal scorer during the regular season. Bobby Smith was Mon-

The Montreal defense was second-best in NHL last season.

treal's leading goal-scorer with 28, one more than Claude Lemieux.

The Montreal press has fanned rumors of a trade which would
bring Denis Savard to the Canadiens. But that seems unlikely and
since there is no Guy Lafleur on the immediate horizon, coach
Jean Perron will turn to some younger forwards for offensive
help. At the top of the list are 6-0, 175-pound center Shayne
Corson, who scored six goals in the playoffs and was a standout
in the series against the Flyers, and 21-year-old center Stephane
Richer, who scored 61 goals in 57 junior games four years ago
but has yet to blossom in the NHL.

Mark Pederson, the club's No. 1 draft pick in 1986, is a long
shot, although the Canadiens may have to rush him along if their
defense does not remain strong enough to overcome a weak offense.

DEFENSE: When they needed it the most, the Canadiens' de-
pendable defense let them down. In the sixth and final game of
the Wales finals against Philadelphia, Montreal blew a 3-1 lead in
the Forum and lost, 4-3. "We lost this series ourselves," said Guy
Carbonneau.

The Canadiens have quality defensemen in Larry Robinson
(but he's sidelined with a fractured right tibia), Craig Ludwig,
Chris Chelios, Petr Svoboda and Rick Green. It is Green who is
emerging as the defensive key as Robinson winds up his career.
Chelios and Ludwig form a tandem which stacks up to any pair-
ing in hockey. Together they literally smothered the Bruins' offense in the playoffs.

Up front, the Canadiens remain sound defensively. Carbonneau, a perennial Selke Trophy candidate, may be the best defensive forward in the game today, while bad boys Chris Nilan and
Lemieux keep opposing forwards honest.

OUTLOOK: Robinson, who has played for some of the greatest
clubs in Montreal history since 1972, says the current Canadiens'
team is not as good as some past Stanley Cup winners, yet the
club is "rock-solid." It is good enough to regain the Stanley Cup
if all the pieces fall into place.

But to win again, the goaltending duo of Brian Hayward and
Patrick Roy must return to the form that showed during the regular season and not the form they displayed against the Flyers in
the playoffs. Secondly, the Canadiens of the future, waiting in the
wings for several seasons, must finally emerge. They include
Richer, Corson, Brent Gilchrist (a 1985 fourth-round draft
choice) and Mike Keane (a free agent).

The Canadiens have not finished first in their division since

CANADIEN ROSTER

No.	Player	Pos.	Ht.	Wt.	Born	1986 – 87	G	A	Pts.	PIM
12	Serge Boisvert	RW	5-9	172	6-1-59/Drummondville, Que.	Sherbrooke	27	54	81	29
						Montreal	0	0	0	0
	Gareme Bonar	C-RW	6-3	205	1-21-66/Toronto, Ont.	Sherbrooke	6	6	12	7
22	Randy Bucyk	RW	6-0	190	11-9-62/Edmonton, Alta.	Sherbrooke	24	37	63	28
21	Guy Carbonneau	C	5-11	175	3-18-60/Sept Isles, Que.	Montreal	18	27	45	68
	Andrew Cassels	C	6-0	167	7-23-69/Bramalee, Ont.	Ottawa	26	66	92	28
	Jose Charbonneau	RW	6-0	195	11-2-66/Fermo Neuve, Que.	Sherbrooke	14	27	41	94
24	Chris Chelios	D	6-1	185	1-25-62/Chicago, Ill.	Montreal	11	33	44	124
27	Shayne Corson	C	6-0	175	8-13-66/Barrie, Ont.	Montreal	12	11	23	144
20	Kjell Dahlin	C	6-0	176	2-2-63/Timra, Swe.	Montreal	12	8	20	0
	Rocky Dundas	RW	6-0	202	1-30-67/Regina, Sask.	Medicine Hat	33	41	74	132
23	Bob Gainey	LW	6-2	196	12-13-53/Peterborough, Ont.	Montreal	8	8	16	19
	Perry Ganchar	RW	5-9	180	10-28-63/Saskatoon, Sask.	Sherbrooke	22	29	51	64
29	Gaston Gingras	D	6-0	191	2-13-59/North Bay, Ont.	Montreal	11	34	45	21
5	Rick Green	D	6-3	210	2-20-56/Belleville, Ont.	Montreal	1	9	10	10
31	John Kordic ·	LW	6-1	188	3-22-65/Edmonton, Alta.	Montreal	5	3	8	151
						Sherbrooke	4	4	8	49
38	Mike Lalor	D	6-0	193	3-8-63/Buffalo, N.Y.	Montreal	0	10	10	47
32	Claude Lemieux	C	6-1	210	7-16-65/Rockinghant, Que.	Montreal	27	26	53	156
17	Craig Ludwig	D	6-2	204	3-15-61/Eagle River, Wis.	Montreal	4	12	16	105
35	Mike McPhee	C	6-2	205	2-14-60/Sydney, N.S.	Montreal	18	21	39	58
36	Sergio Momesso	C	6-3	202	9-4-65/Montreal, Que.	Montreal	14	17	31	96
						Sherbrooke	1	6	7	10
26	Mats Naslund	RW	5-7	160	10-31-59/Sweden	Montreal	25	55	80	16
30	Chris Nilan	RW	6-0	200	2-9-58/Boston, Mass.	Montreal	4	16	20	266
	Mark Pederson	LW	6-1	196	1-14-68/Medicine Hat, Alta.	Medicine Hat	56	46	102	58
44	Stephane Richer	C	6-0	190	6-7-66/Buckingham, Que.	Montreal	20	19	39	80
						Sherbrooke	10	4	14	11
19	Larry Robinson	D	6-3	215	6-2-51/Marvelville, Ont.	Montreal	13	37	50	44
	Guy Rouleau	C	5-9	175	2-16-65/Beloel, Que.	Sherbrooke	4	3	7	2
39	Brian Skrudland	C	6-1	180	7-31-63/Peace River, Alta.	Montreal	11	17	28	107
15	Bobby Smith	C	6-4	210	2-12-58/North Sydney, Nfind.	Montreal	28	47	75	72
	Karel Svoboda	C	6-1	192	12-2-60/Czechoslvakia	Sherbrooke	22	46	68	45
	Petr Svoboda	D	6-0	167	2-14-66/Czechoslovakia	Montreal	5	17	22	73
28	Gilles Thiboudeau	C	5-10	165	3-4-63/Montreal, Que.	Montreal	1	3	4	0
						Sherbrooke	27	40	67	26
11	Ryan Walter	C	6-0	195	4-23-58/New Westminster, B.C.	Montreal	23	23	46	34

No.	Player	Pos.	Ht.	Wt.	Born	1986 – 87	GP	GA	SO	Avg.
1	Brian Hayward	G	5-10	175	6-25-60/Kingston, Ont.	Montreal	37	102	1	2.81
	Vincent Riendeau	G	5-9	173	4-20-66/St. Hyacinthe, Que.	Sherbrooke	41	114	2	2.89
33	Patrick Roy	G	6-0	175	10-5-55/Quebec, Que.	Montreal	46	131	1	2.93

1984-85. Look for them to regain the top spot in the Adams Division and return to the Stanley Cup finals.

CANADIEN PROFILES

MATS NASLUND 28 5-7 160   Left Wing
A throwback to the Canadiens of the 1950s and '60s, despite being born in Sweden...Montreal's best player in the 1987 playoffs, leading the team in scoring with seven goals, 15 assists and 22 points...Will begin second year on a three-year contract at $275,000 per season...Dangerous overtime scorer under playoff pressure...Scored 400th point of his career last season...Tallied only one goal in month of November...Since sensational 1985-86 season (43-67-110), opposing clubs have shadowed him...Born Oct. 31, 1959, in Timra, Sweden.

Year	Club	GP	G	A	Pts.
1982-83	Montreal	74	26	45	71
1983-84	Montreal	77	29	35	64
1984-85	Montreal	80	42	37	79
1985-86	Montreal	80	43	67	110
1986-87	Montreal	79	25	55	80
	Totals	390	165	239	404

CLAUDE LEMIEUX 22 6-1 210   Right Wing
A theatrical player who drew the ire of his teammates during the playoffs...Regarded as a money player as well as an agitator ...Pregame brawl in sixth game of Flyer series was triggered by his ritual of putting a shot the length of the ice into opponents' net...Was a plus-7 in playoffs...Selected for RendezVous '87 ...Bit Jim Peplinski's finger during 1986 Stanley Cup finals against Calgary...Scored game-winning goal in OT in seventh game of '86 Adams final against Hartford...Tallied 10 goals (four game-winners) in '86 playoffs but couldn't repeat last spring...Born July 16, 1965, in Buckingham, Que.

Year	Club	GP	G	A	Pts.
1983-84	Montreal	8	1	1	2
1984-85	Montreal	1	0	1	1
1985-86	Montreal	10	1	2	3
1986-87	Montreal	76	27	26	53
	Totals	95	29	30	59

BOBBY SMITH 29 6-4 210   **Center**

Only Canadien to appear in all 80 regular-season games...
Finished second to Mats Naslund in club scoring, although offensive production dropped to 28 goals and 75 points...One
of hockey's most adept playmaking centers who can also play
the physical game...Twelfth-leading scorer in playoffs with
9 goals, 9 assists...Considered by teammates most underrated
player in lineup...Tied Ryan Walter for team lead in power-play
goals with 11...Led Canadiens with 7 game-winning goals,
3 more than runnersup Walter and Sergio Momesso...Recorded
first hat trick as Canadien on Nov. 6, 1986, at Los Angeles...
Attributes include long reach and long stride...Born Feb. 12,
1958, in North Sydney, Nova Scotia.

Year	Club	GP	G	A	Pts.
1978-79	Minnesota.........	80	30	44	74
1979-80	Minnesota.........	61	27	56	83
1980-81	Minnesota.........	78	29	64	93
1981-82	Minnesota.........	80	43	71	114
1982-83	Minnesota.........	77	24	53	77
1983-84	Minn-Mont........	80	29	43	72
1984-85	Montreal..........	65	16	40	56
1985-86	Montreal..........	79	31	55	86
1986-87	Montreal..........	80	28	47	75
	Totals............	680	257	473	730

GUY CARBONNEAU 27 5-11 175   **Center**

Disappointing regular season and playoffs...Did not reach
20-goal plateau for first time in four seasons...Bothered by
nagging injuries first half of season...Benched early in season
along with Chris Nilan when two broke curfew on West Coast
trip...One of five Canadiens to participate in taping of a rock
video...A perennial Selke Trophy candidate...Still dives face-
first in front of slap shots. Best at that craft in the game...Born
March 18, 1960, in Sept Isles, Que.

Year	Club	GP	G	A	Pts.
1980-81	Montreal..........	2	0	1	1
1982-83	Montreal..........	77	18	29	47
1983-84	Montreal..........	78	24	30	54
1984-85	Montreal..........	79	23	34	57
1985-86	Montreal..........	80	20	36	56
1986-87	Montreal..........	79	18	27	45
	Totals............	395	103	157	260

BRIAN HAYWARD 27 5-10 175   **Goaltender**

Developing as a strong NHL goalie...Recorded best goals-
against average among league's netminders (2.81)...Ranked

fourth with an .893 save percentage... Involved in a multiple-auto accident while driving to the Forum on Feb. 4. His car was damaged but the goalie starred in a 4-3 victory over Quebec that night... Acquired from Winnipeg on Aug. 15, 1986, in deal for Steve Penney... After dismal 1985-86 season for Jets, he made the deal a lopsided success for Montreal GM Serge Savard... Born June 25, 1960, in Georgetown, Ont.

Year	Club	GP	GA	SO	Avg.
1982-83	Winnipeg	24	89	1	3.71
1983-84	Winnipeg	28	124	0	4.86
1984-85	Winnipeg	61	220	0	3.84
1985-86	Winnipeg	52	217	0	4.79
1986-87	Montreal	37	102	1	2.81
	Totals	202	752	2	3.98

CHRIS CHELIOS 25 6-1 185   **Defenseman**
Regarded by many as hockey's dirtiest player... Demands respect from opposing players and usually gets it... Member of RendezVous '87 squad... Canadiens' best player in playoff series against Boston... Paired with Craig Ludwig... Played right wing against the Islanders Feb. 22, marking the first time he played up front since his junior days at Moose Jaw... Ambidextrous. Can shoot from either side... If he can remain injury-free, he is likely to be Larry Robinson's successor... Born Jan. 25, 1962, in Chicago.

Year	Club	GP	G	A	Pts.
1983-84	Montreal	12	0	2	2
1984-85	Montreal	74	9	55	64
1985-86	Montreal	41	8	26	34
1986-87	Montreal	71	11	33	44
	Totals	198	28	116	144

LARRY ROBINSON 36 6-3 215   **Defenseman**
Will be late starting his 16th season as a result of fractured right tibia in a summer polo match... Could hasten the end of distinguished career... Plus-24 rating was tops on club... Had three goals and 17 assists in 17 playoff games... Has written his autobiography... Recorded his 800th career point Feb. 25 in Chicago... Tallied 100th career playoff point with a goal in series opener against Boston... Missed 10 games with a heel

problem in December and knee injury in March... Norris Trophy winner in 1977 and '80... Notched 600th career assist Dec. 11 vs. Rangers... Holds five club records for defensemen... Born June 2, 1951, in Winchester, Ont.

Year	Club	GP	G	A	Pts.
1972-73	Montreal	36	2	4	6
1973-74	Montreal	78	6	20	26
1974-75	Montreal	80	14	47	61
1975-76	Montreal	80	10	30	40
1976-77	Montreal	77	19	66	85
1977-78	Montreal	80	13	52	65
1978-79	Montreal	67	16	45	61
1979-80	Montreal	72	14	61	75
1980-81	Montreal	65	12	38	50
1981-82	Montreal	71	12	47	59
1982-83	Montreal	71	14	49	63
1983-84	Montreal	74	9	34	43
1984-85	Montreal	76	14	33	47
1985-86	Montreal	78	19	63	82
1986-87	Montreal	70	13	37	50
	Totals	1075	187	626	813

RICK GREEN 31 6-3 210   **Defenseman**

Maturing into a reliable old pro... Has been called the Brad Marsh of the Canadiens... Led Montreal with a plus-13 rating during the 1987 playoffs... Voted the winner of the fourth Star Award as the club's unsung hero... Was Canadiens' nominee for Bill Masterton Memorial Trophy... Scored only one goal all season, moving him to within two of 40-goal career plateau ... Compiled only 10 minutes in penalties in 72 games, second-lowest total of career (7 in 1983-84)... Played in 200th game as a Canadien and 600th in NHL last season... Born Feb. 20, 1956, in Belleville, Ont.

Year	Club	GP	G	A	Pts.
1976-77	Washington	45	3	12	15
1977-78	Washington	60	5	14	19
1978-79	Washington	71	8	33	41
1979-80	Washington	71	4	20	24
1980-81	Washington	65	8	23	31
1981-82	Washington	65	3	25	28
1982-83	Montreal	66	2	24	26
1983-84	Montreal	7	0	1	1
1984-85	Montreal	77	1	18	19
1985-86	Montreal	46	3	2	5
1986-87	Montreal	72	1	9	10
	Totals	645	38	181	219

RYAN WALTER 29 6-0 195   **Left Wing**

Scored game-winning goal in pivotal fifth game of Adams final vs. Quebec . . . Tallied 500th point of career Dec. 11 against the Rangers . . . Suspended three games for leading Canadiens off the bench in Nov. 20 Boston Garden fiasco . . . Recorded 200th NHL goal at Edmonton on Nov. 8 . . . Excellent skater without the puck . . . Former No. 1 draft pick by Caps was dealt to Montreal with Rick Green on Sept. 9, 1982, for Brian Engblom, Rod Langway, Doug Jarvis and Craig Laughlin . . . Had his highest goal output (23) in four seasons last year . . . Born April 23, 1958, in New Westminster, B.C.

Year	Club	GP	G	A	Pts.
1978-79	Washington	69	28	28	56
1979-80	Washington	80	24	42	66
1980-81	Washington	80	24	44	68
1981-82	Washington	78	38	49	87
1982-83	Montreal	80	29	46	75
1983-84	Montreal	73	20	29	49
1984-85	Montreal	72	19	19	38
1985-86	Montreal	69	15	34	49
1986-87	Montreal	76	23	23	46
	Totals	677	220	314	534

CHRIS NILAN 29 6-0 200   **Right Wing**

Disappointing playoffs in which he was Montreal's worst minus (−4) player . . . Despite playing only 44 regular-season games, he easily led team with 266 penalty minutes . . . Accidentally shared a Montreal General Hospital room with Hartford's Torrie Robertson after undergoing surgery for torn knee ligaments . . . Sidelined Dec. 8 until All-Star break . . . Hit with 18 minutes of penalties in first game of playoff series vs. Quebec . . . Triggered free-for-all at Boston Garden Nov. 20 when he shoved glove in Ken Linseman's face . . . Had his fewest games played since rookie season . . . Born Feb. 9, 1958, in Boston.

Year	Club	GP	G	A	Pts.
1979-80	Montreal	15	0	2	2
1980-81	Montreal	57	7	8	15
1981-82	Montreal	49	7	4	11
1982-83	Montreal	66	6	8	14
1983-84	Montreal	76	16	10	26
1984-85	Montreal	77	21	16	37
1985-86	Montreal	72	19	15	34
1986-87	Montreal	44	4	16	20
	Totals	412	76	63	139

PATRICK ROY 22 6-0 175   **Goaltender**

MVP in Canadiens' 1986 Stanley Cup triumph but heard boos in
Forum last season...Was 1-3-2 in first six starts...Canadiens'
goalie in NHL's first 0-0 tie in three seasons on Oct. 15, 1986,
facing Buffalo's Tom Barrasso...Runner-up to teammate Brian
Hayward for league's lowest GAA (2.93)...Played in 25 con-
secutive playoff games until sitting for second game of Adams
final vs. Quebec...Youngest player ever to be named playoff
MVP in 1986...Part-time video jock on Canadian TV...
Earned $95,000 last year, a raise of $15,000 over rookie salary
...Born Oct. 5, 1965, in Quebec.

Year	Club	GP	GA	SO	Avg.
1984-85	Montreal.........	1	0	0	0.00
1985-86	Montreal.........	47	150	1	3.39
1986-87	Montreal.........	46	131	1	2.93
	Totals	94	281	2	3.16

COACH JEAN PERRON: Another in a long line of successful
Montreal coaches...Acted as head coach for
the NHL All-Star squad at RendezVous '87 in
Quebec...Rarely shows outward emotion behind the bench. Very businesslike...Became
13th coach to win the Stanley Cup as a rookie
coach when he did it as a 39-year-old fresh-
man in 1986...Succeeded Jacques Lemaire
as Canadiens' coach July 29, 1985...Cracked
down on overconfident Canadiens with two-hour practice ses-
sions during the season and guided team to Wales Conference
finals...Enforces strict curfew...Measures his club on a
10-game system. A 10-game stretch in which Canadiens score
12 points is a success...Born Oct. 5, 1946, in St. Isidore
d'Auckland, Que.

GREATEST COACH

Back during the 1979 playoffs a prominent member of the
Montreal Canadiens was asked about Scotty Bowman. "Impossi-

ble," said the player two weeks before the team won its fourth straight Stanley Cup. "If he left today I'd say, 'Good riddance.' " Not until Bowman did leave later that year did the Canadiens and the city of Montreal realize how much they missed the greatest coach in that proud franchise's history.

Over a span of eight seasons, Bowman led the Canadiens to five Stanley Cup championships while compiling a record of 419-110-105 for a winning percentage of .744. Not even the legendary Toe Blake, who won eight Stanley Cups and 500 games, had a winning percentage to match Scotty's.

The winningest coach in NHL history, a genius at motivating and using his players, Bowman had taken the expansion Blues to the finals three times before going to Montreal after the 1970-71 season to succeed Al MacNeil. His brilliant reign in Montreal came to an end in '79 when he was passed over as GM (Sam Pollack got the job). Scotty took his wisdom to Buffalo.

ALL-TIME CANADIEN LEADERS

GOALS: Steve Shutt, 60, 1976-77
          Guy Lafleur, 60, 1977-78
ASSISTS: Pete Mahovlich, 82, 1974-75
POINTS: Guy Lafleur, 136, 1976-77
SHUTOUTS: George Hainsworth, 22, 1928-29

NEW JERSEY DEVILS

TEAM DIRECTORY: Owner: John McMullen; VP-Operations/ GM: Max McNab; Dir. Player Personnel: Marshall Johnson; Dir. Pub. Rel.: Dave Freed; Coach: Doug Carpenter. Home ice: Byrne Meadowlands Arena (19,040; 200' x 85'). Colors: White, red and green.

SCOUTING REPORT

OFFENSE: There are quite a few NHL teams with a weaker attack than the Devils, who scored 293 goals last season. In fact, only seven teams in the league surpassed that total. Then what's wrong here? Not a heck of a lot.

GM Max McNab likes to brag about his centers, and why not? Kirk Muller, Greg Adams and Mark Johnson are talented playmakers and scorers. At right wing, the Devils are blessed with two 30-goal scorers—Pat Verbeek and John MacLean.

McNab and coach Doug Carpenter are excited about Brendan Shanahan, the second player chosen in last June's draft. The precocious 18-year-old can play either right wing or center. "He's another young prospect who could mature into a franchise player," Carpenter said.

The sore spot is left wing. Once you get beyond team scoring leader Aaron Broten, the talent is a little thin. Perry Anderson is noted more for his toughness than his goal-scoring, and the same applies to newcomers Jim Korn and Dave Maley, two offseason acquisitions.

"Maley is 200 pounds-plus and he can do it all," McNab said. However, the Wisconsin-born husky didn't do much with Montreal, totaling only six goals in 48 games last season.

DEFENSE: "There has never been a team in the NHL with such a young defense," claims Carpenter. Who can dispute him?

The average age of the team's defensemen is about 23. The youngest, Craig Wolanin, 20, is the best. The others include Ken Danyeko (23), Gord Mark (23), Joe Cirella (24) and Bruce Driver (25).

Gone are such old hands as Bob Lorimer, Dave Lewis and Phil Russell. Cirella, for goodness sakes, started the season with the most longevity among the defensemen, having totaled 343 games.

The Devils led the league in goals-allowed last season, surrendering 368. You can't give up an average of 4.6 goals a game and expect to win the Stanley Cup—or even make the playoffs.

What the team needs now are one or two physical defensemen who can keep the crease clean. McNab made a move in that direction by picking up Tom Kurvers from the Sabres for a third-round draft pick. Kurvers, though, has not shown much progress since his rookie season with the Canadiens in 1984-85.

Goaltender Alain Chevrier, who accounted for 24 of the team's 29 victories last season, will have to contend with the newly signed Bob Suave, the 10-year veteran last with Chicago. Promising Chris Terreri will get experience with the U.S. team in the 1988 Olympics, leaving Craig Billington and Kirk McLean as netminder candidates.

Pat Verbeek (35 goals) can score from any angle for Devils.

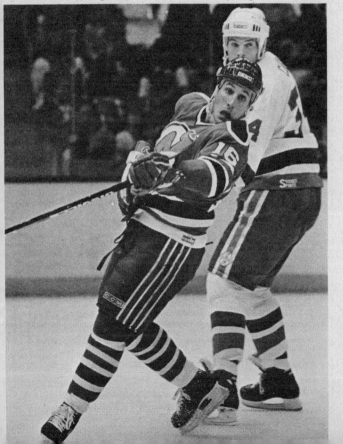

DEVIL ROSTER

No.	Player	Pos.	Ht.	Wt.	Born	1986–87	G	A	Pts.	PIM
24	Greg Adams	C	6-2	185	8-1-63/Nelson, B.C.	New Jersey	20	27	47	19
	Dave Anderson	RW	6-0	190	7-30-62/Vancouver, B.C.	Maine	9	9	18	80
25	Perry Anderson	LW	6-0	195	10-14-62/Barrie, Ont.	New Jersey	10	9	19	105
						Maine	5	4	9	42
5	Timo Blomqvist	D	6-0	200	1-23-61/Finland	New Jersey	0	2	2	29
	Neil Brady	C	6-2	180	4-12-68/Calgary, Alta.	Medicine Hat	19	64	83	126
26	Andy Brickley	C	6-0	185	8-9-61/Melrose, Mass.	New Jersey	11	12	23	8
10	Aaron Broten	RW	5-10	175	11-14-60/Roseau, Minn.	New Jersey	26	53	79	36
	Doug Brown	RW	5-11	190	6-12-64/Southborough, Mass.	New Jersey	0	1	1	0
						Maine	24	34	58	15
11	Rich Chernomaz	RW	5-9	175	9-1-63/Selkirk, Man.	New Jersey	6	4	10	11
						Maine	35	27	62	65
	Chris Cichoki	RW	5-10½	185	9-17-63/Detroit, Mich.	Adir.-Maine	33	36	69	27
						Detroit	0	0	0	2
2	Joe Cirella	D	6-3	210	5-9-63/Hamilton, Ont.	New Jersey	9	22	31	111
	Pat Conacher	C	5-8	185	5-1-59/Edmonton, Alta.	Maine	12	14	26	47
3	Ken Daneyko	D	6-0	195	4-16-64/Windsor, Ont.	New Jersey	2	12	14	183
	Dan Dorian	C	5-9	175	3-2-65/Astoria, N.Y.	Maine	16	22	38	47
23	Bruce Driver	D	6-0	185	4-29-62/Toronto, Ont.	New Jersey	6	28	34	36
	Greg Evtushevski	LW	5-8	181	5-4-65/St. Paul, Alta.	Maine	1	1	2	55
	Larry Floyd	C	5-8	177	5-1-61/Peterborough, Ont.	Maine	30	44	74	50
	Al Hepple	D	5-9	203	8-16-83/England	Maine	6	19	25	137
	Jamie Huscroft	D	6-2	195	1-9-67/Lister, B.C.	Medicine Hat	4	22	26	195
12	Mark Johnson	RW	5-9	160	9-22-57/Minneapolis, Minn.	New Jersey	25	26	51	22
	Jim Korn	D	6-3	210	7-26-57/Hopkins, Minn.	Buffalo	4	10	14	158
	Tom Kurvers	D	6-0	190	9-14-62/Minneapolis, Minn.	Mont.-Buff.	6	17	23	24
	Marc Laniel	D	6-1	187	1-16-68/Scarborough, Ont.	Oshawa	14	32	46	54
33	Tim Lenardon	C	6-2	185	5-11-62/Trail, B.C.	Maine	28	35	63	30
						New Jersey	1	1	2	0
19	Claude Loiselle	C	5-11	171	5-29-63/Ottawa, Ont.	New Jersey	16	24	40	137
15	John MacLean	RW	6-0	195	11-20-64/Oshawa, Ont.	New Jersey	31	36	67	120
	Dave Maley	C	6-2	195	4-24-63/Beaver Dam, Wis.	Montreal	6	12	18	55
						Sherbrooke	1	5	6	25
4	Gordon Mark	D	6-3	205	9-10-64/Edmonton, Alta.	New Jersey	3	5	8	82
						Maine	4	10	14	66
9	Kirk Muller	C	6-0	190	2-8-66/Kingston, Ont.	New Jersey	26	50	76	75
	Lars Persson	D	6-2	205	8-24-69/Sweden	Ostersund	10	11	21	2
8	Dave Pichette	D	6-3	200	2-4-60/Grand Falls, N.S.	Maine	6	16	22	69
21	Steve Richmond	D	6-1	205	12-11-59/Chicago, Ill.	New Jersey	1	7	8	143
	Brendan Shanahan	C	6-3	200	1-23-69/Mimico, Ont.	London	39	53	92	128
	Bud Stefanski	C	5-10	170	4-28-55/S. Porcupine, Ont.	Maine	9	12	21	34
14	Al Stewart	LW	6-0	175	1-31-64/Grande Center, Alta.	Maine	14	24	38	143
						New Jersey	1	0	1	26
22	Doug Sulliman	LW	5-9	195	8-29-59/Glace Bay, N.S.	New Jersey	27	26	53	14
	Rocky Trottier	C	5-11	185	4-11-64/Climax, Sask.	Maine	9	14	23	41
	Steve Tsujiura	C	5-5	165	2-20-62/Coaldale, Alta.	Maine	24	41	65	73
27	Randy Velischek	D	6-1	190	2-10-62/Montreal, Que.	New Jersey	2	16	18	54
12	Pat Verbeek	C	5-9	190	5-24-64/Sarnia, Ont.	New Jersey	35	24	59	120
6	Craig Wolanin	D	6-3	205	7-27-67/Warren, Mich.	New Jersey	4	6	10	109

No.	Player	Pos.	Ht.	Wt.	Born		GP	GA	SO	Avg.
31	Craig Billington	G	5-10	160	9-11-66/London, Ont.	New Jersey	22	89	0	4.79
						Maine	20	70	0	3.65
30	Alain Chevrier	G	5-8	180	4-23-61/Cornwall, Ont.	New Jersey	58	227	0	4.32
32	Kirk McLean	G	6-0	177	6-26-66/Willowdale, Ont.	New Jersey	4	10	0	3.75
						Maine	45	140	1	3.22
	Bob Sauve	G	5-8	185	6-17-55/St. Genevieve, Que.	Chicago	46	159	1	3.59

OUTLOOK: When Lou Lamoriello left his athletic director's job at Providence College to become the Devils' new president, he said: "You can get used to losing . . . I know how to win."

Good. But will he and McNab find the players to help the Devils out of the Patrick Division basement? The team set a franchise record by compiling a 29-45-6 record last season, but again failed to make the playoffs. If they don't make it this season, heads are sure to roll.

DEVIL PROFILES

ALAIN CHEVRIER 26 5-8 180   Goaltender

His favorite subject in high school was math, and now he's learning to play the angles as a major-league goalie . . . Showed marked improvement in his second NHL season . . . Appeared in 58 games and accounted for all but five of the Devils' 29 victories (24-26-2) . . . Had 15 victories by mid-December, then went a month before bagging No. 16 . . . His total victories represented a record for the franchise . . . Extremely aggressive and likes to challenge shooters . . . Born April 23, 1961, in Cornwall, Ont. . . . Ignored in the draft, he signed as a free agent in 1985 after impressing the Devils' scouts during his first pro season with Fort Wayne of the International League . . . Prior to that, he played four seasons of college hockey at Miami of Ohio . . . Posted a 11-19-2 record and a 4.61 goals-against average as a rookie in 1985-86.

Year	Club	GP	GA	SO	Avg.
1985-86	New Jersey.......	37	143	0	4.61
1986-87	New Jersey.......	58	227	0	4.32
	Totals	95	370	0	4.43

JOHN MacLEAN 22 6-0 195   Right Wing

A tireless two-way player, he developed into a scoring threat last season . . . Totaled 31 goals, including four game-winners, and 67 points, both career-highs . . . Strong in the corners and extremely durable, he didn't miss a game . . . "My size is an advantage over the long season, but a lot is mental preparation," he said. "Of course, I'm still learning." . . . Used to rush his shot, but has corrected that... Born Nov. 20, 1964, in Oshawa, Ont... Played his junior hockey with the Oshawa Generals, leading them into the Memorial Cup finals in 1983... Was a first-round pick (sixth overall) in the 1983 draft... Split the 1983-84 season between Oshawa and New Jersey... Failed to score in his first 19 games the following season, but showed his character and determination by playing ruggedly every night.

Year	Club	GP	G	A	Pts.
1983-84	New Jersey........	23	1	0	1
1984-85	New Jersey........	61	13	20	33
1985-86	New Jersey........	74	21	37	58
1986-87	New Jersey........	80	31	36	67
	Totals	238	66	93	159

AARON BROTEN 26 5-10 175   **Left Wing**
Despite his comparative youth, he ranks as the senior member of the franchise... Was Colorado's sixth pick (106th overall) in 1980 draft... Led the Devils in scoring last season with a career-high 26 goals and a team-record 53 assists for a team-record 79 points. Was the Devils' only plus player at plus-5... Good skills, excellent playmaker... Forthright and honest. Admits it's impossible to maintain his intensity for the entire season. "You can't be at the top of your game for 80 games. You try to be consistent and maybe play 60 out of 80."... Born Nov. 14, 1960, in Roseau, Minn.... Has played well in international tournaments for Team USA... Younger brother of North Stars' center Neal Broten. Older brother of Rangers' draftee Paul Broten.

Year	Club	GP	G	A	Pts.
1981-82	Colorado..........	58	15	24	39
1982-83	New Jersey........	73	16	39	55
1984-85	New Jersey........	80	22	35	57
1985-86	New Jersey........	66	19	25	44
1986-87	New Jersey........	80	26	53	79
	Totals	357	98	176	274

PAT VERBEEK 23 5-9 190   **Right Wing**
Nobody on the Devils can match this fellow's courage and perseverance... Suffered a career-threatening injury in 1985 when his left thumb was severed in a farm accident. The thumb

was reattached through microsurgery ... Was the team's second-leading goal scorer in 1985-86 with 25 ... Equalled a team record with 35 goals last season, including a club-record 17 on the power play ... Accomplished this despite a midseason slump and a strained right knee late in the season ... When somebody suggested his slump-buster "got the monkey off his back," he replied: "That was no monkey. That was a piano." ... Born May 24, 1964, in Sarnia, Ont. ... Was the Devils' third-round pick (43rd overall) in 1982 draft ... Named the team's Rookie of the Year in 1983-84.

Year	Club	GP	G	A	Pts.
1982-83	New Jersey	6	3	2	5
1983-84	New Jersey	79	20	27	47
1984-85	New Jersey	78	15	18	33
1985-86	New Jersey	76	25	28	53
1986-87	New Jersey	74	35	24	59
	Totals	313	98	99	197

JOE CIRELLA 24 6-3 210   Defenseman

The franchise's oldest defenseman in length of service ... Born May 9, 1963, in Hamilton, Ont. ... A first-round pick in 1981 draft ... Only 18 when he made his NHL debut that year, but returned to Oshawa of the OHL the following season and sparked the Generals to the Memorial Cup finals ... Appeared in the 1984 NHL All-Star Game at the Meadowlands and set up the winning goal by Don Maloney of the Rangers ... Was benched for a time during the 1984-85 season, but bounced back to lead the team's defensemen in scoring the following season ... Suffered a broken foot last season and missed 15 games. However, he still showed improvement ... "I was a bit mixed up at one point," he admitted. "Sometimes it takes some guys longer to mature."

Year	Club	GP	G	A	Pts.
1981-82	Colorado	65	7	12	19
1982-83	New Jersey	2	0	1	1
1983-84	New Jersey	79	11	33	44
1984-85	New Jersey	66	6	18	24
1985-86	New Jersey	66	6	23	29
1986-87	New Jersey	65	9	22	31
	Totals	343	39	109	148

CRAIG WOLANIN 20 6-3 205   Defenseman

Though he didn't turn 20 until last summer, this is his third NHL season ... Still a growing boy. Grew an inch and added 11 pounds between his rookie and sophomore years with the Devils

. . . Missed 30 games with a broken finger in his rookie season of 1985-86, yet impressed people with his bone-crushing checks . . . Continued to improve last season . . . Ranks as one of his severest critics. "Reaching the rush has been my No. 1 problem. Until I can play like Rod Langway in every game, I won't be satisfied." . . . Crashed into a goal post during a late-season game at St. Louis and suffered a 70-stitch gash on his forehead . . . Born July 27, 1967, in Grosse Pointe, Mich . . . Was the third player chosen, behind Toronto's Wendel Clark and Pittsburgh's Dave Simpson, in the 1985 draft.

Year	Club	GP	G	A	Pts.
1985-86	New Jersey	44	2	16	18
1986-87	New Jersey	68	4	6	10
	Totals	112	6	22	28

GREG ADAMS 24 6-2 185   **Center**
What's a guy from Northern Arizona University doing in the NHL? . . . "I made up my mind when I was about 16 that I was going to a university—not necessarily Northern Arizona, but it was the only (scholarship) offer I got." . . . Led the NCAA in scoring during his senior year with 73 points in 26 games, but Northern Arizona isn't exactly a hockey hotbed, so he wasn't drafted . . . The Devils signed him in 1984 and assigned him to Maine of the AHL. Called up in midseason, he totaled 21 points in 36 games . . . Set New Jersey records with 35 goals, 43 assists and 78 points in 1985-86 . . . Was slow recovering from a concussion last season and his goal production slipped to 20 . . . Born Aug. 15, 1963, in Nelson, B.C. . . . Lean and rangy with great stick extension. Dangerous on the power play.

Year	Club	GP	G	A	Pts.
1984-85	New Jersey	36	12	9	21
1985-86	New Jersey	78	35	43	78
1986-87	New Jersey	72	20	27	47
	Totals	186	67	79	146

KIRK MULLER 21 6-0 190   **Center**
His boyhood hero was Hall of Famer Bobby Clarke, and some people are comparing him to the former Flyers' star . . . Said GM

Max McNab: "We like to think we see a lot of Bobby Clarke in Kirk. He already has become a leader." . . . The Devils' second-leading scorer again last season with 76 points in 79 games . . . Named the team's Most Valuable Player by beat writers . . . Tireless worker, smooth playmaker, fine penalty-killer. Showing improvement defensively . . . Born Feb. 8, 1966, in Kingston, Ont. . . . Member of 1984 Canadian Olympic team . . . Picked second behind Mario Lemieux in the 1984 draft . . . Scored 17 goals as a rookie, added 25 the following season . . . "During my first two years there were times when I became frustrated, mainly because of my offensive production," he admits. "But the idea in New Jersey has been a team thing." . . . Named captain of the Devils during the offseason.

Year	Club	GP	G	A	Pts.
1984-85	New Jersey	80	17	37	54
1985-86	New Jersey	77	25	42	67
1986-87	New Jersey	79	26	50	76
	Totals	236	68	129	197

DOUG SULLIMAN 28 5-9 195   Left Wing

A diligent worker at both ends of the ice . . . Born Aug. 29, 1959, in Glace Bay, Nova Scotia . . . Was a 50-goal scorer with Kitchener of the OHL in 1977-78 . . . First-round pick of the Rangers in 1979 . . . Spent his first two years as a pro commuting between New York and New Haven . . . The Rangers traded him to the Whalers in a five-player deal in 1981 . . . Scored 29 goals with Hartford in 1981-82, but was released after scoring only six goals in 1983-84 . . . Signed with the Devils as a free agent without compensation in 1984 and has proved to be a good pickup . . . Has had 20-or-more goals each of the past three seasons . . . Named the team's Player of the Year in a fans' poll.

Year	Club	GP	G	A	Pts.
1979-80	New York R.	31	4	7	11
1980-81	New York R.	32	4	1	5
1981-82	Hartford	77	29	40	69
1982-83	Hartford	77	22	19	41
1983-84	Hartford	67	6	13	19
1984-85	New Jersey	57	22	16	38
1985-86	New Jersey	73	21	21	42
1986-87	New Jersey	78	27	26	53
	Totals	492	135	143	278

MARK JOHNSON 30 5-9 160   Left Wing

A well-traveled player, he was a third-round pick of the Penguins in 1977 and turned pro with them in 1980. Has also played for Minnesota, Hartford and St. Louis. The Devils obtained him from the Blues prior to the start of the 1985-86 season . . . Scored 25 goals in 68 games last season . . . Had his best years with Hartford when he posted 31- and 35-goal seasons . . . Has exceptional skills with the puck . . . "Mark's a worker," said Devils coach Doug Carpenter. "He can score big goals when he gets the chance." . . . Born Sept. 22, 1957, in Madison, Wis. . . . Played for father, Bob, at University of Wisconsin . . . NCAA Player of the Year in 1978-79 . . . Was the leading scorer on the gold medal-winning 1980 U.S. Olympic team and scored the clinching goal against Finland in final game . . . Nickname: "Magic."

Year	Club	GP	G	A	Pts.
1979-80	Pittsburgh.........	17	3	5	8
1980-81	Pittsburgh.........	73	10	23	33
1981-82	Pitt-Minn	56	12	13	25
1982-83	Hartford	73	31	38	69
1983-84	Hartford	79	35	52	87
1984-85	Hart-St L..........	66	23	34	57
1985-86	New Jersey........	80	21	41	62
1986-87	New Jersey........	68	25	26	51
	Totals	512	160	232	392

COACH DOUG CARPENTER:

Was greeted with cries of "Doug Who?" when he became the Devils' head coach in 1984 . . . Spent 11 years of coaching apprenticeship in junior and minor leagues . . . This is his fourth season with the Devils, and the team has shown improvement every year . . . Flaming red hair hints at his sometimes fiery temperament, but he is a patient teacher . . . Cautious and reserved in dealing with the media . . . Born July 1, 1942, in Cornwall, Ont. . . . Graduate of Loyola College of Montreal . . . Played eight years in the Eastern and International Leagues as a defenseman and left winger . . . Launched his coaching career with Flint of the IHL during the 1973-74 season . . . Coached Cornwall Royals to the Memorial Cup championship in 1980 . . . Served four years as coach of the Toronto Maple Leafs' top minor-league clubs, but was passed over for the Leafs' job that went to Dan Maloney.

GREATEST COACH

The date was May 31, 1984. Doug Carpenter had just been introduced as the Devils' new head coach. He won the job after Tom McVie, who had served as the Devils' interim coach for the final 60 games of the previous season, failed to wrangle a multi-year contract out of club chairman John McMullen.

"The most successful managing and coaching in sports is done with one-year contracts," said McMullen, who is also majority owner of the Houston Astros baseball team.

Carpenter, who never before had coached in the NHL, said: "One-year contracts don't bother me."

So the man who signed on for one year is now in his fourth season with the Devils and has become the most successful coach in the history of the franchise. Under Carpenter's direction, the Devils won 79 games in the past three seasons.

Carpenter also owns a longevity record of sorts. Until his arrival, no coach in the history of the franchise had completed two full seasons on the job.

The old revolving-door policy went back to the birth of the franchise in Kansas City in 1974 when the Scouts had three coaches in their first two years. The franchise shift to Colorado in 1976 didn't improve matters. Coaches—a total of six in seven years—moved in and out.

So even though Carpenter hasn't led the Devils into the playoffs yet, he has brought a semblance of order to the coaching staff.

ALL-TIME DEVIL LEADERS

GOALS: Wilf Paiement, 41, 1976-77
ASSISTS: Wilf Paiement, 56, 1977-78
POINTS: Wilf Paiement, 87, 1977-78
SHUTOUTS: Doug Favell, 1, 1977-78
　　　　　　　Bill Oleschuk, 1, 1978-79
　　　　　　　Bill McKenzie, 1, 1979-80
　　　　　　　Glenn Resch, 1, 1983-84
　　　　　　　Ron Low, 1, 1984-85
　　　　　　　Sam St. Laurent, 1, 1985-86

NEW YORK ISLANDERS

TEAM DIRECTORY: Chairman of the Board: John Pickett; Pres.-GM: Bill Torrey; VP: Al Arbour; Dir. Pub. Rel.: Greg Bouris; Coach: Terry Simpson. Home ice: Nassau Coliseum (16,267; 200' x 85'). Colors: White, blue and orange. Training camp: Hicksville, N.Y.

SCOUTING REPORT

OFFENSE: What's happened to the Islanders' once-potent offense? A good question. Last season they scored only 279 goals —their lowest production in 12 years and the poorest production in the Patrick Division. Even the Devils scored more goals than the Isles.

Mike Bossy's aching back and Denis Potvin's sprained left knee weakened the attack, especially on the power play. New coach Terry Simpson's constant line shuffling also had a deleterious effect.

Left wing reamins the Isles' biggest trouble spot. Rich Kromm was the highest-scoring left winger last season with a mere 12 goals. Maybe Derek King, a 1985 first-round pick, will help. He scored 53 goals in 57 games in his final junior year.

There are some strong points. At center, Bryan Trottier provides experience and leadership, Pat LaFontaine has developed into an exciting, dangerous scorer, and Brent Sutter can hurt you —when he's healthy. Mikko Makela, swift and flashy, has helped shore up right wing, where Bossy has reigned supreme for 10 seasons. "The Boss" was disappointed last season when he failed to reach the 50-goal mark for the first time. If he has to settle for anything less this season, he might go ahead with his plans for an early retirement.

DEFENSE: Twelve other NHL teams allowed more goals than the Isles (281) last season. Credit Simpson for insisting on a return to tight-checking and stronger positional play, though his players didn't catch on fully until the playoffs.

If this is Potvin's final season in Islander blue, he'd like to go out a winner and wipe out memories of last year, when he went from a plus-30 the previous season to minus-8. He isn't as dominant as he once was, but he remains a presence on the backline. And he sets a league record for defensemen every time he scores or sets up a goal.

Another veteran, Ken Morrow, made a strong comeback, but will his scarred knees carry him through another season? Brian

Curran keeps the slot clean and his hands dirty fighting rivals. Ken Leiter and Gord Dineen move the puck well, Steve Konroyd is steady and sturdy, and Gerald Diduck is improving with each game.

No problems in goal where venerable, lovable Bill Smith now backs up Kelly Hrudey.

OUTLOOK: The Isles' record last season (35-33-12) was the worst since their second year in the league (1983-84). If they

Kelly Hrudey has become No. 1 in goal for the Islanders.

ISLANDER ROSTER

No.	Player	Pos.	Ht.	Wt.	Born	1986-87	G	A	Pts.	PIM
28	Bob Bassen	LW	5-10	180	5-6-65/Calgary, Alta.	Islanders	7	10	17	89
22	Mike Bossy	RW	6-0	185	1-22-57/Montreal, Que.	Islanders	38	37	75	33
8	Randy Boyd	D	6-1	192	5-6-60/Coniston, Ont.	Islanders	7	17	24	37
						Springfield	9	30	39	96
	Dean Chynoweth	D	6-1	190	10-30-68/Calgary, Alta.	Medicine Hat	3	18	21	285
36	Neil Coulter	RW	6-2	190	1-2-63/Toronto, Ont.	Islanders	2	1	3	7
						Springfield	12	13	25	63
34	Brian Curran	D	6-4	220	11-5-63/Toronto, Ont.	Islanders	0	10	10	356
	Brad Dalgarno	RW	6-3	205	8-1-67/Vancouver, B.C.	Hamilton	27	32	59	100
4	Gerald Diduck	D	6-2	195	4-6-65/Edmonton, Alta.	Islanders	2	3	5	67
						Springfield	6	8	14	120
2	Gord Dineen	D	5-11	180	9-21-62/Toronto, Ont.	Islanders	4	10	14	110
26	Patrick Flatley	RW	6-2	205	10-3-63/Toronto, Ont.	Islanders	16	35	51	81
17	Greg Gilbert	LW	6-1	194	1-22-62/Mississauga, Ont.	Islanders	6	7	13	26
25	Ari Haanpaa	RW	6-1	185	11-28-65/Finland	Islanders	6	4	10	17
20	Dale Henry	LW	6-0	205	9-24-64/Prince Albert, Sask.	Islanders	3	3	6	46
						Springfield	9	14	23	49
3	Tomas Jonsson	D	5-10	176	4-12-60/Sweden	Islanders	6	25	31	36
10	Alan Kerr	LW	5-10	181	3-28-64/Hazelton, B.C.	Islanders	7	10	17	175
	Derek King	LW	6-2	220	2-11-67/Hamilton, Ont.	Islanders	0	0	0	0
						Oshawa	53	53	106	74
33	Steve Konroyd	D	6-1	195	2-10-61/Scarborough, Ont.	Islanders	5	16	21	70
11	Roger Kortko	G	5-10	182	2-1-63/Hofford, Sask.	Springfield	16	30	46	54
35	Richard Kromm	LW	5-11	190	3-29-64/Trail, B.C.	Islanders	12	17	29	20
16	Pat LaFontaine	C	5-10	177	2-20-65/St. Louis, Mo.	Islanders	38	32	70	70
32	Brad Lauer	RW	6-0	196	10-27-66/Humboldt, Sask.	Islanders	7	14	21	65
29	Ken Leiter	D	6-1	195	4-19-61/Detroit, Mich.	Islanders	9	20	29	30
24	Mikko Makela	C	6-2	193	2-28-65/Finland	Islanders	24	33	57	24
6	Ken Morrow	D	6-4	205	10-17-56/Davison, Mich.	Islanders	3	8	11	32
5	Denis Potvin	D	6-0	205	10-25-53/Ottawa, Ont.	Islanders	12	30	42	70
	Vern Smith	D	6-1½	195	5-30-64/Lethbridge, Alta.	Springfield	1	10	11	58
21	Brent Sutter	C	5-11	180	6-10-62/Viking, Alta.	Islanders	27	36	63	73
12	Duane Sutter	RW	6-1	189	5-6-30/Viking, Alta.	Islanders	14	17	31	169
19	Bryan Trottier	C	5-11	195	7-17-56/Val Marie, Sask.	Islanders	23	64	87	50
11	Randy Wood	C	6-0	195	10-12-63/Princeton, N.J.	Islanders	1	0	1	4

							GP	GA	SO	Avg.
	Roydon Gunn	G	5-10	163	8-5-66/Saskatoon, Sask.	Springfield	29	107	0	4.02
	Jeff Hackett	G	6-0	178	6-1-68/London, Ont.	Oshawa	31	85	2	3.05
30	Kelly Hrudey	G	5-10	180	1-31-61/Edmonton, Alta.	Islanders	46	145	0	3.30
	Gary Johnson	G	5-10	165	2-16-65/Winnipeg, Man.	Springfield	1	0	0	0.00
31	Bill Smith	G	5-10	185	12-12-50/Perth, Ont.	Islanders	40	132	1	3.52
	Mike Volpe	G	5-11	165	1-2-67/Vancouver, B.C.	Toronto (OHL)	10	42	0	5.33

hope to move up, they have to show more unity. There was some bickering between vets and rookies last season.

GM Bill Torrey will continue working fuzzy-cheeked newcomers into the lineup. "Young players have to be given a chance to fail before they succeed," he said.

Bob Bassen, Brad Lauer and Alan Kerr were among the rookies who got their baptism last season. Each scored seven goals. They'll have to contribute more this season.

ISLANDER PROFILES

KELLY HRUDEY 26 5-10 180   Goaltender

Has slowly supplanted Bill Smith as the team's No. 1 goalie.... Completed his fourth season with a career-high 21 victories and a 3.30 goals-against average. Started all the team's 14 playoff games ... One of the heroes in the Isles' four-overtime victory over the Capitals, totaling 73 saves, including 51 straight... Stand-up style, quick glove, plays angles well ... Born Jan. 13, 1961, in Edmonton ... Quit hockey temporarily after being cut from a midget team at age 16. Was invited to join the Medicine Hat juniors a year later and was stunned to make the team. "I think they took me because they had nobody else." ... The Islanders' second-round pick in the 1980 draft ... Surname is pronounced "ROO-dee."

Year	Club	GP	GA	SO	Avg.
1983-84	New York I........	12	28	0	3.14
1984-85	New York I........	41	141	2	3.62
1985-86	New York I	45	137	1	3.21
1986-87	New York I........	46	145	0	3.30
	Totals	144	451	3	3.35

BILL SMITH 36 5-10 185   Goaltender

The last of the original Islanders and still a battler ... Though his work load has been reduced, he finished last season with a 3.52 goals-against average, his lowest in three years ... Owns a league-record 88 playoff victories, but had only two relief jobs in last spring's playoffs ... "I'm a team guy now. I accept what's happened. The only frustrating part is that I still think I can do the job." ... Still fiesty on the ice, but extremely likeable off the ice ... When he won the writers' "Good Guy" award in 1984, he said, "Even my kids won't believe this." . . . Born Dec. 12, 1950, in Perth, Ont. . . . Was the first NHL goalie to score a goal—vs. the Colorado Rockies in 1979.

Year	Club	GP	GA	SO	Avg.
1971-72	Los Angeles	5	23	0	4.60
1972-73	New York I	37	147	0	4.16
1973-74	New York I	46	134	0	3.07
1974-75	New York I	58	156	3	2.78
1975-76	New York I	39	98	3	2.61
1976-77	New York I	36	87	2	2.50
1977-78	New York I	38	95	2	2.65
1978-79	New York I	40	108	1	2.87
1979-80	New York I	38	104	2	2.95
1980-81	New York I	41	129	2	3.28
1981-82	New York I	46	133	0	2.97
1982-83	New York I	41	112	1	2.87
1983-84	New York I	42	130	2	3.42
1984-85	New York I	37	133	0	3.82
1985-86	New York I	41	143	1	3.72
1986-87	New York I.	40	132	1	3.52
	Totals	625	1864	20	3.14

BRENT SUTTER 25 5-11 180   **Center**
His sixth season was one of his best (27-36-63) even though he missed the final 11 regular-season games and the first nine in the playoffs because of a pulled groin muscle . . . Was the team leader with a plus-23 figure and contributed eight game-winning goals . . . Born June 10, 1962, in Viking, Alta. . . . The 17th player taken in the 1980 draft despite the fact that he was just graduating from a Tier II league in Saskatchewan . . . Teamed briefly with brothers Rich and Ron on a line at Lethbridge before the Islanders recalled him midway through the 1981-82 season . . . Was one of the stars in Team Canada's victory in the 1984 Canada Cup tournament . . . Owns and races quarter horses . . . Nickname: "Pup."

Year	Club	GP	G	A	Pts.
1980-81	New York I.	3	2	2	4
1981-82	New York I.	43	21	22	43
1982-83	New York I.	80	21	19	40
1983-84	New York I.	69	34	15	49
1984-85	New York I.	72	42	60	102
1985-86	New York I.	61	24	31	55
1986-87	New York I.	69	27	36	63
	Totals	397	171	185	356

DENIS POTVIN 34 6-0 205   **Defenseman**

When John Ferguson was GM of the Rangers, he referred to this barrel-chested defenseman as "The Navigator." It was an apt description for Potvin, who is navigating his way to certain admission into the Hall of Fame . . . Has smashed all of the league's career records for a defenseman formerly held by Bobby Orr . . . Still thrills fans—and bruises rivals—with solid hip checks he learned from Hall of Famer Leo Boivin, his coach in junior hockey . . . Missed 17 games late last season with a sprained left knee and wound up with his lowest production figures in seven years (12-30-42) . . . Born Oct. 29, 1953, in Ottawa . . . Won Calder Trophy as NHL's Rookie of the Year in 1974 . . . Three-time winner of the Norris Trophy as the league's best defenseman . . . Named to the All-Star team seven times.

Year	Club	GP	G	A	Pts.
1973-74	New York I	77	17	37	54
1974-75	New York I	79	21	55	76
1975-76	New York I	78	31	67	98
1976-77	New York I	80	25	55	80
1977-78	New York I	80	30	64	94
1978-79	New York I	73	31	70	101
1979-80	New York I	31	8	33	41
1980-81	New York I	74	20	56	76
1981-82	New York I	60	24	37	61
1982-83	New York I	69	12	54	66
1983-84	New York I	78	22	63	85
1984-85	New York I	77	17	51	68
1985-86	New York I	74	21	38	59
1986-87	New York I	58	12	30	42
	Totals	988	291	710	1001

BRYAN TROTTIER 31 5-11 195   **Center**

This is his 13th season in the NHL, and he's still regarded as one of the best two-way players in the game . . . His goal production dropped last season from 37 to 23, but he added 64 assists to supplant old buddy Mike Bossy as the team's leading scorer . . . Outspoken president of the NHL Players Association, he was fined $1,000 by league president John Ziegler for publicly criticizing NHL referees . . . Veteran penalty-killer, excellent playmaker, strong on his skates . . . A North American Indian, he was born on July 17, 1956, in Val Marie, Sask. . . . Second-round draft pick in 1974 . . . Named Rookie of the Year in 1976, won the Hart (MVP) Trophy in 1979 and the Smythe (playoff MVP) in 1980.

Year	Club	GP	G	A	Pts.
1975-76	New York I	80	32	63	95
1976-77	New York I	76	30	42	72
1977-78	New York I	77	46	77	123
1978-79	New York I	76	47	87	134
1979-80	New York I	78	42	62	104
1980-81	New York I	73	31	72	103
1981-82	New York I	80	50	79	129
1982-83	New York I	80	34	55	89
1983-84	New York I	68	40	71	111
1984-85	New York I	68	28	31	59
1985-86	New York I	78	37	59	96
1986-87	New York I	80	23	64	87
	Totals	914	440	762	1202

PATRICK FLATLEY 24 6-2 195   Right Wing

A rugged checker, he knocked the Rangers' Barry Beck out of the 1984 playoffs with a shoulder check . . . Has suffered his own share of injuries—broken hand, knee and shoulder ailments . . . Never has scored more than 20 goals in three full seasons with the Isles . . . "I don't look at goals, I look at points and I've been over 50 points each year," he says. "Still, I know I can do better." . . . Good positional player, he was plus-17 last season, second-best on the team . . . Born Oct. 3, 1963, in Toronto . . . A first-round pick in the 1982 draft . . . Attended University of Wisconsin and played for 1984 Canadian Olympic team before joining the Islanders.

Year	Club	GP	G	A	Pts.
1983–84	New York I	16	2	7	9
1984-85	New York I	78	20	31	51
1985-86	New York I	73	18	34	52
1986-87	New York I	63	16	35	51
	Totals	230	56	107	163

MIKKO MAKELA 22 6-2 193   Right Wing

This blond-haired Finn is blossoming into a star . . . An aching back hampered him during his rookie season of 1985-86, but he still managed 16 goals, including three game-winners, in 58 games . . . Increased his production to 24 goals last season and didn't miss a game . . . Excellent skater who has a strong, swift and accurate shot. A good playmaker, too . . . Doesn't back away from the rough stuff... Born Feb. 28, 1965, in Tampere, Finland... A fifth-round pick (66th overall) in the 1983 draft... Was the leading goal-scorer in the Finnish League before joining the Isles.

Year	Club	GP	G	A	Pts.
1985-86	New York I	58	16	20	36
1986-87	New York I	80	24	33	57
	Totals	138	40	53	93

MIKE BOSSY 30 6-0 185 Right Wing

The greatest right wing of his era... Records are his business, so he was disappointed when he failed to score 50 goals for a record 10th consecutive season. Blame it on an aching back that bothered him most of the year and caused him to miss 17 games... He settled for 38 goals and 75 points, his lowest totals since he joined the Islanders as a first-round draft pick in 1977... He entered the current season with 573 lifetime goals, placing him fifth on the all-time list... Born Jan. 22, 1957, in Montreal, the sixth of 10 children... Passed over by 14 teams in the 1977 draft because they didn't think he would check. Now he's considered a solid two-way player... Working on the final year of a contract that earns him more than $700,000 a year.

Year	Club	GP	G	A	Pts.
1977-78	New York I	73	53	38	91
1978-79	New York I	80	69	57	126
1979-80	New York I	75	51	41	92
1980-81	New York I	79	68	51	119
1981-82	New York I	80	64	83	147
1982-83	New York I	79	60	58	118
1983-84	New York I	67	51	67	118
1984-85	New York I	76	58	59	117
1985-86	New York I	80	61	62	123
1986-87	New York I	63	38	37	75
	Totals	752	573	553	1126

PAT LaFONTAINE 22 5-10 177 Center

Once considered too slender and too brittle to make it big in the NHL, he has become one of the Isles' most valuable players... Joined the team after representing the U.S. in the 1984 Olympics and scored 13 goals in 15 games... A bout with mononucleosis hampered his first full season and a shoulder injury slowed him down in 1985-86... Scored a career-high 38 goals last season to tie Mike Bossy for the club lead in that department... Slick and swift, he's getting tougher to knock off the puck... "I try to improve every year," he said... Born Feb. 22, 1965, in St. Louis and grew up in a Detroit suburb.

Year	Club	GP	G	A	Pts.
1983-84	New York I	15	13	6	19
1984-85	New York I	67	19	35	54
1985-86	New York I	65	30	23	53
1986-87	New York I	80	38	32	70
	Totals	227	100	96	196

KEN MORROW 31 6-4 205   Defenseman

Emerged as the NHL's comeback player of the year last season ...Expected to be a part-time performer because of past knee problems, he took regular shifts and led all Isles' defensemen with a plus-7 rating... "I feel as well as I did three years ago," he said... A good shot-blocker, he makes intelligent break-out passes and is adept at steering rebounds to the corners... Born on Oct. 17, 1956, in Flint, Mich.... A fourth-round draft pick in 1976 while attending Bowling Green University... Joined the Isles in 1980 after helping the U.S. team win the gold medal in the Winter Olympics... Nickname: "Wolfman."

Year	Club	GP	G	A	Pts.
1979-80	New York I	18	0	3	3
1980-81	New York I	80	2	11	13
1981-82	New York I	75	1	18	19
1982-83	New York I	79	5	11	16
1983-84	New York I	63	3	11	14
1984-85	New York I	15	1	7	8
1986-87	New York I	64	3	8	11
	Totals	394	15	69	84

COACH TERRY SIMPSON: Made a strong impression in his

rookie year as an NHL coach last season... Was virtually unknown outside of amateur hockey when he was hired to replace Al Arbour, who resigned after 13 seasons as the Islanders' coach... Not as explosive as Arbour, he had some early minor problems dealing with the team's veterans. Gained acceptance, though, with his low-key approach and his sense of fairness . . . One of those veterans, Duane Sutter, said, "We certainly haven't been outcoached by anybody." . . . Said GM Bill Torrey, who hired him: "Terry has given the team direction. He came here not knowing anybody and he had established players who were used to the old coach. He has to be given good marks." . . . Born Aug. 30, 1943, in Brantford, Ont. . . . Played one season as a defenseman for Jacksonville of the defunct Eastern League . . . Had a successful 14-year career with the Prince Albert (Sask.) Raiders: 10 years in Tier II and four in the WHL. Won four Centennial Cups, one Memorial Cup . . . Admits he is still feeling his way in the NHL. "But I feel like I'm part of the team now."

GREATEST COACH

When Al Arbour was dismissed as head coach of the St. Louis Blues in 1972, Sid Salomon, then the team president, said: "Al is a loyal, dutiful sergeant, but he'll never be a general."

Salomon was wrong. Dead wrong.

History now will testify that Arbour was a four-star general—the stars representing four consecutive Stanley Cup championships the Islanders won under the direction of the former defenseman from Sudbury, Ont.

Arbour, who also earned three Stanley Cup rings as a player, coached the Islanders for 13 years (1973-1986). Prior to arriving on Long Island, he put in two brief hitches as the Blues' coach. He is the third-winningest coach in NHL history with 594 regular-season victories, and his 113 playoff victories are just one shy of Scotty Bowman's all-time record.

Arbour was 53 when he stepped down as the Isles' coach in May of 1986 and became a superscout with the title of club vice-president. "It's time for somebody else to take the reins," he said. "Frankly, I'm tired."

ALL-TIME ISLANDER LEADERS

GOALS: Mike Bossy, 69, 1978-79
ASSISTS: Bryan Trottier, 87, 1978-79
POINTS: Mike Bossy, 147, 1981-82
SHUTOUTS: Glenn Resch, 7, 1975-76

NEW YORK RANGERS

TEAM DIRECTORY: Pres.: Richard Evans; VP-GM: Phil Esposito; Alt. Governor: Jack Diller; VP-Finance: Mel Lowell; Asst. to GM: Joe Bucchino; VP-Dir. Communications: John Halligan; Coach: Michel Bergeron. Home ice: Madison Square Garden (17,500; 200' x 85'). Colors: Blue, red and white. Training camp: Rye, N.Y.

SCOUTING REPORT

OFFENSE: Only the Red Wings scored fewer goals than the Rangers in 1985-86. Then along came Phil Esposito, who as general manager and sometime-coach engineered many changes, including a switch from the team's defensive-minded philosophy to one that emphasized a free-wheeling attack. And now, finally, a new coach in Michel Bergeron, who joined the Rangers in June after seven years as leader of the Quebec Nordiques.

The Rangers totaled 307 goals, fifth-best in the league, last season. However, they came up empty in the playoffs against the Flyers when they were shut out twice by Ron Hextall and totaled only 13 goals in six games.

Was this a portent of things to come? Maybe. Walt Poddubny, the team's regular-season scoring leader, had no points in the playoffs; Marcel Dionne and Tomas Sandstrom had only one goal apiece. Dionne is 36 now and looks it, and old age is creeping up on some of the other Ranger forwards, too. Pierre Larouche is 31, Ron Duguay is 30, Don Maloney is 29, and Kelly Kisio is 28.

Esposito is expecting big things from Swedish center Ulf Dahlen, the team's No. 1 pick in the 1985 draft who signed a three-year contract for a reported $1.2 million to turn pro last May. "He's going to be a good one," Esposito said. The GM also is enthusiastic about Brian Mullen, acquired from Winnipeg during the summer.

DEFENSE: Help is needed here for a team that finished 19th in the league with 323 goals allowed last season. And it could come in the form of Barry Beck, who returns after a year's self-imposed retirement.

James Patrick has matured into one of the NHL's top defensemen, but he isn't a physical player. Big Willie Huber hits people, but not consistently. Larry Melnyk is an intense defensive player and Curt Giles makes up in heart what he lacks in size. After them, it's thin.

Tomas Sandstrom keeps his stick and his production high.

Ron Greschner, the 32-year-old dean of the corps, has slowed down considerably. Terry Carkner, a first-round pick in 1984, got into 52 games last season and is still feeling his way.

Last season, Esposito frequently deplored the fact that Patrick was the only Ranger defenseman with natural puck-carrying ability. So during the offseason he made a deal aimed at correcting that shortcoming, dealing Tony McKegney to the St. Louis Blues for Bruce Bell, who is good with the puck and also quite physical.

RANGER ROSTER

No.	Player	Pos.	Ht.	Wt.	Born	1986—87	G	A	Pts.	PIM
5	Barry Beck	D	6-3	215	6-3-57/Vancouver, B.C.	Did not play	—	—	—	—
	Bruce Bell	D	5-11	180	2-15-65/Toronto, Ont.	St. Louis	3	13	16	18
38	Terry Carkner	D	6-3	197	3-7-66/Winchester, Ont.	Rangers	2	13	15	120
						New Haven	2	6	8	56
26	Jay Caufield	LW	6-4	225	7-17-60/Philadelphia, Pa.	Rangers	2	1	3	45
						New Haven	0	0	0	43
						Flint	4	3	7	59
	Jeff Crossman	RW	6-0	200	12-3-64/Toronto, Ont.	New Haven	2	3	5	133
	Ulf Dahlen	C	6-2	195	1-12-67/Sweden	Ostersund	—	—	—	—
32	Lucien DeBlois	RW	5-11	200	6-21-57/Joliette, Que.	Rangers	3	8	11	27
16	Marcel Dionne	C	5-8	190	8-3-51/Drummondville, Que.	LA-Rang.	28	56	84	60
	Mike Donnelly	LW	5-11	185	10-10-63/Detroit, Mich.	Rangers	1	1	2	0
						New Haven	27	34	61	57
	Ken Duggan	D	6-3	210	2-21-63/Toronto, Ont.	Flint	2	23	25	51
44	Ron Duguay	C-RW	6-2	210	7-6-57/Sudbury, Ont.	Pitt.-Rang.	14	25	39	39
20	Jan Erixon	LW	6-0	190	7-8-62/Sweden	Rangers	8	18	26	24
25	Paul Fenton	C	5-11	180	12-22-59/Springfield, Mass.	Rangers	0	0	0	2
						New Haven	37	38	75	45
9	Dave Gagner	C	5-10	183	12-11-64/Chatham, Ont.	Rangers	1	4	5	12
						New Haven	22	41	63	50
6	Curt Giles	D	5-8	180	11-30-58/Humboldt, Minn.	Minn.-Rang.	2	20	22	54
4	Ron Greschner	D-C	6-2	205	12-23-54/Goodsoil, Sask.	Rangers	6	34	40	62
27	Willie Huber	D	6-5	228	1-15-58/West Germany	Rangers	8	22	30	70
14	Jeff Jackson	LW	6-0	195	4-24-65/Chatham, Ont.	Tor.-Rang.	13	8	21	79
						Newmarket	3	6	9	13
15	Chris Jensen	C	5-10	180	10-28-63/Fort St. John, B.C.	Rangers	6	7	13	21
						New Haven	4	9	13	41
11	Kelly Kisio	C	5-9	170	9-18-59/Peace River, Alta.	Rangers	24	40	64	73
18	Stu Kulak	LW	5-10	180	3-10-63/Edmonton, Alta.	Van.-Edm.-Rang.	4	2	6	78
24	Pierre Larouche	C	5-11	175	11-16-55/Teschereau, Que.	Rangers	28	35	63	12
	Brian Leetch	D	5-10	170	3-3-68/Corpus Christi, Tex.	Boston U.	9	38	47	10
37	Norm Maciver	D	5-11	180	9-1-64/Thunder Bay, Ont.	Rangers	0	1	1	0
						New Haven	6	30	36	73
12	Don Maloney	LW	6-1	190	1-5-58/Kitchener, Ont.	Rangers	19	38	57	117
21	George McPhee	LW	5-9	170	7-2-58/Guelph, Ont.	Rangers	4	4	8	34
30	Larry Melnyk	D	6-0	193	2-21-60/New Westminster, B.C.	Rangers	3	12	15	182
	Jayson More	D	6-1	190	1-12-69/Delorme, Man.	New Westminster	8	29	37	217
	Brian Mullen	LW	5-10	170	3-16-62/New York, N.Y.	Winnipeg	19	32	51	20
	Steve Nemeth	C	5-9	175	2-11-67/Calgary, Alta.	Kamloops	10	4	14	0
3	James Patrick	D	6-2	185	6-14-63/Winnipeg, Man.	Rangers	10	45	55	62
8	Walt Poddubny	LW	6-1	205	2-25-60/Thunder Bay, Ont.	Rangers	40	47	87	49
47	Pat Price	D	6-2	200	3-24-55/Nelson, B.C.	Que.-Rang.	0	8	8	130
						Fredericton	0	0	0	14
	Mark Raedeke	RW	5-11	180	1-7-63/Regina, Sask.	Flint	11	15	26	89
						New Haven	10	15	25	56
28	Tomas Sandstrom	RW	6-2	200	9-4-64/Sweden	Rangers	40	34	74	60
41	Mike Siltala	RW	5-10	175	8-5-63/Toronto, Ont.	New Haven	13	6	19	20
						Rangers	0	0	0	0
	Terry Tait	C	6-2	190	9-10-63/Thunder Bay, Ont.	Flint	26	39	65	48
35	Ron Talakoski	LW	6-2	215	6-1-62/Thunder Bay, Ont.	Rangers	0	0	0	21
						New Haven	2	2	4	58
						Flint	2	1	3	12
	Gordie Walker	RW	6-0	185	1-21-65/Castlegar, B.C.	New Haven	24	20	44	58
						Rangers	1	0	1	2
	Simon Wheeldon	C	5-11	175	8-30-66/Vancouver, B.C.	New Haven	11	28	39	39
						Flint	17	53	70	67

No.	Player	Pos.	Ht.	Wt.	Born		GP	GA	SO	Avg.
	Drago Adam	G	5-10	157	9-21-66/N. Battleford, Sask.	New Westminster	55	259	1	5.50
33	Bob Froese	G	5-11	180	6-30-58/St. Catharines, Ont.	Phil.-Rang.	31	100	0	3.63
31	Ron Scott	G	5-8	155	7-21-60/Guelph, Ont.	Rangers	1	5	0	4.62
						New Haven	29	107	2	3.69
34	John Vanbiesbrouck	G	5-7	165	9-4-63/Detroit, Mich.	Rangers	50	161	0	3.64

Goaltending is not a problem. John Vanbiesbrouck didn't have another Vezina Trophy year, but he got little help from his teammates. Bob Froese was streaky after arriving from Philadelphia, but he looked good against his old team in the playoffs.

OUTLOOK: "We're going to improve this team by 15 to 20 percent," Esposito predicted. If the Rangers live up to the GM's prediction, they won't have to wait until the final days of the season to clinch a playoff spot.

One big question mark, though, involves the new coach. Will Esposito give Bergeron free rein? If he doesn't, chaos will reign again in Madison Square Garden.

RANGER PROFILES

PIERRE LAROUCHE 31 5-11 175   Right Wing
It's difficult to believe that this engaging French-Canadian is in his 14th NHL season, for he has retained his youthful exuberance and good looks... He shed no tears when Ted Sator was dismissed as head coach early last season. It was Sator who had exiled Larouche to the minors the previous season... Finished as the Rangers' fifth-leading scorer last season with 28-35-63 stats. Defensively, he was minus-7... Born Nov. 16, 1955, in Taschereau, Quebec, the youngest of 10 children... Was Pittsburgh's first choice (eighth overall) in the 1974 amateur draft... Scored a goal in his first NHL game... Scored 53 goals for the Penguins in 1975-76, becoming the youngest 50-goal scorer in NHL history until Wayne Gretzky came along in 1980... Has also played for Montreal and Hartford.

Year	Club	GP	G	A	Pts.
1974-75	Pittsburgh	79	31	37	68
1975-76	Pittsburgh	76	53	58	111
1976-77	Pittsburgh	65	29	34	63
1977-78	Pitt-Mont	64	23	37	60
1978-79	Montreal	36	9	13	22
1979-80	Montreal	73	50	41	91
1980-81	Montreal	61	25	28	53
1981-82	Mont-Hart	67	34	37	71
1982-83	Hartford	38	18	22	40
1983-84	New York R.	77	48	33	81
1984-85	New York R.	65	24	36	60
1985-86	New York R.	28	20	7	27
1986-87	New York R.	73	28	35	63
	Totals	802	392	418	810

JAMES PATRICK 23 6-2 185 Defenseman

A first-round pick (ninth overall) in 1981 draft, he elected to attend the University of North Dakota for two years and was named to the NCAA All-America team in 1983. Turned pro after playing for the Canadian National team in the 1984 Olympics ... His first Ranger coach was Herb Brooks, who once remarked: "The elevator goes all the way up on his kid." ... Completed his third full season as the team's top-scoring defenseman with 10 goals and 55 points. Was plus-13, second-best on the club... Nickname: "Jeep." ... Bright and congenial, he is a favorite of the New York media... Born June 14, 1963, in Winnipeg... His father, Stephen, was a star football player for the Winnipeg Blue Bombers.

Year	Club	GP	G	A	Pts.
1983-84	New York R.	12	1	7	8
1984-85	New York R.	75	8	28	36
1985-86	New York R.	75	14	29	43
1986-87	New York R.	78	10	45	55
	Totals	240	33	109	142

WALT PODDUBNY 27 6-1 205 Center

One of Esposito's first acts as GM was to snatch Poddubny from the Maple Leafs for Mike Allison on Aug. 18, 1986. It was a steal. Poddubny, converted from left wing to center, emerged as the Rangers' leading scorer with 40 goals and 87 points ... Asked to explain his success in New York, Poddubny said, "I'm having fun playing center and they're letting me go out and do my stuff." ... Born Feb. 14, 1960, in Thunder Bay, Ont. ... Was the Oilers' fourth choice in the 1980 draft and appeared in four games with Edmonton in 1981-82 before being traded to Toronto. Was a 28-goal scorer for the Maple Leafs in 1982-83 ... Possesses an excellent wrist shot and a soft touch around the net.

Year	Club	GP	G	A	Pts.
1981-82	Edm-Tor	15	3	4	7
1982-83	Toronto	72	28	31	59
1983-84	Toronto	38	11	14	25
1984-85	Toronto	32	5	15	20
1985-86	Toronto	33	12	22	34
1986-87	New York R.	75	40	47	87
	Totals	265	99	133	232

MARCEL DIONNE 36 5-8 190   **Center**

Figured in one of last season's most stunning trades when GM
Phil Esposito acquired him from the Los Angeles Kings at the
March trading deadline . . . A veteran of 16 NHL seasons, he
asked to be traded. Yet when he arrived in New York he told a
Los Angeles writer, "My heart is still with the Kings." . . . Scored
four goals in 14 games with the Rangers, finishing the season
with 28 goals and 84 points, but was a disappointment in the
playoffs (one goal in six games against the Flyers) . . . Entered
this season with 1,683 career points, second behind Gordie Howe
(1,850) on the all-time list . . . His new two-year contract with the
Rangers earns him $600,000 a season . . . Born Aug. 3, 1951, in
Drummondville, Que. . . . Started his NHL career with Detroit
in 1971 when he was the second player chosen in the draft behind Guy Lafleur. Signed as a free agent with the Kings in
1975 . . . Has had eight 100-point seasons and has enjoyed six
50-goal seasons.

Year	Club	GP	G	A	Pts.
1971-72	Detroit	78	28	49	77
1972-73	Detroit	77	40	50	90
1973-74	Detroit	74	24	54	78
1974-75	Detroit	80	47	74	121
1975-76	Los Angeles	80	40	54	94
1976-77	Los Angeles	80	53	69	122
1977-78	Los Angeles	70	36	43	79
1978-79	Los Angeles	80	59	71	130
1979-80	Los Angeles	80	53	84	137
1980-81	Los Angeles	80	58	77	135
1981-82	Los Angeles	78	50	67	117
1982-83	Los Angeles	80	56	51	107
1983-84	Los Angeles	66	39	53	92
1984-85	Los Angeles	80	46	80	126
1985-86	Los Angeles	80	36	58	94
1986-87	LA-NYR	81	28	56	84
	Totals	1244	693	990	1683

JOHN VANBIESBROUCK 24 5-7 165   **Goaltender**

His surname is so long it barely fits on the back of his sweater,
but he has fit in nicely with the Rangers since joining the team in
1984 . . . A workhorse, he played in 50 games last season, finishing with an 18-20-5 record and a 3.64 goals-against average . . .
Dreams about being six feet tall ("What an advantage that would
be.") . . . A fifth-round pick (72nd overall) in 1981 draft . . . Was
only 18 when he had a one-game trial with the Rangers that same
year . . . Helped lead the Tulsa Oilers to the Central League championship in 1983-84, then moved up to the Rangers . . . In his

second year with the club, 1985-86, he established a team record by totaling 39 victories—31 during the regular season and eight in the playoffs, and won the Vezina Trophy . . . Born Sept. 4, 1963, in Detroit.

Year	Club	GP	GA	SO	Avg.
1981-82	New York R.	1	1	0	1.00
1983-84	New York R.	3	10	0	3.33
1984-85	New York R.	42	166	1	4.22
1985-86	New York R.	61	184	3	3.32
1986-87	New York R.	50	161	0	3.64
	Totals	157	522	4	3.65

TOMAS SANDSTROM 23 6-2 200   Right Wing

Attained all-star status last season . . . Was heading for a 50-goal season when he suffered a fractured ankle while playing against the Soviets in RendezVous '87 . . . Settled for 40 goals, 74 points and a plus-8 figure. His blazing shot has earned him the nickname "Tommy Gun." However, some feel he should be called "Timex" because he takes a lot of abuse but keeps on ticking . . . Carries his stick high, explaining, "I don't like to take it without giving it back, but I'm not as bad as they say." . . . Born Sept. 4, 1964, in Jacobstad, Finland, but moved with his family to Sweden when very young . . . A second-round pick in the 1982 draft . . . Scored in his first NHL game in 1984 . . . Had problems conversing in English when he first arrived in New York, but has a better grasp of the language now.

Year	Club	GP	G	A	Pts.
1984-85	New York R.	74	29	29	58
1985-86	New York R.	73	25	29	54
1986-87	New York R.	64	40	34	74
	Totals	211	94	92	186

DON MALONEY 29 6-1 190   Left Wing

Made a strong comeback last season after being slowed by leg injuries the previous two years . . . Suffered a broken leg early in the 1984-85 season and tore up his right knee a year later . . . Though not considered a prolific scorer, he has had two 29-goal seasons . . . Has always displayed a strong work ethic, even during the offseason. Has a complete Nautilus setup in his New York suburban home . . . Voted prestigious Players' Player Award twice by his teammates . . . Born Sept. 5, 1958, in Lindsay, Ont. . . .

Was the Rangers' second-round pick in the 1978 draft...Made his NHL debut in 1979 against the Bruins, scoring a goal on his first shift and an assist on his second shift...MVP in the 1984 All-Star Game...Older brother, Don, was his teammate in New York for 6½ years.

Year	Club	GP	G	A	Pts.
1978-79	New York R.	28	9	17	26
1979-80	New York R.	79	25	48	73
1980-81	New York R.	61	29	23	52
1981-82	New York R.	54	22	36	58
1982-83	New York R.	78	29	40	69
1983-84	New York R.	79	24	42	66
1984-85	New York R.	37	11	16	27
1985-86	New York R.	68	11	17	28
1986-87	New York R.	72	19	38	57
	Totals	550	179	278	456

KELLY KISIO 28 5-9 170   Center
Made a large impression on Madison Square Garden fans—and general manager Esposito—after joining the team last season... "He's going to help us a lot," said Esposito. "That's as evident as the nose on my face, which is pretty evident."...Was the team's fourth-leading scorer with 24 goals and 64 points...Acquired with right winger Lane Lambert and defenseman Jim Leavins from Detroit for goalie Glen Hanlon in a 1986 deal that also included a complicated exchange of draft choices...Born on Sept. 18, 1959, in Peace River, Alta...Signed as a free agent with the Red Wings in 1979 after being bypassed in the amateur draft because of his size...Spent two years in the minors and a season in Switzerland before joining the Red Wings in 1983.

Year	Club	GP	G	A	Pts.
1983-84	Detroit	70	23	37	60
1984-85	Detroit	75	20	21	41
1985-86	Detroit	76	21	48	69
1986-87	New York R.	70	24	40	64
	Totals	291	88	146	234

RON DUGUAY 30 6-2 210   Right Wing
Starting to show his age, but still one of the league's most colorful players...Returned to New York midway through last season in a trade with Pittsburgh...Had five goals in 40 games with the Penguins, nine in 34 games with the Rangers...Good penalty-

killer... Born July 6, 1957, in Sudbury, Ont.... First-round pick by the Rangers in 1977. John Ferguson, then the team's GM, chose him over Mike Bossy... Part of a six-player deal between the Rangers and the Red Wings in 1983... Had two good seasons in Detroit, totaling 33 and 38 goals. Red Wings traded him to Pittsburgh for Doug Shedden late in the 1985-86 season... One of the league's last remaining bare-headed players.

Year	Club	GP	G	A	Pts.
1977-78	New York R.	71	20	20	40
1978-79	New York R.	79	27	36	63
1979-80	New York R.	73	28	22	50
1980-81	New York R.	50	17	21	38
1981-82	New York R.	72	40	36	76
1982-83	New York R.	72	19	25	44
1983-84	Detroit	80	33	47	80
1984-85	Detroit	80	38	51	89
1985-86	Det-Pitt	80	25	36	61
1986-87	Pitt-NYR	74	14	25	39
	Totals	731	261	319	580

BOB FROESE 29 5-11 180   Goaltender

His surname is pronounced "Froze," he's nicknamed "Frosty" and he is a cool customer... Acquired from the Flyers on Dec. 18, 1986, for defenseman Kjell Samuelsson and a second-round draft choice in 1989... Admitted he was "ecstatic" to leave Philly, where he had quarreled with coach Mike Keenan. GM Esposito was equally happy to get Froese. "Bob is a quality player, an all-star," the GM said... Froese had a combined 17-11-0 record and a 3.32 goals-against average last season... Born June 30, 1958, in St. Catherines, Ont.... Drafted by the St. Louis Blues in the 10th round (160th overall) of the 1978 draft... Kicked around in the minors for four years... Took over as the Flyers' No. 1 goalie following the tragic death of Pelle Lindbergh early in the 1985-86 season... Led the league that season in average (2.55), record (31-10-3), save percentage (.909) and shutouts (5).

Year	Club	GP	GA	SO	Avg.
1982-83	Philadelphia	24	59	4	2.52
1983-84	Philadelphia	48	150	2	3.14
1984-85	Philadelphia	17	37	1	2.41
1985-86	Philadelphia	51	116	5	2.55
1986-87	Phil-NYR	31	100	0	3.63
	Totals	171	462	12	2.90

BARRY BECK 30 6-3 215   **Defenseman**

Returns after sitting out 1986-87 season in protest initially over differences with then-Ranger coach Ted Sator... Bubba plagued by injuries throughout career... Played in 56 games in 1984-85 and underwent surgery for left shoulder after season, but reinjury kept him to 25 games in 1985-86...A huge defensive plus if he and his body can make the grade again... Devastating body-checker and defensive defenseman who has never scored up to expectations... One of many reasons for the 1985 firing of Herb Brooks, who called him a "coward"... Beck blew up, overturning a stick rack at practice when news of incident hit the papers ... Second player taken in the 1977 draft (by Colorado), traded to Rangers for six players in 1979... Born June 3, 1957, in Vancouver... Year off cost him an estimated $450,000.

Year	Club	GP	G	A	Pts.
1977-78	Colorado..........	75	22	38	60
1978-79	Colorado..........	63	14	28	42
1979-80	Col-NYR	71	15	50	65
1980-81	New York R........	75	11	23	34
1981-82	New York R........	60	9	29	38
1982-83	New York R........	66	12	22	34
1983-84	New York R........	72	9	27	36
1984-85	New York R........	56	7	19	26
1985-86	New York R........	25	4	8	12
	Totals	563	103	244	347

COACH MICHEL BERGERON: Another of Phil Esposito's surprises, Bergeron comes to New York after seven successful seasons with the Nordiques ... They call him "Le Petite Tigre" (The Little Tiger) for good reason... A motivator who screams and goads and is a premier ref-baiter, he'll bring the Rangers the sort of emotion that will at least please the flamboyant Esposito ... He's proven himself as a coach... Overall

he's 253-222-79 and he's the second most-experienced coach in the league, behind Edmonton's Glen Sather... Played and coached in youth hockey in Montreal, where he was born June 12, 1946... Coached junior hockey from 1974 to 1980 with Three Rivers in the Quebec Junior League and joined the Nordiques as assistant coach in 1980... Became head coach early in the 1980-81 season... Was assistant coach of the NHL All-Stars at RendezVous '87 under head coach Jean Perron. Ironically, he refused to shake hands with Perron after the Adams Division final series because he felt Quebec was robbed in the pivotal fifth game . . . Often uses bench like a soap box and sometimes waves a stick for effect.

GREATEST COACH

The Rangers have had 23 coaches in their 61-year history. The first one accounted for two of the team's three Stanley Cup championships. He was Lester Patrick, hockey's legendary "Silver Fox," who served as both the general manager and coach when the Rangers won the Cup in the second year of their existence in 1928. They repeated under Patrick in 1933.

Patrick coached the Rangers for 13 years, during which time his teams won 281 regular-season games, giving Patrick a career winning percentage of .554. Of all the Ranger coaches, only Emile Francis accounted for more victories (347) and had a higher won-lost percentage (.606)

Patrick was born on Dec. 30, 1983, in Drummondville, Que., and was an outstanding defenseman during his playing days. He provided one of hockey's great moments in the 1928 Cup finals against the Montreal Maroons after Lorne Chabot, the Rangers' regular goalie, suffered an eye injury early in the second period. Though Patrick was then 44 years old and long retired as a player, he replaced Chabot and allowed only one goal in the ensuing 43 minutes. The Rangers won, 2-1, on an overtime goal by Frank Boucher and went on to capture the Stanley Cup.

Patrick relinquished his coaching duties to Boucher in 1939, but remained as GM until 1946. Patrick was elected to the Hockey Hall of Fame in 1945. He died in Victoria, B.C., in 1960.

ALL-TIME RANGER LEADERS

GOALS: Vic Hadfield, 50, 1971-72
ASSISTS: Mike Rogers, 65, 1981-82
POINTS: Jean Ratelle, 109, 1971-72
SHUTOUTS: John Roach, 13, 1928-29

PHILADELPHIA FLYERS

TEAM DIRECTORY: Chairman Exec. Comm.: Edward Snider; Chairman of the Board: Joseph Scott; Pres.: Jay Snider; Exec. VP: Keith Allen; GM: Bobby Clarke; Dir. Scouting-Asst. GM: Gary Darling; Dir. Press Rel.: Rodger Gottlieb; Coach: Mike Keenan. Home ice: The Spectrum (17,222; 200' × 85'). Colors: Orange, black and white. Training camps: Voorhees, N.J., and Philadelphia.

SCOUTING REPORT

OFFENSE: The Flyers were beset by injuries last season. At one point they had eight players in the infirmary, but the team carried on and totaled 310 goals, fourth-best in the league.

If you get the idea that the Flyers' cup runneth over with

Tim Kerr has scored 60 power-play goals the past two years.

talented forwards, you are right. They are led by big Tim Kerr, a perennial 50-goal scorer who is in his seventh season with the team, and stocky Brian Propp, who is in his eighth season. It will be interesting to see how Kerr bounces back from offseason shoulder surgery.

The supporting players have far less experience, but possess equal amounts of enthusiasm, intensity and savvy. They include Peter Zezel, team captain Dave Poulin, Pelle Eklund, Rick Tocchet, Murray Craven, Ron Sutter and Scott Mellanby.

Zezel, Poulin, Sutter and Eklund provide the Flyers with great strength at center. Zezel followed up his 33-goal regular season by playing solid two-way hockey in the playoffs. So did Eklund, who emerged as a dangerous game-breaker. Tocchet and Mellanby have helped shore up the right side, while Craven, Derrick Smith and Lindsay Carson share the left side with Propp.

Perhaps the Flyers, like most clubs, could use one more goal-scoring threat. The organization's best prospects include Finnish forward Jukka-Pekka Seppo (No. 2, 1986) and Glen Seabrooke (No. 1, 1985).

DEFENSE: The Flyers finished second in the league with 245 goals allowed last season. They should have finished first, but gave up nine goals in their regular-season finale against the Islanders, permitting the Canadiens to win the Jennings Trophy by a four-goal margin.

Goalie sensation Ron Hextall received most of the credit for the Flyers' high finish, but he had help from the rearguards. And when the defensemen failed to clear the slot of intruders, Hextall prodded them with his large goalie stick.

Darren Jensen, who shared the Jennings Trophy with Bob Froese in 1985-86, spent last season at Hershey. Management obviously had doubts if he could replace retired Chico Resch as Hextall's backup, so Mark LaForest was obtained from the Red Wings in the offseason.

Coach Mike Keenan has relied on four defensemen since he took charge in 1984, and all have been around the block more than once. They are 32-year-old Mark Howe, Brad Marsh (29), Brad McCrimmon (28) and Doug Crossman (27). Is help on the way? Well, Kjell Samuelsson provided splendid relief in the playoffs and J.J. Daigneault has shown flashes of promise.

OUTLOOK: Hextall sounded the rallying cry after the Flyers came within one victory of winning the Stanley Cup against the Oilers last spring. "We have a lot of good young players . . . a great team that's going to be here for many years," he said.

FLYER ROSTER

No.	Player	Pos.	Ht.	Wt.	Born	1986 – 87	G	A	Pts	PIM
	Hay Allison	RW	5-9	178	3-4-59/Cranbrook, B.C.	Hershey	29	55	84	57
						Philadelphia	0	0	0	0
34	Craig Berube	LW	6-2	195	12-17-65/Calhoo, Alta.	Philadelphia	0	0	0	57
						Hershey	7	17	24	325
21	Dave Brown	RW	6-5	205	10-12-62/Saskatoon, Sask.	Philadelphia	7	3	10	274
18	Lindsay Carson	C	6-2	190	11-21-60/Oxbow, Sask.	Philadelphia	11	15	26	141
6	Jeff Chychrun	D	6-4	186	5-3-66/LaSalle, Que.	Philadelphia	0	0	0	4
						Hershey	1	17	18	239
32	Murray Craven	C	6-2	170	7-20-64/Medicine Hat, Alta.	Philadelphia	19	30	49	38
3	Doug Crossman	D	6-2½	180	6-13-60/Peterborough, Ont.	Philadelphia	9	31	40	29
15	J.J. Daigneault	D	5-11	180	10-12-65/Montreal, Que.	Philadelphia	6	16	22	56
7	Brian Dobbin	RW	5-11	195	8-18-66/Petrolia, Ont.	Philadelphia	2	1	3	14
						Hershey	26	35	61	66
9	Pelle Eklund	C	5-10	170	3-22-63/Sweden	Philadelphia	14	41	55	2
	Ross Fitzpatrick	LW	6-0	195	10-7-60/Penticton, B.C.	Hershey	45	40	85	34
17	Ed Hospodar	D-RW	6-2	200	2-5-59/Bowling Green, Ohio	Philadelphia	2	2	4	136
2	Mark Howe	D	5-11	190	5-28-55/Detroit, Mich.	Philadelphia	15	43	58	37
	Kerry Huffman	D	6-2	180	1-3-68/Peterborough, Ont.	Philadelphia	0	0	0	2
						Guelph	4	31	35	20
12	Tim Kerr	RW	6-3	225	3-31-58/Windsor, Ont.	Philadelphia	58	37	95	57
	Mitch Lamoureaux	C	5-6	175	8-22-62/Ottawa, Ont.	Hershey	43	46	89	122
10	Brad MacCrimmon	D	5-10	185	3-29-59/Dodsland, Sask.	Philadelphia	10	29	39	52
8	Brad Marsh	D	6-3	220	3-31-58/London, Ont.	Philadelphia	2	9	11	124
	Kevin Maxwell	C	5-9	165	3-30-60/Edmonton, Alta.	Hershey	12	20	32	139
36	Kevin McCarthy	D	5-11	185	7-14-57/Winnipeg, Man.	Hershey	6	44	50	86
						Philadelphia	0	0	0	0
19	Scott Mellanby	RW	5-11	195	6-11-66/Montreal, Que.	Philadelphia	11	21	32	94
42	Don Nachbaur	C	6-2	200	1-30-59/Kitimat, B.C.	Hershey	18	17	35	274
						Philadelphia	0	2	2	89
20	Dave Poulin	C	5-11	180	12-17-58/Timmins, Ont.	Philadelphia	25	45	70	53
26	Brian Propp	LW	5-10	190	2-15-59/Neudorf, Sask.	Philadelphia	31	36	67	45
	Darren Rumble	D	6-1	187	1-23-69/Barrie, Ont.	Kitchener	11	32	43	44
28	Kjell Samuelsson	D	6-6	227	10-18-58/Sweden	Phil.-Rang.	3	12	15	136
23	Ilkka Sinisalo	LW	6-1	190	7-10-58/Finland	Philadelphia	10	21	31	8
24	Derrick Smith	LW	6-1	190	1-22-65/Scarborough, Ont.	Philadelphia	11	26	37	191
5	Steve Smith	D	5-10	210	4-4-63/Toronto, Ont.	Philadelphia	0	0	0	6
						Hershey	11	26	37	191
40	Greg Smyth	D	6-3	213	4-23-66/Mississauga, Ont.	Hershey	0	2	2	158
						Philadelphia	0	0	0	0
44	Mike Stothers	D	6-4	210	2-22-62/Toronto, Ont.	Philadelphia	0	0	0	4
						Hershey	5	11	16	283
14	Ron Sutter	C	5-11	175	12-2-63/Viking, Alta.	Philadelphia	10	17	27	69
29	Darryl Stanley	D	6-2	200	12-2-62/Winnipeg, Man.	Philadelphia	1	2	3	76
22	Rick Tocchet	RW	6-0	195	4-9-64/Scarborough, Ont.	Philadelphia	21	26	47	286
	Tim Tookey	C	5-11	180	8-29-60/Edmonton, Alta.	Hershey	51	78	129	45
25	Peter Zezel	C	5-9	200	4-22-65/Toronto, Ont.	Philadelphia	33	39	72	71

No.	Player	Pos.	Ht.	Wt.	Born		GP	GA	SO	Avg.
27	Ron Hextall	G	6-3	175	5-3-64/Winnipeg, Man.	Philadelphia	66	190	1	3.00
30	Darren Jensen	G	5-8	165	5-27-60/Cresto, B.C.	Hershey	60	215	0	3.76
	John Kemp	G	6-0	180	7-31-63/Burlington, Ont.	Hershey	30	80	1	3.56
	Mark Laforest	G	5-10	178	7-10-62/Welland, Ont.	Detroit	5	12	0	3.29
						Adirondack	37	105	3	2.83

The precocious goalie will be hard-pressed to match his rookie season, but don't bet against it. And don't bet against the Flyers going all the way in next spring's playoffs.

FLYER PROFILES

RON HEXTALL 24 6-3 175   Goaltender

Wayne Gretzky said, "This is probably the best goalie I've ever played against." . . . Hall of Famer Eddie Giacomin said, "Ron Hextall is the best puck-handling goalie I've ever seen." . . . High praise, indeed, for this newcomer to greatness . . . As a rookie last season he won the Vezina (outstanding goalie) Trophy, led the league in victories (37) and save percentage (.902) and set an NHL record for most penalty minutes by a goalie (107). His goals-against average was 3.00 . . . Continued his astounding work in the playoffs, starting all 26 games for the Flyers and winning the Smythe (MVP) Trophy . . . Extremely intense and aggressive. Uses his stick like a scythe . . . Born May 3, 1964, in Brandon, Manitoba . . . A hockey purebred. His father, Bryan Jr., was a rugged NHL forward for nine years and his late grandfather, Bryan Sr., was a star winger for the Rangers from 1936 to 1948 . . . In late June, Ron was suspended by the NHL for the first eight games of the 1987-88 season for a stick-swinging incident in Game 4 of the Stanley Cup finals.

Year	Club	GP	GA	SO	Avg.
1986-87	Philadelphia	66	190	1	3.00

PETER ZEZEL 22 5-9 200   Center

He's last alphabetically but first in the hearts of Philly's female fans . . . Handsome and personable, he had a bit role in the movie "Youngblood." . . . Took giant strides toward stardom last season when he finished second behind Tim Kerr in goals scored (33), points (72) and game-winners (7) . . . Strong skater and deft passer, he reminds some people of a young Bryan Trottier the way he finishes his checks. "When I bump, I play better," he claims . . . Born April 22, 1965, in Toronto . . . Second-round pick in the 1983 draft . . . Gave up a budding soccer career—he played briefly for the Toronto Blizzard of the NASL—to concentrate on hockey.

Year	Club	GP	G	A	Pts.
1984-85	Philadelphia	65	15	46	61
1985-86	Philadelphia	79	17	37	54
1986-87	Philadelphia	71	33	39	72
	Totals	215	65	122	187

PELLE EKLUND 24 5-10 170   Center
Was a revelation for the Flyers in the playoffs, totaling 27 points on 7 goals and 20 assists . . . Scored five goals in two consecutive games against the Canadiens in the semifinals, prompting Montreal's Stephane Richer to say, "He thinks he's Gretzky." . . . Wasn't quite as spectacular during the regular season, scoring 14 goals . . . Must improve his defensive work (minus-2) . . . Plays the point on the power play . . . Born March 22, 1963, in Stockholm . . . Was an eighth-round pick (167th overall) in the 1983 draft . . . Played for Sweden in the 1984 Olympics in Yugoslavia, recording eight points in seven games . . . Had an impressive rookie season with the Flyers in 1985-86, finishing third among all NHL rookies with 66 points.

Year	Club	GP	G	A	Pts.
1985-86	Philadelphia	70	15	51	66
1986-87	Philadelphia	72	14	41	55
	Totals	142	29	92	121

BRIAN PROPP 28 5-10 190   Left Wing
Made a strong comeback in the playoffs after missing one-third of the regular season with a knee injury that required major surgery . . . Totaled team-high 12 goals and 28 points in 26 playoff games . . . A perennial 40-goal scorer, he settled for 31 in 53 regular-season games . . . Quick and aggressive, he is a valued penalty-killer. "He's like one of those Russian skaters," says GM Clarke. "He takes those short, quick strides." . . . Born Feb. 15, 1959, in Lanisan, Sask. . . . A first-round pick in the 1979 draft . . . As a rookie, he scored the game-winning goal in the

Flyers' season opener against the Rangers and totaled 34 goals in 80 games...Only survivor of the Flyer team that lost to the Islanders in the 1980 finals.

Year	Club	GP	G	A	Pts.
1979-80	Philadelphia	80	34	41	75
1980-81	Philadelphia	79	26	40	66
1981-82	Philadelphia	80	44	47	91
1982-83	Philadelphia	80	40	42	82
1983-84	Philadelphia	79	39	53	92
1984-85	Philadelphia	76	43	53	96
1985-86	Philadelphia	72	40	57	97
1986-87	Philadelphia	53	31	36	67
	Totals	599	297	369	666

RON SUTTER 23 5-11 175   Center

One of the top defensive centers in the league, he missed the second half of last season with a stress fracture in his lower back ...Had 10 goals in 39 regular-season games...His recuperation took longer than expected, causing much concern. "There's pressure on me to play," he admitted. He returned in time to help the Flyers fight off the Canadiens in the Wales Conference final... Has all the dogged traits that put five of his brothers into the NHL...Born Dec. 2, 1963, in Viking, Alta., he is 30 minutes younger than twin brother Rich of the Canucks...Fourth player taken in the 1982 draft...Had an excellent rookie season in 1983-84, totaling 51 points on 19 goals and 32 assists.

Year	Club	GP	G	A	Pts.
1982-83	Philadelphia	10	1	1	2
1983-84	Philadelphia	79	19	32	51
1984-85	Philadelphia	73	16	29	45
1985-86	Philadelphia	75	18	41	59
1986-87	Philadelphia	39	10	17	27
	Totals	276	64	120	184

BRAD MARSH 29 6-3 220   Defenseman

A throwback to hockey's earlier days. Might be the league's best at shot-blocking, plus clutch and grab tactics...One of the last bareheaded players, he showed up for last spring's playoffs with a brush cut. "I wanted it short—it makes me go faster," he joked ...Though an awkward skater, he rarely gets caught out of position...Born March 31, 1958, in London, Ont....First-round pick of the Atlanta Flames in 1978...Served as the Flames' captain when they moved to Calgary...Dealt to Philly for Mel Bridgman in 1981 . . . Competes in triathlons during the offseason.

Year	Club	GP	G	A	Pts.
1978-79	Atlanta	80	0	19	19
1979-80	Atlanta	80	2	9	11
1980-81	Calgary	80	1	12	13
1981-82	Calg-Phil	83	2	23	25
1982-83	Philadelphia	68	2	11	13
1983-84	Philadelphia	77	3	14	17
1984-85	Philadelphia	77	2	18	20
1985-86	Philadelphia	79	0	13	13
1986-87	Philadelphia	77	2	9	11
	Totals	701	14	128	142

TIM KERR 27 6-3 225   Right Wing

The most dangerous power-play sniper since Phil Esposito, he gives rival defensemen and goalies fits when he plants himself in front of the net . . . Scored a league-record 34 power-play goals during the 1985-86 season . . . Led the Flyers last season with 58 goals, including 26 on the power play, and 95 points. Contributed 10 game-winners . . . A damaged left shoulder limited his playoff participation to 12 games and caused him to miss both the Montreal and Edmonton series . . . Not overly aggressive. "I'm big but they don't pay me to punch out people. I'm lucky, I suppose, that I can contribute other ways." . . . Born Jan. 5, 1960, in Windsor, Ont. . . . One of the greatest free-agent finds in NHL history. Signed as an underage player after being ignored during an abbreviated six-round draft in 1979.

Year	Club	GP	G	A	Pts.
1980-81	Philadelphia	68	22	23	45
1981-82	Philadelphia	61	21	30	51
1982-83	Philadelphia	24	11	8	19
1983-84	Philadelphia	79	54	39	93
1984-85	Philadelphia	74	54	44	98
1985-86	Philadelphia	76	58	26	84
1986-87	Philadelphia	75	58	37	95
	Totals	457	278	207	485

MARK HOWE 32 5-11 190   Defenseman

This son of hockey immortal Gordie Howe is the Flyers' most consistent player. "It used to be I'd play 40 great games a year, 40 bad," he said. "Now I play five great games, five bad games and the rest are the same—consistent." . . . Very effective defensively, he finished last season with a plus-57 rating and was named to the All-Star first team for second consecutive year . . .

Led all NHL players the previous season at plus-85 . . . Has an awesome wrist shot which some feel is as good as the one his dad once used to terrify goalies. "No way," he says . . . Born May 28, 1955, in Detroit . . . Broke in as an 18-year-old on the same line with dad and brother Marty with Houston of the WHA in 1973 . . . Acquired by the Flyers in 1982 in a three-way deal with the Whalers and the Oilers.

Year	Club	GP	G	A	Pts.
1973-74	Houston (WHA)	76	38	41	79
1974-75	Houston (WHA)	74	36	40	76
1975-76	Houston (WHA)	72	39	37	76
1976-77	Houston (WHA)	57	23	52	75
1977-78	New Eng. (WHA) ...	70	30	61	91
1978-79	New Eng. (WHA) ...	77	42	65	107
1979-80	Hartford	74	24	56	80
1980-81	Hartford	63	19	46	65
1981-82	Hartford	76	8	45	53
1982-83	Philadelphia	76	20	47	67
1983-84	Philadelphia	71	19	34	53
1984-85	Philadelphia	73	18	39	57
1985-86	Philadelphia	77	24	58	82
1986-87	Philadelphia	69	15	43	58
	NHL Totals	579	147	368	515
	WHA Totals........	426	208	296	504

RICK TOCCHET 23 6-0 195   Right Wing

Rough and tough, he has led the Flyers in penalties in each of his three seasons with the team. More important, he's developing into a good goal-scorer. After accounting for 14 goals in each of his first two seasons, he totaled 21 last season, then added 11 in the playoffs. Was particularly effective in the playoffs against the Rangers, scoring five goals in six games . . . "My first two years I just wanted to play tough and fit in," he says. "Now it's comes to the point where I think I can score goals, too." . . . Born April 9, 1964, in Scarborough, Ont. . . . Drafted from Sault Ste. Marie of OHL in sixth round (121st overall) in 1983 draft.

Year	Club	GP	G	A	Pts.
1984-85	Philadelphia	75	14	25	39
1985-86	Philadelphia	69	14	21	35
1986-87	Philadelphia	69	21	26	47
	Totals	213	49	72	121

DAVE POULIN 28 5-11 180   **Center**

The man who filled the shoes of Bobby Clarke... Excellent
penalty-killer and strong checker. Good on faceoffs... A
plus-47 player last season, he won the Selke Trophy as the
league's top defensive forward... Five of his 25 goals were
game-winners... Hampered by sore ribs and a busted finger in
the playoffs... Scored the winning goal for the NHL All-Stars in
their first game against the Soviets in the RendezVous'87 series
... "I never visualized what it would be like to play against the
Soviets," he said. "Hey, I never even visualized playing in the
NHL."... Born Dec. 17, 1958, in Timmins, Ont....
Overlooked in the draft after a fine four-year career at Notre
Dame University... Spent a season playing in Sweden before
signing with the Flyers as a free agent in 1983

Year	Club	GP	G	A	Pts.
1982-83	Philadelphia	2	2	0	2
1983-84	Philadelphia	73	31	45	76
1984-85	Philadelphia	73	30	44	74
1985-86	Philadelphia	79	27	42	69
1986-87	Philadelphia	75	25	45	70
	Totals	402	115	176	291

COACH MIKE KEENAN: One of the league's most complex

personalities. Appears arrogant behind the
bench with his Scotty Bowman posture—head
tilted back, jaw thrust forward, eyes narrowed.
Called "a jerk" by Phil Esposito, he engaged
in a shouting match with Wayne Gretzky during the playoff finals... Though he has trouble projecting a friendly attitude, there is no
questioning his coaching ability. In his three
years in Philly, he has directed the Flyers to three Patrick Division championships and into the Stanley Cup finals twice...
Named Coach of the Year in 1984-85 season... His teams have
also won championships in Junior B, Major Junior, Canadian
University and American Hockey League... Not as stern with
his players as he was two years ago. "I want them to enjoy playing hockey," he says... Born Oct. 21, 1949, in Toronto...
Played defense at St. Lawrence University, University of Toronto
and one year with Roanoke Valley Rebels of the defunct Southern
Hockey League... Enjoys music. Used to sing with a group of
college chums named Nik and the Nice Guys.

GREATEST COACH

He was known as "Freddie the Fog," but there is nothing foggy about Fred Shero's coaching record with the Flyers. Using many unique motivational techniques, he led the Flyers to four first-place finishes and two consecutive Stanley Cup championships in the '70s.

Not all his players understood Shero, an avid reader who collected quotes from sources as varied as Dag Hammarskjold, Tolstoy and the Beatles. Said former Philly defenseman Joe Watson: "I never understood most of the things Freddie wrote on the blackboard. I used to have to look up some of the words."

The Flyers became the first expansion team to win the Stanley Cup when they turned back Bobby Orr and the Bruins in the 1974 finals. They repeated as champions the following spring.

Shero was a hero then. However, he turned his back on Philadelphia in 1978 to become coach and general manager of the Rangers, leading them into the Cup finals in his first season in New York. In his second season, the team fell apart and so did Shero. He was dismissed in 1980.

Shero, who underwent successful surgery for stomach cancer in 1984, currently is serving as an analyst on broadcasts of New Jersey Devils' games.

ALL-TIME FLYER LEADERS

GOALS: Reggie Leach, 61, 1975-76
ASSISTS: Bobby Clarke, 89, 1974-75, 1975-76
POINTS: Bobby Clarke, 119, 1975-76
SHUTOUTS: Bernie Parent, 12, 1973-74, 1974-75

PITTSBURGH PENGUINS

TEAM DIRECTORY: Owner: Edward J. DeBartolo; GM: Ed Johnston; Asst. GM: Ken Schinkel; Coach: Pierre Creamer; Dir. Press Rel.: Cindy Himes; Home ice: Civic Arena (16,033; 200′ × 85′). Colors: Black and gold. Training camp: Pittsburgh.

SCOUTING REPORT

OFFENSE: Any team with Mario Lemieux in its lineup shouldn't have to worry about goal-scoring. Right? Well . . . the Penguins totaled 297 goals last season, seventh in the league, but

"The Franchise"—Mario Lemieux—had 107 points.

they again failed to make the playoffs. So there's room for improvement here.

Wilf Paiement, the free-agent Sabre veteran who signed with the Penguins in July, should fill a pressing need at right wing, where Dan Frawley was the most productive goal-scorer last season with 14. Ron Duguay returned to the Rangers late in the season and Willy Lindstrom retired. Maybe rookie Dwight Mathiasen is ready to move up after a year in the minors.

The left wingers include Randy Cunneyworth, Bob Errey, Warren Young and Kevin LaVallee. Cunneyworth led this group last season with 26 goals and a plus-14 rating.

Center is the Penguins' strong suit. In addition to Lemieux, new coach Pierre Creamer can call on Dan Quinn, Craig Simpson and Dave Hannan. And general manager Eddie Johnston is high on rookie Rob Brown, who became the first 17-year-old to lead the Western League in scoring two seasons ago. "Brown will play in our league, for sure," Johnston said.

The Penguins need help on their specialty teams. They were 14th in power plays and 15th in penalty-killing last season.

DEFENSE: This is a team that once allowed 13 goals in a game and close to 400 in a season. But that was several years ago. The Pens have tightened their defense considerably, thanks to young hands like Doug Bodger, Jim Johnson, Moe Mantha, Rod Buskas and Ville Siren.

Added to the cast this season is Zarley Zalapski, a first-round pick (fourth overall) in the 1986 draft. The outstanding member of Canada's Olympic team is not expected to be available until after the closing ceremonies at Calgary in February. GM Johnston can hardly wait. "We're getting a heckuva fine hockey player," he said. "I'm very pleased with his progress."

In goal, the Penguins have veterans Gilles Meloche and Pat Riggin. Either could lose his job to rookie Steve Guenette, who performed extremely well on the Baltimore farm last season (3.10 GAA in 54 games). He had a two-game trial with the parent club, lost both starts, but played well.

Guenette was signed as a free agent after leading Guelph to the 1986 Memorial Cup championship. "Steve has played exceptionally well . . . he could stick with us this season," Johnson said.

OUTLOOK: Remember when the Penguins were called "The Bores of Winter?" It was a bad rap that no longer applies. The Pens are an exciting club now and they're putting people in the seats, drawing a record 598,614 fans at home last season.

PENGUIN ROSTER

No.	Player	Pos.	Ht.	Wt.	Born	1986—87	G	A	Pts.	PIM
24	Roger Belanger	C	6-0	188	12-1-65/Welland, Ont.	Baltimore	9	11	20	14
22	Neil Belland	D	5-11	175	4-3-61/Parry Sound, Ont.	Pittsburgh	0	1	1	0
						Baltimore	6	18	24	12
26	Mike Blaisdell	RW	6-1	195	1-18-60/Regina, Sask.	Pittsburgh	1	1	2	2
						Baltimore	12	12	24	47
3	Doug Bodger	D	6-2	200	6-18-66/Chernanius, B.C.	Pittsburgh	11	38	49	52
29	Phil Bourque	LW	6-0	179	6-8-62/Chelmsford, Mass.	Pittsburgh	2	3	5	32
						Baltimore	15	16	31	183
	Ron Brown	C	5-11	170	4-10-68/Kingston, Ont.	Kamloops	76	136	212	101
7	Rod Buskas	D	6-1	197	1-7-61/Wetaskiwin, Alta.	Pittsburgh	3	15	18	123
	Todd Charlesworth	D	6-1	191	3-22-65/Ottawa, Ont.	Pittsburgh	0	0	0	0
						Baltimore	5	21	26	64
15	Randy Cunneyworth	C	6-0	183	5-10-61/Etobicoke, Ont.	Pittsburgh	26	27	53	142
2	Chris Dahlquist	D	6-1	190	12-14-62/Fridley, Man.	Pittsburgh	0	1	1	20
						Baltimore	1	16	17	50
10	Bob Errey	LW	5-10	183	9-21-64/Montreal, Que.	Pittsburgh	16	18	34	46
						Baltimore	13	14	27	134
28	Dan Frawley	RW	6-0	170	6-2-62/Sturgeon Falls, Ont.	Pittsburgh	14	14	28	218
	Lee Giffin	RW	5-11	175	4-1-67/Chatham, Ont.	Pittsburgh	1	1	2	0
						Oshawa	31	69	100	46
32	Dave Hannan	C	5-10	180	11-26-61/Sudbury, Ont.	Pittsburgh	10	15	25	56
23	Randy Hillier	D	6-0	185	3-20-60/Toronto, Ont.	Pittsburgh	4	8	12	97
6	Jim Johnson	D	6-0	186	8-9-62/Minneapolis, Minn.	Pittsburgh	5	25	30	116
	Chris Joseph	D	6-2	194	9-10-69/Burnaby, B.C.	Seattle	13	45	58	156
14	Chris Kontos	C	6-1	186	12-10-63/Toronto, Ont.	Pittsburgh	8	9	17	6
						New Haven	14	17	31	29
16	Kevin LaVallee	LW	5-8	180	9-16-61/Sudbury, Ont.	Pittsburgh	8	20	28	4
	Alain Lemieux	C	6-0	185	5-29-61/Montreal, Que.	Baltimore	41	56	97	62
						Pittsburgh	0	0	0	0
66	Mario Lemieux	C	6-4	200	10-5-65/Montreal, Que.	Pittsburgh	54	53	107	57
19	Willy Lindstrom	RW	6-0	180	8-5-51/Sweden	Pittsburgh	10	13	23	6
24	Troy Loney	LW	6-3	210	9-21-63/Bow Island, Alta.	Pittsburgh	8	7	15	22
						Baltimore	13	14	27	134
20	Moe Mantha	D	6-2	197	1-21-61/Lakewood, Ohio	Pittsburgh	9	31	40	44
11	Dwight Mathiason	RW	6-1	185	12-5-63/Vancouver, B.C.	Pittsburgh	0	1	1	2
						Baltimore	23	22	45	48
	Jim McGeough	LW	5-8	170	4-13-63/Regina, Sask.	Pittsburgh	1	4	5	8
						Baltimore	18	19	37	37
	Dave McIlwain	C	6-0	180	6-9-67/Seaforth, Ont.	North Bay	46	73	119	35
	Carl Mokosak	LW	6-1	180	9-22-62/Ft. Saskatchewan, Sask.	Pittsburgh	0	0	0	4
						Baltimore	23	27	50	228
27	Wilf Paiement	RW	6-1	210	10-15-55/Earlton, Ont.	Buffalo	20	17	37	108
14	Dan Quinn	C	5-10	175	6-1-65/Ottawa, Ont.	Cal.-Pittsburgh	31	49	80	54
	Mike Richard	C	5-10	175	7-9-66/Toronto, Ont.	Toronto (OHL)	57	50	107	38
						Baltimore	5	2	7	2
33	Mike Rowe	D	6-1	212	3-8-65/Kingston, Ont.	Pittsburgh	0	0	0	0
						Baltimore	1	18	19	64
25	Norm Schmidt	D	5-11	190	1-24-63/Sault Ste. Marie, Ont.	Pittsburgh	1	5	6	4
						Baltimore	4	7	11	25
4	Dwight Schofield	D	6-3	195	3-15-56/Waltham, Mass.	Pittsburgh	1	6	7	59
						Baltimore	1	5	6	58
18	Craig Simpson	C	6-2	192	2-15-67/London, Ont.	Pittsburgh	26	25	51	57
5	Ville Siren	D	6-1	170	2-11-64/Finland	Pittsburgh	5	17	22	50
	Mitch Wilson	C	5-8	190	7-5-57/Kelowna, B.C.	Pittsburgh	2	1	3	83
						Baltimore	8	9	17	358
	Zarley Zalapski	D	6-1	190	4-22-68/Leduc, Alta.	Team Canada				

No.	Player	Pos.	Ht.	Wt.	Born	1986—87	GP	GA	SO	Avg.
31	Brian Ford	G	5-10	165	9-12-61/Edmonton, Alta.	Pittsburgh	32	99	0	3.85
	Steve Guenette	G	5-9	170	11-13-65/Montreal, Que.	Pittsburgh	2	8	0	4.25
						Baltimore	54	157	5	3.10
27	Gilles Meloche	G	5-9	182	7-12-50/Montreal, Que.	Pittsburgh	43	134	0	3.43
1	Pat Riggin	G	5-9	163	5-26-59/Kitchener, Ont.	Bos.-Pitt.	27	84	0	3.36
						Moncton	14	34	1	2.56

Management has offered season-ticket holders a $1 rebate on each ticket sold if the Pens fail to make the playoffs this season. It's a good gimmick, but many are predicting the fans won't collect.

Much depends on Lemieux, of course. Can he stay healthy and free of fatigue? He missed 17 games last season because of injuries.

PENGUIN PROFILES

MARIO LEMIEUX 22 6-4 200   Center
He's been called "The Franchise," and no wonder. Missed 13 games after suffering a sprained right knee in a game against the Flyers last season, and the Penguins won only two games (2-7-4) during his absence . . . Finished the season with a career-high 54 goals and 107 points . . . Wears No. 66, Wayne Gretzky's 99 upside down . . . Is he in the same league with Gretzky? "The best player in the business today is Gretzky, but if anybody's close to him it's our guy Mario," says Eddie Johnston, the Pens' GM . . . Born Oct. 5, 1965, in Montreal . . . Totaled an incredible 282 points (133-149) in his final junior season with Laval Voisins . . . The first player chosen in the 1984 draft . . . Won Calder Trophy as NHL's Rookie of the Year.

Year	Club	GP	G	A	Pts.
1984-85	Pittsburgh.........	73	43	57	100
1985-86	Pittsburgh.........	79	48	93	141
1986-87	Pittsburgh.........	63	54	53	107
	Totals	215	145	203	348

DOUG BODGER 21 6-2 200   Defenseman
When the Penguins traded Randy Carlyle to Winnipeg for Moe Mantha late in the 1983-84 season, GM John Ferguson of the Jets also surrendered a first-round draft pick. It was a good deal for the Penguins. They used that pick in the 1984 draft to grab Bodger . . . Was only 18 when he made the big jump from juniors to the Penguins and struggled a little in his rookie season . . . "Maybe I didn't push myself enough," he admits. "I'm more aware of what's going on now." . . . Finished his rookie season at minus-24, but has shown steady improvement since. Was the

team's top-scoring defenseman last season with 11 goals and 49 points and had a plus-6 figure . . . Born June 18, 1966, in Chemainus, B.C.

Year	Club	GP	G	A	Pts.
1984-85	Pittsburgh.........	65	5	26	31
1985-86	Pittsburgh.........	79	4	33	37
1986-87	Pittsburgh.........	76	11	38	49
	Totals	220	20	97	117

DAVE HANNAN 25 5-10 180   Left Wing

He followed a circuitous route to the NHL. Played for three different junior teams during his days in the OHL. In his final season of junior hockey (1980-81), he scored 46 goals in 56 games with Brantford. Despite these impressive numbers, he was virtually ignored in the 1981 draft when he was the Penguins' 10th-round pick (196th overall) . . . Spent his first four years as a pro by splitting his time between Pittsburgh and its AHL affiliates . . . Finally lasted a full season with the Penguins in 1985-86 when he developed into an accomplished checker, penalty killer and occasional scorer (17 goals) . . . Born Nov. 26, 1961, in Sudbury, Ont.

Year	Club	GP	G	A	Pts.
1981-82	Pittsburgh.........	1	0	0	0
1982-83	Pittsburgh.........	74	11	22	33
1983-84	Pittsburgh.........	24	2	3	5
1984-85	Pittsburgh.........	30	6	7	13
1985-86	Pittsburgh.........	75	17	18	35
1986-87	Pittsburgh.........	58	10	15	25
	Totals	262	46	65	111

RANDY CUNNEYWORTH 26 6-0 183   Left Wing

Another member of the Penguins' Overachievers' Club . . . Was the team's top-scoring winger last season with 26 goals and 53 points. Had a plus-14 figure . . . Has always been a sturdy, rugged body-checker. "I enjoy laying a good body-check on somebody," he says . . . Born May 10, 1961, in Toronto suburb of Etobicoke . . . Scored 54 goals with Ottawa of the OHL in 1980-81 . . . Was the Sabres' ninth-round pick (167th overall) in the 1980 draft . . . Spent five years in the Buffalo organization before the Sabres finally gave up on him and traded him to the Penguins prior to the 1985-86 season . . . Had 15 goals and 45 points in his rookie season.

Year	Club	GP	G	A	Pts.
1980-81	Buffalo	1	0	0	0
1981-82	Buffalo	20	2	4	6
1985-86	Pittsburgh	75	15	30	45
1986-87	Pittsburgh	79	26	27	53
	Totals	175	43	61	104

CRAIG SIMPSON 20 6-2 192   Center

Appeared to find himself last season while Lemieux was recuperating from a knee injury. Scored nine goals in 10 games and finished with 26 goals, 51 points and a plus-11 figure . . . "I looked at it (Lemieux's absence) as a chance to prove myself and try to become a little bit of a leader," he said. "Hopefully, I'll continue to be counted on." . . . Born Feb. 15, 1967, in London, Ont. . . . Attended Michigan State for two years . . . Was the second player chosen, behind Wendel Clark, in the 1985 draft . . . Got off to a slow start as a rookie with 11 goals and 28 points . . . A good playmaker, strong on the power play . . . Mother was a member of Canada's 1952 Olympic track team . . . Brother, Dave, was in the Islander organization.

Year	Club	GP	G	A	Pts.
1985-86	Pittsburgh	76	11	17	28
1986-87	Pittsburgh	72	26	25	51
	Totals	148	37	42	79

MOE MANTHA 26 6-2 195   Defenseman

Has developed into one of the NHL's best playmaking defensemen since being obtained from Winnipeg in 1984 . . . Totaled 83 assists over the past two seasons . . . Extremely dangerous as a point man on the power play. Eight of his nine goals last season came on the power play; the previous season it was 11 of 15 . . . His father, Moe Sr., is a former minor-league defenseman . . .

Born Jan. 21, 1961, in Lakeland, Ohio, when his dad was playing for the Cleveland Barons... Played his junior hockey with the Toronto Marlboros of the OHL... Was the Jets' second-round pick in the 1980 draft... Captained the U.S. National team in the 1985 world championships.

Year	Club	GP	G	A	Pts.
1980-81	Winnipeg	58	2	23	25
1981-82	Winnipeg	25	0	12	12
1982-83	Winnipeg	21	2	7	9
1983-84	Winnipeg	72	16	38	54
1984-85	Pittsburgh.........	71	11	40	51
1985-86	Pittsburgh.........	78	15	52	67
1986-87	Pittsburgh.........	62	9	31	40
	Totals	387	55	203	258

JIM JOHNSON 25 6-0 186   Defenseman

One of the league's best free-agent "finds."... Signed with the Penguins in June 1985 after graduating from University of Minnesota-Duluth... Was named to the All-Academic Team each year at UMD and was a second-team All-American for three years... Played for Team USA in the 1985 World Championships in Prague and again in 1986 in the USSR... As a rookie during the 1985-86 season, he led all Pittsburgh defensemen with a plus-12 rating... Finished last season at minus-6... Extremely durable, he was the only Penguin to appear in all 80 games last season... Born Aug. 9, 1962, in New Hope, Minn.... Enjoys hunting and fishing... Took business courses during the off-season to prepare for a career in sales marketing.

Year	Club	GP	G	A	Pts.
1985-86	Pittsburgh.........	80	3	26	29
1986-87	Pittsburgh.........	80	5	25	30
	Totals	160	8	51	59

GILLES MELOCHE 37 5-9 182   Goaltender

Was the busiest of four Pittsburgh goaltenders last season, appearing in 43 games. Had a 13-9-7 record and a 3.43 goals-against average... Stand-up style, good puck-handler... Born July 12, 1950, in Montreal... A fifth-round pick by the Blackhawks in 1970 draft... Played two games with the Blackhawks in 1970-71, traded to the California Golden Seals early in the 1971-72 season... Wept openly after being bombed for 11 goals in a game against the Rangers at Madison Square Garden in the early '70s... Moved with the Seals to Cleveland in 1976... Acquired by the Penguins in 1985.

Year	Club	GP	GA	SO	Avg.
1970-71	Chicago	2	6	0	3.00
1971-72	California	56	173	4	3.33
1972-73	California	59	235	1	4.06
1973-74	California	47	198	1	4.24
1974-75	California	47	186	1	4.03
1975-76	California	41	140	1	3.44
1976-77	Cleveland	51	171	2	3.47
1977-78	Cleveland	54	195	1	3.77
1978-79	Minnesota	53	173	2	3.33
1979-80	Minnesota	54	160	1	3.06
1980-81	Minnesota	38	120	2	3.25
1981-82	Minnesota	51	175	1	3.47
1982-83	Minnesota	47	160	1	3.57
1983-84	Minnesota	52	201	2	4.18
1984-85	Minnesota	32	115	0	3.80
1985-86	Pittsburgh	34	119	0	3.59
1986-87	Pittsburgh	43	134	0	3.43
	Totals	761	2661	20	3.63

DAN QUINN 22 5-10 175   Center

Acquired early last season from the Flames for Mike Bullard in a trade of malcontents. Quinn admitted he was happy to leave Calgary. "I was suffocating there," he said... Produced immediately for the Pens. Finished second behind Lemieux in scoring with 31 goals and 80 points, both career-highs... Has quick hands and some nifty finesse moves... Born June 1, 1965, in Ottawa... Totaled 59 goals, 88 assists and 147 points for Belleville of the OHL in 1982-83... Was the Flames' No. 1 draft choice in 1983 ... Only 18 when he joined the Flames and scored his first NHL goal against Edmonton on Dec. 23, 1983... His father, Peter, played pro football for Ottawa of the CFL.

Year	Club	GP	G	A	Pts.
1983-84	Calgary	54	19	33	52
1984-85	Calgary	74	20	38	58
1985-86	Calgary	78	30	42	72
1986-87	Calg-Pitt.	80	31	49	80
	Totals	286	100	162	262

WILF PAIEMENT 32 6-1 210   **Right Wing**

A grizzled old veteran by NHL standards who may be nearing the end of the line . . . Until he hangs up his skates, he will continue to play above his fading talents . . . Fan of Gil Perreault and Rick Martin who always wanted to play in Buffalo . . . Earned a reported $260,000 last season . . . Scored first hat trick as a Sabre Feb. 26, 1987, against St. Louis . . . Reached 20-goal plateau for the 12th time in his NHL career . . . Underwent arthroscopic surgery on right knee . . . Picked up by Sabres Oct. 6 in waiver draft off Rangers' unprotected list for $2,500 . . . Tallied 800th career point Feb. 8 against Chicago . . . Born Oct. 16, 1955, in Earlton, Ont.

Year	Club	GP	G	A	Pts.
1974-75	Kansas City	78	26	13	39
1975-76	Kansas City	57	21	22	43
1976-77	Colorado	78	41	40	81
1977-78	Colorado	80	31	56	87
1978-79	Colorado	65	24	36	60
1979-80	Col-Tor	75	30	44	74
1980-81	Toronto	77	40	57	97
1981-82	Tor-Que	77	25	46	71
1982-83	Quebec	80	26	38	64
1983-84	Quebec	80	39	37	76
1984-85	Quebec	68	23	28	51
1985-86	Que-NYR	52	8	18	26
1986-87	Buffalo	56	20	17	37
	Totals	923	354	452	806

COACH PIERRE CREAMER: Became the team's 10th coach in the 20-year history of the franchise last June, succeeding Bob Berry . . . Was the last of eight men interviewed for the job . . . Had no previous NHL experience as a player or coach . . . Spent the past three seasons as coach of the Sherbrooke Canadiens of the AHL, Montreal's No. 1 farm club, where his teams compiled a 120-104-14 record . . . Guided Sherbrooke to the Calder Cup championship in 1985 . . . Brother-in-law of Mike Bossy . . . "Mike played for me when I coached a Midget team in Laval. He was 14 then and big for his age. He was great even in those days," Creamer said . . . Has been a coach for 16 of his 43 years . . . His career took him from Laval to the Junior A team at Verdun, where he coached Pat LaFontaine of the Islanders . . .

Also coached many of the current Montreal players at Sherbrooke, including goalie Patrick Roy and winger Claude Lemieux... A chunky man, he speaks softly but carries a big stick... Born July 6, 1944, in Chomedey, Que.

GREATEST COACH

The Penguins called him "Popeye," and the organist at the Civic Arena used to play "I'm Popeye, the Sailor Man" when the Pens were wrapping up a victory.

Under Marc (Popeye) Boileau, the Penguins enjoyed their most successful season ever in 1974-75. They established several team records that still stand, including most victories (37), most points (89) and fewest home losses (5).

Some of the joy was wiped out during the playoffs that season when the Penguins were eliminated by the Islanders in the quarterfinals after winning the first three games of the series. However, Boileau remains as one of the most successful coaches in the team's history.

He spent most of his career in the minor leagues, though he did play one season with the Detroit Red Wings (1961-62), filling in briefly as a center on a the same line with Gordie Howe.

"Not too many guys can brag about that," he once bragged.

Boileau got his first coaching job with Fort Wayne of the old International Hockey League and led the Komets to the league and playoff championships in 1973. He coached the Penguins for parts of three seasons—from February 1974 to January 1976.

ALL-TIME PENGUIN LEADERS

GOALS: Rick Kehoe, 55, 1980-81
ASSISTS: Mario Lemieux, 93, 1985-86
POINTS: Mario Lemieux, 141, 1985-86
SHUTOUTS: Les Binkley, 6, 1967-68

QUEBEC NORDIQUES

TEAM DIRECTORY: Pres.: Marcel Aubut; GM: Maurice Filion; Coach: Andre Savard. Home ice: Quebec Coliseum (15,153; 200' x 85'). Training camp: Quebec City.

SCOUTING REPORT

OFFENSE: The misfortune of the 1986-87 season, second-worst in Quebec's eight-year NHL history, should benefit the squad this

Michel Goulet eyes a return to 50 goals in Quebec.

season. But the Nordiques will have to do it without Michel Bergeron, who signed as coach of the New York Rangers in June after seven years at the Nordiques' helm. Former Nordique Andre Savard takes his place.

Injuries to centers Peter Stastny and Dale Hunter caused the team's offensive production to fall off. However, when Stastny and Hunter were sidelined, Paul Gillis and rookie Jason LaFreniere received valuable experience.

Quebec is deep at left wing, where Michel Goulet (49 goals) and John Ogrodnick lead the way and Basil McRae, obtained last season from Detroit, has strengthened the team. However, Alain Cote and Anton Stastny were far from awesome on the right side. In fact, Anton seems to perform much better at left wing.

Peter Stastny and Goulet are snipers capable of carrying a club, as they did when Quebec fell behind, 2-0, in the playoff series against Hartford before bouncing back to win. It was Stastny who beat Mike Liut for the series-winning goal.

The big offseason trade with the Capitals brings Alan Haworth and Gaetan Duchesne to Quebec City, where they will be counted on for forechecking. They will help to replace Hunter, who was dealt to Washington along with goaltender Clint Malarchuk.

DEFENSE: McRae, a tough checker who stands 6-2, 205, greatly improved Quebec's defense upon his arrival from the Red Wings. Although the Nords dropped in the Adams Division standings from first to fourth, they actually improved their defense and lowered their goals-against total from 289 to 276.

The line of Cote, Gillis and Mike Eagles was clearly the best defensive unit in the playoffs for Quebec. The backline is anchored by two veterans—Robert Picard and Normand Rochefort.

Although Malarchuk played in more regular-season games (54) than Mario Gosselin (30), it was the younger Gosselin who emerged as Bergeron's No. 1 netminder during the playoffs. Gosselin played in 11 of Quebec's 13 postseason games and fashioned a 3.39 GAA. Even if Malarchuk hadn't been traded, it was obvious that Gosselin would be the goalie on which Quebec's fortunes would ride this season.

OUTLOOK: After finishing first in the Adams Division two seasons ago, the Nordiques appeared to be on the verge of challenging for the Stanley Cup. What the hockey world has discovered since is that they remain an inferior playoff team, incapable of winning the big game or overcoming the Montreal mystique.

Sure, the Nordiques felt they won last season's Adams Division final series against the Canadiens, only to be robbed by

NORDIQUE ROSTER

No.	Player	Pos.	Ht.	Wt.	Born	1986—87	G	A	Pts.	PIM
28	Jeff Brown	D	6-1	185	4-30-66/Ottawa, Ont.	Quebec	7	22	29	16
						Fredericton	2	14	16	16
19	Alain Cote	LW	5-10	205	5-3-47/Matane, Que.	Quebec	12	24	36	38
10	Bill Derlago	C	5-10	194	8-25-58/Beulah, Man.	Winn.-Que.	6	11	17	18
						Fredericton	7	8	15	2
34	Gord Donnelly	D	6-3	195	4-5-62/Montreal, Que.	Quebec	0	2	2	143
	Gaetan Duchesne	LW	5-11	195	7-11-62/Quebec City, Que.	Washington	17	35	52	53
11	Mike Eagles	C	5-10	180	3-7-63/Sussex, N.B.	Quebec	13	19	32	55
29	Steve Finn	D	6-0	195	8-20-66/Laval, Que.	Fredericton	7	19	26	73
						Quebec	2	5	7	40
	Bryan Fogarty	D	6-1	194	6-11-69/Brantford, Ont.	Kingston	20	50	70	46
	Jean Marc Gaulin	LW	6-1	185	3-3-62/West Germany	Fredericton	1	1	2	15
23	Paul Gillis	C	5-11	190	2-31-63/Toronto, Ont.	Quebec	13	26	39	267
16	Michel Goulet	LW	6-1	185	4-21-60/Perihonqua, Que.	Quebec	49	47	96	61
	Alan Haworth	LW	5-10	190	9-11-60/Drumondville, Que.	Washington	25	16	41	43
	Yves Heroux	RW	5-11	185	4-27-65/Terrebonna, Que.	Fredericton	8	6	14	13
						Quebec	0	0	0	0
31	Mike Hough	RW	6-1	190	2-6-63/Montreal, Que.	Quebec	6	8	14	79
						Fredericton	1	3	4	20
15	Jason Lafreniere	C	6-0	184	12-6-66/North Bay, Ont.	Quebec	13	15	28	8
						Fredericton	3	11	14	0
7	Lane Lambert	RW	5-11	180	11-18-64/Melfort, Sask.	Rang.-Que.	7	8	15	51
						New Haven	3	3	6	19
	Dave Latta	LW	6-0	181	1-3-67/Thunder Bay, Ont.	Kitchener	32	46	78	46
	Greg Malone	C	6-0	190	3-8-56/Fredericton, N.B.	Quebec	0	1	1	0
						Fredericton	13	22	35	50
	Ken McRae	C	6-1	196	4-23-68/Finch, Ont.	Sud.-Ham.	19	27	46	65
10	Ken Middendorf	RW	6-4	197	8-18-67/Syracuse, N.Y.	Quebec	1	4	5	4
						Sud.-Kitch.	38	44	82	13
21	Randy Moller	D	6-2	205	8-23-63/Calgary, Alta.	Quebec	5	9	14	144
25	John Ogrodnick	RW	6-0	190	6-20-59/Edmonton, Alta.	Det.-Que.	23	44	67	10
24	Robert Picard	D	6-2	205	5-25-57/Montreal, Que.	Quebec	8	20	28	71
2	Daniel Poudrier	D	6-2	185	2-15-64/Thetford Mines, Ont.	Fredericton	8	18	26	11
44	Ken Quinney	RW	6-0	190	5-23-65/New Westminster, B.C.	Quebec	2	7	9	16
						Fredericton	14	27	41	20
5	Normand Rochefort	D	6-1	200	1-28-61/Three Rivers, Que.	Quebec	6	9	15	46
	Joe Sakik	C	5-11	181	7-7-69/Burnaby, B.C.	Swift Current	60	73	133	31
14	J.F. Sauve	C	5-6	175	1-23-60/Ste. Genevieve, Que.	Quebec	2	3	5	4
6	Scott Shaunessy	D	6-4	220	1-22-64/Newport, R.I.	Quebec	0	0	0	7
4	Dave Shaw	D	6-2	187	12-25-64/St. Thomas, Ont.	Quebec	0	19	19	69
9	Doug Sheddon	C	6-0	184	4-16-61/Wallaceburg, Ont.	Det.-Que.	6	14	20	14
20	Anton Stastny	LW	6-0	185	8-5-59/Czechoslovakia	Quebec	27	35	62	8
26	Peter Stastny	C	6-1	195	9-18-56/Czechoslovakia	Quebec	24	52	76	73
14	Trevor Stienberg	RW	6-1	180	5-13-66/Moscow, Ont.	Quebec	1	0	1	12
						Fredericton	14	12	26	123
37	Rich Zemlak	C	6-2	190	3-3-63/Wynard, Sask.	Quebec	0	2	2	47
						Fredericton	9	6	15	201

No.	Player	Pos.	Ht.	Wt.	Born		GP	GA	SO	Avg.
33	Mario Gosselin	G	5-8	160	6-13-63/Thetford Mines, Que.	Quebec	30	86	0	3.18
1	Richard Sevigny	G	5-8	172	4-11-57/Montreal, Que.	Quebec	4	11	0	4.58
						Fredericton	16	62	0	4.21

controversial officiating, but good playoff clubs find ways to win despite bad breaks and questionable officiating. You have to wonder if Quebec will ever escape from the shadow of the arch-rival Canadiens.

Barring serious injuries to Peter Stastny and Goulet, Quebec will again be a powerful club. Why then are so many players unhappy playing in Quebec City? Money can't be the entire reason. After all, you don't hear those complaints in Montreal.

NORDIQUE PROFILES

MICHEL GOULET 27 6-1 185   Left Wing
Needs 34 goals to reach 400 for his brilliant career ... After four straight seasons of 53, 55, 56 and 57 goals, he did not reach 50-goal plateau ... Scored 49 goals in 75 games ... Drop in offensive production attributed to broken finger courtesy of Brad Maxwell slash in October and injury to linemate Dale Hunter ... Finished eighth among scorers with 96 points ... Defines the word "sniper" with his accurate, explosive shot ... Ranked sixth among NHL goal-scorers ... One of two players in top 12 scorers to have a minus rating (-12). Doug Gilmour of the Blues was minus-2 ... Played in 600th NHL game and passed 700-point mark last season ... Born April 21, 1960, in Peribonqua, Que.

Year	Club	GP	G	A	Pts.
1978-79	Birmingham (WHA) .	78	28	30	58
1979-80	Quebec............	77	22	32	54
1980-81	Quebec............	76	32	39	71
1981-82	Quebec............	80	42	42	84
1982-83	Quebec............	80	57	48	105
1983-84	Quebec............	75	56	65	121
1984-85	Quebec............	69	55	40	95
1985-86	Quebec............	75	53	50	103
1986-87	Quebec............	75	49	47	96
	NHL Totals	607	366	363	729
	WHA Totals........	78	28	30	58

PETER STASTNY 31 6-1 195   Center
Missed 12 games with a broken finger and finished second to Michel Goulet in scoring for first time since 1983-84 ... His 76 points were by far his lowest total in seven NHL seasons ... Beat Mike Liut at 6:05 of OT in sixth game of opening round to eliminate Whalers from playoffs ... Shorthanded goal, one of three goals he scored in third game vs. Hartford, turned series around for Nords ... Most talented forward in Adams Divi-

sion . . . Led Quebec in playoff scoring with 6-9-15 in 13 games, edging Goulet's 9-5-14 . . . Played in 500th NHL game last season and needs 25 goals to reach 300 in career . . . Born Sept. 18, 1956, in Bratislava, Czechoslovakia.

Year	Club	GP	G	A	Pts.
1980-81	Quebec	77	39	70	109
1981-82	Quebec	80	46	93	139
1982-83	Quebec	75	47	77	124
1983-84	Quebec	80	46	73	119
1984-85	Quebec	75	32	68	100
1985-86	Quebec	76	41	81	122
1986-87	Quebec	64	24	52	76
	Totals	527	275	514	789

JOHN OGRODNICK 28 6-0 190　　　　　　　**Left Wing**

Like Michel Goulet, he is always the topic of trade rumors . . . A deal finally came about when Detroit traded him to Quebec in a six-player deal Jan. 17, 1987 . . . Nords got Ogrodnick, Doug Shedden and Basil McRae for Brent Ashton, Gilbert Delorme and Mark Kumpel . . . Scored twice in first game as Nordique . . . Subpar season, including lowest full-season goal total of his NHL career (23) . . . Skated on a line with Peter and Anton Stastny . . . Finished strong, hinting he may be adjusting to Quebec . . . Born June 20, 1959, in Ottawa, Ont.

Year	Club	GP	G	A	Pts.
1979-80	Detroit	41	8	24	32
1980-81	Detroit	80	35	35	70
1981-82	Detroit	80	28	26	54
1982-83	Detroit	80	41	44	85
1983-84	Detroit	64	42	36	78
1984-85	Detroit	79	55	50	105
1985-86	Detroit	76	38	32	70
1986-87	Det-Que	71	23	44	67
	Totals	571	270	291	561

MARIO GOSSELIN 24 5-8 160　　　　　　　**Goaltender**

May have changed his status from a solid backup to Quebec's No. 1 man in playoffs . . . Proclaimed in French Canadian newspapers for fans to "bet their farms" on Nordiques in third playoff game vs. Hartford and then stopped 57 of 59 shots in Games 3 and 4 to even series while giving Quebec the momentum . . . Three seasons ago, he played in 17 playoff games and posted a 3.06 GAA after going 19-11-3 in his best season to date . . . Was 13-11-1 with 3.18 GAA last season behind the since-traded Clint

Malarchuk... Played for 1984 Canadian Olympic team... Born June 15, 1963, in Thetford Mines, Que.

Year	Club	GP	GA	SO	Avg.
1983-84	Quebec	3	3	1	1.21
1984-85	Quebec	35	109	1	3.34
1985-86	Quebec	31	111	2	3.86
1986-87	Quebec	30	86	0	3.18
	Totals	97	309	4	3.36

ALAIN COTE 30 5-10 205   Right Wing

On a team of goal-scorers, he has never been able to crack the 20-goal plateau... After eight NHL seasons he is still three goals shy of 100 for his career... Holdover from Quebec's WHA days ... Key member of superior checking line of Cote, Paul Gillis and Mike Eagles... Apparent goal in pivotal fifth game of Adams Division finals was disallowed by referee Kerry Fraser, turning series in Montreal's favor... Claimed by Nordiques from

Alain Cote embarks on his second decade as a pro.

Montreal roster in 1979 NHL expansion draft... Born May 3, 1957, in Matane, Que.

Year	Club	GP	G	A	Pts.
1977-78	Quebec (WHA)	27	3	5	8
1978-79	Quebec (WHA)	79	14	13	27
1979-80	Quebec...........	41	5	11	16
1980-81	Quebec...........	51	8	18	26
1981-82	Quebec...........	79	15	16	31
1982-83	Quebec...........	79	12	28	40
1983-84	Quebec...........	77	19	24	43
1984-85	Quebec...........	80	13	22	35
1985-86	Quebec...........	78	13	21	34
1986-87	Quebec...........	80	12	24	36
	NHL Totals	565	97	164	261
	WHA Totals........	106	17	18	35

PAUL GILLIS 23 5-11 190   **Center**

A checking center who is not afraid to mix it up, he led the Nordiques with 267 minutes in penalties... Addition of Basil McRae gave Nords two players to keep the penalty-box seat warm... Suspended for three games early in the season for scratching Hartford's Dean Evason on the face during a fight... Collected three game-winning goals... Beginning sixth NHL season and will play in 300th career game three games into schedule... Born Dec. 31, 1963, in Toronto.

Year	Club	GP	G	A	Pts.
1982-83	Quebec...........	7	0	2	2
1983-84	Quebec...........	57	8	9	17
1984-85	Quebec...........	77	14	28	42
1985-86	Quebec...........	80	19	24	43
1986-87	Quebec...........	76	13	26	39
	Totals	297	54	89	143

ALAN HAWORTH 27 5-10 190   **Center**

Part of the four-player deal that sent Dale Hunter and Clint Malarchuk to Washington... Missed 30 games last season with an assortment of injuries, including a ligament tear in his right knee that required an arthroscope. However, he still wound up with 25 goals... Spunky and swift... "Alan has always been fast and he's quick in his reactions, but he lacked stamina," former coach Bryan Murray admitted. "He's a lot stronger now."... Born

Sept. 1, 1960, in Drummondville, Que. . . . His father, Gord, is a former pro hockey player . . . Was a fifth-round draft choice of the Sabres in the 1979 draft . . . Traded to the Capitals in 1982.

Year	Club	GP	G	A	Pts.
1980-81	Buffalo	49	16	20	36
1981-82	Buffalo	57	21	18	39
1982-83	Washington	74	23	27	50
1983-84	Washington	75	24	31	55
1984-85	Washington	76	23	26	49
1985-86	Washington	71	34	39	73
1986-87	Washington	50	25	16	41
	Totals	452	166	177	343

ROBERT PICARD 30 6-2 205   Defenseman

His experience helped Quebec cut down its goals-against . . . Physical checker who begins his 11th season in the NHL . . . Had outstanding playoff series against Hartford . . . Has cut down on his mistakes caused by gambling style . . . Is playing for his fifth NHL club . . . Acquired by Nordiques on Nov. 27, 1985, from Winnipeg for Mario Marois . . . Played in 700th game last season . . . Scored only eight goals all season, but three of those were game-winners . . . Born May 25, 1957, in Montreal.

Year	Club	GP	G	A	Pts.
1977-78	Washington	75	10	27	37
1978-79	Washington	77	21	44	65
1979-80	Washington	78	11	43	54
1980-81	Tor-Mont.	67	8	21	29
1981-82	Montreal	62	2	26	28
1982-83	Montreal	64	7	31	38
1983-84	Mont-Winn	69	6	18	24
1984-85	Winnipeg	78	12	22	34
1985-86	Winn-Que	68	9	32	41
1986-87	Quebec	78	8	20	28
	Totals	716	94	284	378

GAETAN DUCHESNE 25 5-11 195   Left Wing

They call him "The Shadow" and with good reason . . . Does an excellent job checking rival gunners. Just ask Mike Bossy. Outscored the Isles' star, 4-1, in the Caps' opening-round sweep in the 1986 playoffs . . . Totaled a career-high 52 points (17-35), plus four game-winning goals, last season . . . He and former linemate Bob Gould finished with plus-18 figures . . . Durable, he has missed just six games over the past two seasons . . . Was an eighth-round selection (152nd overall) in the 1981 draft . . . Born July 11, 1962, in Quebec City, Que. . . . One of 11 children . . . A brother, Yves, works as a linesman in the Quebec Major Junior

Hockey League...Name is pronounced "GAY-ton Doo-SHAYNE."

Year	Club	GP	G	A	Pts.
1981-82	Washington	74	9	14	23
1982-83	Washington	77	18	19	37
1983-84	Washington	79	17	19	36
1984-85	Washington	67	15	23	38
1985-86	Washington	80	11	28	39
1986-87	Washington	74	17	35	52
	Totals	451	87	138	225

COACH ANDRE SAVARD: "It has been my ambition to coach the Nordiques ever since I played for them," Savard said when named to replace Ranger-bound Michel Bergeron last June...A 12-year NHL forward (Boston, Buffalo, Quebec), Savard went from his final season with the Nordiques (1984-85) to coaching Quebec's AHL affiliate (Fredericton) the last two seasons...Known as a taskmaster, in the mold of Scotty Bowman, his coach at Buffalo...GM Maurice Filion was impressed with Savard's ability to work with younger players...He'll have to deal as well with veterans like Michel Goulet and Peter and Anton Stastny, with whom he played at Quebec...As a player, he never quit...And he'll expect same from his charges...Born Sept. 2, 1953, in Temiscamingue, Que.

GREATEST COACH

In hockey's fiercest rivalry—Montreal vs. Quebec—no one was hated more in the Montreal Forum than Michel Bergeron. In fact, Bergeron asked for protective glass to shield himself and his players from garbage-throwing fans during last year's Adams Division final games in the Forum. He was denied, which only made him more of a target.

Bergeron, who became coach of the Rangers in June, has always considered himself a target. If he is persecuted by referees, the league and opposing fans, he has overcome and remains one of the NHL's top coaches. In Quebec's eight seasons in the league, Bergeron was at the Nordiques' helm in all but the first campaign. He was appointed coach on Oct. 20, 1980, succeeding GM Maurice Filion behind the bench despite only a few days of professional hockey experience. During his stay in Quebec he compiled a 253-222-79 record (.528). On Dec. 1, 1986, against Hartford, he coached his 500th NHL game.

Only Glen Sather has more experience than Bergeron behind the bench. Yet Bergeron's flamboyance and fire never diminished; in fact, they have grown as he seeks to add a Stanley Cup to his accomplishments.

ALL-TIME NORDIQUE LEADERS

GOALS: Michel Goulet, 57, 1982-83
ASSISTS: Peter Stastny, 93, 1981-82
POINTS: Peter Stastny, 139, 1981-82
SHUTOUTS: Clint Malarchuk, 4, 1985-86

WASHINGTON CAPITALS

TEAM DIRECTORY: Chairman: Abe Pollin; Pres.: Richard M. Patrick; VP/GM: David Poile; Dir. Pub. Rel.: Lou Corletto; Coach: Bryan Murray. Home ice: Capital Centre (18,130; 200′ × 85′). Colors: Red, white and blue. Training camp: Alexandria, Va.

SCOUTING REPORT

OFFENSE: When a defenseman is your leading scorer, well . . . as general manager David Poile says, "We're a team not blessed with much depth." Or accurate gunners.

The Capitals scored 285 goals last season—13th in the league. Their power-play specialists ranked 18th during the regu-

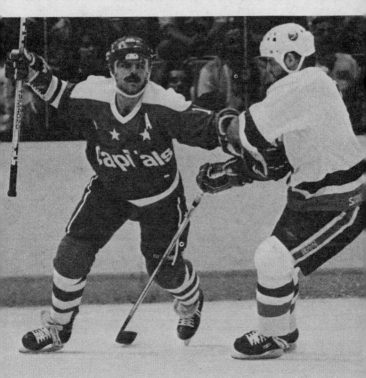

Mike Gartner netted 10 game-winning goals in 1986-87.

lar season and looked even more feeble in the playoffs against the Islanders, converting only two of 36 chances. "We were brutal," Poile admits.

Bengt Gustafsson, back with the Caps after a one-year sabbatical in his native Sweden, and newly-acquired Dale Hunter are being counted on to shore up the specialty teams. But the Caps will miss Gaetan Duchesne and Alan Haworth, who were part of Poile's four-player summer deal with the Nordiques.

Hunter, extremely feisty during his seven years with the Nordiques, isn't expected to change his stripes now that he's wearing a Caps' sweater. He is considered an ideal replacement for Haworth on Washington's "Shift Disturbers" line with Craig Laughlin and Greg Adams.

Duchesne's departure broke up the Capitals' solid checking line of Duchesne, Bob Gould and Kelly Miller. Gustafsson, though, should fit in nicely on this line. Then there are the two Mikes—Gartner and Ridley—who became linemates midway through last season when Ridley was acquired from the Rangers. They totaled 72 goals and barely missed catching defenseman Larry Murphy in the team scoring race.

The Capitals' principal shortcoming remains at left wing. Dave Christian was the only 20-goal scorer at that position last season and he was expected to be shifted to the right side this season. Jeff Greenlaw and Yvon Corriveau, both first-round picks, failed to impress in brief trials last season.

DEFENSE: The Capitals have always stressed close checking under coach Bryan Murray, but some minor leaks developed last season when they allowed 278 goals to finish eighth in the league.

The hundreds of miles Rod Langway has skated on the backline might be catching up with the 30-year-old team captain. However, he remains a sturdy workhorse and has helped immensely in the development of his partner, Kevin Hatcher. Murphy, a finalist for the Norris Trophy last season, and Scott Stevens complement each other extremely well. The backup tandem of Greg Smith and John Barrett could be injury-prone; both suffered broken kneecaps last season.

In goal, the Capitals lost Bob Mason to the Blackhawks via the free-agent route, but picked up Clint Malarchuk in that big deal with the Nordiques. Malarchuk, who is a workhorse, appeared in 54 games with Quebec last season and had an 18-26-9 record. Pete Peeters, a 17-game winner with the Caps, celebrated his 30th birthday over the summer and might be slowing down, but don't tell him that.

CAPITAL ROSTER

No.	Player	Pos.	Ht.	Wt.	Born	1986 – 87	G	A	Pts.	PIM
22	Greg Adams	LW	6-1	190	5-31-60/Duncan, B.C.	Washington	14	30	44	154
	Jeff Ballantyne	D	6-1	190	1-7-69/Elmira, Ont.	Ottawa	2	13	15	75
6	John Barrett	D	6-1	210	7-2-58/Ottawa, Ont.	Washington	2	2	4	43
30	Paul Cavallini	D	6-2	202	10-13-65/Toronto, Ont.	Washington	0	2	2	8
						Binghamton	12	24	36	35
27	Dave Christian	C	5-11	180	5-12-59/Wayroad, Minn.	Washington	23	27	50	8
26	Yvon Corriveau	LW	6-1	195	2-8-67/Wellant, Ont.	Washington	1	2	2	4
						Binghamton	0	0	0	2
32	Lou Franceschetti	LW	5-11	180	3-28-52/Toronto, Ont.	Washington	12	9	21	127
12	Gary Galley	D	5-11	190	4-16-63/Ottawa, Ont.	LA-Wash.	6	21	27	67
11	Mike Gartner	RW	6-0	185	10-29-59/Ottawa, Ont.	Washington	41	32	73	61
23	Bob Gould	RW	5-11	195	9-2-57/Petrolia, Ont.	Washington	23	27	50	74
24	Jeff Greenlaw	LW	6-2	195	2-28-68/Toronto, Ont.	Washington	0	3	3	44
						Binghamton	0	2	2	0
16	Bengt Gustafsson	RW	6-0	190	3-23-56/Sweden	Team Sweden				
4	Kevin Hatcher	D	6-3	185	9-9-66/Sterling Heights, Mich.	Washington	8	16	24	144
	Dale Hunter	C	5-9	190	7-31-60/Oil Springs, Ont.	Quebec	10	29	39	135
	Grant Jennings	D	6-3	202	5-5-65/Hudson Bay, Sask.	Binghamton	1	5	6	125
9	Dave Jensen	LW	6-1	180	8-19-65/Needham, Mass.	Washington	8	8	16	12
						Binghamton	2	5	7	0
29	Ed Kastelic	RW	6-2	208	1-29-64/Toronto, Ont.	Washington	1	1	2	83
						Binghamton	17	11	28	124
5	Rod Langway	D	6-3	215	5-3-57/Taiwan	Washington	2	25	27	53
18	Craig Laughlin	RW	5-11	198	9-19-57/Toronto, Ont.	Washington	22	30	52	67
21	Steve Leach	RW	5-11	180	1-16-66/Cambridge, Mass.	Washington	1	0	1	6
						Binghamton	18	21	39	39
	Grant Martin	LW	5-10	190	3-13-62/Smooth Rock Falls, Ont.	Washington	0	0	0	4
						Binghamton	30	23	53	86
	Scott McCrory	C	5-10	178	2-27-67/Sudbury, Ont.	Oshawa	51	99	150	35
10	Kelly Miller	LW	5-11	185	3-3-65/Detroit, Mich.	Rang.-Wash.	16	26	42	48
8	Larry Murphy	D	6-0	200	3-8-61/Scarborough, Ont.	Washington	23	58	81	39
20	Michal Pivonka	C	6-2	192	1-28-66/Czechoslovakia	Washington	18	25	43	41
17	Mike Ridley	C	6-1	200	8-7-63/Winnipeg, Man.	Rang.-Wash.	31	39	70	40
12	Gary Sampson	RW	6-0	190	8-24-59/Atkoken, Ont.	Washington	1	2	3	4
						Binghamton	12	16	28	10
19	Greg Smith	D	6-0	190	7-8-55/Ponoka, Alta.	Washington	0	9	9	31
37	Jim Thomson	RW	6-1	196	12-30-65/Edmonton, Alta.	Binghamton	13	10	23	360
3	Scott Stevens	D	5-11	200	4-1-64/Kitchener, Ont.	Washington	10	51	61	285

No.	Player	Pos.	Ht.	Wt.	Born		GP	GA	SO	Avg.
	Clint Malarchuk	G	5-10	170	5-1-61/Edmonton, Alta.	Quebec	54	175	1	3.40
1	Pete Peeters	G	6-0	185	8-1-57/Edmonton, Alta.	Washington	37	107	0	3.21
						Binghamton	4	4	1	0.98
	Alain Raymond	G	5-10	177	6-24-55/Rimouski, Que.	Fort Wayne	45	134	1	3.30

OUTLOOK: Many questions, including the big one: Will the Capitals finally advance past the second round of the playoffs and save Murray's job? The odds are not good.

CAPITAL PROFILES

MIKE GARTNER 28 6-0 185   **Right Wing**
You need a flak jacket when facing this guy... Has a cannon shot and uses it often... Led the Caps in shots on goal again last season with 317, second in the league to Boston's Ray Bourque (334)... Knows how to score, too. Collected 41 goals and 73 points last season... Turned in 10 game-winners and six short-handed goals... Had only seven goals at Christmas, then went on goal-scoring streaks of nine and seven games during the second half of the season. Collected 12 goals in each streak... Smiles when kidded about being a square peg in a round hole on this defensive-minded team. "I work on my defense," he said. "Let's just say I get to practice a lot on my defense."... Born Oct. 29, 1959, in Oshawa, Ont.... Turned pro with Cincinnati of the World Hockey Association in 1978 and joined the Caps the following year... Has never scored less than 35 goals in a season... Tapes a daily radio show in the Washington area.

Year	Club	GP	G	A	Pts.
1978-79	Cincinnati(WHA)....	78	27	25	52
1979-80	Washington	77	36	32	68
1980-81	Washington	80	48	46	94
1981-82	Washington	80	35	45	80
1982-83	Washington	73	38	38	76
1983-84	Washington	80	40	45	85
1984-85	Washington	80	50	52	102
1985-86	Washington	74	35	40	75
1986-87	Washington	78	41	32	73
	NHL Totals	622	323	330	653
	WHA Totals........	78	27	25	52

BENGT GUSTAFSSON 29 6-0 190   **Right Wing**
"King Gus" is back. That's the nickname awarded him by the Swedish media after he captained Sweden to its first world championship in 25 years last May in Vienna... Spent last season playing for Bofors in the Swedish Second Division... Agreed to rejoin the Caps when offered a new contract that is worth slightly less than $1 million over two years... Strong defensive player, neat playmaker and capable goal-scorer... "Bengt is a top player who can be effective in offensive and defensive situations," coach Bryan Murray said... Born March 23, 1958, in Karls-

koga, Sweden . . . Caps' fourth-round pick in 1978 and joined the team in 1979 after the Caps won a legal battle against the Oilers for his services . . . Suffered a broken leg in a playoff game against the Islanders in 1986.

Year	Club	GP	G	A	Pts.
1979-80	Washington	80	22	38	60
1980-81	Washington	72	21	34	55
1981-82	Washington	70	26	34	60
1982-83	Washington	67	22	42	64
1983-84	Washington	69	32	43	75
1984-85	Washington	51	14	29	43
1985-86	Washington	70	23	52	75
1986-87	Washington		Did Not Play		
	Totals	479	160	272	432

DALE HUNTER 27 5-9 190   Center
Former captain of the Nordiques came in June trade with Clint Malarchuk for Gaetan Duchesne, Alan Haworth and a first-round draft choice . . . Last year's totals of 10 goals, 29 assists and 39 points were all career lows . . . Broken leg suffered Nov. 25 limited him to 46 games all season . . . Caught skate in a rut at Montreal Forum after check from Petr Svoboda . . . Required surgery on lower fibula . . . Uses aluminum stick . . . Appeared in 500th NHL game last season and is 41 points shy of 500 for career . . . An instigator in front of the net, he is a master at cashing in on rebounds . . . Brothers are NHL veterans Dave and Mark Hunter . . . Born July 31, 1960, in Petrolia, Ont.

Year	Club	GP	G	A	Pts.
1980-81	Quebec	80	19	44	63
1981-82	Quebec	80	22	50	72
1982-83	Quebec	80	17	46	63
1983-84	Quebec	77	24	55	79
1984-85	Quebec	80	20	52	72
1985-86	Quebec	80	28	43	71
1986-87	Quebec	46	10	29	39
	Totals	523	140	319	459

LARRY MURPHY 26 6-0 200   Defenseman
Turned the fans' jeers to cheers at the Capital Centre last season when he emerged as the team's leading scorer . . . Scored 23 goals, 58 assists and 81 points, all club records for a defenseman . . . Was plus-20 over the final 24 regular-season games to wind up as the team leader at plus-25 . . . "I'm pleased about the statistics, especially the plus-minus," he said . . . Has shown marked improvement in the defensive area, where he was downgraded by the experts in the past . . . "He understands our defensive philoso-

phy now," coach Bryan Murray said . . . Born March 8, 1961, in Scarborough, Ont. . . . Began his NHL career with the Los Angeles Kings in 1980 after they made him their first-round pick in the draft that year . . . Collected 76 points as a rookie, which still stands as an NHL record for a first-year defenseman . . . Acquired by the Caps early in the 1983-84 season for Brian Engblom and Ken Houston.

Year	Club	GP	G	A	Pts.
1980-81	Los Angeles	80	16	60	76
1981-82	Los Angeles	79	22	44	66
1982-83	Los Angeles	77	14	48	62
1983-84	LA-Wash.	78	13	36	49
1984-85	Washington	79	13	42	55
1985-86	Washington	78	21	44	65
1986-87	Washington	80	23	58	81
	Totals	551	122	332	454

SCOTT STEVENS 23 5-11 200   Defenseman

Like Murphy, he has shown considerable improvement in the past two years . . . A good shot-blocker and rugged body-checker . . . Offensively, he moves the puck well and has a dynamite shot from the point . . . Was the team's fourth-leading scorer last season (10-51-61) and was plus-13 . . . Extremely durable, having missed only 15 games in his past five seasons . . . Intense and fiery . . . People keep saying he's learning to control his temper, but he again led the team in penalty minutes (285) last season . . . Born April 1, 1964, in Kitchener, Ont. . . . Fifth player taken in the 1982 draft . . . Was named to the NHL's All-Rookie team and finished third in the voting for the Calder Trophy in 1982-83.

Year	Club	GP	G	A	Pts.
1982-83	Washington	77	9	16	25
1983-84	Washington	78	13	32	45
1984-85	Washington	80	21	44	65
1985-86	Washington	73	15	38	53
1986-87	Washington	77	10	51	61
	Totals	385	68	181	249

ROD LANGWAY 30 6-3 215   Defenseman

As the team captain goes, so go the Capitals . . . Last season, he struggled during the first half and so did the team. He suffered a stretch where he was on the ice for at least one even-strength opposition goal in nine straight games; the Caps didn't win any of the nine . . . With the captain showing the way, the Caps lost only five of their final 23 games to finish second in the Patrick Division . . . Born May 3, 1957, in Taiwan (his father was in the

U.S. Navy)...Family later settled in Randolph, Mass....
Played football and hockey at the University of New Hampshire
...Montreal's second-round pick in the 1977 draft...Was the
key man in the Montreal-Washington six-player trade in 1982...
Winner of the Norris Trophy as the league's top defenseman in
1983 and 1984...Signed a lifetime contract with the Caps in
1984.

Year	Club	GP	G	A	Pts.
1977-78	Birmingham (WHA) .	52	3	18	21
1978-79	Montreal	45	3	4	7
1979-80	Montreal	77	7	29	36
1980-81	Montreal	80	11	34	45
1981-82	Montreal	66	5	34	39
1982-83	Washington	80	3	29	32
1983-84	Washington	80	9	24	33
1984-85	Washington	79	4	22	26
1985-86	Washington	71	1	17	18
1986-87	Washington	78	2	25	27
	NHL Totals	656	45	218	263
	WHA Totals	52	3	18	21

CLINT MALARCHUK 26 5-10 170   Goaltender

Misjudgment cost Quebec dearly in playoffs, and may have led to
his trade to the Capitals...Victim of unusual goal in Adams
Division finals when he left his crease on a penalty call he
thought was against Montreal. Guy Carbonneau scored into the
open net...For two months last season he may have been the
best goalie in hockey, but he finished below .500 (18-26-9) with
a 3.40 GAA...Topped Nords with 54 games played...Should
get plenty of playing time in Washington...Must cut down on
wandering to be a consistent winner...Born May 1, 1961, in
Grande, Alta.

Year	Club	GP	GA	SO	Avg.
1981-82	Quebec	2	14	0	7.00
1982-83	Quebec	15	71	0	4.43
1983-84	Quebec	23	80	0	3.95
1985-86	Quebec	46	142	4	3.21
1986-87	Qubec	54	175	1	3.40
	Totals	140	482	5	3.62

MIKE RIDLEY 24 6-1 200   Center

Was unhappy when the Rangers traded him and Kelly Miller to
the Capitals for Bobby Carpenter in the middle of last season and
seems intent on proving that Ranger GM Phil Esposito was
wrong...He didn't eat for two days after the trade and it af-
fected his play..."A trade mentally affects you, and your legs

don't have the usual jump," he said at the time. "But I'll hit my stride soon." ... He had 16 goals when traded and finished with 31, second on the team to linemate Mike Gartner's 41 ... "We're very pleased with Mike, but we expect him to get even better," said general manager David Poile ... Born July 8, 1963, in Winnipeg ... Overcame a broken collarbone and a fractured leg during his amateur career ... Was a walk-on at the Rangers' 1985 training camp ... Scored a goal in his first NHL game and wound up as the Rangers' leading scorer with 22 goals and 65 points ... Named to the NHL's All-Rookie team.

Year	Club	GP	G	A	Pts.
1985-86	New York R.	80	22	43	65
1986-87	NYR-Wash.	78	31	39	70
	Totals	158	53	82	135

PETE PEETERS 30 6-0 185   Goaltender

A standup guy—on and off the ice. "I've never been a flashy goaltender," he admits. "I try to play the angles." ... Can be extremely moody on occasions ... Maligned in the past as a poor playoff goalie, he was sensational in the 1986 preliminary round, when he limited the Islanders to four goals in three games ... Earned nine straight victories last season on his way to a 17-11-4 record and a goals-allowed average of 3.21. Was 1-2 in three playoff starts against the Islanders ... Born Aug. 1, 1957, in Edmonton ... Eighth-round choice of the Flyers in 1977 draft ... Traded to the Bruins for Brad McCrimmon in 1982 ... Won the Vezina Trophy in his first season with the Bruins ... Traded to the Caps for Pat Riggin in 1985.

Year	Club	GP	GA	SO	Avg.
1978-79	Philadelphia	5	16	0	3.43
1979-80	Philadelphia	40	108	1	2.73
1980-81	Philadelphia	40	115	2	2.96
1981-82	Philadelphia	44	160	0	3.71
1982-83	Boston	62	142	8	2.36
1983-84	Boston	50	151	0	3.16
1984-85	Boston	51	172	1	3.47
1985-86	Bos-Wash.	42	144	1	3.45
1986-87	Washington	37	107	0	3.21
	Totals	373	1115	13	3.12

DAVE CHRISTIAN 28 5-11 180   Right Wing

One of the team's most versatile players. Has played all three forward positions and a little defense during his pro career ...

Led the Caps in goals (41) and points (83) in 1985-86 . . . His production fell off last season when he settled for 23 goals and 50 points . . . A speedy, excellent two-way player . . . Not too aggressive. Totaled only eight minutes in penalties last season . . . Was Winnipeg's second-round pick in 1979 draft . . . Played three full seasons with the Jets, who traded him to Washington in 1983 mainly because of a salary dispute . . . Born May 12, 1959, in Warroad, Minn. . . . Played his college hockey at the University of North Dakota . . . Member of the gold medal-winning U.S. Olympic hockey team in 1980 . . . Father, Bill, and uncles, Roger and Gordon, are also former Olympians.

Year	Club	GP	G	A	Pts.
1979-80	Winnipeg	15	8	10	18
1980-81	Winnipeg	80	28	43	71
1981-82	Winnipeg	80	25	51	76
1982-83	Winnipeg	55	18	26	44
1983-84	Washington	80	29	52	81
1984-85	Washington	80	26	43	69
1985-86	Washington	80	41	42	83
1986-87	Washington	76	23	27	50
	Totals	546	198	294	492

BOB GOULD 30 5-11 195   Center

Was twice voted the Caps' Unsung Hero award . . . Has been attracting more attention in recent years . . . Originally a right winger, he centers the team's checking line . . . Strong penalty-killer . . . Has a knack for scoring important goals . . . From Jan. 1 to the end of last season, the Caps were 12-0 in games in which he scored a goal . . . He finished with 23 goals and 50 points, both career-highs . . . Born Sept. 2, 1957, in Petrolia, Ont. . . . Played four seasons of college hockey at the University of New Hampshire. His teammate for two of those years was fellow Cap Rod Langway . . . Was a seventh-round pick (118th overall) of the Atlanta Flames in 1977 . . . Spent three years in the Flames' farm system . . . Was still an unknown quality when the Caps acquired him from the Flames early in November, 1981. He's no longer unknown.

Year	Club	GP	G	A	Pts.
1979-80	Atlanta	1	0	0	0
1980-81	Calgary	3	0	0	0
1981-82	Calg-Wash	76	21	13	34
1982-83	Washington	80	22	18	40
1983-84	Washington	78	21	19	40
1984-85	Washington	79	19	19	38
1986-87	Washington	78	23	27	50
	Totals	473	120	115	235

COACH BRYAN MURRAY: Has been the Capitals' head coach since Nov. 11, 1981, when he replaced Gary Green . . . Has 246-160-60 regular-season record, but is 15-18 in five postseasons . . . Won the Jack Adams Trophy as the NHL's Coach of the Year in 1984 . . . Born on Dec. 5, 1942, in Shawville, Que. . . . A graduate of Montreal's McGill University, where he served as the college's hockey coach and athletic director for four years . . . Coached Tier II teams in Rockland and Pembroke, Ont., for five years . . . "I was teaching high school at Shawville and I used to drive 75 miles to coach in Rockland," he said . . . Also coached high-school track and basketball teams . . . Owned a sporting goods store in Pembroke when he agreed to coach the Regina Pats, leading that junior team into the Memorial Cup finals in 1980 . . . Moved on to the Hershey Bears and was named the AHL's Coach of the Year in 1981 . . . Considered an excellent game coach, but has a short fuse . . . Younger brother, Terry, a former NHL defenseman, is his principal assistant.

GREATEST COACH

Jim Anderson, Red Sullivan, Milt Schmidt, Tommy McVie— these were some of the men who got caught in the Capitals' revolving door for coaches in the '70s. All tried hard to turn the Caps into winners, and when they were replaced they expressed similar regrets.

"It hurts," said Anderson when he was replaced by Sullivan just 54 games into the Capitals' initial season of 1974-75. The Caps won only four games under Anderson and two of 19 under Sullivan before he was replaced by Schmidt late in that first season.

It was McVie who took his firing the hardest. "I gave my soul to this team . . . I pushed and pulled and I put everything into it," he said when he was fired at the start of the 1978-79 season.

Three years and three coaches later, Bryan Murray moved behind the Washington bench. He promised to turn the Capitals into winners, and he kept his promise. The Caps climbed over the .500 mark for the first time in Murray's first full season on the job (1982-83) and have not dipped below that mark since.

It has been quite a turnaround for the Capitals, who had a 1-13 record when club owner Abe Pollin chose him to replace Gary Green early in the 1981-82 season. For his efforts, Murray was named NHL Coach of the Year in 1984.

ALL-TIME CAPITAL LEADERS

GOALS: Dennis Maruk, 60, 1981-82
ASSISTS: Dennis Maruk, 76, 1981-82
POINTS: Dennis Maruk, 136, 1981-82
SHUTOUTS: Al Jensen, 4, 1983-84
　　　　　　　Pat Riggin, 4, 1983-84

Former Ranger Mike Ridley fit in well in Washington.

CALGARY FLAMES

TEAM DIRECTORY: Pres.-GM: Cliff Fletcher; Asst. to Pres.: Al Coates; Asst. GM: Al MacNeil; Dir. Pub. Rel.: Rick Skaggs; Coach: Terry Crisp. Home ice: Olympic Saddledome (16,683; 200′ × 85′). Colors: Red, white and gold. Training camp: Calgary.

Joe Mullen: 40 or more goals four years in a row.

SCOUTING REPORT

OFFENSE: To snuff out the Flames, stop Joe Mullen. Or so the story went.

Mullen is still the best, but beware of Mike Bullard and Brett Hull, the second-youngest son of the legendary Bobby Hull. Like his father, Hull has an intimidating shot and an uncanny knack of knowing where to be. He comes from Moncton and the American Hockey League, where he scored 50 goals waiting for the Flames to take notice.

Bullard is a genuine scoring threat, too, with a repertoire of fancy moves inside the blue line. This will be his first full season in Calgary.

Mullen should become the second American-born player to score 50 goals in the NHL. It only makes sense. Of those who qualify, he is the purest goal scorer.

Badly needed is an infusion of new bodies. Lanny McDonald is more popular than horses in Calgary, but he's 34 and much of the zip is gone. He needs 21 goals for a lifetime mark of 500. It would be nice, but is he pushing a good thing too far?

Joel Otto, Jim Peplinski and John Tonelli are big men who relish the grinding game.

DEFENSE: Calgary's best defenseman, by a country kilometer, is Jamie Macoun. Leather tough, he treats his opponents roughly. Although he's the team's fastest skater, he lets his teammates lug the puck while he takes care of defensive matters.

However, he had a difficult spring. First, he was accidentally speared by a teammate, Kari Eloranta, and suffered a bruised kidney. Then he smashed up his sports car, incurring nerve and muscle damage in his left arm.

Al MacInnis and Paul Reinhart finished 2-3 in team scoring. They play a prominent role in the team's offense as well as defense. Gary Suter, the 1985-86 Rookie of the Year, is coming off a poor season. Rock-hard Neil Sheehy is improving every year.

Mike Vernon was a 30-game winner in goal. The job is his, no matter how hard veteran Reggie Lemelin tries.

OUTLOOK: No fewer than five Flames have either retired or are preparing to do so. Doug Risebrough and Paul Baxter are done. McDonald, Tonelli and Nick Fotiu are close. Suddenly, the key people are Vernon, Macoun, Mullen, Otto, Hull, MacInnis and Terry Crisp, the new coach, who believes this team can go all the way.

FLAME ROSTER

No.	Player	Pos.	Ht.	Wt.	Born	1986–87	G	A	Pts.	PIM
21	Perry Berezan	C	6-1	178	12-25-64/Edmonton, Alta.	Calgary	5	3	8	24
26	Steve Bozek	C	5-11	186	11-26-60/Castlegar, B.C.	Calgary	17	18	35	22
14	Brian Bradley	C	5-10	179	1-21-65/Kitchener, Ont.	Calgary	10	18	28	16
						Moncton	12	16	28	8
25	Mike Bullard	C	5-10	193	3-10-61/Ottawa, Ont.	Pitt.-Calgary	30	36	66	51
	Bryan Deasly	LW	6-3	205		U. Michigan	13	11	24	74
28	Dale DeGray	RW/LW	6-0	200	9-1-63/Oshawa, Ont.	Calgary	6	7	13	29
						Moncton	10	22	32	57
6	Brian Engblom	D	6-2	200	1-27-57/Winnipeg, Man.	Calgary	0	4	4	28
22	Nick Fotiu	LW	6-2	210	5-25-52/Staten Island, N.Y.	Calgary	5	3	8	145
	Kevin Guy	D	6-3	202	7-16-65/Edmonton, Alta.	Calgary	0	4	4	19
						Moncton	2	10	12	38
15	Brett Hull	RW	5-11	200	8-9-64/Vancouver, B.C.	Moncton	50	42	92	16
						Calgary	1	0	1	0
19	Tim Hunter	RW	6-1	186	9-10-60/Calgary, Alta.	Calgary	6	15	21	357
12	Hakan Loob	LW	5-9	178	7-3-60/Sweden	Calgary	18	26	44	26
2	Al MacInnis	D	6-1	195	7-11-63/Inverness, N.B.	Calgary	20	56	76	97
34	Jamie Macoun	D	6-2	197	8-17-61/Newmarket, Ont.	Calgary	7	33	40	111
9	Lanny McDonald	LW	6-0	194	2-16-53/Hanna, Alta.	Calgary	14	12	26	54
7	Joe Mullen	RW	5-9	180	2-16-57/New York, N.Y.	Calgary	47	40	87	14
	Rick Nattress	D	6-2	208	5-25-62/Hamilton, Ont.	St. Louis	6	22	28	24
18	Joe Nieuwendyk	C	6-1	175	9-10-66/Oshawa, Ont.	Calgary	5	1	6	0
29	Joel Otto	C	6-4	220	10-29-61/St. Cloud, Minn.	Calgary	19	31	50	185
	Rick Paterson	D	6-0	196	2-22-64/Ottawa, Ont.	Moncton	6	21	27	112
11	Colin Patterson	RW	6-2	196	5-11-60/Rexdale, Ont.	Calgary	13	14	27	41
24	Jim Peplinski	RW	6-2	201	10-24-60/Renfrew, Ont.	Calgary	18	32	50	185
23	Paul Reinhart	D	5-11	205	1-8-60/Kitchener, Ont.	Calgary	15	54	69	22
32	Gary Roberts	LW	6-2	185	5-23-66/Whitby, Ont.	Calgary	5	9	14	85
						Moncton	20	18	38	72
5	Neil Sheehy	D	6-2	215	2-9-60/Ft. Francis, Ont.	Calgary	4	6	10	151
20	Gary Suter	D	6-0	190	6-24-64/Madison, Wis.	Calgary	9	40	49	70
27	John Tonelli	LW	6-1	200	3-23-57/Hamilton, Ont.	Calgary	20	31	51	72
33	Carey Wilson	C	6-2	205	5-19-62/Winnipeg, Man.	Calgary	20	36	56	42

No.	Player	Pos.	Ht.	Wt.	Born	1986–87	GP	GA	SO	Avg.
	Doug Dadswell	G	5-10	175	2-7-64/Scarborough, Ont.	Calgary	2	10	0	4.80
1	Marc D'Amour	G	5-9	185	4-29-61/Sudbury, Ont.	Moncton	42	138	1	3.64
31	Rejean Lemelin	G	5-11	160	11-19-54/Sherbrooke, Que.	Calgary	34	94	2	3.25
33	Mike Vernon	G	5-9	155	2-24-63/Calgary, Alta.	Calgary	54	178	1	3.61

FLAME PROFILES

JOEY MULLEN 30 5-9 180   **Right Wing**
Classified as as natural goal scorer, a title reserved for only a few...Pounces on his opportunities...Flames' opponents key on him...Led his tseam in goals (47), points (87) and power-play goals (15) and led the NHL in game-winning goals (12) in 1986-87...Had three penalty shots and scored on all of them, though the third was wiped out because he used an illegal stick ...Captured the Lady Byng Trophy as the NHL's most gentlemanly player in 1986-87...A wise investment on the part of the Flames who made him one of the NHL's best-paid players after they got him in six-player swap with St. Louis in February 1986 ...Born Feb. 26, 1957, in New York City, a product of Hell's Kitchen on Manhattan's West Side...As a youth, he played most of his hockey on roller skates...Signed as a free agent out of Boston College...Has a younger brother, Brian, who now plays for the Rangers...Once scored 110 goals in 45 games in the Metropolitan Junior Hockey Association of New York.

Year	Club	GP	G	A	Pts.
1981-82	St. Louis..........	45	25	34	59
1982-83	St. Louis..........	49	17	30	47
1983-84	St. Louis..........	80	41	44	85
1984-85	St. Louis..........	79	40	52	92
1985-86	St L-Calg	77	44	46	90
1986-87	Calgary............	79	47	40	87
	Totals	409	214	246	460

AL MacINNIS 24 6-1 195   **Defenseman**
Warranted All-Star consideration in 1986-87...Takes fewer chances than most offensive-minded defensemen...Team leader in assists (56) and shots (262) in 1986-87...Has a lethal right-handed shot...The sight of him winding up in the slot is one all goaltenders dread...On power plays, teams try to stay on top of him at the point...Born July 11, 1963, in Inverness, N.S., on Cape Breton Island...A two-time All-Star in junior hockey in Ontario...Tied Bobby Orr's junior record for goals (38) by a

defenseman in a single season as a member of the 1982-83
Kitchener Rangers . . . A movie buff.

Year	Club	GP	G	A	Pts.
1981-82	Calgary	2	0	0	0
1982-83	Calgary	14	1	3	4
1983-84	Calgary	51	11	34	45
1984-85	Calgary	67	14	52	66
1985-86	Calgary	77	11	57	68
1986-87	Calgary	79	20	56	76
	Totals	290	57	202	259

JAMIE MACOUN 26 6-2 197   **Defenseman**
Pillar of strength on Flames' defense . . . As tough as he is
talented . . . Hard-luck guy, however . . . Suffered 40 lacerations
and a deep gash on his left arm, doing nerve and muscle damage,
when he smashed up his sports car last May . . . Knocked out of
the 1987 playoffs with bruised kidney when accidentally speared
by teammate Kari Eloranta . . . Team's Emery Edge Award winner
with +31 in 1986-87 . . . Born Aug. 17, 1961, in Newmarket,
Ont . . . Named to the NHL's All-Rookie team in 1984 . . .
Acclaimed as the Flames' fastest skater . . . Good endurance . . .
Never drafted and signed as a free agent out of Ohio State in
1983 . . . Regarded as the Flames' fastest skater.

Year	Club	GP	G	A	Pts.
1982-83	Calgary	22	1	4	5
1983-84	Calgary	72	9	23	32
1984-85	Calgary	70	9	30	39
1985-86	Calgary	77	11	21	32
1986-87	Calgary	79	7	33	40
	Totals	320	37	111	148

JOEL OTTO 26 6-4 220   **Center**
One of the NHL's biggest forwards . . . Tracks down defensemen
with impacting results . . . Skates better than most big men in the
game . . . Flames try to match him against Mark Messier when
they meet arch-rival Oilers . . . A knee injury caused him to miss
the 1987 playoffs, a factor in the Flames' quick demise . . . Born
Oct. 29, 1961, in St. Cloud, Minn . . . A finalist for the Hobey
Baker Award given the top U.S. collegian in 1984 . . . Chosen as
the best player in Division II hockey that same year . . . Signed as
a free agent out of Bemidji State University on Sept. 11, 1984

. . . Had a hat trick on March 17, 1987, as Flames beat the Buffalo Sabres, 6-2, in Calgary.

Year	Club	GP	G	A	Pts.
1984-85	Calgary	17	4	8	12
1985-86	Calgary	79	25	34	59
1986-87	Calgary	68	19	31	50
	Totals	164	48	73	121

MIKE BULLARD 26 5-10 193   Center

Acquired from Pittsburgh for center Dan Quinn on Nov. 12, 1986 . . . Had his problems with coach Bob Berry, prompting the trade . . . Flames sent the team's psychologist to the airport to pick him up . . . Had eight goals and nine assists in an eight-game stretch and four goals and six assists in four games in March 1987 . . . Scored in sudden-death overtime in Winnipeg to give the Flames' one of their two wins in the 1987 playoffs . . . Born March 10, 1961, in Ottawa, Ont. . . . Has an excellent lateral movement into the slot . . . Weight has been known to fluctuate . . . Eats well.

Year	Club	GP	G	A	Pts.
1980-81	Pittsburgh	15	1	2	3
1981-82	Pittsburgh	75	36	27	63
1982-83	Pittsburgh	57	22	22	44
1983-84	Pittsburgh	76	51	41	92
1984-85	Pittsburgh	68	32	31	63
1985-86	Pittsburgh	77	41	42	83
1986-87	Pitt.-Calg.	71	30	36	66
	Totals	439	213	201	414

PAUL REINHART 27 5-11 205   Defenseman

Coming off one of his healthiest, most productive seasons . . . Strong skater and excellent puck-handler who frequently takes shifts as a center . . . Has had a career that has been plagued by a chronic back injury . . . Makes the game appear simple to play . . . Amazes people by coming off long layoffs and being at the top of his game . . . He and goaltender Rejean Lemelin are the only Flames who were with the team when it was based in Atlanta . . . Born Jan. 8, 1960, in Kitchener, Ont. . . . Has consistently represented Canada in international tournaments . . . Works

with Wayne Gretzky on anti-drug programs for the RCMP...
Owns a popular Calgary nightspot called Three Cheers...
Shrewd businessman...Team's psychologist goes to him for
investment advice.

Year	Club	GP	G	A	Pts.
1979-80	Atlanta	79	9	38	47
1980-81	Calgary	74	18	49	67
1981-82	Calgary	62	13	48	61
1982-83	Calgary	78	17	58	75
1983-84	Calgary	27	6	15	21
1984-85	Calgary	75	23	46	69
1985-86	Calgary	32	8	25	33
1986-87	Calgary	76	15	54	69
	Totals	503	109	333	442

JOHN TONELLI 30 6-1 200   Left Wing

Still identified as one of the New York Islanders during their
dynasty and makes his home on Long Island...Renowned for
his relentless drive down his side of the ice...Budges many
defensemen out of position with his intensity in the attacking
zone...Named MVP playing for Canada in the 1984 Canada
Cup...Twice selected to the NHL's second All-Star team...
Shaken when the Islanders traded him to Calgary for Richard
Kromm and Steve Konroyd on March 11, 1986...Born
March 23, 1957, in Milton, Ont.... Signed as an 18-year-old by
Houston Aeros of the now-defunct World Hockey Association
...Owns a beautiful home that includes a par-3 golf hole and
tennis courts.

Year	Club	GP	G	A	Pts.
1975-76	Houston (WHA)	79	17	14	31
1976-77	Houston (WHA)	80	24	31	55
1977-78	Houston (WHA)	65	23	41	64
1978-79	New York I	73	17	39	56
1979-80	New York I	77	14	30	44
1980-81	New York I	70	20	32	52
1981-82	New York I	80	35	58	93
1982-83	New York I	76	31	40	71
1983-84	New York I	73	27	40	67
1984-85	New York I	80	42	58	100
1985-86	NYI-Calgary	74	23	45	68
1986-87	Calgary	78	20	31	51
	NHL Totals	681	229	373	602
	WHA Totals	224	64	86	150

MIKE VERNON 24 5-9 155   Goaltender

Only Lanny McDonald is more in demand than he is in Calgary
. . . Star of the Flames' drive to the Stanley Cup final in 1986 . . .
Posted a 30-21-1 record in 1986-87 . . . Only Ron Hextall (37) of
Philadelphia and Mike Liut (31) of Hartford had more wins . . .
Still qualified as a rookie in 1986-87 . . . Debonair individual who
could qualify as a model . . . Born Feb. 24, 1963, in Calgary . . .
Was unbeaten for two months during 1985-86 season . . . Selected
twice as the Western Hockey League's Most Valu-
able Player in his junior years . . . Colorful . . . Helped Portland
Winterhawks win the Memorial Cup in 1983.

Year	Club	GP	GA	SO	Avg.
1982-83	Calgary	2	11	0	6.59
1983-84	Calgary	1	4	0	21.82
1985-86	Calgary	18	52	1	3.39
1986-87	Calgary	54	178	1	3.61
	Totals	75	245	2	3.69

GARY SUTER 23 6-0 190   Defenseman

Did not have quite the same impact on the team as he had a year
earlier when he was named the NHL's Rookie of the Year . . .
Nagged by a knee injury through most of 1986-87 . . . Lost some
of his tenacity, according to Flame watchers . . . His − 13 was the
team's worst . . . A ninth-round pick who made the Calgary scouts
look like geniuses . . . Born June 24, 1964, in Madison, Wis. . . .
Attended the University of Wisconsin . . . Older brother, Bob,
was a member of the U.S. gold-medal hockey team in the 1980
Winter Olympics . . . Basically a shy person . . . Played for Team
USA in the world hockey championships.

Year	Club	GP	G	A	Pts.
1985-86	Calgary	80	18	50	68
1986-87	Calgary	68	9	40	49
	Totals	148	27	90	117

LANNY McDONALD 34 6-0 194   Right Wing

Mention the name "Lanny" anywhere in Canada and people auto-
matically think of him . . . A legend in his own right, he's the

Flames' most popular player... Figures have dropped considerably as the seasons pass... Burdened by a knee injury through most of the 1986-87 season... Shot has lost much of its zip... Holds the franchise record for most goals (66) in a single season ... Born Feb. 16, 1953, in Hanna, Alta.... One-time winner of the Bill Masterton Trophy for his perserverance and dedication ... Scored the Flames' first goal in the Saddledome... Lends credibility to every advertisement or cause he endorses... Mustache is a classic.

Year	Club	GP	G	A	Pts.
1973-74	Toronto	70	14	16	30
1974-75	Toronto	64	17	27	44
1975-76	Toronto	75	37	56	93
1976-77	Toronto	80	46	44	90
1977-78	Toronto	74	47	40	87
1978-79	Toronto	79	43	42	85
1979-80	Tor-Col	81	40	35	75
1980-81	Colorado	80	35	46	81
1981-82	Col-Calg	71	40	42	82
1982-83	Calgary	80	66	32	98
1983-84	Calgary	65	33	33	66
1984-85	Calgary	43	19	18	37
1985-86	Calgary	80	28	43	71
1986-87	Calgary	58	14	12	26
	Totals	1000	479	486	965

COACH TERRY CRISP: Hired after Bob Johnson announced his resignation to become the executive director of the U.S. Amateur Hockey Association ...No fewer than three teams—Vancouver Canucks, New York Rangers and Pittsburgh Penguins—had expressed an interest in hiring him when the Calgary job came open... He pounced on it... Spent the past two seasons as coach and general manager of the Flames' American Hockey League franchise in Moncton, N.B.... Claims his coaching techniques were greatly influenced by Fred Shero, Scotty Bowman and Harry Sinden... Helped Philadelphia win Stanley Cups in 1974 and 1975... Twice was named Coach of the Year in the Ontario Hockey League while leading his team, the Sault Ste. Marie Greyhounds, to three junior hockey titles ... "He is a winner," said Calgary general manager Cliff Fletcher... Born May 28, 1943, in Perry Sound, Ont.

GREATEST COACH

"Badger" Bob Johnson left his mark on Calgary and the Flames. His five years behind the bench produced a 193-155-52 record, culminated by a 1986-87 mark of 46-31-3, the team's all-time best.

He took the Flames to one Stanley Cup final, 1985-86, only to lose to Montreal in five games. Johnson waged a war of words with Glen Sather from the arch-rival Edmonton Oilers while trying to co-exist in the same province—Alberta.

He was known for taking copious notes during the course of games, though the players said he rarely brought the contents to their attention in meetings that were held almost daily. Johnson loved to regale listeners with his hockey stories.

He won three national titles at the University of Wisconsin before leaving to coach the Flames in 1982-83. He left the Flames to become executive director of the U.S. Amateur Hockey Association in May 1987.

ALL-TIME FLAME LEADERS

GOALS: Lanny McDonald, 66, 1982-83
ASSISTS: Kent Nilsson, 82, 1980-81
POINTS: Kent Nilsson, 131, 1980-81
SHUTOUTS: Dan Bouchard, 5, 1973-74
                Phil Myre, 5, 1974-75

CHICAGO BLACK HAWKS

TEAM DIRECTORY: Pres.: William W. Wirtz; VP: Arthur M. Wirtz Jr.; VP: Tommy Ivan; Dir. Pub. Rel.: Jim DeMaria; Coach: Bob Murdoch. Home ice: Chicago Stadium (17,300; 188' × 85'). Colors: Red, black and white. Training camp: Chicago.

SCOUTING REPORT

OFFENSE: One would think that a team graced by the presence of an offensive star such as Denis Savard and a shooter such as Doug Wilson would have a respectable power play. Not so. The Hawks' power play is the NHL's worst.

Not surprisingly, the hiring of former Calgary assistant Bob Murdoch as coach is intended to rectify the situation. It is more than a coincidence that the architect of Calgary's power play was hired. It's the NHL's best.

Better specialty teams are the key to the success of the Blackhawks. Not unnoticed is their penalty-killing, almost as bad.

Certainly, Steve Larmer and Troy Murray are key performers, and younger Hawks such as Ed Olczyk and Bill Watson must have improved seasons. Al Secord is wearing down and, mercifully, Darryl Sutter has retired.

A name to watch is Everett Sanipass, the rookie who starred at Granby last year.

DEFENSE: Age, injuries and burnout are eroding the Hawks' defense. Doug Wilson, 30, is a victim of all three. Even older is Bob Murray, 33. Yet they remain Chicago's top defensemen.

On the plus side, Gary Nylund and Keith Brown are having the best years of their careers. Marc Bergevin is young and tidy defensively, as is Dave Manson.

The signing of free agent Bob Mason (Washington) should improve the goaltending situation. However, he has yet to experience one of the Hawks' frequent defensive lapses, the scourge of Murray Bannerman and Bob Sauve (now a Devil) last season.

Most apparent, however, is the need to reform the team's penalty-killing, especially at home, where the Hawks were touched for power-play goals no less than 27.3 percent of the time.

OUTLOOK: The Chicago crowd is the envy of most of the teams in the league. But take the boys out of the Stadium and

Troy Murray has scored 99 goals the past three seasons.

they are among weakest in the NHL. Murdoch has one enormous advantage. He doesn't have big shoes to fill.

BLACKHAWK PROFILES

DENIS SAVARD 26 5-10 167   **Center**
Chicago Stadium swings to the beat of his rushes . . . Certainly one of the NHL's most exciting players . . . Teammates marvel over his moves . . . Holds six club records, including most points (121) in a single season . . . Led his team in goals (40), points (90) and game-winning goals (7) in 1986-87 . . . Among his goals were three hat tricks . . . Only Mario Lemieux of Pittsburgh had more . . . Born Feb. 4, 1961, in Pointe Gatineau, Que. . . . Kicked the smoking habit . . . Loves the race track . . . Has a horse named after him . . . Canadiens are constantly chided in Montreal for

BLACKHAWK ROSTER

No.	Player	Pos.	Ht.	Wt.	Born	1986–87	G	A	Pts.	PIM
2	Marc Bergevin	D	5-11	178	8-11-65/Montreal, Que.	Chicago	4	10	14	66
32	Bruce Boudreau	C	5-9	175	1-9-55/Toronto, Ont.	Nova Scotia	35	47	82	40
4	Keith Brown	D	6-1	191	5-6-60/Cornerbrook, Nfld.	Chicago	4	23	27	86
25	Jim Camazzola	C	5-11	190	1-5-64/Vancouver, B.C.	Chicago	0	0	0	0
						Nova Scotia	13	18	31	31
32	Bruce Cassidy	D	5-11	176	5-20-65/Ottawa, Ont.	Nova Scotia	2	8	10	4
						Saginaw	2	13	15	6
10	Dave Donnelly	C	5-11	185	2-2-62/Edmonton, Alta.	Chicago	6	12	18	81
8	Curt Fraser	LW	6-0	190	1-12-58/Winnipeg, Man.	Chicago	25	25	50	182
28	Steve Larmer	RW	5-10	189	6-26-61/Peterborough, Ont.	Chicago	28	56	84	22
15	Mark Lavarre	RW	5-11	170	2-21-65/Evanston, Ill.	Chicago	8	15	23	33
						Nova Scotia	12	8	20	8
29	Steve Dudzik	C	5-11	170	4-3-61/Toronto, Ont.	Chicago	5	12	17	34
3	Dave Manson	D	6-2	190	1-27-67/Prince Albert, Sask.	Chicago	1	8	9	146
6	Bob Murray	D	5-10	183	11-26-54/Kingston, Ont.	Chicago	6	38	44	80
19	Troy Murray	C	6-1	195	7-31-62/Edmonton, Alta.	Chicago	28	43	71	59
22	Gary Nylund	D	6-3	210	10-28-63/Vancouver, B.C.	Chicago	7	20	27	190
5	Jack O'Callahan	D	6-1	185	7-24-57/Charleston, Mass.	Chicago	1	13	14	59
16	Ed Olczyk	RW-C	6-1	195	8-26-66/Chicago, Ill.	Chicago	16	35	51	119
26	Rick Paterson	C	5-9	187	2-10-58/Kingston, Ont.	Chicago	1	2	3	6
						Nova Scotia	5	7	12	2
34	Vic Posa	C	6-0	193	11-5-66/Italy	Nova Scotia	1	0	1	2
						Saginaw	13	27	40	203
17	Wayne Presley	RW	5-11	172	3-23-65/Detroit, Mich.	Chicago	32	29	61	114
11	Rich Preston	RW	6-0	185	5-22-52/Regina, Sask.	Chicago	8	9	17	19
7	Everett Sanipass	LW	6-1	192	2-13-68/Big Cove, N.B.	Chicago	1	3	4	2
						Grancy	34	48	82	220
18	Denis Savard	C	5-10	167	2-2-61/Pt. Gatineau, Que.	Chicago	40	50	90	108
	Darrin Sceviour	RW	5-10	185	11-30-65/Lacombe, Alta.	Chicago	0	0	0	0
						Saginaw	13	18	31	4
20	Al Secord	LW	6-1	212	9-20-58/Sudbury, Ont.	Chicago	29	29	58	196
12	Mike Stapleton	C	5-10	173	5-5-66/Sarnia, Ont.	Chicago	3	6	9	6
11	Bill Watson	D	6-0	180	3-30-64/Pine Falls, Man.	Chicago	13	19	32	6
23	Behn Wilson	D	6-3	210	12-19-58/Kingston, Ont.	Injured—Did Not Play				
24	Doug Wilson	D	6-1	190	7-5-57/Ottawa, Ont.	Chicago	16	32	48	36
	Rik Wilson	D	6-0	180	6-17-62/Long Beach, Cali.	Nova Scotia	8	13	21	109
	Trent Yawney	D	6-3	185	9-29-65/Hudson Bay, Sask.	Team Canada	–	–	–	–

No.	Player	Pos.	Ht.	Wt.	Born	1986–87	GP	GA	SO	Avg.
30	Murray Bannerman	G	5-11	184	4-27-57/Ft. Frances, Ont.	Chicago	39	142	0	4.14
	Ed Belfour	G				U. N. Dakota	33			2.43
	Bob Mason	G	6-1	180	4-22-61/International Falls, Ont.	Washington	45	137	0	3.24
						Binghamton	2	4	0	2.02
	Darren Pang	G	5-5	155	2-17-64/Medford, Ont.	Saginaw	44	151	0	3.12
						Nova Scotia	7	21	0	3.24
40	Warren Skorodenski	G	5-8	165	3-22-60/Winnipeg, Man.	Chicago	3	7	0	2.71
						Nova Scotia	32	121	2	4.00
						Saginaw	6	21	0	3.95
	Jim Waite	G	6-0	163		Chicoutimi	50	209	2	4.88

overlooking him in the 1981 draft . . . Death of his mother was a setback in 1986-87.

Year	Club	GP	G	A	Pts.
1980-81	Chicago	76	28	47	75
1981-82	Chicago	80	32	87	119
1982-83	Chicago	78	35	86	121
1983-84	Chicago	75	37	57	94
1904-05	Chicago	79	38	67	105
1985-86	Chicago	80	47	69	116
1986-87	Chicago	70	40	50	90
	Totals	538	257	463	720

TROY MURRAY 25 6-1 195   **Center**
The 1986 winner of the Selke Trophy as the NHL's premier defensive forward . . . Posted more modest numbers in 1986-87 but his defensive play was as sound as ever . . . Lost his regular linemates, Curt Fraser and Ed Olczyk, nicknamed the "Clydesdales," when injuries elsewhere forced them to fill holes on other lines . . . Averaged less than two shots per game but scored on 22 percent of them . . . Born July 31, 1962, in Calgary, Alta. . . . Helped the Fighting Sioux at the University of North Dakota win the NCAA championship in 1982 . . . Starred in Canada's victory in the 1981 world junior championship.

Year	Club	GP	G	A	Pts.
1981-82	Chicago	1	0	0	0
1982-83	Chicago	54	8	8	16
1983-84	Chicago	61	15	15	30
1984-85	Chicago	80	26	40	66
1985-86	Chicago	80	45	54	99
1986-87	Chicago	77	28	43	71
	Totals	353	122	160	282

STEVE LARMER 26 5-10 189   **Right Wing**
The one who complements Denis Savard the most . . . Left-hand shooter who plays on his off wing . . . Team leader in assists (56), power-play goals (10) and plus/minus (+ 20) . . . Extremely quiet individual who lets his actions speak for themselves . . . Named the NHL's Rookie of the Year in 1983 . . . A sixth-round choice (120th overall) who has made his scouts look good . . . Born June 16, 1961, in Peterborough, Ont. . . . Reacts smartly under hectic situations in the attacking zone . . . Nickname is

"Grandpa" . . . A member of the NHL's All-Rookie team in 1983
. . . One-times shots out of the slot most effectively.

Year	Club	GP	G	A	Pts.
1980-81	Chicago	4	0	1	1
1981-82	Chicago	3	0	0	0
1982-83	Chicago	80	43	47	90
1983-84	Chicago	80	35	40	75
1984-85	Chicago	80	46	40	86
1985-86	Chicago	80	31	45	76
1986-87	Chicago	80	28	56	84
	Totals	407	183	229	412

AL SECORD 29 6-1 212   Left Wing

One of the cruel prospects of playing against Chicago is to have
this guy run you . . . Wild crowds grow wilder when he asserts
himself . . . Not as rambunctious as he once was . . . One of two
left wingers in Blackhawk history who has scored 50 or more
goals in a single season . . . The other, Bobby Hull, had five
of them . . . Spent some time playing as a center in 1986-87 . . .
Born March 3, 1958, in Sudbury, Ont. . . . A one-time boxer . . .
A minus-20 rating was the Hawks' worst in 1986-87 . . . Penalty
leader again . . . Two of the best years of his career were ruined
by torn stomach muscles, the bane of all hockey players . . . Had
two hat tricks in 1986-87.

Year	Club	GP	G	A	Pts.
1978-79	Boston	71	16	7	23
1979-80	Boston	77	23	16	39
1980-81	Bos-Chi	59	13	12	25
1981-82	Chicago	80	44	31	75
1982-83	Chicago	80	54	32	86
1983-84	Chicago	14	4	4	8
1984-85	Chicago	51	15	11	26
1985-86	Chicago	80	40	36	76
1986-87	Chicago	77	29	29	58
	Totals	589	238	178	416

ED OLCZYK 21 6-1 195   Right Wing

Production fell off badly, largely because of a dismal shooting
percentage of 8.8 in 1986-87 . . . Move to center ice was
ineffective . . . His potential is one reason the Hawks think their
future is promising . . . A Chicago product who grew up to realize
his dream of playing for the Blackhawks . . . Became the first
American-born player to be drafted in the first-round by a team
from his own city . . . Deplored the Hawks' lack of spirit in

1986-87... Born Aug. 16, 1966, in Chicago... Brushed up on his shooting skills as a kid firing tennis balls at his mother... His parents own the "Ed-Mar" chain of food stores... Played on U.S. entry in the 1984 Winter Olympics in Sarajevo, Yugoslavia ... The NHL's youngest player in his rookie season.

Year	Club	GP	G	A	Pts.
1984-85	Chicago	70	20	30	50
1985-86	Chicago	79	29	50	79
1986-87	Chicago	79	16	35	51
	Totals	228	65	115	180

DOUG WILSON 30 6-1 190   Defenseman

People say the best thing that could happen to him is a change of scenery... Although he's reached the dreaded 30s, he has a ton of talent to offer any team... Shot is still considered lethal... Received an enormous amount of ice time in 1986-87 and tired noticeably... Led his team in shots (249)... Holds club records for goals (39), assists (54) and points (85) by a defenseman in a single season (1981-82)... The NHL's Norris Trophy winner in 1982 as the league's outstanding defenseman... Born July 5, 1957, in Ottawa, Ont.... Represented NHL at Rendez-Vous '87 ... Cites playing for Team Canada in the 1984 Canada Cup as his biggest thrill... Perceptive interview... Friendly person.

Year	Club	GP	G	A	Pts.
1977-78	Chicago	77	14	20	34
1978-79	Chicago	56	5	21	26
1979-80	Chicago	73	12	49	61
1980-81	Chicago	76	12	39	51
1981-82	Chicago	76	39	46	85
1982-83	Chicago	74	18	51	69
1983-84	Chicago	66	13	45	58
1984-85	Chicago	78	22	54	76
1985-86	Chicago	79	17	47	64
1986-87	Chicago	69	16	32	48
	Totals	724	168	404	572

GARY NYLUND 24 6-3 210   Defenseman

Despite serious knee injuries early in his career, he was one of only three Hawks to appear in all 80 games in 1986-87... Involves himself in situations that often result in fights... Played out his option in Toronto and signed with Chicago as a free agent in 1986...Hawks lost Ken Yaremchuk and Jerome Dupont as compensation...Handsome chap who dedicates himself to staying fit...Born Oct. 23, 1963, in the Vancouver suburb of Surrey...Helped Canada win the 1981 world junior hockey championship...Selected third overall in the 1982 draft after being named the top defenseman in the Western Hockey League ..."Beaker" spends his summers catching salmon off the coast of British Columbia.

Year	Club	GP	G	A	Pts.
1982-83	Toronto	16	0	3	3
1983-84	Toronto	47	2	14	16
1984-85	Toronto	76	3	17	20
1985-86	Toronto	79	2	16	18
1986-87	Chicago	80	7	20	27
	Totals	298	14	70	84

BOB MASON 26 6-1 180   Goaltender

Was a much-coveted free agent without compensation...Teams lined up trying to sign him...Opted to sign with Hawks after coming close to an agreement with Vancouver...Came out of Binghamton to post a 20-18-5 record with Washington in 1986-87...Waged a goaltending duel with Islanders' Kelly Hrudey in the seven-period marathon in the seventh and deciding game of the divisional semifinals...Born April 22, 1961, in International Falls, Minn....Catches with the right hand...Performed for the U.S. in the 1984 Winter Olympics.

Year	Club	GP	GA	SO	Avg.
1983-84	Washington	2	3	0	1.50
1984-85	Washington	12	31	1	2.81
1985-86	Washington	1	0	0	0.00
1986-87	Washington	45	137	0	3.24
	Totals	60	171	1	3.08

WAYNE PRESLEY 22 5-11 172   Right Wing

A bright spot in the Windy City...In Wayne's first-full year with the Hawks, only Denis Savard scored more goals...Scored on 19.22 percent of his shots...Not very big, but has plenty of gumption...Pokes his nose into skirmishes and usually pays for it... Excellent speed and good defensively... Born March 23, 1965, in Detroit... Scored four game-winners in 1986-87... Scored eight first goals, too, to rank fourth in that department in the NHL... Uses a short stick.

Year	Club	GP	G	A	Pts.
1984-85	Chicago	3	0	1	1
1985-86	Chicago	38	7	8	15
1986-07	Chicago	80	32	29	61
	Totals	121	39	38	77

KEITH BROWN 27 6-1 191   Defenseman

Enjoyed his finest year in 1986-87... Emerged as the Hawks' best defenseman after Doug Wilson went down with a knee injury in March... Partner on defense is Gary Nylund, a former Portland Winterhawk, like Keith... Coach Bob Murdoch feels he has more to offer offensively and intends to bring him out of his shell... Born May 6, 1960, in Cornerbrook, Nfld... Excellent skater... Powerful upper body, thanks to weightlifting ... Despite his strength, he isn't noted as a good fighter... An interesting interview.

Year	Club	GP	G	A	Pts.
1979-80	Chicago	76	2	18	20
1980-81	Chicago	80	9	34	43
1981-82	Chicago	33	4	20	24
1982-83	Chicago	50	4	27	31
1983-84	Chicago	74	10	25	35
1984-85	Chicago	56	1	22	23
1985-86	Chicago	70	11	29	40
1986-87	Chicago	73	4	23	27
	Totals	512	45	198	243

COACH BOB MURDOCH: Succeeds GM Bob Pulford as the Hawks' coach... Becomes the 29th coach in the history of the franchise... Spent five years working as an assistant coach in Calgary... In 17 years as a player and a coach, his teams have never missed the playoffs... Defenseman who helped Montreal win two Stanley Cups (1970-71 and 1972-73)... Easily identified by his bushy mustache...

Greatly influenced by Bob Johnson in Calgary and Bob Pulford, his coach in Los Angeles...A power-play specialist who must improve team's weakness in that area...Charged with the responsibility of reviving the careers of some tired pros in Chicago ...Born Nov. 20, 1946, in Kirkland Lake, Ont....Chose University of Waterloo over junior hockey.

Hawks count on Steve Larmer for good assist—and more.

GREATEST COACH

In a 13½ career that began in 1963-64, Billy Reay reeled off six first-place finishes, but never won a Stanley Cup.

The last coach to wear a fedora behind the bench, Reay posted a 517-334-160 record. Oddly enough, he was a coach before he started an eight-year playing career as a forward, briefly in Detroit and then in Montreal. Reay performed as a playing coach in Quebec City, Victoria and Seattle on the way to the NHL as a player.

He coached in Toronto for less than two seasons prior to being hired as leader of the Blackhawks during the halcyon years of Bobby Hull.

Today he lives in Chicago, where he works for a corrugated box company.

ALL-TIME BLACK HAWK LEADERS

GOALS: Bobby Hull, 58, 1968-69
ASSISTS: Denis Savard, 87, 1981-82
POINTS: Denis Savard, 121, 1982-83
SHUTOUTS: Tony Esposito, 15, 1969-70

DETROIT RED WINGS

TEAM DIRECTORY: Owner: Michael Ilitch; GM: Jim Devellano; Dir. Pub. Rel.: Bill Jamieson; Coach: Jacques Demers. Home ice: Joe Louis Arena (19,275; 200' × 85'). Training camp: Flint, Mich.

SCOUTING REPORT

OFFENSE: There is room to star in Jacques Demers' rigid, team-first doctrine. Steve Yzerman knows how. So does Gerard Gallant and Brent Ashton. Darren Veitch understands what's expected of him—tidy defense and hard shots from the point when the opportunities arise.

They wear red, but their collars are blue. Players who work will play for Demers, who puts one-dimensional performers such as Petr Klima on the front step of his doghouse. But Demers saw enough in John Chabot to sign the free-agent Penguin.

This is a team that doesn't score a lot of goals—fewest in the NHL in 1986-87—but gets a disproportionate amount of mileage out of those it does score. Thank their stingy defensive play for such a phenomenon.

A power play that clicked 23.3 percent of the time on the road was a large factor in the team's success.

DEFENSE: Defense is a joint effort in Detroit. Non-conformists beware. Last in offense, the Red Wings are winners because they are one of the five best defensive teams in the NHL.

Players who would seem to be making the last stop in their careers have contributed greatly to the defensive effort. Among them are goaltender Glen Hanlon and defensemen Mike O'Connell, Doug Halward, Dave Lewis, Lee Norwood and Harold Snepsts.

The only prime-time star behind the Detroit blueline is goaltender Greg Stefan, a 20-game winner last season. If he keeps his cool, he can beat any team any given night.

Up front, the Red Wings have the best young defensive forward in the game in Shawn Burr. He not only checks the enemy's stars, he is the backbone of the Wings' penalty-killing unit.

OUTLOOK: Detroit's love affair with the Red Wings is beginning to evoke the unbridled passions of another era. Demers has fixed ideas on what it takes to win in the NHL. He doesn't ask for miracles for his players. He expects them to be man-made.

Gerard Gallant had 17 power-play goals last season.

RED WING PROFILES

STEVE YZERMAN 22 5-11 180   Center
Team captain and its undisputed leader... To the surprise of
some, he became an even better hockey player under Jacques
Demers' highly-disciplined doctrine... Led Red Wings in points,
assists and shots (217) in 1986-87... Plays well in traffic but is
equally at home in open ice... As a rookie, he was the youngest
player to appear in an All-Star Game in the 40-year history of the
event... Born May 9, 1965, in Cranbrook, B.C., but raised in
the Ottawa, Ont., suburb of Nepean... His father is a high-
ranking official in the social services department of the Cana-

RED WING ROSTER

No.	Player	Pos.	Ht.	Wt.	Born	1986–87	G	A	Pts.	PIM
14	Brent Ashton	LW	6-1	210	5-18-60/ Saskatoon, Sask.	Que.-Det.	31	59	90	43
22	Dave Barr	C	6-1	180	11-30-60/Edmonton, Alta.	Hart-Stl.-Det.	15	17	32	68
15	Mel Bridgman	C	6-0	190	4-28-55/Victoria, B.C.	N.J.-Det.	10	33	43	99
11	Shawn Burr	C	6-1	180	7-1-66/Sarnia, Ont.	Detroit	22	25	47	107
	John Chabot	C	6-2	195	3-18-62/Riverside, PEI	Pittsburgh	14	22	36	8
3	Steve Chasson	D	6-0	210	4-14-67/Barrie, Ont.	Detroit	1	4	5	73
	Gilbert Delorme	D	6-1	205	11-25-62/Longgueil, Que.	Detroit	4	3	7	47
	Brent Fedyk	RW	6-0	180	3-6-67/Yankton, Sask.	Portland	19	21	40	24
17	Gerard Gallant	RW	5-11	168	9-2-63/Summerside, PEI	Detroit	38	34	72	216
	Adam Graves	C	5-11	184	4-12-68/Toronto, Ont.	Windsor	45	55	100	70
7	Doug Halward	D	6-1	184	11-1-55/Toronto, Ont.	Van.-Det.	0	6	6	53
20	Tim Higgins	RW	6-0	181	2-2-58/Ottawa, Ont.	Detroit	12	14	26	124
	Doug Houda	D	6-2	190	6-3-66/Blairmore, Alta.	Adirondack	6	23	29	142
	Kris King	LW	6-0	193	2-18-66/Bracebridge, Ont.	Peterborough	23	33	56	160
85	Petr Klima	LW	6-0	190	12-23-64/Czechoslovakia	Detroit	30	23	53	42
26	Joe Kocur	RW	6-1	204	12-21-64/Calgary, Alta.	Detroit	9	9	18	276
28	Dale Krentz	C	5-11	187	12-19-61/Steinbach, Man.	Detroit	0	0	0	0
						Adirondack	32	39	71	68
	Gord Kruppke	D	6-2	200	4-2-69/Slave Lake, Alta.	Prince Albert	2	10	12	129
18	Mark Kumpel	RW	6-0	190	3-7-61/Wakefield, Mass.	Adirondack	2	3	5	0
						Que.-Det.	1	9	10	16
8	Mark Lamb	C	5-9	167	8-3-64/Swift Current, Sask.	Detroit	2	1	3	8
						Adirondack	14	36	50	45
52	Dave Lewis	D	6-2	205	7-3-53/Kindersley, Sask.	Detroit	2	5	7	66
	Barry Melrose	D	6-2	205	2-15-56/Kelvington, Sask.	Adirondack	4	9	13	170
	Glen Merkosky	C	5-10	175	11-4-53/Belleville, Ont.	Adirondack	54	31	85	66
10	Joe Murphy	C-RW	6-1	190	10-16-67/London, Ont.	Adirondack	21	38	59	61
						Detroit	0	1	1	2
23	Lee Norwood	D	6-0	195	2-2-60/Oakland, Cal.	Detroit	6	21	27	163
						Adirondack	0	3	3	0
34	Adam Oates	C	5-11	185	8-27-62/Weston, Man.	Detroit	15	32	47	21
2	Mike O'Connell	D	5-9	180	11-25-58/Chicago, Ill.	Detroit	5	26	31	70
24	Bob Probert	LW	6-3	208	6-5-65/Windsor, Ont.	Detroit	13	11	24	221
						Adirondack	1	4	5	15
	Yves Racine	D	6-1	183		Longueuil	7	43	50	50
	Geordie Robertson	C	6-0	163	8-1-59/Victoria, B.C.	Adirondack	28	41	69	94
16	Ric Seiling	RW	5-11	178	12-15-57/Elmira, Ont.	Detroit	3	8	11	49
4	Jeff Sharples	D	6-1	185	7-28-67/Terrace, B.C.	Detroit	0	1	1	2
						Portland	25	35	60	92
	Bill Shibicky	C	5-8	165	1-25-64/Burnaby, B.C.	Michigan State	43	36	79	–
27	Harold Snepsts	D	6-5	215	10-24-54/Edmonton, Alta.	Detroit	1	13	14	129
	Ted Speers	LW	5-11	190	1-21-61/Ann Arbor, Mich.	Adirondack	24	37	61	39
5	Darren Veitch	D	6-0	190	4-24-60/Saskatoon, Sask.	Detroit	13	45	58	52
35	Warren Young	C-LW	6-3	205	1-11-56/Weston, Ont.	Pittsburgh	8	13	21	103
19	Steve Yzerman	C	5-11	180	5-9-63/Cranbrook, B.C.	Detroit	31	59	90	43
	Rick Zombo	D	6-1	195	5-8-63/Des Plaines, Ill.	Adirondack	0	6	6	22

No.	Player	Pos.	Ht.	Wt.	Born	1986–87	GP	GA	SO	Avg.
	Darren Eliot	G	6-1	175	11-26-61/Milton, Ont.	New Haven	4	15	0	3.77
						Los Angeles	24	103	1	4.40
1	Glen Hanlon	G	6-0	171	2-20-57/Brandon, Man.	Detroit	36	104	1	3.18
	Chris Pusey	G	6-0	180	6-20-65/Brantford, Ont.	Adirondack	11	40	0	3.89
34	Sam St. Laurent	G	5-10	186	2-16-59/Arvida, Que.	Detroit	6	16	22	2.81
						Adirondack	25	98	1	4.21
30	Greg Stefan	G	5-11	180	2-11-61/Brantford, Ont.	Detroit	45	135	1	3.45

dian government...A first-round choice (fourth overall) in 1983...Well-spoken person.

Year	Club	GP	G	A	Pts.
1983-84	Detroit	80	39	48	87
1984-85	Detroit	80	30	59	89
1985-86	Detroit	51	14	28	42
1986-87	Detroit	80	31	59	90
	Totals	291	114	194	308

GERARD GALLANT 24 5-11 168   Left Wing

Received serious consideration as the NHL's all-star left winger in 1986-87...Coach Jacques Demers describes him as "my Brian Sutter in Detroit" because of his fiesty nature, dressing-room influence and zeal to win...A favorite of Detroit fans... Led his team in goals, power-play goals (17) and game-tying goals (2) in 1986-87...Rookie season in the NHL was marred by a broken jaw...Born Sept. 2, 1963, in Summerside, Prince Edward Island, Canada's smallest province...A sixth-round choice (107th overall) in 1981...A former linemate of the Islanders' Pat LaFontaine at Verdun in the Quebec Junior League.

Year	Club	GP	G	A	Pts.
1984-85	Detroit	32	6	12	18
1985-86	Detroit	52	20	19	39
1986-87	Detroit	80	38	34	72
	Totals	164	64	65	129

BRENT ASHTON 27 6-1 210   Left Wing

Yet another reason why the Red Wings have one of the NHL's best left sides...Plays even bigger than he is, skates hard and has soft hands...Acquired from the Nordiques along with Gilbert Delorme and Mark Kumpel for John Ogrodnick, Doug Shedden and Basil McRae on Jan. 17, 1987...Performed as a center in Quebec when the Nordiques lost Dale Hunter and Peter Stastny for stretches in 1986-87...An accomplished penalty-killer...Born May 18, 1960, in Saskatoon, Sask...His older brother, Ron, played briefly in the NHL with Winnipeg...Has been a competitive water skier... Every team that traded him would love to have him now.

Year	Club	GP	G	A	Pts.
1979-80	Vancouver.........	47	5	14	19
1980-81	Vancouver.........	77	18	11	29
1981-82	Colorado..........	80	24	36	60
1982-83	New Jersey........	76	14	19	33
1983-84	Minnesota.........	68	7	10	17
1984-85	Minn-Que.........	78	31	31	62
1985-86	Quebec...........	77	26	32	58
1986-87	Que-Det	81	40	35	75
	Totals	584	165	188	353

PETR KLIMA 22 6-0 190   Left Wing

Wears No. 85 to commemorate the year he gained his freedom by defecting from Czechoslovakia... The only NHL player who tapes his stick in stripes... Possesses outstanding offensive talents with game-breaking qualities... Led Detroit in game-winning goals (5) in 1986-87... Abhors defense, which causes him unbelievable grief with coach Jacques Demers... Born Dec. 23, 1964, in Chaomutov, Czechoslovakia... "He's just going to have to take some time off and learn how to check," said Demers... A fifth-round draft choice (88th overall) in 1983... Served two years in the Czech army... Loves fast cars, rock concerts and his two Great Danes... Received a five-minute standing ovation from Detroit fans on his first night in Joe Louis Arena in 1985.

Year	Club	GP	G	A	Pts.
1985-86	Detroit	74	32	24	56
1986-87	Detroit	77	30	23	53
	Totals	151	62	47	109

GREG STEFAN 26 5-11 180   Goaltender

Cooled down after a bizarre 1985-86 season when he was suspended twice for stick-swinging altercations with Chicago's Al Secord and Pittsburgh's Dan Frawley... Red Wings successfully impressed upon him the importance of having him in their lineup ... Posted a 20-17-3 record for the Wings in 1986-87... Became a tad indignant in the 1987 playoffs when Glen Hanlon starred in the Norris Division final against Toronto... At one point, he refused to dress as his backup... Born Feb. 11, 1961, in Brantford, Ont., growing up in the same neighborhood as Wayne Gretzky... An excellent golfer... Stages a golf tournament in supported of abused children... A seventh-round choice (128th overall) in 1981.

Year	Club	GP	GA	SO	Avg.
1981-82	Detroit	2	10	0	5.00
1982-83	Detroit	35	139	0	4.52
1983-84	Detroit	50	152	2	3.51
1904-85	Detroit	46	190	0	4.33
1985-86	Detroit	37	155	1	4.50
1986-87	Detroit	43	135	1	3.45
	Totals	213	781	4	4.03

DARREN VEITCH 27 6-0 190   Defenseman

Is coming off what ranks as his best season in the NHL... Was the Red Wings' Emory Edge Award winner in 1986-87 with plus-14... Offensively, he led Detroit defensemen in goals and assists, thanks to a bristling righthand shot and creative playmaking... Required arthoscopic knee surgery in the 1987 playoffs... Finished in a 10th-place tie with Mark Howe of Philadelphia among the NHL's highest-scoring defensemen in 1986-87... Born April 24, 1960, in Saskatoon, Sask., but calls Regina, Sask., home... One of Canada's top amateur golfers ... Known to clutch and grab, discreetly.

Year	Club	GP	G	A	Pts.
1980-81	Washington	59	4	21	25
1981-82	Washington	67	9	44	53
1982-83	Washington	10	0	8	8
1983-84	Washington	46	6	18	24
1984-85	Washington	75	3	18	21
1985-86	Wash-Det	75	3	14	17
1986-87	Detroit	77	13	45	58
	Totals	409	38	168	206

MIKE O'CONNELL 31 5-9 180   Defenseman

One of the few players in the NHL who performs without the security of a helmet... Blocks shots zealously, a feature statistics cannot reflect... An accomplished rusher... An assistant captain of the Red Wings... One of the NHL's older players, but plays as effectively as ever... Durable performer who rarely misses a game... Born Nov. 29, 1955, in Chicago and raised near Boston... Older brother, Tim, played for the San Diego Mariners of the now-defunct World Hockey Association... His father, Tommy, was a quarterback at Illinois and played pro ball with the Cleveland Browns ... A career in real estate waits to be pursued when he retires.

Year	Club	GP	G	A	Pts.
1977-78	Chicago	6	1	1	2
1978-79	Chicago	48	4	22	26
1979-80	Chicago	78	8	22	30
1980-81	Chi-Buf	82	15	38	53
1981-82	Boston	80	5	34	39
1982-83	Boston	80	14	39	53
1983-84	Boston	75	18	42	60
1984-85	Boston	78	15	40	55
1985-86	Bos-Det	76	9	28	37
1986-87	Detroit	77	5	26	31
	Totals	680	94	292	386

ADAM OATES 25 5-11 185   Center

The only free agent out of college who has had some impact on the team ... Signed the same year (1985) as two other celebrated free agents—Ray Staszak and Tim Friday ... Plays an all-round game to suit the needs of Jacques Demers ... Born Aug. 27, 1962, in Weston, Ont., a suburb of Toronto ... Set scoring records at Rensselaer Polytechnic Institute for points (91) and assists (60) in his junior year (1984-85), leading his school to the NCAA championship ... Instructs at a hockey school in Albany, N.Y. ... Has established himself as one of Detroit's starting centers along with Shawn Burr and Steve Yzerman.

Year	Club	GP	G	A	Pts.
1985-86	Detroit	38	9	11	20
1986-87	Detroit	76	15	32	47
	Totals	114	24	43	67

JOHN CHABOT 25 6-2 195   Center

In late June he turned his Penguin free-agent status into a contract with the Red Wings ... Not a big scorer, he has totaled only 55 goals in four NHL seasons. Earns his salary as a solid checker and playmaker ... "I was told I could help the team more in a defensive role, so that's where I wound up and I like it," he said ... Born May 18, 1962, in Summerside, P.E.I., of North American Indian heritage. Family name originally was Kahibaitche ... Spends considerable time visiting Indian reservations in Canada, lecturing on drug and alcohol abuse ... Played his junior hockey for Hull and Sherbrooke of the QMJHL... Was the Canadiens' third choice (40th overall) in the 1980 draft... Played one year in the AHL before being promoted to the Canadiens in 1983... Has scored 14 goals in each of his last two seasons.

Year	Club	GP	G	A	Pts.
1983-84	Montreal	56	18	25	43
1984-85	Mont-Pitt	77	9	51	60
1985-86	Pittsburgh	77	14	31	45
1986-87	Pittsburgh	72	14	22	36
	Totals	282	55	129	184

SHAWN BURR 21 6-1 180   Center

Jacques Demers' kind of hockey player... Checks the stars into a frazzled frame of mind... Neatly negated Wayne Gretzky in the Campbell Conference final in 1987... Good skater who can pounce on a break... Scored two shorthanded goals for the Wings last season... Born July 1, 1966, in Sarnia, Ont., only a few miles up river from Detroit... Warranted serious consideration for the NHL's All-Rookie Team in 1987... A first-round choice (seventh overall) in 1984.

Year	Club	GP	G	A	Pts.
1984-85	Detroit	9	0	0	0
1985-86	Detroit	5	1	0	1
1986-87	Detroit	80	22	25	47
	Totals	94	23	25	48

JOE   KOCUR 22 6-1 204   Right Wing

Largely responsible for the fact the Red Wings led the entire NHL in penalty minutes with 2209 in 1986-87... Sixth-most penalized player in the league... Fought often and rarely lost ... Found time to score two game-winning goals... Refused to fight his cousin, Wendel Clark of Toronto, for family reasons... Clark was ninth on the penalty list... Born Dec. 21, 1984, in Calgary and raised on a farm near Kelvington, Sask.... Barry

Melrose, a Red Wing farmhand, is another cousin . . . A fifth-round choice (91st overall) in 1983.

Year	Club	GP	G	A	Pts.
1984-85	Detroit	17	1	0	1
1985-86	Detroit	59	9	6	15
1986-87	Detroit	77	9	9	18
	Totals	153	19	15	34

COACH JACQUES DEMERS: Coach of the Year in 1986-87

. . . Under his command, the Red Wings went from last place in the NHL's overall standing to 11th . . . Even better, they were a powerhouse in the playoffs, reaching the Campbell Conference final before being eliminated . . . Widely recognized as the NHL coach who gets the most from his players . . . Signed a five-year, $1 million contract to become the Red Wings' coach on June 13, 1986 . . . The Blues protested loudly, claiming he had made a verbal agreement to remain with them. The issue is not dead . . . To play for him, a player is obliged to put the team above himself . . . The sacrifices that checking requires are mandatory . . . Failure to comply can lead to instant banishment to the minors or, at the extremes, a stretch of inactivity or a trade to another team . . . Disgusted with his players' lack of effort one night, he ordered them to put in a full day's work like everyone else in society . . . The Red Wings practiced, watched films and heard lectures from 9 until 5 . . . They were a different team the next night . . . A career coach.

GREATEST COACH

During his 20-year coaching career (1927-28 to 1946-47), his Red Wing teams won 12 league championships, including seven in a row, and seven Stanley Cups. All told, Jack Adams served

35 years as general manager and the Red Wings failed to make the playoffs only seven times.

His greatest personal satisfaction was the development of Gordie Howe into a superstar and the highest scorer of all time. Adams' arrival in Detroit in 1927 coincided with the opening of The Olympia. Born June 14, 1895, in Fort William, Ont., now known as Thunder Bay, he played as a 16-year-old in the Northern Michigan Hockey League. He helped the Toronto Arenas win the 1918 Stanley Cup and he won on a scoring title in the Pacific Coast League at Vancouver in 1923-24.

Adams, known of hockey's farm system, left Detroit in 1962 to serve as president of the Central Professional Hockey League. Nicknamed "Jolly," Adams was inducted into the Hall of Fame in 1959. He died May 1, 1968.

ALL-TIME RED WING LEADERS

GOALS: John Ogrodnick, 55, 1984-85
ASSISTS: Marcel Dionne, 74, 1974-75
POINTS: Marcel Dionne, 121, 1974-75
SHUTOUTS: Terry Sawchuk, 12, 1951-52, 1954-55
                Glenn Hall, 12, 1955-56

EDMONTON OILERS

TEAM DIRECTORY: Owner: Peter Pocklington; Pres.-GM-Co-Coach: Glen Sather; Co-Coach: John Muckler; Dir. Player Personnel: Barry Fraser; Dir. Pub. Rel.: Bill Tuele. Home ice: Northlands Coliseum (17,502; 200' × 85'). Colors: Royal blue, orange and white. Training camp: Edmonton.

SCOUTING REPORT

OFFENSE: Ask them and they say the reason why the Oilers won their third Stanley Cup last spring was because they finally learned how to play defense.

The Oilers did impress with their occasional demonstrations of discipline, but not before unleashing their lethal attack that presented them with a lead substantial enough to protect.

Lurking beneath the guise was a yearning to let loose . . . to see who could get to 10 first.

Wayne Gretzky won his seventh consecutive scoring championship with his lowest point total (183) in six years, a tribute to his commitment to defense. Once again, he had more assists than his nearest challenger and teammate, Jari Kurri, had points (108).

So what's new?

The Oilers have lost the perfect playmate for Mark Messier and Glenn Anderson. Never was hockey as much fun for Messier and Anderson as it was when Kent Nilsson was there. For three months, it was pure bliss . . . climaxed by a Stanley Cup. But the Magic Man has returned to Europe to play the remaining years of his career. It won't be the same without him.

DEFENSE: The apparent retirement of Dr. Randy Gregg poses a problem for Glen Sather's Oilers. He was their purest defensive defenseman, as reliable as snow in the nearby Rockies. He may play for Canada in the Winter Olympics and be tempted to join the Oilers about playoff time. But if he's left unprotected in the waiver draft, another team is expected to take his rights.

Also gone is Reijo Ruotsalainen, the short but speedy Finn. He has returned to Europe, though the Oilers might be tempted to bring him back, too, when the playoffs roll around.

Kevin Lowe is a free agent with compensation and there are persistent rumors out of the East that Paul Coffey is trade material. But both men are critical to the Oilers' defense. The loss of either could severely affect the flow up front.

To prop up the defense, the Oilers are ready to trade Andy Moog, a 28-game winner in goal. Obviously, Grant Fuhr is their

Jari Kurri has had four straight 50-goal seasons.

first choice, as evidenced in the playoffs. Darryl Reaugh is a logical successor if Moog is moved.

OUTLOOK: Changes are occurring in Edmonton. And this is where the expertise of management comes into effect. Glen Sather has made outstanding moves in the past. He needs more of the same again. The Oilers won't win another Stanley Cup unless they can add a quality defenseman without giving up one.

OILER PROFILES

WAYNE GRETZKY 26 6-0 170   **Center**
Hockey's single greatest asset...A mega-star who gives the sport its most glowing image...Has not lost the common touch

OILER ROSTER

No.	Player	Pos.	Ht.	Wt.	Born	1986–87	G	A	Pts.	PIM
9	Glenn Anderson	RW	5-11	175	10-2-60/Vancouver, B.C.	Edmonton	35	38	73	65
6	Jeff Beukeboom	D	6-4	208	3-28-65/Ajax, Ont.	Edmonton	3	8	11	124
						Nova Scotia	1	7	8	35
	Kelly Buchberger	LW	6-0	188	12-2-66/Langenburg, Sask.	Nova Scotia	12	20	32	257
7	Paul Coffey	D	6-0	200	6-1-61/Weston, Ont.	Edmonton	17	50	67	49
	Murray Eaves	C	5-10	183	5-10-60/Calgary, Alta.	Nova Scotia	26	38	64	46
15	Steve Graves	LW	6-0	180	4-7-64/Ottawa, Ont.	Edmonton	2	0	2	0
						Nova Scotia	18	10	28	22
99	Wayne Gretzky	C	6-0	170	1-26-61/Brantford, Ont.	Edmonton	62	121	183	28
22	Charlie Huddy	D	5-11	204	6-2-59/Oshawa, Ont.	Edmonton	4	15	19	35
12	Dave Hunter	LW	5-11	195	1-1-58/Petrolia, Ont.	Edmonton	6	9	15	75
	Kim Issel	RW	6-4	184	9-25-67/Calgary, Alta.	Prince Albert	31	44	75	55
17	Jari Kurri	LW	6-0	190	5-18-60/Finland	Edmonton	54	54	108	41
26	Mike Krushelnyski	LW-C	6-2	200	4-27-70/Montreal, Que.	Edmonton	16	35	51	67
19	Norm Lacombe	RW	5-11	205	10-18-64/Pierrefonds, Que.	Buff.-Edm.	4	7	11	10
						Roch.N. Scotia	9	10	19	8
25	Moe Lemay	LW	5-11	187	2-18-62/Saskatoon, Sask.	Van.-Edm.	10	19	29	164
4	Kevin Lowe	D	6-2	195	4-15-59/Hawksbury, Ont.	Edmonton	8	29	37	94
14	Craig MacTavish	C	6-0	190	8-15-58/London, Ont.	Edmonton	20	19	39	55
24	Kevin McClelland	RW	6-0	180	7-4-62/Oshawa, Ont.	Edmonton	12	13	25	238
33	Marty McSorley	LW	6-1	185	5-18-63/Hamilton, Ont.	Edmonton	2	4	6	159
						Nova Scotia	2	2	4	48
11	Mark Messier	C	6-1	205	1-18-61/Edmonton, Alta.	Edmonton	37	70	107	73
28	Craig Muni	D	6-2	200	7-19-62/Toronto, Ont.	Edmonton	7	22	29	85
16	Selmar Odelein	D	6-3	195	4-11-66/Quill Lake, Sask.	Team Canada	–	–	–	–
	Jim Playfair	D	6-3	186	5-22-64/Vanderhoof, B.C.	Edmonton	2	3	5	6
						Nova Scotia	1	21	22	82
5	Steve Smith	D	6-2	200	4-30-63/Scotland	Edmonton	7	15	22	165
	Peter Soberlak	LW	6-2	185	5-12-69/Kamloops, B.C.	Swift Current	33	42	75	45
10	Esa Tikkanen	LW	5-11	185	1-25-64/Finland	Edmonton	34	44	78	120
	Alfie Turcotte	C	5-9	170	1-15-65/Gary, Ind.	Nova Scotia	27	41	68	37
8	Wayne Van Dorp	LW	6-5	225		Edmonton	0	0	0	25
						Roch.-N. Scotia	9	6	15	229
	Jim Wiemer	D	6-4	197	1-9-61/Sudbury, Ont.	N. Haven-N. Scotia	9	32	41	78

No.	Player	Pos.	Ht.	Wt.	Born		GP	GA	SO	Avg.
31	Grant Fuhr	G	5-10	185	9-28-62/Spruce Grove, Alta.	Edmonton	44	137	0	3.44
35	Andy Moog	G	5-9	170	2-18-60/Princeton, B.C.	Edmonton	46	144	0	3.51
32	Darryl Reaugh	G	6-4	200	2-13-65/Prince Albert, B.C.	Nova Scotia	46	168	1	3.72

... Wherever the game is played, he is a household word ... One of the world's most identifiable superstars ... Owns 41 NHL records ... Ranks fourth among all-time point leaders ... Should be No. 2, with Gordie Howe's all-time record of 1,850 points within reach, by the end of this season ... Had more assists than his nearest challenger—linemate Jari Kurri—had total points in 1986-87 ... Holds the NHL records for goals (92), assists (163) and points (215) in a single season ... The only NHL player who has collected more than 200 points in one season ... Has scored 40 hat tricks in the NHL ... Has won seven consecutive NHL scoring championships and has been named the league's MVP for the last eight years ... Born Jan. 26, 1961, in Brantford, Ont ... The highest-paid player in professional hockey, earning $1 million per year ... Once labelled as "too scrawny" by a former general manager ... A fear of flying threatens to shorten his career ... Played in the now-defunct World Hockey Association with the Indianapolis Racers, prior to joining the Oilers.

Year	Club	GP	G	A	Pts.
1978-79	Ind-Edm (WHA)	80	46	64	110
1979-80	Edmonton.........	79	51	86	137
1980-81	Edmonton.........	80	55	109	164
1981-82	Edmonton.........	80	92	120	212
1982-83	Edmonton.........	80	71	125	196
1983-84	Edmonton.........	74	87	118	205
1984-85	Edmonton.........	80	73	135	208
1985-86	Edmonton.........	80	52	163	215
1986-87	Edmonton.........	79	62	121	183
	NHL Totals	632	543	977	1520
	WHA Totals........	80	46	64	110

PAUL COFFEY 26 6-0 200   **Defenseman**
Knee and shoulder injuries interrupted 1986-87 season, preventing him from winning his third consecutive Norris Trophy as the NHL's top defenseman ... Outstanding skater who acts as the trailer on many rushes ... Rink-long rushes are his bag ... Holds the NHL records for goals (48) in a single season by a defenseman, breaking the mark set by Bobby Orr in 1974-75 ... Earned assists in 17 consecutive games in 1985-86 to set another NHL record for defensemen ... Born June 1, 1961, in Weston, Ont. ... Holds NHL playoff records for defensemen for points (6) in a single game, most assists (3) in one period, most goals (12) in a playoff year and most points (38) in a playoff year ... Articulate individual ... Has had his differences with coach Gien Sather

over his occasional disappearances on defense...A five-time NHL All-Star.

Year	Club	GP	G	A	Pts.
1980-81	Edmonton.........	74	9	23	32
1981-82	Edmonton.........	80	29	60	89
1982-83	Edmonton.........	80	29	67	96
1983-84	Edmonton.........	80	40	86	126
1984-85	Edmonton.........	80	37	84	121
1985-86	Edmonton.........	79	48	90	138
1986-87	Edmonton.........	59	17	50	67
	Totals	532	209	460	669

MARK MESSIER 26 6-1 205   Center

Considered by many to be the NHL's most complete player... Powerful individual who beats his opponents physically and artistically...A two-time All-Star (1982-83) as a left winger... Joined with Glenn Anderson and Kent Nilsson to form an awesome line in 1986-87...Prides himself as a playmaker...Torments goaltenders with his forays off right wing...Born Jan. 18, 1961, in Edmonton...The son of a former pro, Doug Messier...Brother-in-law is Boston defenseman John Blum...Turned pro as a 17-year-old with Indianapolis of the now-defunct WHA...Gives spell-binding speeches within the walls of the dressing room when the need arises.

Year	Club	GP	G	A	Pts.
1978-79	Ind-Cin (WHA)	52	1	10	11
1979-80	Edmonton.........	75	12	21	33
1980-81	Edmonton.........	72	23	40	63
1981-82	Edmonton.........	78	50	38	88
1982-83	Edmonton.........	77	48	58	106
1983-84	Edmonton.........	73	37	64	101
1984-85	Edmonton.........	55	23	31	54
1985-86	Edmonton.........	63	35	49	84
1986-87	Edmonton.........	77	37	70	107
	NHL Totals	570	265	371	636
	WHA Totals........	52	1	10	11

JARI KURRI 27 6-0 190   Right Wing

Noted as the perfect complement to the outstanding talents of Wayne Gretzky...Their act goes down as one of hockey's all-time best...Led the Oilers with 10 game-winning goals last season...First European to score more than 60 goals in the NHL and one of only three players in league history to have scored 70 goals in a single season...Scores on a high percentage of his shots...Born May 18, 1960, in Helsinki, Finland...A hero in his country... A first-team All-Star in 1984-85 and a second-team All-Star in 1983-84 and 1985-86... Won Lady Byng Trophy as the league's most gentlemanly player in 1984-85... The father of twin sons... An accomplished tennis player who has won a tournament for celebrities in Finland three times.

Year	Club	GP	G	A	Pts.
1980-81	Edmonton.........	75	32	43	75
1981-82	Edmonton.........	71	32	54	86
1982-83	Edmonton.........	80	45	59	104
1983-84	Edmonton.........	64	52	61	113
1984-85	Edmonton.........	73	71	64	135
1985-86	Edmonton.........	78	68	63	131
1986-87	Edmonton.........	79	54	54	108
	Totals	520	354	398	752

GLENN ANDERSON 27 5-11 175   Right Wing

Equally at home on the left or right side... Incredibly fast skater who, given lots of room, leaves his opponents standing still... A free spirit who excels under pressure... Scored two overtime goals during the 1986-87 regular season and had another in the playoffs... Scored the clinching goal and set up the first with a spectacular rush in the seventh game of the 1987 Stanley Cup final against Philadelphia... Upsets his opponents by carrying his stick a little high... Competed for the NHL in Rendez-Vous '87... Born Oct. 2, 1960, in Vancouver... Has scored 55 game-winning goals for the Oilers in his career. Only Gretzky has scored more... Competed for Canada in the 1980 Winter Olympics... Quotes Soviet center Alexander Maltsev as his boyhood idol.

Year	Club	GP	G	A	Pts.
1980-81	Edmonton.........	58	30	23	53
1981-82	Edmonton.........	80	38	67	105
1982-83	Edmonton.........	72	48	56	104
1983-84	Edmonton.........	80	54	45	99
1984-85	Edmonton.........	80	42	39	81
1985-86	Edmonton.........	72	54	48	102
1986-87	Edmonton.........	80	35	38	73
	Totals	522	301	316	617

GRANT FUHR 25 5-10 185   Goaltender

Wayne Gretzky calls him the greatest goaltender he's never faced ... Has played a major role in Oilers' three Stanley Cups and says he's planning on four or five more... Posted a 22-13-3 record in 1986-87... Always seems to be required to make three or four sensational saves to allow the Oilers to build a lead...

Relaxed during the 1987 Stanley Cup final by playing golf on his off days . . . Starred for the NHL against the Russians in Rendez-Vous series . . . Born in the Edmonton suburb of Spruce Grove on Sept. 28, 1962 . . . Became the first black goaltender in NHL history in 1981 . . . Named Player of the Game in the 1986 All-Star Game in Hartford . . . One of only two goaltenders in the NHL who was a first-round draft choice; the other is Tom Barrasso of the Sabres.

Year	Club	GP	GA	SO	Avg.
1981-82	Edmonton........	48	157	0	3.31
1982-83	Edmonton........	32	129	0	4.29
1983-84	Edmonton........	45	171	1	3.91
1984-85	Edmonton........	46	165	1	3.87
1985-86	Edmonton........	40	143	0	3.93
1986-87	Edmonton........	44	137	0	3.44
	Totals	255	902	2	3.76

CRAIG MacTAVISH 29 6-0 190   Center

Responded to the challenge of increased ice time as the Oilers resorted to a four-line system in 1986-87 . . . Softens his opponents with his intense forechecking . . . Loves to handle the puck and make creative plays . . . Usually has Dave Hunter and Marty McSorley as his wingers . . . Kills penalties and accounted for four shorthanded goals in 1986-87 . . . Missed the entire 1984-85 season while serving time for vehicular homicide . . . Signed as a free agent by the Oilers upon his release . . . Has dedicated his life to the social awareness of the evils of drinking and driving . . . Born Aug. 15, 1958, in London, Ont . . . A two-time ECAC All-Star at Lowell University . . . Grew up with Flyers' Brad Marsh and Doug Crossman on the south side of London . . . Skinny as a kid, he's developed into a rugged pro.

Year	Club	GP	G	A	Pts.
1979-80	Boston	46	11	17	28
1980-81	Boston	24	3	5	8
1981-82	Boston	2	0	1	1
1982-83	Boston	75	10	20	30
1983-84	Boston	70	20	23	43
1985-86	Edmonton.........	74	23	24	47
1986-87	Edmonton.........	79	20	19	39
	Totals	370	87	109	196

KEVIN LOWE 28 6-2 195   Defenseman

Considered by many to be the Oilers' best all-around defenseman . . . Throws a mean open-ice hit and keeps the front of the net clear . . . One of the most engaging and enlightening interviews in the NHL... The Oilers' first-ever draft choice, taken 21st overall in 1979... Played out his option in 1986-87, claiming, "It's a case of the U.S. dollar vs. the Canadian dollar and the U.S. tax system vs. the Canadian tax system."... Born April 15, 1959, in Lachute, Que.... Fluent in French and English... Has written a newspaper column and had his own radio show... His brother is a trainer with the Edmonton Eskimos of the Canadian Football League... An excellent cook.

Year	Club	GP	G	A	Pts.
1979-80	Edmonton	64	2	19	21
1980-81	Edmonton	79	10	24	34
1981-82	Edmonton	80	9	31	40
1982-83	Edmonton	80	6	34	40
1983-84	Edmonton	80	4	42	46
1984-85	Edmonton	80	4	22	26
1985-86	Edmonton	74	2	16	18
1986-87	Edmonton	77	8	29	37
	Totals	614	45	217	262

ESA TIKKANEN 22 5-11 185   Left Wing

Inherited the most coveted position in professional hockey when he joined Wayne Gretzky and Jari Kurri on the same line... Scored on 27 percent of his shots in 1986-87; only Ray Ferraro of Hartford had a better shooting percentage... Burly individual who does the line's heavy work in the attacking zone... Born Jan. 25, 1965, in Helsinki, Finland... Travelled extensively as a youth through his father's diplomatic postings... Spent a season with the Regina Blues of the Saskatchewan Junior League... Named a first team All-Star at the world junior championships in 1985.

Year	Club	GP	G	A	Pts.
1985-86	Edmonton	35	7	6	13
1986-87	Edmonton	76	34	44	78
	Totals	111	41	50	91

ANDY MOOG 27 5-9 170   Goaltender

Looks all of 19... Played out his option, saying he wants to be the No. 1 starter somewhere in the NHL... Displeased with only two starts—both wins—in the 1987 playoffs... Posted a 28-11-3 record in 1986-87... Only three goaltenders—Ron Hextall of

Philadelphia, Mike Liut of Hartford and Mike Vernon of Calgary
—had more wins... Once went 17 starts (14-0-3) without a loss
... Born Feb. 18, 1960, in Penticton, B.C.... Nickname is
"Peach"... Plays prominent role in Okanagan Hockey Schools in
the B.C. Interior.

Year	Club	GP	GA	SO	Avg.
1980-81	Edmonton........	7	20	0	3.83
1981-82	Edmonton........	8	32	0	4.81
1982-83	Edmonton........	50	167	1	3.54
1983-84	Edmonton........	38	139	1	3.77
1984-85	Edmonton........	39	111	1	3.30
1985-86	Edmonton........	47	164	1	3.69
1986-87	Edmonton........	46	144	0	3.51
	Totals	235	777	4	3.61

COACH GLEN SATHER: Always wears an impish smile and

drives officials crazy... Holds more titles than
any other coach in the NHL... Also the general manager and team president... Named
one of Canada's 10 sexiest men... Ranks
eighth among all-time coaches for series victories in the playoffs... Passed Punch Imlach
and Emile Francis with his 19th, 20th, 21st
and 22nd series victories in the 1987 playoffs
... Can be cute and cutting during interviews... Drew raves
from fellow coaches in 1986-87 for teaching his team how to play
defense... Born Sept. 2, 1943, in High River, Alta....
Perceptive individual with all sorts of theories... Blames "social-
ists" for everything from rules changes in the NHL to the snub
Wayne Gretzky received in fans' balloting for RendezVous...
Nickname is "Slats" because of the time he served sitting on the
bench as a player... His teams have recorded 364 wins in 640
games in the NHL... Named Coach of the Year in 1985-86, the
only season in the last four in which the Oilers did not win the
Stanley Cup.

GREATEST COACH

The person who displaces Glen Sather as the greatest coach in
the history of Edmonton Oilers will have to improve upon a

364-191-85 record, six first-place finishes overall and three Stanley Cups. Good luck!

Sather was hired as the Oilers' playing coach in the WHA on Jan. 27, 1977, succeeding Bep Guidolin. He'd started the season as a player following a career as a forward that began with Boston in 1966-67 and took him to Pittsburgh, New York (Rangers), St. Louis, Montreal, Minnesota and the last stop in Edmonton.

A disciple of Sammy Pollock, then the Canadiens' storied general manager, Sather was recommended as having coaching potential by Pollock and Emile Francis, then coach and general manager of the St. Louis Blues.

He surrounds himself with a solid support system that includes John Muckler, Ted Green, Barry Fraser and Bruce MacGregor.

ALL-TIME OILER LEADERS

GOALS: Wayne Gretzky, 92, 1981-82
ASSISTS: Wayne Gretzky, 163, 1985-86
POINTS: Wayne Gretzky, 215, 1985-86
SHUTOUTS: Andy Moog, 2, 1985-86

LOS ANGELES KINGS

TEAM DIRECTORY: Owner: Dr. Jerry Buss; Pres.: Lou Baumeister; GM: Rogie Vachon; Dir. Pub. Rel.: David Courtney; Coach: Mike Murphy. Home ice: The Forum (16,005; 200' × 85'). Colors: Purple and gold. Training camp: Victoria, B.C.

SCOUTING REPORT

OFFENSE: The Kings are stirring, thanks to a coterie of restless kids. In one year, they have unearthed a 45-goal left winger, Luc Robitaille; a 79-point center, Jimmy Carson; a former 50-goal scorer, Bobby Carpenter, 24; and two quality defensemen, Tom Laidlaw and Steve Duchesne.

The total cost: Marcel Dionne, a 36-year-old center now with the Rangers.

Good drafting produced Robitaille, Carson and Duchesne, half the members of the NHL's 1987 All-Rookie team.

Add the likes of Bernie Nicholls, Dave Taylor, Jimmy Fox and Butsy Erickson, plus a couple of hard-shooting defensemen such as Grant Ledyard and Jay Wells, and it becomes apparent that the Kings are going to score a ton of goals.

A contributing factor, too, could be the Kings' power play, the NHL's third best in 1986-87. Among them, Carson, Robitaille and Nicholls had 46 power-play goals.

DEFENSE: The only team that picked more goals out of its net than the Kings last season was the New Jersey Devils. Clearly, there were many nights when Robitaille, Carson, Taylor and Nicholls couldn't score often enough to keep up to the number of goals they were giving up.

Defensively, Ledyard is scary. His −40 was appalling. Mark Hardy, Dean Kennedy, Laidlaw, Wells and Duchesne are solid, but, as is the rule in hockey, they are nothing without some help from the forwards.

Most importantly, measures are being taken to improve the Kings' defense. Their first-round selection in the 1987 draft was Wayne McBean, a 6-2, 200-pound defenseman, the third pick overall. Some scouts considered him the best player available in the draft.

Among all their discoveries last season the Kings found a starting goaltender. Roland Melanson produced points in 53.5 percent of his starts, reeling off 18 wins and six ties in 45 decisions.

Luc Robitaille netted 45 goals for L.A. in rookie season.

OUTLOOK: The Kings—under Mike Murphy—should tighten up the Smythe Division standings. Third place would seem attainable at the expense of either Calgary or Winnipeg, providing they can tighten up defensively and come up with a better penalty-killing unit.

KING ROSTER

No.	Player	Pos.	Ht.	Wt.	Born	1986–87	G	A	Pts.	PIM
14	Bob Bourne	C	6-3	202	6-11-54/Kindersley, Sask.	Los Angeles	13	9	22	35
21	Bob Carpenter	C	6-1	190	7-13-63/Beverley, Mass.	Wash.-Rang.-LA	9	18	27	47
17	Jimmy Carson	C	6-0	185	7-20-68/Detroit, Mich.	Los Angeles	37	42	79	22
	Glen Currie	C	6-2	180	7-18-58/Montreal, Que.	New Haven	12	16	28	16
25	Pete Dineen	D	5-11	180	11-19-60/Kingston, Ont.	Los Angeles	0	2	2	8
						New Haven	2	17	19	140
28	Steve Duchesne	D	5-11	190	6-30-65/Sept. Isles, Que.	Los Angeles	13	25	38	74
32	Craig Duncanson	LW	6-0	190	3-17-67/Haughton, Ont.	Los Angeles	0	0	0	24
						Cornwall	22	45	67	88
15	Bryan Erickson	LW	5-9	170	3-7-60/Roseau, Minn.	Los Angeles	20	30	50	26
19	Jim Fox	RW	5-8	185	5-18-60/Comiston, Ont.	Los Angeles	19	42	61	48
	Dan Gratton	C	6-1	184	12-7-66/Brantford, Ont.	New Haven	6	10	16	45
8	Paul Guay	RW	6-0	193	9-2-63/N. Smithfield, R.I.	Los Angeles	2	5	7	16
						New Haven	1	3	4	11
	Ken Hammond	D	6-1	190	8-22-63/Port Credit, Ont.	Los Angeles	0	2	2	11
						New Haven	1	15	16	76
5	Mark Hardy	D	5-11	195	2-1-59/Switzerland	Los Angeles	3	27	30	120
6	Dean Kennedy	D	6-2	196	1-18-63/Redver, Sask.	Los Angeles	6	14	20	91
3	Tom Laidlaw	D	6-2	215	4-15-58/Brampton, Ont.	Rang.-LA	1	13	14	69
4	Grant Ledyard	D	6-2	190	11-15-61/Winnipeg, Man.	Los Angeles	14	23	37	93
12	Morris Lukowich	RW	5-9	175	6-1-56/Speers, Sask.	Los Angeles	14	21	35	64
	Wayne McBean	D	6-2	190	2-21-69/Calgary, Alta.	Medicine Hat	12	41	53	163
10	Sean McKenna	C	6-0	186	3-17-62/Asbestoes, Que.	Los Angeles	14	19	33	10
	Chris McSorley		5-11	185	3-22-62/Hamilton, Ont.	Muskegon	18	17	35	293
						New Haven	2	2	4	116
9	Bernie Nicholls	C	6-0	185	6-24-61/Haliburton, Ont.	Los Angeles	33	48	81	101
27	Joe Paterson	LW-C	6-1	208	6-25-60/Calgary, Alta.	Los Angeles	2	1	3	158
11	Lyle Phair	LW	5-11	195	3-8-61/Pilot Mound, Man.	Los Angeles	2	0	2	2
						New Haven	19	27	46	77
23	Larry Playfair	D	6-4	202	6-23-58/Calgary, Alta.	Los Angeles	2	7	9	181
2	Craig Redmond	D	5-10	190	9-22-65/Langley, B.C.	Los Angeles	1	7	8	8
						New Haven	2	2	4	6
20	Luc Robitaille	LW	6-0	178	2-17-56/Montreal, Que.	Los Angeles	45	39	84	28
7	Phil Sykes	LW	6-0	178	5-18-59/Dawson Creek, B.C.	Los Angeles	6	15	21	133
18	Dave Taylor	RW	6-0	190	12-4-55/Sudbury, Ont.	Los Angeles	18	44	62	84
24	Jay Wells	D	6-1	210	5-18-59/Paris, Ont.	Los Angeles	7	29	36	155
26	Brian Wilks	C	5-11	175	2-27-66/N. York, Ont.	Los Angeles	0	0	0	0
						New Haven	16	20	36	23
22	Tiger Williams	LW	5-11	190	2-3-54/Weyburn, Sask.	Los Angeles	16	18	34	358

							GP	GA	SO	Avg.
	Mark Fitzpatrick	G	6-1	195	11-13-68/Kitimat, B.C.	Medicine Hat	50	159	4	3.35
	Glen Healy	G	5-9	183	8-23-62/Pickering, Ont.	New Haven	47	173	1	3.67
1	Bob Janecyk	G	6-1	180	5-18-57/Chicago, Ill.	Los Angeles	7	34	0	4.86
29	Al Jensen	G	5-10	180	11-27-58/Hamilton, Ont.	Washington-LA	11	54	0	5.19
						Binghamton	13	42	0	3.68
30	Roland Melanson	G	5-10	180	6-28-60/Moncton, N.B.	Los Angeles	46	168	1	3.69

KING PROFILES

LUC ROBITAILLE 21 6-0 178   **Left Wing**
The choice of many as Rookie of the Year in 1986-87 ... Waged
a season-long battle with Philadelphia goalie Ron Hextall for the
attention of voters ... Hit Los Angeles like a breath of fresh air
... A new crown jewel ... Could be the NHL's best left winger
already ... Led the Kings in goals (45), points (84), and power-
play goals (18) ... Set club records for goals and points by a
rookie ... Born Feb. 17, 1966, in Montreal, Que. ... A ninth-
round draft choice (171st overall) in 1984 ... Became Canada's
top junior in 1985-86 with 68 goals and 123 assists at Hull,
Que. ... Taken under Marcel Dionne's wing in Los Angeles ...
Was "orphaned" when Dionne was traded to the Rangers, but
fared even better.

Year	Club	GP	G	A	Pts.
1986-87	Los Angeles	79	45	39	84

JIMMY CARSON 19 6-0 185   **Center**
The NHL's youngest player in 1986-87 ... Selected to the NHL's
All-Rookie team ... Played so well the Kings decided the time
had come to trade Marcel Dionne ... Caused a hometown crowd
of 16,053 in Detroit to cheer for him as he scored two goals and
assisted on another in leading the Kings to a 4-3 win over the Red
Wings ... Born July 20, 1968, in Southfield, Mich., a suburb of
Detroit ... His father owned a parking lot outside of the old
Olympia ... Of Greek ancestry, his Grandfather changed the
family's name from Kyriazopoulos to Carson.

Year	Club	GP	G	A	Pts.
1986-87	Los Angeles	80	37	42	79

BERNIE NICHOLLS 26 6-0 185   Center

Assumes the No. 1 center slot since the trade that sent Marcel Dionne to New York... Despite all the distractions of Los Angeles, he's forged a good career in the NHL... The Kings' top playmaker in 1986-87 with 48 assists... Plays some of his best hockey in the clutch... When scoring chances are needed most, he finds a way to create one or two... Born June 24, 1961, in Haliburton, Ont.... Holds the Kings' club record for the longest points streak—25 games, Oct. 16, 1984, until Dec. 10, 1984 ... Had 21 goals and 19 assists in that streak, the fourth-longest in NHL history... One of five children... Father is a trapper ... Enjoys horse racing.

Year	Club	GP	G	A	Pts.
1981-82	Los Angeles	22	14	18	32
1982-83	Los Angeles	71	28	22	50
1983-84	Los Angeles	78	41	54	95
1984-85	Los Angeles	80	46	54	100
1985-86	Los Angeles	80	36	61	97
1986-87	Los Angeles	80	33	48	81
	Totals	411	198	257	455

DAVE TAYLOR 31 6-0 190   Right Wing

The sole survivor of the Triple Crown Line, once the most productive in the NHL... Spent seven seasons on the line with Marcel Dionne and Charlie Simmer... Adopted a new center, Jimmy Carson, in 1986-87... Second among Kings' all-time scorers ... Holds the club record for most goals (47), assists (65) and points (112) by a right winger in a single season... Born Dec. 4, 1955, in Levack, Ont.... A fluke in the draft... Wasn't taken until the 15th round (210th overall) in 1975... A former All-American at Clarkson in 1976-77... Bothered by a knee injury in 1986-87... Has suffered two broken wrists in his career... Plays the game hard... Nickname is "Stitch".

Year	Club	GP	G	A	Pts.
1977-78	Los Angeles	64	22	21	43
1978-79	Los Angeles	78	43	48	91
1979-80	Los Angeles	61	37	53	90
1980-81	Los Angeles	72	47	65	112
1981-82	Los Angeles	78	39	67	106
1982-83	Los Angeles	46	21	37	58
1983-84	Los Angeles	63	20	49	69
1984-85	Los Angeles	79	41	51	92
1985-86	Los Angeles	76	33	38	71
1986-87	Los Angeles	67	18	44	62
	Totals	684	321	473	794

BRYAN ERICKSON 27 5-9 170 **Right Wing**

Became a principal player in 1986-87 . . . Handled the right side on a line with Luc Robitaille and Marcel Dionne, then Bob Carpenter . . . A digger who stays on top of defenders in the attacking zone . . . Short in stature but long in enthusiasm . . . "Butsy" led the Kings in game-winning goals (4) in 1986-87 . . . Born March 7, 1960, in Roseau, Minn., the same hometown as the Broten brothers, Neal and Aaron . . . A student of Dave Taylor's style of play . . . A former WCHA All-Star with the University of Minnesota . . . Acquired from Washington for a defenseman, Bruce Shoebottom, on Oct. 31, 1985 . . . Competed for the U.S. in the 1987 world hockey championships in Vienna.

Year	Club	GP	G	A	Pts.
1983-84	Washington	45	12	17	29
1984-85	Washington	57	15	13	28
1985-86	Los Angeles	55	20	23	43
1986-87	Los Angeles	68	20	30	50
	Totals	225	67	83	150

BOB CARPENTER 24 6-1 190 **Center**

A newsmaker, if nothing else, in 1986-87 . . . Traded twice in the same year after staging a strike in Washington . . . Sent to the Rangers in a 3-for-1 swap, then exiled to Los Angeles, where he shouldn't be such an issue . . . Acquired from the Rangers along with defenseman Tom Laidlaw for Marcel Dionne . . . Seems haunted by his one great season . . . Washington coach Bryan Murray said he lost it with the Caps when he stopped playing in traffic . . . Born July 13, 1963, in Beverly, Mass. . . . Made the jump from high school (St. John's Prep of Danvers, Mass.) hockey to the NHL as an 18-year-old . . . Selected in the first round (third overall) by the Caps in 1981 . . . Until then, no American had been drafted as high.

Year	Club	GP	G	A	Pts.
1981-82	Washington	80	32	35	67
1982-83	Washington	80	32	37	69
1983-84	Washington	80	28	40	68
1984-85	Washington	80	53	42	95
1985-86	Washington	80	27	29	56
1986-87	Wash-NYR-LA	60	9	18	27
	Totals	460	181	201	382

DAVE WILLIAMS 33 5-11 190 **Left Wing**

A controversial individual who never spares the words or the actions that immediately come to mind . . . Three incidents were the highlights of his most penalty-prone season (1986-87)... A blind-side hit on Randy Carlyle wrenched his neck and drew the wrath of the Jets, who launched a "Tiger Hunt"; the Canucks claimed he speared Stan Smyl near the eye, and Detroit accused him of head-butting Gerard Gallant... Nosed out Tim Hunter of Calgary Flames and Brian Curran of New York Islanders by one and two minutes, respectively, as the NHL's most-penalized player in 1986-87... Born Feb. 3, 1954, in Weyburn, Sask.... Bears the lumps and scars of numerous feuds over 934 games.

Year	Club	GP	G	A	Pts.
1974-75	Toronto	42	10	19	29
1975-76	Toronto	78	21	19	40
1976-77	Toronto	77	18	25	43
1977-78	Toronto	78	19	31	50
1978-79	Toronto	77	19	20	39
1979-80	Tor–Van	78	30	23	53
1980-81	Vancouver	77	35	27	62
1981-82	Vancouver	77	17	21	38
1982-83	Vancouver	68	8	13	21
1983-84	Vancouver	67	15	16	31
1984-85	Det-LA	67	7	11	18
1985-86	Los Angeles	72	20	29	49
1986-87	Los Angeles	76	16	18	34
	Totals	934	235	272	507

STEVE DUCHESNE 22 5-11 190   Defenseman

One of three outstanding rookies introduced by the Kings in 1986-87... Paled by the media coverage Luc Robitaille and Jimmy Carson received... Deserved serious consideration to the NHL's All-Rookie team... Handled himself with remarkable composure for a first-year player... Played a regular shift from the first days of training camp... Born June 30, 1965, in Sept-Iles, Que.... Never drafted, he was signed as a free agent by general manager Rogie Vachon... One of only five Kings who had a plus rating (plus-8).

Year	Club	GP	G	A	Pts.
1986-87	Los Angeles	75	13	25	38

JAY WELLS 28 6-1 210   Defenseman

Scored all of his goals in the first 40 games in 1986-87... Rugged sort who commands respect... Most effective when he's mean... Plays the power-play on which the Kings take advantage of his heavy shot . . . Missed three games in 1986-87 when struck in the eye with a shot . . . Born May 18, 1959, in Paris, Ont., where his family has a farm . . . Collects antiques . . . Nickname is "Jaybird" . . . Lives only two minutes from the beach in El Segundo, Calif. . . . Collects old John Wayne movies.

Year	Club	GP	G	A	Pts.
1979-80	Los Angeles	43	0	0	0
1980-81	Los Angeles	72	5	13	18
1981-82	Los Angeles	60	1	8	9
1982-83	Los Angeles	69	3	12	15
1983-84	Los Angeles	69	3	18	21
1984-85	Los Angeles	77	2	9	11
1985-86	Los Angeles	79	11	31	42
1986-87	Los Angeles	77	7	29	36
	Totals	546	32	120	152

ROLAND MELANSON 27 5-10 180   Goaltender

Clearly established himself as the Kings' No. 1 goaltender in the second half of 1986-87 . . . Posted an 18-21-6 record for a team that finished 10 games under .500 . . . A second-team All-Star and co-holder of the William Jennings Trophy with Billy Smith in 1982-83 . . . Recorded his second NHL shutout on Jan. 14, 1987, beating Vancouver, 4-0 . . . Born June 28, 1960, in Moncton, N.B. . . . Aspires for a career in business in life after hockey . . . Has sold cars for Chrysler in offseason . . . Missed three games with food poisoning and set a team record for goaltenders with six assists in 1986-87.

Year	Club	GP	GA	SO	Avg.
1980-81	New York I	11	32	0	3.10
1981-82	New York I	36	114	0	3.23
1982-83	New York I	44	109	1	2.66
1983-84	New York I	37	110	0	3.27
1984-85	NYI-Minn.	28	113	0	4.33
1985-86	Minn-LA	28	111	0	4.24
1986-87	Los Angeles	46	168	1	3.69
	Totals	230	757	2	3.47

COACH MIKE MURPHY: Entering his 14th season with the Kings . . . Appointed coach early in 1987 under bizarre circumstances . . . He inherited the job when his predecessor, Pat Quinn, was suspended by the NHL for accepting money from another team (Vancouver) in anticipation of becoming their general manager . . . Most personable individual . . . Sincere and honest . . . A great believer in the benefits of defensive hockey . . . Availed himself as a close-checking, low-scoring forward in a 12-year playing career that netted 194 goals and 262 assists in 673 games . . . A feared fighter in his time . . . Felt he was ready to coach in the NHL after working as Quinn's assistant for two seasons, little realizing the Los Angeles job would be his.

GREATEST COACH

The five seasons Bob Pulford spent behind the Kings' bench will long be remembered in Los Angeles. Hired in 1972, he promptly brought respectability to a franchise that had struggled from its start five years earlier. He posted an overall record of 178-150-68 for a winning percentage of .535, with the most notable year 1974-75, when the Kings put together a 42-17-21 record for 105 points, by far a club record.

Pulford's Los Angeles teams played tight, defensive hockey, relying on the superb goaltending of Rogie Vachon and the modest outputs of such players as Butch Goring, Juha Widing and Bob Nevin. An inordinate number of his players became coaches and general managers in the NHL, among them Vachon, Bob Berry, Mike Murphy, Bob Murdoch, Dan Maloney and Goring.

On and off a coach of the Blackhawks since the late 1970s, Pulford today is Chicago's general manager.

ALL-TIME KING LEADERS

GOALS: Marcel Dionne, 59, 1978-79
ASSISTS: Marcel Dionne, 84, 1979-80
POINTS: Marcel Dionne, 137, 1979-80
SHUTOUTS: Rogatien Vachon, 8, 1976-77

MINNESOTA NORTH STARS

TEAM DIRECTORY: Co-Chairmen: George Gund III and Gordon Gund; Pres.: John Karr; GM: Lou Nanne; Dir. Media Info.: Dick Dillman; Coach: Herb Brooks. Home ice: Met Center (15,499, 200′ × 85′). Colors: Green, white, gold and black. Training camp: Bloomington, Minn.

Neal Broten had 53 points in just 46 games for Minnesota.

SCOUTING REPORT

OFFENSE: It's hard to imagine, but the highest-scoring team in the Norris Division last season failed to make the playoffs. The North Stars scored more goals than the Hartford Whalers, the Adams Division champions, but they couldn't catch a playoff spot in the NHL's weakest division.

Herb Brooks becomes the North Stars' 14th coach in 20 seasons and, by the time No. 15 is hired, he'll have left his mark on the team. If anything, the team will be scoring even more goals . . . perhaps even more than it allows, which would be novel.

Dino Ciccarelli, Neal Broten, Craig Hartsburg, Brian Bellows and Brian Lawton should enjoy playing hockey Herb's way. The season will be one long skating party.

He'll find room for smaller centers such as Dennis Maruk and Keith Acton by using free agent Basil McRae and Willi Plett in assertive roles. McRae's presence should rejuvenate Plett.

But the North Stars are drifting toward sizeable centers again. Bob Brooke is one. Another is Dave Archibald, their first-round draft choice and a clone of Jean Ratelle.

Terry Ruskowski, 32, who signed as a free-agent Penguin, could make a contribution in what figures as his final campaign.

DEFENSE: Here's the rub. This team gave up far too many goals, due to forwards who couldn't give a damn about back-checking, inconsistent goaltending and defensemen who are either too inexperienced, too old or too deep over their heads.

Frantisek Musil is a burly Czech and Jari Gronstrand is a tall Finn, and both are a lot wiser after their rookie year. Bob Rouse is improving every year and Paul Boutilier has good seasons ahead of him.

Gord Roberts, 30, has some hard years on him, as has Ron Wilson, 32. Brad Maxwell, 30, wore out welcomes in Quebec City, Toronto and Vancouver prior to coming back.

On the positive side, the oft-injured Craig Hartsburg has responded with his most productive year since 1982-83, showing all the stickhandling and skating skills that were so badly missed for two seasons.

In goal, neither Don Beaupre nor Kari Takko has treated the North Stars to particularly brilliant evenings without leaving a few bummers, too. Takko may be taking over.

OUTLOOK: No one in the world is better suited for the Minnesota coaching job than Brooks. Undyingly faithful to his home state, he has been cast in the role of a redeemer, someone who

NORTH STAR ROSTER

No.	Player	Pos.	Ht.	Wt.	Born	1986–87	G	A	Pts.	PIM
12	Keith Acton	C	5-8	167	4-13-58/Peterborough, Ont.	Minnesota	16	29	45	56
	Dave Archibald	C	6-1	190	4-14-69/Chilliwack, B.C.	Portland	50	57	107	40
23	Brian Bellows	RW	5-11	195	9-1-64/St. Catharines, Ont.	Minnesota	26	27	53	34
	Todd Bergen	LW	6-3	190	7-11-63/Prince Albert, Sask.	Springfield	12	11	23	14
14	Scott Bjugstad	C	6-1	185	6-2-61/New Brighton, Minn.	Minnesota	4	9	13	43
						Springfield	6	4	10	7
13	Bob Brooke	LW	6-2	205	12-28-60/Melrose, Mass.	Rang.-Minn.	13	23	36	98
7	Neil Broten	C	5-9	169	11-29-59/Roseau, Minn.	Minnesota	18	35	53	35
	Colin Chisholm	D	6-2	185	3-18-66/Minneapolis, Minn.	Minnesota	0	0	0	0
						Springfield	1	11	12	141
20	Dino Ciccarelli	C	5-10	180	2-8-60/Sarnia, Ont.	Minnesota	52	51	103	92
29	Tim Coulis	LW	6-0	200	2-24-58/Kenora, Ont.	Springfield	12	19	31	212
31	Larry DePalma	LW	6-0	180	10-27-65/Trenton, Mich.	Minnesota	9	6	15	219
						Springfield	2	2	4	82
21	Dirk Graham	RW	5-11	190	7-29-59/Regina, Sask.	Minnesota	25	29	54	142
5	Jari Gronstrand	D	6-3	197	11-14-62/Tampere, Fin.	Minnesota	1	6	7	27
	Marc Habscheid	C	5-11	169	3-1-63/Swift Current, Sask.	Minnesota	2	0	2	2
28	Mats Hallin	RW	6-2	205	3-19-58/Sweden	Minnesota	0	0	0	4
4	Craig Hartsburg	D	6-1	193	6-29-59/Stratford, Ont.	Minnesota	11	50	61	93
15	Raimo Helminen	C	6-0	185	3-11-64/Finland	Rang.-Minn.	2	5	7	2
						New Haven	0	2	2	0
	Tom Hirsch	D	6-4	210	1-27-63/Minneapolis, Minn.	Injured—Did Not Play				
37	Paul Houck	RW	5-11	185	8-12-63/N. Vancouver, B.C.	Minnesota	0	2	2	2
98	Brian Lawton	C	6-0	173	6-29-65/New Brunswick, N.J.	Minnesota	21	23	44	86
27	Brian MacLellan	LW	6-3	212	10-27-58/Guelph, Ont.	Minnesota	32	31	63	69
9	Dennis Maruk	C	5-8	165	11-17-55/Toronto, Ont.	Minnesota	16	30	46	50
55	Brian Maxwell	D	6-2	197	7-7-57/Brandon, Man.	Van.-Rang.-Minn.	3	18	21	65
	Basil McRae	LW	6-2	205	1-5-61/Beaverton, Ont.	Det.-Que.	11	7	18	342
6	Frantisek Musil	D	6-3	205	12-17-64/Czechoslovakia	Minnesota	2	9	11	148
16	Mark Pavelich	C	5-8	170	2-28-56/Eveleth, Minn.	Minnesota	4	6	10	10
44	Steve Payne	LW	6-2	205	9-16-58/Toronto, Ont.	Minnesota	4	6	10	19
24	Willi Plett	RW	6-3	205	6-7-55/Paraguay	Minnesota	6	5	11	263
36	Chris Pryor	D	6-0	200	1-23-61/St. Paul, Minn.	Minnesota	1	3	4	49
						Springfield	0	2	2	17
10	Gordie Roberts	D	6-0	195	10-2-57/Detroit, Mich.	Minnesota	3	10	13	68
3	Bob Rouse	D	6-2	212	6-19-64/Surrey, B.C.	Minnesota	2	10	12	179
8	Terry Ruskowski	C	5-9	183	12-31-54/Prince Albert, Sask.	Pittsburgh	14	37	51	147
32	Randy Smith	C	6-3	175	7-7-65/Saskatoon, Sask.	Springfield	20	44	64	24
11	Sean Toomey	LW	6-2	190	6-27-65/St. Paul, Minn.	Minnesota	0	0	0	0
18	Emanuel Viveiros	D	5-11	175	1-8-66/St. Albert, Alta.	Minnesota	0	1	1	0
						Springfield	7	35	42	38
2	Ron Wilson	D	5-10	170	5-28-55/Windsor, Ont.	Minnesota	12	29	41	36

No.	Player	Pos.	Ht.	Wt.	Born	1986–87	GP	GA	SO	Avg.
33	Don Beaupre	G	5-8	162	9-19-61/Waterloo, Ont.	Minnesota	47	174	1	3.98
30	Jon Casey	G	5-9	155	8-29-62/Grand Rapids, Minn.	Springfield	13	56	0	4.36
35	Mike Sands	G	5-9	150	4-6-53/Sudbury, Ont.	Minnesota	3	12	0	4.42
						Springfield	19	77	0	4.41
1	Kari Takko	G	6-2	182	6-23-63/Finland	Minnesota	38	119	0	3.44
						Springfield	5	16	1	3.20

will restore the franchise's dignity. One can expect a more entertaining, harder-working team than the one that missed the playoffs last spring, yet finished only nine points out of first place.

NORTH STAR PROFILES

DINO CICCARELLI 27 5-10 180   Right Wing
To many, 1986-87 was his best . . . Proved he could maintain high standards despite missing his center, Neal Broten, for 34 games . . . Led his team in goals (52), assists (51), points (103), power-play goals (22), game-tying goals (3) and shots (255) . . . Finished sixth overall in NHL scoring race . . . Scored goals—10 of them —in six consecutive games in October 1986 . . . Notched the 13th hat trick of his career on Nov. 26, 1986, in Minnesota's 5-2 win over Chicago . . . Holds the club record for goals (55) in a single season (1981-82) and has the NHL record for goals (14) by a rookie in the Stanley Cup playoffs (1981) . . . Born Feb. 8, 1960, in Sarnia, Ont. . . . Never drafted, but signed as a free agent by GM Lou Nanne in what has turned out to be the best move he ever made . . . Scouts lost interest in him after he suffered a broken leg in his final year of junior . . . Skated with a metal rod in his leg for one season and kept it as a souvenir . . . Left off NHL's Rendez-Vous '87 team amid much hollering . . . Invited to play for Team Canada in 1987 Canada Cup.

Year	Club	GP	G	A	Pts.
1980-81	Minnesota	32	18	12	30
1981-82	Minnesota	76	55	52	107
1982-83	Minnesota	77	37	38	75
1983-84	Minnesota	79	38	33	71
1984-85	Minnesota	51	15	17	32
1985-86	Minnesota	75	44	45	89
1986-87	Minnesota	80	52	51	103
	Totals	470	259	248	507

NEAL BROTEN 27 5-9 169   Center
Two shoulder separations caused him much grief and hurt the team immeasurably . . . Regarded as the North Stars' best player . . . Skilled playmaker and tenacious forechecker . . . Holds the team record for assists (76) in a single season (1985-86) . . . Scored in overtime to beat Toronto, 6-5, on Dec. 18, 1986, and added a hat trick in a 5-4 loss to Winnipeg eight days later . . . Born Nov. 29, 1959, in Roseau, Minn. . . . Starred for Roseau in two state high-school tournaments . . . The 1981 recipient of the

Hobey Baker Award as the top college player in the U.S. . . . An All-American at the University of Minnesota . . . A member of the gold-medal U.S. team at the 1980 Winter Olympics in Lake Placid, N.Y. . . . Younger brother, Aaron, is a member of the New Jersey Devils . . . Never played a game in the minors.

Year	Club	GP	G	A	Pts.
1980-81	Minnesota.........	3	2	0	2
1981-82	Minnesota.........	73	38	59	97
1982-83	Minnesota.........	79	32	45	77
1983-84	Minnesota.........	76	28	61	89
1984-85	Minnesota.........	80	19	37	56
1985-86	Minnesota.........	80	29	76	105
1986-87	Minnesota.........	46	18	35	53
	Totals	437	166	313	479

CRAIG HARTSBURG 28 6-1 195   Defenseman

Received a glowing compliment in Vienna, Austria, of all places, when he was named the MVP—playing for Canada—in the 1987 world hockey championships . . . A key performer in Minnesota's game plan . . . Tempered his style, slightly, to reduce the risk of another serious injury . . . Missed virtually two complete seasons with knee and hip injuries . . . Finished seventh among the NHL's highest-scoring defensemen in 1986-87 . . . The 11th team captain in the history of the franchise . . . Born June 29, 1959, in Stratford, Ont. . . . Collected points in 11 consecutive games, Nov. 22 to Dec. 15, 1986 . . . Holds club records for assists (60) and points (77) by a defenseman in a single season . . . One of the few remaining players in the NHL who once played in the World Hockey Association.

Year	Club	GP	G	A	Pts.
1978-79	Birmingham (WHA) .	77	9	40	49
1979-80	Minnesota.........	79	14	30	44
1980-81	Minnesota.........	74	13	30	43
1981-82	Minnesota.........	76	17	60	77
1982-83	Minnesota.........	78	12	50	62
1983-84	Minnesota.........	26	7	7	14
1984-85	Minnesota.........	32	7	11	18
1985-86	Minnesota.........	75	10	47	57
1986-87	Minnesota.........	73	11	50	61
	NHL Totals	513	91	285	376
	WHA Totals........	77	9	40	49

BRIAN MacLELLAN 29 6-3 212   Left Wing

Rewarded the North Stars with 13 power-play goals and five game-winners in his career-high total of 32 . . . Ranked No. 2 in team scoring . . . A big man who plays lighter than he is . . . Uses his strength more than his nerve to get where he wants... Looks like a matinee idol... Well-spoken and educated, he spent four years at Bowling Green... Born Oct. 17, 1958, in Guelph, Ont. ... Signed as a free agent by Los Angeles Kings, who considered him another Dave Taylor... As a boy, he contracted Legges Perches and was told he might never walk correctly... As a junior, he sustained a broken neck while playing hockey... Traded to Minnesota by the New York Rangers for North Stars' fifth-round draft choice (Michael Sullivan) in 1987.

Year	Club	GP	G	A	Pts.
1982-83	Los Angeles	8	0	3	3
1983-84	Los Angeles	72	25	29	54
1984-85	Los Angeles	80	31	54	85
1985-86	LA-NYR	78	16	29	45
1986-87	Minnesota.........	76	32	31	63
	Totals	314	104	146	250

BRIAN LAWTON 22 6-0 173　　　　　　　　　　**Center**
The only American who has ever been taken first overall in the NHL's entry draft... Came out of a Rhode Island high school, Mount St. Charles, to play in the NHL in 1983... Some will say he was rushed... Couldn't see eye to eye with coach Lorne Henning, prior to latter's dismissal... Still, he should respond to Herb Brooks' modern techniques... Born June 29, 1965, in New Brunswick, N.J.... Selected as Rhode Island High School Athlete of the Year by *USA Today* in 1983... Seems to gain greater pleasure from a nice pass leading to a goal rather than scoring it himself... Recorded his second NHL hat trick on March 15, 1987, in North Stars' 4-2 win over Chicago.

Year	Club	GP	G	A	Pts.
1983-84	Minnesota.........	58	10	21	31
1984-85	Minnesota.........	40	5	6	11
1985-86	Minnesota.........	65	18	17	35
1986-87	Minnesota.........	66	21	23	44
	Totals	229	54	67	121

BRIAN BELLOWS 23 5-11 195　　　　　　　　　**Right Wing**
Captain of the faction of players that Lorne Henning divorced himself from... What hurt him most—a wrist injury or Henning—is not clear... A grinding style of forward who has averaged

almost a point per game . . . Nobody is satisfied they have seen
the best of him yet . . . Interim captain of the team in 1983-84
when Craig Hartsburg went down with an injury . . . Born
Sept. 1, 1964, in St. Catharines, Ont. . . . Led his junior team,
Kitchener Rangers, to the Memorial Cup in 1981 . . . Selected
second overall in the 1982 draft . . . Gord Kluzak of Boston
Bruins was the only player taken ahead of him . . . Holds the
North Stars' record for consecutive games (20) with one or more
points.

Year	Club	GP	G	A	Pts.
1982-83	Minnesota	78	35	30	65
1983-84	Minnesota	78	41	42	83
1984-85	Minnesota	78	26	36	62
1985-86	Minnesota	77	31	48	79
1986-87	Minnesota	65	26	27	53
	Totals	376	159	183	342

DON BEAUPRE 26 5-8 162   Goaltender

Plagued by a lack of consistency . . . Hot or cold . . . Once reeled
off 14 wins in a row, three short of the NHL record . . . Appeared
in 47 games in 1986-87, compiling a 17-20-6 record . . .
Recorded the third shutout of his career in a 5-0 win over Buffalo
on Jan. 20, 1987 . . . "Bobo" splits starts with Kari Takko, a Finn
. . . Small but combative when annoyed . . . A reflex goaltender
. . . Born Sept. 19, 1961, in Kitchener, Ont. . . . Started for the
Campbell Conference in the 1981 All-Star Game in Los Angeles
. . . Named the *Hockey News'* Comeback Player of the Year in
1986 after posting a 25-20-6 record, infinitely better than the
previous season's 10-17-3 . . . A pro wrestling buff.

Year	Club	GP	GA	SO	Avg.
1980-81	Minnesota	44	138	0	3.20
1981-82	Minnesota	29	101	0	3.71
1982-83	Minnesota	36	120	0	3.58
1983-84	Minnesota	33	123	0	4.12
1984-85	Minnesota	21	109	1	3.69
1985-86	Minnesota	52	182	1	3.55
1986-87	Minnesota	47	174	1	3.93
	Totals	262	947	3	3.67

DIRK GRAHAM 28 5-11 190   Right Wing

One of the few penalty-killers in the NHL who spends a lot of
time watching others trying to kill off his own . . . Not many
were . . . Minnesota's penalty-killing ranked 19th in 1986-87 . . .

Only four players in the NHL scored more shorthanded goals than he (5)...Hard-working, quick-skating winger who plays either side adeptly...Served his time in the minors, winning All-Star recognition in the International and Central Leagues... Born July 29, 1959, in Regina, Sask....A fifth-round draft choice (89th overall) by Vancouver in 1979 who signed as a free agent with Minnesota in 1983.

Year	Club	GP	G	A	Pts.
1983-84	Minnesota.........	6	1	1	2
1984-85	Minnesota.........	36	12	11	23
1985-86	Minnesota.........	80	22	33	55
1986-87	Minnesota.........	76	25	29	54
	Totals	198	60	74	134

SCOTT BJUGSTAD 26 6-1 185   Left Wing

Living evidence that one's career can suddenly take a turn for the worse...It was as if he forgot how to score...Haunted by bad luck...Felt he was doing the same things as the year before, but 39-goal dip could not be explained...Injuries to Neal Broten caused the breakup of his line, which contributed to his slide... Born June 2, 1961, in St. Paul, Minn....Noted as a sniper through high school and college...A 1983 finalist from the University of Minnesota for the Hobey Baker Award given the outstanding player in U.S. college hockey...Played for the U.S. in the 1984 Winter Olympics in Sarajevo, Yugoslavia...Drafted 181st overall by the North Stars in 1981.

Year	Club	GP	G	A	Pts.
1983-84	Minnesota.........	5	0	0	0
1984-85	Minnesota.........	72	11	4	15
1985-86	Minnesota.........	80	43	33	76
1986-87	Minnesota.........	39	4	9	13
	Totals	196	58	46	104

BOB BROOKE 26 6-2 205   Center

One of only two players in the NHL who wears No. 13...The other is Ken Linseman of Boston Bruins...The only player on the North Stars' current roster who has played for Herb Brooks, the team's new coach...Grinding style of forward who drives to the net, a quality Minnesota centers have lacked in the past... Acquired from the Rangers on Nov. 13, 1986, in what amounted to be a 2-for-1 trade for Curt Giles and Tony McKegney... Born Dec. 16, 1960, in Melrose, Mass.... A Hobey Baker Award winner after his senior year at Yale... Worked at a brokerage firm in the offseason... A shortstop in college who played behind the Mets' Ron Darling.

Year	Club	GP	G	A	Pts.
1983-84	Ne York R	9	1	2	3
1984-85	New York R	72	7	9	16
1985-86	New York R	79	24	20	44
1986-87	NYR-Minn	80	13	23	36
	Totals	240	45	54	99

TERRY RUSKOWSKI 32 5-9 183   **Forward**

One of the NHL's most vigorous, aggressive forwards, he has been called "a monument to overachievement."... And his latest achievement as the Penguins' free-agent captain was to sign with the North Stars for more money and a chance to become an assistant coach after this season... He doesn't score a lot but makes it with his playmaking and teamwork... Drafted by the Blackhawks in the fourth round (70th overall) in the 1974 draft... Turned pro with Houston of the WHA in 1974. Completed his WHA career with Winnipeg's Avco Cup champions in '79... Reclaimed by the Blackhawks from Winnipeg in the 1979 expansion draft... Traded to Los Angeles in 1982, signed by the Pens as a free agent in '85... Born Dec. 31, 1954, in Prince Albert, Sask.

Year	Club	GP	G	A	Pts.
1974-75	Houston (WHA)	71	10	36	46
1975-76	Houston (WHA)	65	14	35	49
1976-77	Houston (WHA)	80	24	60	84
1977-78	Houston (WHA)	78	15	57	72
1978-79	Winnipeg (WHA)	75	20	66	86
1979-80	Chicago	74	15	55	70
1980-81	Chicago	72	8	51	59
1981-82	Chicago	60	7	30	37
1982-83	Chi-LA	76	14	32	46
1983-84	Los Angeles	77	7	25	32
1984-85	Los Angeles	78	16	33	49
1985-86	Pittsburgh	73	26	37	63
1986-87	Pittsburgh	70	14	37	51
	NHL Totals	580	107	300	407
	WHA Totals	369	83	254	337

COACH HERB BROOKS: Signed to coach the North Stars in

a tremendously popular move by the club . . .
The first native son to coach the team in its
20-year history . . . Club's failure to make the
playoffs for the first time in 10 years prompted
the ownership to demand the man Minnesotans
believe will lead the team to its Utopia . . .
Stickler for discipline and good physical
conditioning . . . Endeared himself to all Amer-
icans by coaching the U.S. to the gold medal in the 1980 Winter
Olympics in Lake Placid, N.Y. . . . Had an interesting change of
pace last season when he introduced the hockey program at
St. Cloud State . . . Represented a ring company (Jostens) after
leaving the Rangers . . . Coached the Blueshirts for 3½ seasons,
compiling a 131-113-41 record for a winning percentage of .532
. . . Known to have a large ego, which could put him in a con-
flicting position with GM Lou Nanne . . . Born Aug. 5, 1937, in
St. Paul, Minn. . . . Coached University of Minnesota, where he
once played, to three NCAA championships in seven seasons.

GREATEST COACH

The near-miss of a Stanley Cup in the spring of 1981 is regarded as the most exciting period in the history of the franchise.
Not surprisingly, Glen Sonmor was the man behind the bench.

Bubbling with excitement, his enthusiasm rubbed off on
players and management alike. Players drove themselves for him.
From the time he replaced Harry Howell during the 1978-79 season to 1982-83, when Murray Oliver took over the reins, Sonmor
compiled a 174-160-81 record.

A favorite in Minnesota, Sonmor has remained in the organization and on two occasions has made cameo appearances behind
the bench following the firings of Bill Mahoney and Lorne Henning. Today he is the North Stars' assistant general manager and
director of player development.

ALL-TIME NORTH STAR LEADERS

GOALS: Dino Ciccarelli, 55, 1981-82
ASSISTS: Neal Broten, 76, 1985-86
POINTS: Bobby Smith, 114, 1981-82
SHUTOUTS: Cesare Maniago, 6, 1967-68

ST. LOUIS BLUES

TEAM DIRECTORY: Chairman: Michael Shanahan; Pres.: Jack Quinn; VP-GM: Ronald Caron; Pub. Dir.: Susie Mathieu; Coach: Jacques Martin. Home ice: St. Louis Arena (17,640; 200′ × 85′). Colors: White, blue, gold and red. Training camp: Peoria, Ill.

SCOUTING REPORT

OFFENSE: The emergence of Doug Gilmour as one of the NHL's most productive centers has eased the diminishing years of

It's tough to stop the Blues' Doug Gilmour.

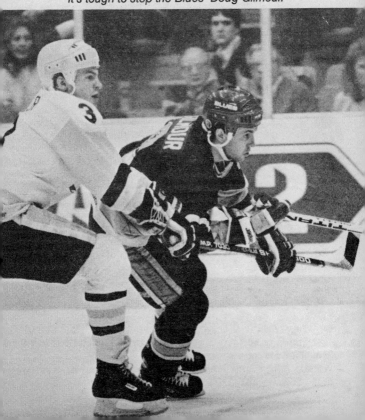

Bernie Federko, the team's top scorer for nine consecutive seasons.

If anything, the Blues have a dirth of effective wingers. Mark Hunter is 50-goal material in a stable year and Greg Paslawski is showing signs of developing into a scorer, too.

But the left side, noticeably deficient since potentially career-ending injuries to Brian Sutter and Eddie Beers, has undergone reconstruction. Back in the fold is Perry Turnbull, once swapped to Montreal for three starters. Upon his trade from Winnipeg, he said St. Louis was on his mind so much he felt he had never left.

Acquired, too, was Tony McKegney, a much-traveled left winger who managed 31 goals—his highest total in five years—splitting the past season between Minnesota and the Rangers. Not to be overlooked are Gino Cavallini, Ron Flockhart and two rookies, Jocelyn Lemieux and Doug Evans.

Lest one forget, the Blues won the Norris Division with those four playing the left side, though the team's record (32-33-15) would have got them fourth place in the other divisions.

A player to watch: tiny Cliff Ronning.

DEFENSE: No one expected Brian Benning to have the kind of year he had. Destined to play for Canada's Olympic team, he opted for the NHL and promptly established himself as a quick, hard-shooting defenseman for St. Louis, though his photo never appeared in the Blues' media guide.

Receiving on the job training from Rob Ramage, a tutor of great repute, Benning was able to impress enough people to win selection to the NHL's All-Rookie team.

Gone is Ric Nattress, traded to Calgary, which puts added pressure on Tim Bothwell, Charlie Bourgeois and Jim Pavese. There are stronger collections of defensemen in the NHL.

There is a desire on the part of the Blues to trade one of their two starting goaltenders, probably Greg Millen more than Rick Wamsley, for another starting defenseman. Minor-league netminder Darrell May is ready to graduate to the NHL.

OUTLOOK: The Blues should be an even better team in a division that is there for the taking. Coach Jacques Martin has the benefit of a year's experience in the NHL. He and the Blues' veterans have learned to live with each other. There is also peace in the board room.

BLUE ROSTER

No.	Player	Pos.	Ht.	Wt.	Born	1986 – 87	G	A	Pts.	PIM
19	Ed Beers	LW	6-2	200	10-12-59/Merritt, B.C.	Injured—Did Not Play				
2	Brian Benning	D	6-0	175	6-10-66/Edmonton, Alta.	St. Louis	13	36	49	110
6	Tim Bothwell	D	6-3	190	5-6-55/Vancouver, B.C.	St. Louis	6	16	22	46
4	Charles Bourgeois	D	6-3	204	11-11-59/Moncton, N.B.	St. Louis	2	12	14	164
	Kent Carlson	D	6-3	200	1-11-62/Concord, N.Y.	Injured—Did Not Play				
17	Gino Cavallini	LW	6-2	215	11-24-62/Toronto, Ont.	St. Louis	18	26	44	54
	Michael Dark	D	6-3	210	9-17-63/Sarnia, Ont.	St. Louis	2	0	2	2
						Peoria	4	11	15	93
	Robert Dirk	D	6-4	218	8-20-66/Regina, Sask.	Peoria	5	17	22	135
32	Doug Evans	C	5-9	178	6-2-63/Peterborough, Ont.	St. Louis	3	13	16	91
						Peoria	10	15	25	39
21	Todd Ewen	RW	6-2	180	3-26-66/Saskatoon, Sask.	St. Louis	2	0	2	84
						Peoria	3	3	6	110
24	Bernie Federko	C	6-0	190	5-12-56/Foam Lake, Sask.	St. Louis	20	52	72	32
12	Rob Flockhart	C	5-11	174	10-10-60/Smithers, B.C.	St. Louis	16	19	35	12
18	Doug Gilmour	C	5-11	165	6-23-63/Kingston, Ont.	St. Louis	42	63	105	58
20	Mark Hunter	RW	6-0	195	11-12-62/Petrolia, Ont.	St. Louis	36	33	69	169
18	Tony Hrkac	C	5-11	165	7-7-66/Thunder Bay, Ont.	U. N. Dakota	46	70	116	–
	Tony McKegney	LW	6-1	198	2-15-58/Sarnia, Ont.	Minn.Rang.	31	20	51	72
16	Jocelyn Lemieux	RW	5-11	207	11-18-67/Mont Larrier, Que.	St. Louis	10	8	18	94
22	Rick Meagher	C	5-8	175	11-4-53/Belleville, Ont.	St. Louis	18	21	39	54
	Keith Osborne	RW	6-1	181	4-2-69/Toronto, Ont.	North Bay	34	55	89	31
28	Greg Paslawski	LW	5-11	189	8-25-61/Kindersley, Sask.	St. Louis	29	35	64	27
33	Jim Pavese	D	6-2	204	6-9-62/New York, N.Y.	St. Louis	2	9	11	129
34	Mike Posavad	D	5-11	196	1-3-64/Brantford, Ont.	St. Louis	0	0	0	0
						Peoria	2	15	17	77
25	Herb Raglan	RW	6-0	204	8-5-67/Peterborough, Ont.	St. Louis	6	10	16	159
5	Rob Ramage	D	6-2	195	1-11-59/Bryon, Ont.	St. Louis	11	28	39	106
15	Mark Reeds	RW	5-10	188	1-24-60/Burlington, Ont.	St. Louis	9	16	25	16
7	Cliff Ronning	C	5-8	157	10-1-65/Vancouver, B.C.	St. Louis	11	14	25	6
11	Brian Sutter	LW	5-11	180	10-7-56/Viking, Alta.	St. Louis	3	3	6	18
	Dave Thomlinson	LW	6-2	190	10-22-66/Andrew, N.B.	Moose Jaw	44	37	81	126
	Larry Trader	D	6-1	197	7-7-63/Barry Bay, Ont.	St. Louis	0	0	0	8
	Perry Turnbull	LW	6-2	200	3-9-59/Bentley, Alta.	Winnipeg	1	5	6	44
	Rob Whistle	D	6-2	195	4-30-61/Thunder Bay, Ont.	New Haven	4	12	16	30
14	Doug Wickenheiser	C	6-1	197	3-30-61/Regina, Sask.	St. Louis	13	15	28	37

No.	Player	Pos.	Ht.	Wt.	Born		GP	GA	SO	Avg.
1	Darrell May	G	6-0	175	3-6-62/Edmonton, Alta.	Peoria	58	214	0	3.75
29	Greg Millen	G	5-9	175	6-25-57/Toronto, Ont.	St. Louis	42	146	0	3.53
	Alan Perry	G	5-8	162	1-30-66/Johnson, R.I.	Belleville	15	64	0	4.56
						Peoria	6	36	0	6.92
30	Rick Wamsley	G	5-11	185	5-25-59/Simcoe, Ont.	St. Louis	41	142	0	3.54

BLUE PROFILES

DOUG GILMOUR 24 5-11 165   Center
Finished fifth in NHL scoring in 1986-87, the highest finish by a
member of the Blues since Phil Goyette's fourth place in 1969-
70...Also placed fifth in voting for the Hart Trophy as the
NHL's MVP...Selected as the Player of the Month in March
after 12-18-30 binge...Team leader in goals (42), assists (63),
points (105), power-play goals (17) and shots (207)...Ended
Bernie Federko's nine-year reign as the Blues' leader in points
...Ranked second in NHL in first goals (9)...Longest point
streak was eight games...A steal by the Blues, who selected
him 134th overall in the 1982 draft when other teams dismissed
him as too light...Born June 25, 1963, in Kingston, Ont....
Nickname is "Killer"...As a junior, he set an OHL record with
points in 55 consecutive games for Cornwall Royals.

Year	Club	GP	G	A	Pts.
1983-84	St. Louis	80	25	28	53
1984-85	St. Louis	78	21	36	57
1985-86	St. Louis	74	25	28	53
1986-87	St. Louis	80	42	63	105
	Totals	312	113	155	268

MARK HUNTER 24 6-0 195   Right Wing
One of the NHL's top goal-scorers...Production fell in 1986-87
when his regular linemates, Bernie Federko and Brian Sutter,
went down with injuries...Distressed when a shoulder injury
kept him out of the lineup for four games in the Blues' stretch
drive...Led his team in game-winning goals (4) and, regrett-
ably, penalty minutes (169)...Born Nov. 12, 1962, in Petrolia,
Ont....Youngest of three Hunter brothers in the NHL. Dave is
with Edmonton and Dale is with Washington...Needed only
5 minutes, 15 seconds to score a hat trick in a 4-3 win over
Quebec on Feb. 21, 1987...Traded to St. Louis by the Montreal
Canadiens on June 15, 1985.

Year	Club	GP	G	A	Pts.
1981-82	Montreal	71	18	11	29
1982-83	Montreal	31	8	8	16
1983-84	Montreal	22	6	4	10
1984-85	Montreal	72	21	12	33
1985-86	St. Louis	78	44	30	74
1986-87	St. Louis	74	36	33	69
	Totals	348	133	98	231

BERNIE FEDERKO 31 6-0 190   **Center**

Suffered a broken jaw—the most serious injury of his career—in a mid-ice collision with linemate Mark Hunter ... Missed 16 games while recuperating and finished with his lowest point total in nine years ... Did not readily adjust to the Blues' new coach, Jacques Martin ... Blues' all-time leader in games (790), goals (310), assists (607) and points (917) ... Grossly underrated in his prime ... Born May 12, 1956, in Foam Lake, Sask. ... Blues held a night for him last season and presented him with a membership at a golf course, hoping they might see more of him in the summer time.

Year	Club	GP	G	A	Pts.
1976-77	St Louis	31	14	9	23
1977-78	St Louis	72	17	24	41
1978-79	St Louis	74	31	64	95
1979-80	St Louis	79	38	56	94
1980-81	St Louis	78	31	73	104
1981-82	St Louis	74	30	62	92
1982-83	St Louis	75	24	60	84
1983-84	St Louis	79	41	66	107
1984-85	St Louis	76	30	73	103
1985-86	St. Louis	80	34	68	102
1986-87	St. Louis	64	20	52	72
	Totals	782	310	607	917

BRIAN BENNING 21 6-0 175   **Defenseman**

Came off the roster of Canada's Olympic team on Oct. 13, 1986, and proceeded to star ... Selected to the NHL's All-Rookie team ... A bonus considering the fact he was not included in the Blues' 1986-87 plans ... Finished fourth among rookie scorers and led all rookie defensemen in scoring ... Seven of his goals were scored on power plays, where he shared the point with Rob Ramage ... Defensive skills improved remarkably under the tutelage of Dave King, the Canadian Olympic coach ... Born June 10, 1966, in Edmonton, Alta. ... The Blues' first choice (26th overall) in 1984 ... The choice originally belonged to Hartford ... A younger brother of Vancouver's Jim Benning ... Junior career was interrupted by wrist and leg fractures.

Year	Club	GP	G	A	Pts.
1984-85	St. Louis	4	0	2	2
1986-87	St. Louis	78	13	36	49
	Totals	82	13	38	51

ROB RAMAGE 28 6-2 195   Defenseman

Served as captain of the Blues in the 66-game absence of Brian Sutter in 1986-87 . . . Agonized through a 21-game hiatus of his own with tendonitis in his knee . . . Had two four-point nights, earning four assists on Jan. 3, 1987, against Calgary and adding two more, plus two goals, against Toronto on March 3, 1987 . . . Considered the bulwark of the Blues' defense . . . Born Jan. 11, 1959 in Byron, Ont. . . . Inherited a kid, Brian Benning, as his defense partner and helped him crack the NHL's All-Rookie team . . . Team's player rep . . . In retrospect, the trade that sent him to St. Louis for two first-round draft choices—Rocky Trottier (1982) and John MacLean (1983), both by New Jersey—was a good one . . . The Devils have no one of his ilk on defense.

Year	Club	GP	G	A	Pts.
1979-80	Colorado	75	8	20	28
1980-81	Colorado	79	20	42	62
1981-82	Colorado	80	13	29	42
1982-83	St. Louis	78	16	35	51
1983-84	St. Louis	80	15	45	60
1984-85	St. Louis	80	7	31	38
1985-86	St. Louis	77	10	56	66
1986-87	St. Louis	59	11	28	39
	Totals	608	100	286	386

GREG PASLAWSKI 26 5-11 189   Right Wing

Set personal highs for goals and assists, not to mention points, in 1986-87 . . . Led the Blues in game-winning goals (7) . . . Swift winger with good work ethics . . . Stolen on Dec. 21, 1983, from Montreal along with Doug Wickenheiser and Gilbert Delorme for Perry Turnbull, a left winger the Habs dumped six months later . . . Scored overtime goals to give Blues a 4-3 win over Quebec and a 3-2 win over Toronto only 16 days apart in 1986-87 . . . Born Aug. 25, 1961, in Kindersley, Sask. . . . Never drafted, but signed as a free agent by Montreal in July 1981 . . . Recorded a hole-in-one in the summer of 1986 . . . Nickname is "Mud".

Year	Club	GP	G	A	Pts.
1983-84	Mont-St L	60	9	10	19
1984-85	St. Louis	72	22	20	42
1985-86	St. Louis	56	22	11	33
1986-87	St. Louis	76	29	35	64
	Totals	264	82	76	158

GREG MILLEN 30 5-9 175   **Goaltender**

A quick left-hander who is entering his 10th season in the NHL
...Posted a 15-18-9 record in 1986-87...Best stretch was a
six-game unbeaten streak in March in the Blues' drive to first
place...Registered an 8-4-4 record against Norris Division
rivals...Exciting to watch...Explodes out of the box as he
leads his team onto the ice...Engaging personality, always interesting, always approachable...Born June 25, 1957, in Toronto
...Signed as a free agent by Hartford on June 15, 1981...As
compensation, the Whalers had to send Pat Boutette and Kevin
McClelland to Pittsburgh...Aspires to stay in the game as either
a coach or broadcaster.

Year	Club	GP	GA	SO	Avg.
1978-79	Pittsburgh	28	86	2	3.37
1979-80	Pittsburgh	44	157	2	3.64
1980-81	Pittsburgh	63	258	0	4.16
1981-82	Hartford	55	229	0	4.29
1982-83	Hartford	60	282	1	4.81
1983-84	Hartford	60	221	2	3.70
1984-85	Hart-St L	54	222	1	4.08
1985-86	St. Louis	36	129	1	3.57
1986-87	St. Louis	42	146	0	3.53
	Totals	442	1730	9	3.98

RICK MEAGHER 33 5-8 175   **Center**

One of the NHL's older players and one of its busiest, too...
Frantic work ethic inspires teammates and excites fans...
Usually assigned to checking roles, though he did manage two
power-play goals in 1986-87...Led the team in shorthanded
goals (2)...Waited seven years to play in the Stanley Cup
playoffs...Born Nov. 4, 1953, in Belleville, Ont....A three-
time All-American at Boston University...Enshrined in BU's
Hall of Fame...Never drafted, but signed as a free agent by
Montreal in 1977...Skating is his forte.

Year	Club	GP	G	A	Pts.
1979-80	Montreal..........	2	0	0	0
1980-81	Hartford	27	7	10	17
1981-82	Hartford	65	24	19	43
1982-83	Hart-NJ...........	61	15	14	29
1983-84	New Jersey........	52	14	14	28
1984-85	New Jersey........	71	11	20	31
1985-86	St. Louis.........	79	11	19	30
1986-87	St. Louis.........	80	18	21	39
	Totals	457	100	117	217

RICK WAMSLEY 28 5-11 185   **Goaltender**

Greatest compliment is his record... Has never finished below .500 in seven seasons in the NHL... Posted a 17-15-6 mark in 1986-87... Went 6-2-2 in his last 10 starts and had a 9-4-3 record against Norris Division opponents... A protege of the late Jacques Plante... Stands up and makes quick, compact moves ... A co-winner of the William Jennings Trophy with Denis Herron for fewest goals allowed as members of Montreal Canadiens in 1982... Born May 25, 1959, in Simcoe, Ont.... Played for Canada in the 1983 world championships.

Year	Club	GP	GA	SO	Avg.
1980-81	Montreal.........	5	8	1	1.90
1981-82	Montreal.........	38	101	2	2.75
1982-83	Montreal.........	46	151	0	3.51
1983-84	Montreal.........	42	144	2	3.70
1984-85	St. Louis	40	126	0	3.26
1985-86	St. Louis	42	144	1	3.43
1986-87	St. Louis	41	142	0	3.54
	Totals	254	816	6	3.35

TONY McKEGNEY 29 6-1 198   **Left Wing**

St. Louis will be his fifth NHL stop in the past six years... The North Stars traded him and defenseman Curt Giles to the Rangers on Nov. 13, 1986... Blues acquired him in May for Bruce Bell ... Coming off a good (31 goals, 51 points) season... Can play all three forward positions... Speedy, strong and durable... Born Feb. 15, 1958, in Montreal, and grew up on the same street in Sarnia, Ont., as Dino Ciccarelli... Won Nordiques' award as best-conditioned player in 1983-84... Two older brothers, Ian and Mike, played minor-league hockey... Launched NHL career in 1978 with the Sabres, who picked him in the second round of the draft.

Year	Club	GP	G	A	Pts.
1978-79	Buffalo	52	8	14	22
1979-80	Buffalo	80	23	29	52
1980-81	Buffalo	80	37	32	69
1981-82	Buffalo	73	23	29	52
1982-83	Buffalo	78	36	37	73
1983-84	Quebec...........	75	24	27	51
1984-85	Que-Minn	57	23	22	45
1985-86	Minnesota.........	70	15	25	40
1986-87	Minn-NYR.........	75	31	20	51
	Totals	640	220	235	455

COACH JACQUES MARTIN: Coached his team to a first-place finish in his first season in the NHL . . . Did this despite a losing (32-33-15) record, commonplace in the Norris Division . . . Filled big shoes admirably, succeeding Jacques Demers, who bolted the Blues to become a millionaire in Detroit as coach of the Red Wings . . . Guided his team to a 17-8-7 record against teams in the Norris Division, which contributed largely to the first-place finish . . . Task made more difficult by serious injuries to key players such as Brian Sutter, Bernie Federko and Rob Ramage . . . Born Oct. 11, 1952, in Ottawa, Ont. . . . A great believer in the merits of defensive hockey . . . Doesn't mind scolding his players publicly if the need arises . . . A brother-in-law of Joe Clark, the Canadian Minister of External Affairs, the equivalent of the United States' George Schultz . . . Played goal for the University of Ottawa and on one occasion played in St. Louis area against St. Louis University.

GREATEST COACH

His players were older and most had had productive years somewhere else, but, as Blues, Scotty Bowman took them to three straight Stanley Cup finals. He posted a 110-83-46 record during his three-year stint starting in 1967-68. Such early success as an expansion franchise was unmatched by the many coaches who followed.

Among Bowman's most notable players were Red Berenson, Gary Sabourin, Frank St. Marseille, Noel Picard, Al Arbour and the Plager brothers, Barclay and Bob. Bowman was succeeded by Arbour, who would go on to coach the New York Islanders to four Stanley Cups.

Berenson, Barclay Plager and Emile Francis all did turns behind the Blues' bench.

As for Bowman, he went on to win five Stanley Cups with the Canadiens.

ALL-TIME BLUE LEADERS

GOALS: Wayne Babych, 54, 1980-81
ASSISTS: Bernie Federko, 73, 1980-81
POINTS: Bernie Federko, 107, 1983-84
SHUTOUTS: Glenn Hall, 8, 1968-69

TORONTO MAPLE LEAFS

TEAM DIRECTORY: Pres.: Harold E. Ballard; Chairman: Paul McNamara; GM: Gerry McNamara; Asst. GM: Gord Stellick; Dir. Pub. Rel.: Bob Stellick; Coach: John Brophy. Home ice: Maple Leaf Gardens (16,382; 200' × 85'). Colors: Blue and white. Training camp: Toronto.

SCOUTING REPORT

OFFENSE: An assistant coach from the Smythe Division—where the Edmonton Oilers live—insists that the Maple Leafs have the best collection of forwards in the NHL. Admittedly, it's a thought. No fewer than eight forwards scored 20 or more goals last season—a claim no other team could make.

Charged by the tenacity of Wendel Clark, guided by the sagacity of Rick Vaive and tuned to the beat of Russ Courtnall, the Leafs' forwards offer an exciting package to Toronto fans. Add a sniper such as Steve Thomas and an already-indoctrinated youngster like Vincent Damphousse, and the possibilities of becoming even better are real.

Curiously, with all the scorers in their lineup, the Leafs' power play has been the pits. In a day and age when specialty teams are so important, a miserable power play is a serious burden. Prospects would improve if Peter Ihnacak can come back from a knee injury and if Tom Fergus can shake that mystery virus.

DEFENSE: Goaltender Ken Wregget has emerged as one of the team's stars, though his statistics (22-28-3 and 3.97) are nothing special. He's portrayed as an heroic performer behind a piecemeal defense and forwards who are often missing in action.

Borje Salming, the 36-year-old patriarch of the Leafs' defense, must bear much of the responsibility for the team's poor play in its own end. On the bright side, Todd Gill and Al Iafrate have progressed to the point of encouragement. Rick Lanz and Chris Kotsopoulos offer a tad of experience and/or toughness.

Not unexpectedly, the Leafs' first-round draft choice, Luke Richardson, is a defenseman. Described as having ample amounts of raw power and skill, the 6-4, 203-pound product of the Peterborough Petes has two shortcomings, according to scouts. He is called a "gentle" giant and has a tendency to make the wrong play. It sounds as if he's ready for the Leafs.

Wendel Clark had 37 goals and 271 penalty minutes.

OUTLOOK: The late-season addition of a defensive forward, Mark Osborne, from the Rangers, has helped considerably. The Leafs could use one or two more. Two quality defensemen would put Toronto in the NHL's top seven. But they'll be hard-pressed to stay in contention in their own division.

MAPLE LEAF ROSTER

No.	Player	Pos.	Ht.	Wt.	Born	1986–87	G	A	Pts.	PIM
8	Mike Allison	C	6-0	200	3-28-61/Ft. Frances, Ont.	Toronto	7	16	23	66
17	Wendel Clark	D-LW	5-11	190	10-25-66/Kelvington, Sask.	Toronto	37	23	60	271
	Rich Costello	RW	6-0	175	6-27-63/Framington, Mass.	Newmarket	6	11	17	53
9	Russ Courtnall	C	5-11	180	1-2-63/Duncan, B.C.	Toronto	29	44	73	90
10	Vincent Damphousse	C	6-0	190	12-17-67/Anjou, Que.	Toronto	21	25	46	26
24	Dan Daoust	C	5-11	160	2-29-60/Kirkland Lake, Ont.	Toronto	4	3	7	35
						Newmarket	0	0	0	4
	Jerome Dupont	D	6-3	190	2-21-62/Ottawa, Ont.	Toronto	0	0	0	23
						Newmarket	1	8	9	47
	Darryl Evans	LW	5-9	185	1-21-61/Toronto, Ont.	Newmarket	27	46	73	17
19	Tom Fergus	C	6-0	180	6-16-62/Chicago, Ill.	Toronto	21	28	49	57
						Newmarket	0	1	1	0
14	Miroslav Frycer	C	6-0	196	9-17-59/Czechoslovakia	Toronto	7	8	15	28
23	Todd Gill	D	6-1	180	11-9-65/Cardinals, Ont.	Toronto	4	27	31	92
						Newmarket	1	8	9	33
33	Al Iafrate	D	6-3	215	3-21-66/Livonia, Mich.	Toronto	9	21	30	55
27	Miroslav Ihnacak	C	5-11	178	11-19-62/Czechoslovakia	Toronto	7	8	15	12
						Newmarket	11	17	28	6
18	Peter Ihnacak	C	5-11	182	5-3-57/Czechoslovakia	Toronto	12	27	39	16
						Newmarket	2	6	8	0
28	Val James	D-RW	6-2	205	2-14-57/Ocala, Fla.	Newmarket	4	3	7	71
						Toronto	0	0	0	14
	Wes Jarvis	C	5-11	185	5-30-58/Toronto, Ont.	Newmarket	28	50	78	32
20	Terry Johnson	D	6-3	210	11-28-58/Calgary, Alta.	Toronto	0	1	1	104
						Newmarket	0	1	1	37
26	Chris Kotsopoulos	D	6-3	215	11-27-58/Toronto, Ont.	Toronto	2	10	12	75
4	Rick Lanz	D	6-2	195	9-16-61/Czechoslovakia	Van.-Tor.	3	25	28	42
11	Gary Leeman	LW	5-11	175	2-19-64/Wilcox, Sask.	Toronto	21	31	52	66
15	Bob McGill	D	6-0	202	4-27-62/Edmonton, Alta.	Toronto	1	4	5	103
12	Mark Osborne	LW	6-2	200	8-13-61/Toronto, Ont.	Rang.-Tor.	22	25	47	113
	Cam Plante	D	6-1	196	3-12-64/Brandon, Man.	Newmarket	3	4	7	14
						Milwaukee	7	47	54	44
	Luke Richardson	D	6-4	208	3-26-69/Ottawa, Ont.	Peterborough	13	32	45	70
34	Bill Root	D	6-0	197	9-6-59/Toronto, Ont.	Newmarket	4	11	15	23
						Toronto	3	3	6	37
21	Borje Salming	D	6-1	198	4-17-51/Kiruna, Swe.	Toronto	4	16	20	42
29	Brad Smith	C	6-1	195	4-13-58/Windsor, Ont.	Toronto	5	7	12	174
7	Greg Terrion	C	6-0	190	3-2-60/Peterborough, Ont.	Toronto	7	8	15	6
32	Steve Thomas	RW	5-10	185	7-15-63/England	Toronto	35	27	62	114
22	Rick Vaive	RW	6-1	190	4-14-59/Ottawa, Ont.	Toronto	32	34	66	61
	Blake Wesley	D	6-1	200	7-20-59/Red Deer, Alta.	Newmarket	1	12	13	170
16	Ken Yaremchuk	C	5-11	185	1-1-64/Edmonton, Alta.	Toronto	3	8	11	16
						Newmarket	2	4	6	21

No.	Player	Pos.	Ht.	Wt.	Born		GP	GA	SO	Avg.
1	Tim Bernhardt	G	5-9	159	4-19-58/Sarnia, Ont.	Toronto	1	3	0	9.00
						Newmarket	31	117	1	4.12
30	Allan Bester	G	5-7	150	3-26-64/Hamilton, Ont.	Toronto	36	110	2	3.65
						Newmarket	3	6	0	1.89
	Jeff Reese	G	5-9	150	3-24-66/Brantford, Ont.	Newmarket	50	193	1	4.10
31	Ken Wregget	G	6-1	195	3-25-64/Medley, Alta.	Toronto	56	200	0	3.97

MAPLE LEAF PROFILES

WENDEL CLARK 21 5-11 190   Left Wing

The Maple Leafs dance to his beat... His arrival triggered the
revival of the team... Rock-hard winger whose unsolicited hits
are the scourge of his opponents... Likened to the legendary
Charlie Conacher by Leaf historians... Became more of a playmaker in 1986-87 while leading the team in goals for the second
year in a row... Has a wrist shot that ranks with the NHL's
best... Born Oct. 10, 1966, in Kelvington, Sask., where his father, a former pro, operates a huge farm... Attended Notre
Dame High School in Wilcox, Sask., with Russ Courtnall and
Gary Leeman, frequent linemates and current teammates in
Toronto... Dyed his hair blue and white for the 1987 playoffs.

Year	Club	GP	G	A	Pts.
1985-86	Toronto	66	34	11	45
1986-87	Toronto	80	37	23	60
	Totals	146	71	34	105

STEVE THOMAS 24 5-10 185   Left Wing

A much-coveted free agent in the summer of 1987... The Red
Wings and Blues were particularly interested in him...
Described as "a young Yvan Cournoyer" by Ron Caron, the
Blues' director of hockey operations... A natural scorer, if there
is such a person... Team leader with seven game-winning goals
in 1986-87... One of his game-winners was scored in overtime
Dec. 13, 1986, giving the Leafs a 3-2 win in Pittsburgh... Born
July 15, 1963, in Stockport, England... Signed as a free agent
by the Leafs, who watched him slip through three drafts unde-
tected.

Year	Club	GP	G	A	Pts.
1984-85	Toronto	18	1	1	2
1985-86	Toronto	65	20	37	57
1986-87	Toronto	78	35	27	62
	Totals	161	56	65	121

RUSS COURTNALL 22 5-11 180   Center

Won the team's scoring title in 1986-87 . . . Leafs' fastest skater
. . . Double-shifted in the playoffs . . . Tends to carry the puck a
lot, if not too much . . . Scored six shorthanded goals in 1986-87;
only Wayne Gretzky had more . . . He and his linemates, Gary
Leeman and Wendel Clark, form the "Hounds Line" . . . They
were Hounds at Notre Dame College High School in 1981-82
. . . Born June 2, 1965, in Duncan, B.C., on Vancouver Island
. . . Had a six-point game (3-3) against Detroit on Nov. 23,
1985 . . . Nickname is "Rusty" . . . Has grown one inch and 15
pounds since his rookie season in Toronto.

Year	Club	GP	G	A	Pts.
1983-84	Toronto	14	3	9	12
1984-85	Toronto	69	12	10	22
1985-86	Toronto	73	22	38	60
1986-87	Toronto	79	29	44	73
	Totals	235	66	101	167

RICK VAIVE 28 6-1 192   Right Wing

Called the Leafs' leader by the writers who follow the team . . .
Although his numbers were approximately the same, many say
1986-87 was his best season in the past three . . . Hard-shooting
and hard-hitting . . . More mature than the individual he was in
1985-86 when he was stripped of his captaincy . . . Acquired in
one of the best trades ever conceived by Leaf management when
he and Bill Derlago went to Toronto for Tiger Williams and Jerry
Butler on Feb. 18, 1980 . . . Born May 14, 1959, in Ottawa,
Ont. . . . The only member of the Leafs who has ever scored 50
goals in a single season . . . Idolized the Montreal Canadians as a
youngster . . . Nickname is "Squid" . . . Wears a visor.

Year	Club	GP	G	A	Pts.
1978-79	Birmingham (WHA)	75	26	33	59
1979-80	Van-Tor	69	22	15	37
1980-81	Toronto	75	33	29	62
1981-82	Toronto	77	54	35	89
1982-83	Toronto	78	51	28	79
1983-84	Toronto	76	52	41	93
1984-85	Toronto	72	35	33	68
1985-86	Toronto	61	33	31	64
1986-87	Toronto	73	32	34	66
	NHL Totals	581	312	246	558
	WHA Totals	75	26	33	59

GARY LEEMAN 23 5-11 175   **Right Wing**
The Leafs' most versatile player... Although primarily a forward, he does play defense and takes the point on the power play... Kills penalties, too... A minus-26 rating in 1986-87 was the team's worst... Regarded as an excellent athlete... As a younger man, he was a member of Ontario's junior soccer team ... Born Feb. 19, 1964, in Toronto... Other teams have asked about him in trade talks... As a junior, he was named the Western Hockey League's top defenseman in 1983.

Year	Club	GP	G	A	Pts.
1983-84	Toronto	52	4	8	12
1984-85	Toronto	53	5	26	31
1985-86	Toronto	53	9	23	32
1986-87	Toronto	80	21	31	52
	Totals	238	39	88	127

AL IAFRATE 21 6-3 215   **Defenseman**
Distinguished himself in the 1987 playoffs by clearly establishing himself as the Leafs' top defenseman... Only player faster than him on the team is Russ Courtnall... Puck-handling skills are immense... Born March 21, 1966, in Dearborn, Mich.... Once ballooned to 240 pounds after a lengthy visit by his grandmother from Italy... A first-round choice (fourth overall) in 1984... Taken ahead of him were Mario Lemieux (Pittsburgh), Kirk Muller (New Jersey) and Ed Olczyk (Chicago).

Year	Club	GP	G	A	Pts.
1984-85	Toronto	68	5	16	21
1985-86	Toronto	65	8	25	33
1986-87	Toronto	80	9	21	30
	Totals	213	22	62	84

KEN WREGGET 23 6-1 195   **Goaltender**
Better eating habits are said to be responsible for his new-found stamina... Disposed of junk food and felt he was more agile because of it... Posted a personal record of 22-28-3 in 1986-87 ... Definitely, the Leafs' No. 1 netminder... Standup style is not unlike that of the team's goaltending coach, Johnny Bower... Born March 25, 1964, in Brandon, Man.... His wife, Holly-

Lee, won $25,000 in a lottery in 1987... Spends the offseason working for his father-in-law's contracting firm.

Year	Club	GP	GA	SO	Avg.
1983-84	Toronto	3	14	0	5.09
1984-85	Toronto	23	103	0	4.84
1985-86	Toronto	30	113	0	4.33
1986-87	Toronto	56	200	0	3.97
	Totals	112	430	0	4.28

BORJE SALMING 36 6-1 195   Defenseman

The NHL's oldest active player... Although he tired in the playoffs, the 1986-87 season was one of his best... Won the Leafs' Emery Edge Award with a plus-12 mark... Suspended for eight games when he admitted using cocaine at one time... Highest-paid member of the team, pulling down $400,000... The first European to be named to the NHL's first All-Star Team in 1977... Born April 17, 1951, in Kiruna, Sweden... Once described as the world's best defenseman... Travelled to the Cayman Islands with team president Harold Ballard... Dyed his hair blue and white prior to the 1987 playoffs... Plays a mean game of tennis.

Year	Club	GP	G	A	Pts.
1973-74	Toronto	76	5	34	39
1974-75	Toronto	60	12	25	37
1975-76	Toronto	78	16	41	57
1976-77	Toronto	76	12	66	78
1977-78	Toronto	80	16	60	76
1978-79	Toronto	78	17	56	73
1979-80	Toronto	74	19	52	71
1980-81	Toronto	72	5	61	66
1981-82	Toronto	69	12	44	56
1982-83	Toronto	69	7	38	45
1983-84	Toronto	68	5	38	43
1984-85	Toronto	73	6	33	39
1985-86	Toronto	41	7	15	22
1986-87	Toronto	56	4	16	20
	Totals	970	143	579	722

MARK OSBORNE 26 6-2 200   Left Wing

John Brophy's kind of hockey player... The Toronto coach coveted him a long time and instigated the trade that brought him from the Rangers for Jeff Jackson and a third-round draft choice, on March 5, 1987... Works the corners exceedingly well and expects to win every battle for the puck... Leafs were leading

Norris Division final, 3 games to 1, when he went down with a knee injury...Detroit won the series, 4-3...Born Aug. 13, 1961, in Toronto...Fervent supporter of Toronto Blue Jays.

Year	Club	GP	G	A	Pts.
1981-82	Detroit	80	26	41	67
1982-83	Detroit	80	19	24	43
1983-84	New York R.	73	23	28	51
1984-85	New York R.	23	4	4	8
1985-86	New York R.	62	16	24	40
1986-87	NYR-Tor.	74	22	25	47
	Totals	392	110	146	256

TOM FERGUS 25 6-0 180   Center

Missed 23 games with a mysterious viral infection in the last half of the 1986-87 season...At one point, doctors prescribed rest in Florida...His absence broke up the Leafs' top line of himself, Rick Vaive and Steve Thomas...Noted as a hard worker and intense checker...Team's top faceoff man...Born June 16, 1962, in Chicago...A steal from Boston on Oct. 11, 1985, when Toronto acquired him even-up for Bill Derlago...An assistant captain...Enjoys killing penalties.

Year	Club	GP	G	A	Pts.
1981-82	Boston	61	15	24	39
1982-83	Boston	80	28	35	63
1983-84	Boston	69	25	36	61
1984-85	Boston	79	30	43	73
1985-86	Toronto	78	31	42	73
1986-87	Toronto	57	21	28	49
	Totals	424	150	208	358

COACH JOHN BROPHY: Glaring eyes and a red face under a mop of snow-white hair is a sight to behold behind the Toronto bench...Knows precisely what he wants and what he can realistically expect from his players...A firm believer that intense checking is the key to success...Likes a lot of toughness, too...Has had an ongoing war of words with Detroit coach Jacques Demers...Talks in staccato outbursts...Prized by Leaf president Harold Ballard, who likes his hard-line approach...Claims he's either played or coached in every league in professional hockey . . . The 52-year-old native of Antigonish, N.S., succeeded Dan Maloney on July 2, 1986 . . . Likes his golf; he shot two holes-in-one in the summer of 1985.

GREATEST COACH

The most successful and longest-serving coach in the 70-year history of the team was Hap Day. During a 10-year span (1940-41 to 1949-50), Day's Maple Leafs won five Stanley Cups. Only once did they fail to make the playoffs.

As a Toronto defenseman, Day led the team in penalty minutes and assists in 1927-28 and helped them with the Stanley Cup in 1931-32. He was the only one who has ever served the Leafs as a player, captain, coach and general manager. Known as a practical joker who turned dead serious when the games began, Day had this philosophy: "If you can master defensive hockey, you can win."

He later worked as an NHL linesman and was elected to the Hall of Fame in 1961.

ALL-TIME MAPLE LEAF LEADERS

GOALS: Rick Vaive, 54, 1981-82
ASSISTS: Darryl Sittler, 72, 1977-78
POINTS: Darryl Sittler, 117, 1977-78
SHUTOUTS: Harry Lumley, 13, 1953-54

VANCOUVER CANUCKS

TEAM DIRECTORY; Chairman: Frank A. Griffiths; Pres.-GM:
Pat Quinn; VP-Dir. Hockey Operations: Brian Burke; Sr. Advi-
sor: Jack Gordon; Dir. Team Services: Norm Jewison; Coach:
Bob McCammon. Home ice: Pacific Coliseum (15,613;
200′ × 85′). Colors: Black, red and yellow. Training camp:
Vancouver.

SCOUTING REPORT

OFFENSE: The Canucks ache for big wingers who can play,
which makes their year-old trade of Cam Neely all the more
ludicrous. Almost as bad, they shipped their first-round draft
choice to Boston, too. Today, under new management, they are
paying the price for the stupidity of others.

The Philadelphia connection of Pat Quinn, Brian Burke and
new coach Bob McCammon has a mandate to take what's avail-

Tony Tanti led the Canucks in five offensive categories.

able, shape a team and make alterations as the need and opportunities arise.

Offensively, they have four light but exciting forwards in Tony Tanti, Petri Skriko, Patrik Sundstrom and Barry Pederson. Stan Smyl is short but feisty and has had a serious knee injury.

Raimo Summanen and Steve Tambellini play small and produce modestly. The same can be said for Dan Hodgson.

But where's the beef?

Rich Sutter plays like a commando and he weighs 165 pounds! Jim Sandlak weighs 205 and plays with all the intensity of a golfer.

DEFENSE: Light, uninvolved forwards don't make life any easier for defensemen or goaltenders. Nobody crosses the Vancouver blue line on his knees . . . a situation that is going to be changed dramatically before Quinn, the new president and GM, is through with the Canucks.

As a group, Doug Lidster, Garth Butcher, Michel Petit, Dave Richter, Jim Benning and Robin Bartel are often ridiculed, though unfairly. More than respect they need a moment to gather their thoughts when waves of forwards bent on buzzing them swarm over the blue line.

Efforts to sign free-agent goaltender Bob Mason fell short. The Canucks realize Richard Brodeur's days are numbered. He's 35. Philadelphia would love to have him to back up Ron Hextall, but, unless the Flyers can fill one of the Canucks' needs, a deal won't be made.

Troy Gamble, a second-round pick in 1985, shows signs he's ready to tend goal in the NHL.

OUTLOOK: Hopefully, the Canucks have bottomed out. An apathetic public in Vancouver has welcomed changes at the management level, though the owners have been roasted for the less than ethical, if not illegal, manner in which they hired Quinn as he coached the division-rival Los Angeles Kings. The spirit of Inspector Clousseau lives!

CANUCK PROFILES

TONY TANTI 24 5-9 185   **Right Wing**
Where would the Canucks have been without him? . . . In 1986-87, he led the team in goals (41), points (79), power-play goals (15), game-winning goals (7) and shots (242) . . . A natural scorer who seems to catch goaltenders off guard . . . A master of

CANUCK PROFILES

No.	Player	Pos.	Ht.	Wt.	Born	1986—87	G	A	Pts.	PIM
	Jim Agnew	D	6-1	185	3-21-66/Hartney, Man.	Vancouver	0	0	0	0
						Fredericton	0	5	5	261
32	Robin Bartel	D	6-0	200	5-16-61/Drake, Sask.	Vancouver	0	1	1	14
						Fredericton	0	2	2	15
4	Jim Benning	D	6-0	183	4-29-63/Edmonton, Alta.	Tor.-Van.	2	11	13	44
						Newmarket	1	5	6	0
25	David Bruce	RW-C	5-11	170	10-7-64/Thunder Bay, Ont.	Vancouver	9	7	16	109
						Fredericton	7	6	13	73
5	Garth Butcher	D	6-0	195	10-8-63/Regina, Sask.	Vancouver	5	15	20	207
29	Glen Cochrane	D	6-2	189	1-29-58/Cranbrook, B.C.	Vancouver	0	0	0	52
	Craig Coxe	LW	6-4	196	1-21-64/Chula Vista, Calif.	Vancouver	1	0	1	31
						Fredericton	1	12	13	168
18	Marc Crawford	LW	5-11	185	2-13-61/Belleville, Ont.	Vancouver	0	3	3	67
8	Taylor Hall	LW	5-11	188	2-20-64/Regina, Sask.	Vancouver	0	0	0	0
						Fredericton	21	20	41	23
23	Dan Hodgson	C	5-10	170	8-29-65/Ft. Murray, Alta.	Tor.-Van.	9	13	22	25
						Newmarket	7	12	19	16
16	Mark Kirton	C	5-10	170	2-3-58/Toronto, Ont.	Fredericton	27	37	64	20
28	J.M. Lanthier	D	6-2	195	3-27-63/Montreal, Que.	Fredericton	15	38	53	24
27	John Leblanc	KW	6-1	190	2-21-64/Campelton, N.B.	Vancouver	1	0	1	0
						Fredericton	40	30	70	27
2	Craig Levie	D	6-1	185	8-17-59/Calgary, Alta.	Vancouver	0	1	1	13
3	Doug Lidster	D	6-1	195	10-18-60/Kamloops, B.C.	Vancouver	12	51	63	40
22	Dave Lowry	LW	6-1	185	1-15-65/Sudbury, Ont.	Vancouver	8	10	18	176
	Rob Murphy	C				Laval	35	54	89	86
7	Barry Pederson	C	5-11	185	3-13-61/Big River, Sask.	Vancouver	24	52	76	50
10	Brent Peterson	C	6-0	190	2-15-58/Calgary, Alta.	Vancouver	7	15	22	77
24	Michel Petit	D	6-1	180	2-12-64/St. Malo, Que.	Vancouver	12	13	25	131
6	Dave Richter	D	6-5	220	4-8-60/Winnipeg, Man.	Vancouver	2	15	17	172
19	Jim Sandlak	RW	6-3	209	12-12-66/Kitchener, Ont.	Vancouver	15	21	36	66
26	Petri Skriko	LW	5-10	172	3-12-62/Finland	Vancouver	33	41	74	44
12	Stan Smyl	RW	5-8	185	1-28-58/Glendon, Alta.	Vancouver	20	23	43	84
	Mike Stevens	RW	5-11	195	12-30-65/Vancouver, B.C.	Fredericton	7	18	25	258
14	Raimo Summanen	RW	5-9	178	3-2-62/Finland	Edm.-Van.	14	11	25	15
17	Patrik Sundstrom	C	6-0	203	12-14-61/Sweden	Vancouver	29	42	71	40
15	Rich Sutter	RW	5-11	165	12-2-63/Viking, Alta.	Vancouver	20	22	42	113
20	Steve Tambellini	C	6-0	190	5-14-58/Trail, B.C.	Vancouver	16	20	36	14
9	Tony Tanti	C	5-9	185	9-7-63/Toronto, Ont.	Vancouver	41	38	79	84
	Claude Vilgrain	C	6-0	190	3-1-63/Haiti	Team Canada	28	42	70	
	Dan Woodley	LW	5-11	185	12-29-67/Oklahoma City, Okla.	Portland	30	50	80	81

							GP	GA	SO	Avg.
35	Richard Brodeur	G	5-7	175	9-15-52/Montreal, Que.	Vancouver	53	178	1	3.59
30	Frank Caprice	G	5-9	147	5-2-62/Hamilton, Ont.	Vancouver	25	89	0	3.84
						Fredericton	12	47	0	4.11
	Troy Gamble	G	5-11	170	4-7-67/Wetaslowin, Alta.	Vancouver	1	4	0	4.00
						Spokane	49	209	0	4.48
1	Wendell Young	G	5-8	178	8-1-63/Halifax, N.S.	Vancouver	8	35	0	5.00
						Fredericton	30	118	0	4.22

the tip-in and deflection... Became the first player in the history of the Canucks to score 40 or more goals on two occasions... Forms an excellent line with Petri Skirko and Patrik Sundstrom ... Not noted for his skating or, certainly, his size or, most definitely, his flashiness... All he does is score... Born Sept. 7, 1963, in Toronto... Broke Wayne Gretzky's record for goals by a rookie in the Ontario Junior Hockey League with 81 in 1980-81 ... Led Team Canada in goals (6) at the 1987 world hockey championships in Vienna.

Year	Club	GP	G	A	Pts.
1982-83	Chi-Van.	40	9	8	17
1983-84	Vancouver	79	45	41	86
1984-85	Vancouver	68	39	20	59
1985-86	Vancouver	77	39	33	72
1986-87	Vancouver	77	41	38	79
	Totals	341	173	140	313

PETRI SKRIKO 25 5-10 172　　　　　　　Right Wing

A former Finnish fireman... Son of a Finnish army major who grew up only a few miles from the Soviet border... Sheer excitement on ice with an abundance of speed and slick moves... "The Streak" is considered one of the NHL's best-kept secrets... Selected as the NHL's Player of the Week, Nov. 17-23, 1986, when he had 12 goals and two assists in a five-game span... Later, in March, he went on another tear with nine goals and eight assists in a six-game stretch... Born March 12, 1962, at Laapeenranta, Finland... A seventh-round draft choice (157th overall) in 1981... Ranked second in NHL with six shorthanded goals in 1986-87.

Year	Club	GP	G	A	Pts.
1984-85	Vancouver	72	21	14	35
1985-86	Vancouver	80	38	40	78
1986-87	Vancouver	76	33	41	74
	Totals	228	92	95	187

BARRY PEDERSON 26 5-11 185　　　　　　　Center

Second-guessers have had a field day thrashing the Canucks for giving up Cam Neely and their first-round draft choice in 1987 to Boston for Pederson... It wasn't his fault... He will have to have phenomenal seasons in Vancouver for them to forget... A quality player, nonetheless . . . Give him a sniper of Rick Middleton's ilk to play with and watch what will happen . . . His passes are gift-wrapped . . . Born March 31, 1961, in Big River, Sask. . . . Underwent serious surgery Jan. 11, 1985, when a large portion of his left bicep was removed . . . A first-round draft choice (18th overall) of Boston's in 1980 . . . Finished second to Dale Hawerchuk of Winnipeg in the 1981-82 voting for Rookie of the Year.

Year	Club	GP	G	A	Pts.
1980-81	Boston	9	1	4	5
1981-82	Boston	80	44	48	92
1982-83	Boston	77	46	61	107
1983-84	Boston	80	39	77	116
1984-85	Boston	22	4	8	12
1985-86	Boston	79	29	47	76
1986-87	Vancouver	79	24	52	76
	Totals	426	187	297	484

RICHARD BRODEUR 35 5-7 175   Goaltender

A veritable institution in Vancouver . . . No. 1 on the Coast for the last seven seasons . . . King Richard . . . Only two active NHL players—Marcel Dionne and Larry Robinson—are older than him . . . Posted 20 or more wins for the third time in his career in 1986-87 . . . Had a record of 20-25-5 for a team that finished 14 games under .500 . . . Born Sept. 15, 1952, in Longueuil, Que. . . . A workhorse who has averaged 50 starts and 3,000 minutes per season . . . An accomplished artist in the offseason . . . His paintings of rural scenes in Quebec have been exhibited . . . Shares in the ownership of a Quebec radio station.

Year	Club	GP	GA	SO	Avg.
1972-73	Quebec (WHA)	24	102	0	4.75
1973-74	Quebec (WHA)	30	89	1	3.32
1974-75	Quebec (WHA)	51	188	0	3.84
1975-76	Quebec (WHA)	69	244	2	3.69
1976-77	Quebec (WHA)	53	167	2	3.45
1977-78	Quebec (WHA)	36	121	0	3.70
1978-79	Quebec (WHA)	42	126	3	3.11
1979-80	New York I	2	6	0	4.50
1980-81	Vancouver	52	177	0	3.51
1981-82	Vancouver	52	168	2	3.35
1982-83	Vancouver	58	208	0	3.79
1983-84	Vancouver	36	141	1	4.02
1984-85	Vancouver	51	228	0	4.67
1985-86	Vancouver	64	240	2	4.07
1986-87	Vancouver	53	178	1	3.59
	NHL Totals	368	1346	11	3.85
	WHA Totals	305	1037	8	3.64

PATRIK SUNDSTROM 25 6-0 203 Center

Holds Canuck club records for points (91) and game-winning goals (7) in a single season and points (7) and assists (6) in a single game... Shy and reticent individual who lets his actions speak for himself... The Canucks' Emory Edge Award winner in 1986-87 with a plus-9 rating... Linemate Tony Tanti describes him as the "best center I've ever played beside. He skates like the wind, and is as tough as nails in the corners"... Born Dec. 14, 1961, in the northern city of Skelleftea, Sweden... A twin brother of Peter Sundstrom, a former New York Ranger... Set his single-game point and assist records Feb. 29, 1984, against Pittsburgh.

Year	Club	GP	G	A	Pts.
1982-83	Vancouver.........	74	23	23	46
1983-84	Vancouver.........	78	38	53	91
1984-85	Vancouver.........	71	25	43	68
1985-86	Vancouver.........	79	18	48	66
1986-87	Vancouver.........	72	29	42	71
	Totals	374	133	209	342

DOUG LIDSTER 27 6-1 195 Defenseman

Considered the Canucks' best defenseman... A sickly minus-35 rating was one of the NHL's worst in 1986-87... Simply put, he played a lot for a bad hockey team... Set the team record for points (63) by a defenseman in 1986-87... The youngest of seven children... Born Oct. 18, 1960, in Kamloops, B.C... An All-American at Colorado College in 1982-83... Competed for Canada in the 1984 Winter Olympics... A sixth-round choice (133rd overall) in 1980... During the offseason, he rides a bicycle every day to the Pacific Coliseum to work out.

Year	Club	GP	G	A	Pts.
1983-84	Vancouver.........	8	0	0	0
1984-85	Vancouver.........	78	6	24	30
1985-86	Vancouver.........	78	12	16	28
1986-87	Vancouver.........	80	12	51	63
	Totals	244	30	91	121

BRENT PETERSON 29 6-0 190 Center

Strictly a specialist... One of the NHL's most accomplished checkers... Coaches value his ability to contain the NHL's best scorers... Most adept on faceoffs... Loathes the losing that keeps occurring in Vancouver... Born Feb. 15, 1958, in

Calgary... Acquired from Buffalo in the 1985 waiver draft...
Considered a steal at the time... An infrequent scorer who manages no more than a goal a month... Most cooperative with the media... Aspires to be a broadcaster when his playing days are over.

Year	Club	GP	G	A	Pts.
1978-79	Detroit	5	0	0	0
1979-80	Detroit	18	1	2	3
1980-81	Detroit	53	6	18	24
1981-82	Det-Buff	61	10	5	15
1982-83	Buffalo	75	13	24	37
1983-84	Buffalo	70	9	12	21
1984-85	Buffalo	74	12	22	34
1985-86	Vancouver	77	8	23	31
1986-87	Vancouver	69	7	15	22
	Totals	502	66	121	187

RICH SUTTER 23 5-11 165   Right Wing

He and his twin brother, Ron, are the youngest of the five Sutter brothers in the NHL... The only Sutter brother who has ever been traded or has ever played in the minors... The lightest, too... Involved in two complex deals involving 12 players...
Started slowly with the Canucks, but salvaged the year with the first 20-goal season of his career... Arrived 30 minutes before his twin brother on Dec. 2, 1963, in Viking, Alta... Typical of the Sutter mold, he plays bigger that he is... In Philadelphia, the brothers were called "Slash and Spear."

Year	Club	GP	G	A	Pts.
1982-83	Pittsburgh	4	0	0	0
1983-84	Pitt-Phil	75	16	12	28
1984-85	Philadelphia	56	6	10	16
1985-86	Philadelphia	78	14	25	39
1986-87	Vancouver	74	20	22	42
	Totals	287	56	69	125

STAN SMYL 29 5-8 185   Right Wing

A serious knee injury left him merely a shadow of his former self at first... Given little chance of extending his 20-goal scoring streak to eight consecutive seasons, he got there by scoring three times in his 79th game—a 6-4 win over Winnipeg on April 3, 1987... Most effective when he's hitting and being a general irritant... Opponents hate him with a passion... Born Jan. 28, 1958, in Glendon, Alta.... Edmonton offered its first-round draft choice for him prior to the 1987 trading deadline...
Canucks considered but refused in the belief their captain has

more good years ahead of him...Detests losing...Loves the outdoor life—canoeing, rafting, sailing and hiking...Nickname is "Steamer"...A third-round choice (40th overall) in 1978... Holds the Canucks' club record for points by a right winger with 88 in 1982-83.

Year	Club	GP	G	A	Pts.
1978-79	Vancouver.........	62	14	24	38
1979-80	Vancouver.........	77	31	47	78
1980-81	Vancouver.........	80	25	38	63
1981-82	Vancouver.........	80	34	44	78
1982-83	Vancouver.........	74	38	50	88
1983-84	Vancouver.........	80	24	43	67
1984-85	Vancouver.........	80	27	37	64
1985-86	Vancouver.........	73	27	35	62
1986-87	Vancouver.........	66	20	23	43
	Totals	692	240	341	581

JIM SANDLAK 20 6-3 209   Right Wing

Follows in Cam Neely's skates as the Canucks' big right winger ...Despite his size, he is less than assertive...Warranted serious consideration for a position on the NHL's 1987 All-Rookie team...Ninth in the NHL rookies' scoring derby...Born Dec. 12, 1966, in Kitchener, Ont...A first-round choice (fourth overall) in 1985...His father, Jim Sandlak Sr., is a former American Hockey League linesman...Played for Canada's national junior team which won the world championship in 1985.

Year	Club	GP	G	A	Pts.
1985-86	Vancouver.........	23	1	3	4
1986-87	Vancouver.........	78	15	21	36
	Totals	101	16	24	40

COACH BOB McCAMMON:

Affable individual who tells great stories...Came out of the cold to sign as coach with the Canucks, joining a Philadelphia reunion on the West Coast...His predecessor, Tom Watt, knew his days were numbered the day the Canucks handed Pat Quinn an envelope containing $100,000 with the understanding he would become their president and general manager...Bided his time as Edmonton's director of player development while waiting for his last Philadelphia contract to run out... Spent his last season behind the bench in 1983-84 while serving as Philadelphia's coach and general manager... Oddly enough, the man he replaced was Pat Quinn... In four seasons, he posted a record of 119-68-31 for a .617 winning percentage... Conversely, his record in the playoffs is a miserable 1-9... Nickname is "Cagey"... Resides in Portland, Me., which is about as far as you can get from Vancouver and still be in North America... Born April 14, 1941, in Kenora, Ont.... Played 13 years as a minor-league defenseman.

GREATEST COACH

One of hockey's classic photographs shows Roger Neilson waving a white towel on the end of a hockey stick in a mock surrender to referee Bob Myers, during the Campbell Conference final against Chicago in 1982. His gesture prompted his players to do the same and fans followed by waving towels in Vancouver.

Most importantly, he took a team playing below .500 to the Stanley Cup final against the Islanders that season. Neilson was elevated to coach when the NHL suspended Harry Neale for wading into a Quebec crowd during an altercation in March 1982. Until his arrival, no Vancouver team had ever won a playoff series. During his stay behind the bench, the Canucks compiled a 47-61-21 record.

For his towel escapade, he was fined $1,000. But the incident is cherished a memorable happening in the most exciting days of the franchise.

ALL-TIME CANUCK LEADERS

GOALS: Tony Tanti, 45, 1983-84
ASSISTS: Andre Boudrias, 62, 1974-75
POINTS: Patrik Sundstrom, 91, 1983-84
SHUTOUTS: Gary Smith, 6, 1974-75

WINNIPEG JETS

TEAM DIRECTORY: Pres.: Barry Shenkarow; VP-GM: John Ferguson; Dir. Media Inf.: Ralph Carter; Dir. Player Personnel: Mike Smith; Coach: Dan Maloney. Home ice: Winnipeg Arena (15,401; 200' × 85'). Colors: Blue, red and white. Training Camp: Winnipeg.

SCOUTING REPORT

OFFENSE: This is a team that rose 11 notches (17th to 6th) in the overall standings last season by preventing goals rather than scoring them.

By allowing 101 fewer goals than the year before, the Jets moved into the NHL's top third for the second time in three years.

Players sacrificed a few goals of their own to spoil the scoring chances of opponents in response to the dictums of coach Dan Maloney.

Mention the Jets and one thinks of Dale Hawerchuk, a five-time 100-point man, or his ever-present right winger, Paul MacLean, a burly, mustached, plodding forward with the hands of a musician.

Gone is their left winger, Brian Mullen, traded to the New York Rangers. Now, we shall see how easily he's replaced, as the pundits predicted.

Newcomers will include Roger Ohman, a 6-3, 200-pound winger from Sweden and Iain Duncan, a 195-pound left winger from Bowling Green. A sneak preview of Duncan in the playoffs suggested he'll be Mullen's successor.

What must improve is the power play, ranked 19th last season. Someone to watch: Hannu Jarvenpaa, the Finnish winger.

DEFENSE: Thanks to the drafting expertise of someone, probably assistant general manager Mike Smith, the Jets have come up with an outstanding young defenseman in Fredrik Olausson, a Swede who starred as a rookie in 1986-87.

Olausson provides a much-needed dash of speed to the defense, dominated by the likes of Randy Carlyle, Mario Marois and Dave Ellett. All three are coming off solid seasons.

Six-foot-five Jim Kyte has proved he can play as well as fight and Brad Berry just quietly does his job.

"Pokey and the Bandit" is a Winnipeg ice show that has attracted international attention.

Eldon (Pokey) Reddick, a black Gump Worsley, won 21

Dale Hawerchuk looks for his sixth 100-point season.

games while his partner, Daniel Berthiaume, a rookie, too, won
18 of his 28 starts. Reddick claimed he didn't know it was Mike
Bossy he had just robbed while Berthiaume knew exactly who his
victims were. They were good, even great and refreshingly
quaint.

Instrumental in every Winnipeg win is its superb penalty-

JET ROSTER

No.	Player	Pos.	Ht.	Wt.	Born	1986–87	G	A	Pts.	PIM
40	Joel Baillargeon	LW	6-2	215	10-6-64/Charlesbourg, Que.	Winnipeg	0	1	1	15
						Sherbrooke	9	18	27	137
29	Brad Berry	D	6-2	190	4-1-65/Bashaw, Alta.	Winnipeg	2	8	10	60
16	Laurie Boschman	C	5-11	175	6-4-60/Karrobert, Man.	Winnipeg	17	24	41	152
8	Randy Carlyle	D	5-10	200	4-19-56/Sudbury, Ont.	Winnipeg	16	26	42	93
5	Bobby Dollas	D	6-2	195	1-31-65/Montreal, Que.	Sherbrooke	6	18	24	87
36	Ian Duncan	LW	6-1	180	8-4-63/Weston, Ont.	Winnipeg	1	2	3	0
12	Peter Douris	C	6-1	192	2-19-66/Toronto, Ont.	Winnipeg	0	0	0	0
						Sherbrooke	14	28	42	24
	Pat Elynuik	RW	6-0	182	10-30-67/Foam Lake, Sask.	Prince Albert	51	62	113	40
2	Dave Ellett	D	6-1	200	3-30-64/Cleveland, Ohio	Winnipeg	13	31	44	53
14	Craig Endean	RW	5-11	175	4-13-68/Kamloops, B.C.	Winnipeg	0	1	1	0
						Regina	69	77	146	34
11	Gilles Hamel	RW	6-0	185	12-15-57/Asbestoes, Que.	Winnipeg	27	21	48	24
10	Dale Hawerchuk	C	5-11	185	4-4-63/Toronto, Ont.	Winnipeg	47	53	100	54
13	Hannu Jarvenpaa	RW	6-0	193	5-19-63/Ives, Fin.	Winnipeg	1	8	9	8
38	Brad Jones	C	6-0	185	6-26-65/Sterling Heights, Mich.	Winnipeg	1	0	1	0
15	Paul MacLean	RW	6-0	205	1-15-58/France	Winnipeg	32	42	74	75
	Bryan Marchment	D	6-1	195	5-1-69/Scarborough, Ont.	Belleville	6	38	44	106
22	Mario Marois	D	5-11	190	12-15-57/Lovette, Que.	Winnipeg	4	40	44	106
20	Andrew McBain	RW	6-1	190	2-18-65/Toronto, Ont.	Winnipeg	11	21	32	106
28	Ray Neufeld	RW	6-2	215	4-13-59/St. Boniface, Man.	Winnipeg	18	18	36	105
17	Jim Nill	D-LW	6-0	186	4-11-58/Hanna, Alta.	Winnipeg	3	4	7	52
4	Fredrick Olaussen	D	6-2	200	10-5-66/Sweden	Winnipeg	7	29	36	24
	Steve Rooney	LW	6-2	185	6-28-62/Canton, Mass.	Winnipeg	2	3	5	79
						Sherbrooke	4	11	15	66
9	Doug Smail	LW	5-9	175	9-2-57/Moose Jaw, Sask.	Winnipeg	25	18	43	36
23	Thomas Steen	C	5-10	195	6-8-60/Sweden	Winnipeg	17	33	50	59
	Ryan Stewart	C	6-1	175	6-1-67/Houston, B.C.	Portland	12	11	23	27
32	Peter Taglianetti	D	6-2	195	8-15-63/Framingham, Mass.	Winnipeg	0	0	0	12
						Sherbrooke	5	14	19	104
7	Tim Watters	D	5-11	180	7-25-59/Kamloops, B.C.	Winnipeg	3	13	16	119
24	Ron Wilson	LW	5-9	168	5-13-56/Toronto, Ont.	Winnipeg	3	13	16	13

No.	Player	Pos.	Ht.	Wt.	Born		GP	GA	SO	Avg.
30	Daniel Berthiaume	G	5-9	150	1-26-66/Longeuil, Que.	Winnipeg	31	93	1	3.17
						Sherbrooke	7	23	0	3.29
	Marc Behrand	G	6-1	185	1-11-61/Madison, Wis.	Sherbrooke	19	62	0	3.31
37	Steve Penney	G	6-1	190	2-2-61/Ste. Foy, Que.	Winnipeg	7	25	0	4.59
						Sherbrooke	4	12	0	3.62
33	Pokey Reddick	G	5-8	170	10-6-64/Halifax, N.S.	Winnipeg	48	149	0	3.24

killing team, led by veteran Ron Wilson. It was the NHL's best in 1986-87.

OUTLOOK: Learning how to win playing defensive hockey is as important as perfecting any style of play. The Jets think they know how to use the means to achieve the end. We'll see. If so, second place in the Smythe will be attainable.

JET PROFILES

DALE HAWERCHUK 24 5-11 185   Center
Crashed the 100-point barrier for the fifth time in six seasons while making a concerted effort to improve his defensive play ...Most identifiable member of the Jets...Holds a plethora of club records, including most goals (53), most assists (77) and most points (130) in a single season...Has league record for most assists (5) in a single period, a feat he performed in a 7-3 win in Los Angeles on March 6, 1984...Team captain...Owns one of the NHL's best contracts, believed to be worth $4 million over eight years...Known as a game-breaker...Team leader in goals (47), assists (53), points (100) and shots (267) in 1986-87 ...Scored goals in six consecutive games from Feb. 20 to March 1, 1987...Has always been upstaged by Wayne Gretzky and his friends in Winnipeg-Edmonton playoff matchups...Played for Team NHL in Rendez-Vous '87...Lives on a farm outside of Manitoba...Born April 4, 1963, in Toronto...An accomplished golfer...Excelled at soccer as a kid.

Year	Club	GP	G	A	Pts.
1981-82	Winnipeg	80	45	58	103
1982-83	Winnipeg	79	40	51	91
1983-84	Winnipeg	80	37	65	102
1984-85	Winnipeg	80	53	77	130
1985-86	Winnipeg	80	46	59	105
1986-87	Winnipeg	80	47	53	100
	Totals	479	268	363	631

RANDY CARLYLE 31 5-10 200   Defenseman
Says a lot and does a lot on the ice...Gives a running commentary of game situations, offering advice and direction to teammates and taunts to opponents...A former Norris Trophy winner (with Pittsburgh in 1980-81) as the NHL's top defenseman... Plays even better defensively today than he did back then, but the

points are not quite as plentiful... Yet, only five NHL defensemen had more goals than he did in 1986-87... Four of them were game-winners... Missed nine games with a neck injury when hit from behind by Tiger Williams of Los Angeles... Answers to the name of "Kitty"... Plays lighter than he did in his earlier days... Plays the stock market... Loves the ponies, especially the harness variety... Owns standardbreds... Born April 19, 1956, in Sudbury, Ont.

Year	Club	GP	G	A	Pts.
1976-77	Toronto............	45	0	5	5
1977-78	Toronto............	49	2	11	13
1978-79	Pittsburgh.........	70	13	34	47
1979-80	Pittsburgh.........	67	8	28	36
1980-81	Pittsburgh.........	76	16	67	83
1981-82	Pittsburgh.........	73	11	64	75
1982-83	Pittsburgh.........	61	15	41	56
1983-84	Pitt-Winn	55	3	26	29
1984-85	Winnipeg	71	13	38	51
1985-86	Winnipeg	68	16	33	49
1986-87	Winnipeg	71	16	26	42
	Totals	706	113	373	486

MARIO MAROIS 29 5-11 190   Defenseman

Unquestionably one of the NHL's top defensemen in 1986-87... Hard-nosed performer who makes his opponents pay dearly for taking liberties near him... Brought the best out of Jim Kyte playing in his company... Has a piercing tenor voice that can be heard by teammates over the din of a large crowd... Put his mind at ease when he signed a three-year contract... Shoots hard and often but scoring percentage was low (2.1 percent) in 1986-87... Born Dec. 15, 1957, in Ancienne Lorette, Que.... One of his biggest supporters is John Ferguson, the Jets' GM, who drafted him for the Rangers in 1977... Cunning individual who knows all the tricks that can help him win.

Year	Club	GP	G	A	Pts.
1977-78	New York R........	8	1	1	2
1978-79	New York R........	71	5	26	31
1979-80	New York R........	79	8	23	31
1980-81	NYR-Van-Que.	69	5	21	26
1981-82	Quebec............	71	11	32	43
1982-83	Quebec............	36	2	12	14
1983-84	Quebec............	80	13	36	49
1984-85	Quebec............	76	6	37	43
1985-86	Que-Winn	76	5	40	45
1986-87	Winnipeg	79	4	40	44
	Totals	645	60	268	328

PAUL MacLEAN 29 6-2 205   **Right Wing**
One of the NHL's largest snipers . . . The Tim Kerr of the Campbell Conference . . . Has a scoring touch as he's bowling over
people . . . Ultra-dangerous when the game is on the line . . . Led
the Jets in game-winning goals (6) and shooting percentage
(20.6) in 1986-87 and shared the lead for power-play goals (10)
. . . Dale Hawerchuk's right winger for the last six seasons . . .
Born March 9, 1959, in Grostenquin, France . . . Holds the NHL
record for overtime goals (3) in a single season (1983-84) . . .
Inhibited by a pinched nerve in his stomach for most of the
1985-86 season . . . Has one of the NHL's bushiest mustaches . . .
Wears contact lenses when he plays . . . Competed for Canada in
the 1980 Winter Olympics . . . An intelligent interview.

Year	Club	GP	G	A	Pts.
1980-81	St. Louis	1	0	0	0
1981-82	Winnipeg	74	36	25	61
1982-83	Winnipeg	80	32	44	76
1983-84	Winnipeg	76	40	31	71
1984-85	Winnipeg	79	41	60	101
1985-86	Winnipeg	69	27	29	56
1986-87	Winnipeg	72	32	42	74
	Totals	451	208	231	439

POKEY REDDICK 23 5-8 170   **Goaltender**
One of the two rookie goaltenders who delivered 39 wins for the
Jets in 1986-87 . . . Posted a personal record of 21-21-4 . . . First
name is actually Eldon, but teammates and fans alike call him by
his nickname, pinned on him by his father who said he was a
slo-poke around the house . . . Style is somewhat similar to that of
Hall of Famer Gump Worsley . . . Actually patterned himself after
Rogie Vachon from studying him on television . . . Played for a
series of bad junior teams that exposed him to thousands of shots
. . . Born Oct. 6, 1964, in Halifax, N.S. . . . The second black
goaltender to play in the NHL; the first being Grant Fuhr of
Edmonton . . . Signed by the Jets as a free agent in September,
1985.

Year	Club	GP	GA	SO	Avg.
1986-87	Winnipeg	48	149	0	3.24

DAVE ELLETT 23 6-1 200   Defenseman

Regained his confidence and positive results followed... Won the Jets' Emery Edge Award with a +19, a marked contrast to a mind-boggling −38 in 1985-86... Strong and benevolent... Snarls at his opponents but rarely drops his gloves... Should have dropped them sooner on Jan. 27, 1987, before Alan Kerr of the Islanders swung and broke his nose... Gradually adopting a leadership role on the team... Born March 30, 1964, in Cleveland, the son of a pro hockey player... Staggered by the trade that sent his mentor, Dave Babych, to Hartford in November 1985... Hard shooter, soft passer.

Year	Club	GP	G	A	Pts.
1984-85	Winnipeg	80	11	27	38
1985-86	Winnipeg	80	15	31	46
1986-87	Winnipeg	78	13	31	44
	Totals	238	39	89	128

THOMAS STEEN 26 5-10 195   Center

A shoulder injury prevented him from playing his best hockey in the 1987 playoffs... Quietly, he has become a main man on the team... Scored a controversial shorthanded goal with no time left on the clock to give Jets a 3-2 win and a 2-0 lead in their series victory over Calgary... Had enough good scoring chances to score 35 goals in 1986-87... Born June 8, 1960, in Tocksmark, Sweden... Led the Jets in shorthanded goals (3)... Tough, by anybody's standards... A cousin of former NHL forward Dan Labraaten... Starred for Sweden in the 1984 Canada Cup with seven goals in eight games.

Year	Club	GP	G	A	Pts.
1981-82	Winnipeg	73	15	29	44
1982-83	Winnipeg	75	26	33	59
1983-84	Winnipeg	78	20	45	65
1984-85	Winnipeg	79	30	54	84
1985-86	Winnipeg	78	17	47	64
1986-87	Winnipeg	75	17	33	50
	Totals	458	125	241	366

GILLES HAMEL 27 6-0 185   Left Wing

Scotty Bowman said he and Scott Arniel were 20-goal scorers

when they were traded for each other in June 1986...But he responded with 27 goals, a career high, while Arniel scored 11, a career low, in Buffalo...Found the added room in Winnipeg Arena to his liking...A skater who has a knack for creating a scoring chance out of a bad situation, especially in the clutch... Kills penalties, too...Younger brother of Jean Hamel, a NHL defenseman for 12 years, whose career was ended by an eye injury...Born March 18, 1960, in Asbestos, Que....Basically shy...Uses some unique and interesting thoughts to express himself...His shot is a blast.

Year	Club	GP	G	A	Pts.
1980-81	Buffalo	51	10	9	19
1981-82	Buffalo	16	2	7	9
1982-83	Buffalo	66	22	20	42
1983-84	Buffalo	75	21	23	44
1984-85	Buffalo	80	18	30	48
1985-86	Buffalo	77	19	25	44
1986-87	Winnipeg	79	27	21	48
	Totals	444	119	135	254

FREDRIK OLAUSSON 21 6-2 200   Defenseman
Scored the Jets' most spectacular goal in 1986-87 on a solo, end-to-end rush, capped by bursting between two Hartford defenders to let loose a shot into the roof of the net...GM John Ferguson was furious when he was left off the American Express All-Rookie team...Definitely, a star of the future...Played in the Elite Division in Sweden as a 17-year-old...Happy-go-lucky sort whose command of English is better than some Canadians ...Born Oct. 5, 1966, in Vaxsjo, Sweden...Grew up dreaming of being a pro...Skates low to the ice...Took some shifts as a right winger in the 1987 playoffs...Considers himself a defenseman, however.

Year	Club	GP	G	A	Pts.
1986-87	Winnipeg	72	7	29	36

DANIEL BERTHIAUME 21 5-9 150   Goaltender
The latter in the Jets' goaltending act, known as Pokey and The Bandit...Small but ultra-quick...Posted a personal record of

18-7-3 with one shutout—3-0 over Hartford on Jan. 9, 1987... Went 8-0-1 over a nine-game stretch... Named the third star twice and first star once in the Jets' six-game dismissal of Calgary in the 1987 playoffs... Reminds many of Quebec's Mario Gosselin... Born Jan. 16, 1966, in Longeuil, Que., a suburb of Montreal... Won the scoring title as a forward in a summer hockey tournament in 1986... His father, a former goaltender, is his most constructive critic.

Year	Club	GP	GA	SO	Avg.
1986-87	Winnipeg	31	93	1	3.17

COACH DAN MALONEY: A finalist for Coach of the Year after guiding the Jets to a 40-32-8 record in his first season in Winnipeg... A stickler for tidy, defensive hockey... Everyone, including the stars, must follow suit to make his system work... In doing so, his team surrendered 101 fewer goals than the year before... Stern individual who commands respect from his players... Very careful never to rap officials publicly but gives them a tough time from behind the bench if their decisions are going against his team... Spent 12 years in the NHL as a player with Los Angeles, Detroit, Chicago and Toronto... Can be terse, but, generally speaking, he is cooperative with the media... His summer hobby is boating... Born Sept. 24, 1950, in Barrie, Ont.

GREATEST COACH

Modest as his accomplishments may seem, Barry Long qualifies as the Jets' greatest coach. On a team that has gone through eight coaches in as many years, his 205-game stay was considerable. His record was 87-93-25, spoiled to a large extent by a 19-41-6 mark in 1985-86.

A players' coach, he expressed great confidence in his men. In many respects, he felt betrayed when the Jets traded defenseman Dave Babych to Hartford for Ray Neufeld. A former defenseman himself, he knew the value of a good one.

A low-key individual, he offered little emotion behind the bench. In so many respects, he was the antithesis of general manager John Ferguson. It was apparent his mandate to coach would not be a long one.

ALL-TIME JET LEADERS

GOALS: Bobby Hull, 77, 1974-75
ASSISTS: Ulf Nilsson, 94, 1974-75
POINTS: Bobby Hull, 142, 1974-75
SHUTOUTS: Joe Daley, 5, 1975-76

Official NHL Statistics

1986-1987

FINAL STANDINGS

CLARENCE CAMPBELL CONFERENCE

NORRIS DIVISION

	GP	W	L	T	GF	GA	PTS	PCTG
St. Louis	80	32	33	15	281	293	79	.494
Detroit	80	34	36	10	260	274	78	.488
Chicago	80	29	37	14	290	310	72	.450
Toronto	80	32	42	6	286	319	70	.438
Minnesota	80	30	40	10	296	314	70	.438

SMYTHE DIVISION

	GP	W	L	T	GF	GA	PTS	PCTG
Edmonton	80	50	24	6	372	284	106	.663
Calgary	80	46	31	3	318	289	95	.594
Winnipeg	80	40	32	8	279	271	88	.550
Los Angeles	80	31	41	8	318	341	70	.438
Vancouver	80	29	43	8	282	314	66	.413

PRINCE OF WALES CONFERENCE

ADAMS DIVISION

	GP	W	L	T	GF	GA	PTS	PCTG
Hartford	80	43	30	7	287	270	93	.581
Montreal	80	41	29	10	277	241	92	.575
Boston	80	39	34	7	301	276	85	.531
Quebec	80	31	39	10	267	276	72	.450
Buffalo	80	28	44	8	280	308	64	.400

PATRICK DIVISION

	GP	W	L	T	GF	GA	PTS	PCTG
Philadelphia	80	46	26	8	310	245	100	.625
Washington	80	38	32	10	285	278	86	.538
NY Islanders	80	35	33	12	279	281	82	.513
NY Rangers	80	34	38	8	307	323	76	.475
Pittsburgh	80	30	38	12	297	290	72	.450

STANLEY CUP: EDMONTON

INDIVIDUAL LEADERS

Goals: Wayne Gretzky, Edmonton, 62
Assists: Wayne Gretzky, Edmonton, 121
Points: Wayne Gretzky, Edmonton, 183
Power-Play Goals: Tim Kerr, Philadelphia, 26
Shorthanded Goals: Wayne Gretzky, Edmonton, 7
Game-Winning Goals: Joe Mullen, Calgary, 12
Shooting Percentage: Ray Ferraro, Hartford, 28.1
Shutouts: Mike Liut, Hartford, 4
Goaltender Wins: Ron Hextall, Philadelphia, 37
Goals-Against Average: Brian Hayward, Montreal, 2.81
Save Percentage: Ron Hextall, Philadelphia, .902

INDIVIDUAL SCORING LEADERS

PLAYER	TEAM	GP	G	A	PTS	+/−	PIM	PP	SH	GW
Wayne Gretzky	Edmonton	79	62	121	183	70	28	13	7	4
Jari Kurri	Edmonton	79	54	54	108	35	41	12	5	10
Mario Lemieux	Pittsburgh	63	54	53	107	13	57	19	0	4
Mark Messier	Edmonton	77	37	70	107	21	73	7	4	5
Doug Gilmour	St. Louis	80	42	63	105	2−	58	17	1	2
Dino Ciccarelli	Minnesota	70	52	51	103	10	92	22	0	5
Dale Hawerchuk	Winnipeg	70	47	53	100	3	54	10	0	4
Michel Goulet	Quebec	75	49	47	96	12−	61	17	0	6
Tim Kerr	Philadelphia	75	58	37	95	38	57	26	0	10
Ray Bourque	Boston	78	23	72	95	44	36	6	1	3
Ron Francis	Hartford	75	30	63	93	10	45	7	0	7
Denis Savard	Chicago	70	40	50	90	15	108	7	0	7
Steve Yzerman	Detroit	80	31	59	90	1−	43	9	1	2
Joe Mullen	Calgary	79	47	40	87	18	14	15	0	12
Walt Poddubny	NY Rangers	75	40	47	87	16	49	11	0	5
Bryan Trottier	NY Islanders	80	23	64	87	2	50	13	0	1
Luc Robitaille	Los Angeles	79	45	39	84	18−	28	18	0	3
Steve Larmer	Chicago	80	28	56	84	20	22	10	0	4
Marcel Dionne	LA-NYR	81	28	56	84	16−	60	10	0	2
Bernie Nicholls	Los Angeles	80	33	48	81	25	101	10	1	2
Larry Murphy	Washington	80	23	58	81	25	39	8	0	4
Dan Quinn	Calgary-Pitts.	80	31	49	80	8	54	11	3	4
Mats Naslund	Montreal	79	25	55	80	3−	16	10	0	3

PLAYER	TEAM	GP	G	A	PTS	+/−	PIM	PP	SH	GW
Ray Bourque	Boston	78	23	72	95	44	36	6	1	3
Cam Neely	Boston	75	36	36	72	23	143	7	0	3
Charlie Simmer	Boston	80	29	40	69	20	59	11	0	4
Rick Middleton	Boston	76	s1	37	68	7	6	4	4	3
Tom McCarthy	Boston	68	30	29	59	10	31	7	0	6
Keith Crowder	Boston	58	22	30	52	20	106	4	0	5
Steve Kasper	Boston	79	20	30	50	4	51	4	2	3
Ken Linseman	Boston	64	15	23	49	15	126	3	0	3
Thomas Gradin	Boston	64	12	31	43	4	18	2	3	3
Geoff Courtnall	Boston	65	13	23	36	4−	117	2	0	1
Reed Larson	Boston	66	12	24	36	9	95	9	0	1
Greg Johnston	Boston	76	12	15	27	7−	79	0	0	1
Mike Milbury	Boston	68	6	16	22	22	96	0	1	1
Michael Thelven	Boston	34	5	15	20	2	18	3	0	0
Nevin Markwart	Boston	64	10	9	19	6−	225	0	0	2
Dwight Foster	Boston	47	4	12	16	1	37	0	1	0
Allen Pedersen	Boston	79	1	11	12	15−	71	0	0	0
Kraig Neinhuis	Boston	16	4	2	6	5−	2	2	0	0
Dave Reid	Boston	12	3	3	6	1−	0	0	0	0
Robert Sweeney	Boston	14	2	4	6	5−	21	0	0	0

PLAYER	TEAM	GP	G	A	PTS	+/-	PIM	PP	SH	GW
Lyndon Byers	Boston	18	2	3	5	1−	53	0	0	0
Randy Burridge	Boston	23	1	4	5	6−	16	0	0	1
Jay Miller	Boston	55	1	4	5	11−	208	0	0	0
Mats Thelin	Boston	59	1	3	4	8−	69	0	0	0
Wade Campbell	Boston	14	0	3	3	1−	24	0	0	0
Doug Keans	Boston	36	0	2	2	0	24	0	0	0
Frank Simonetti	Boston	25	1	0	1	6−	17	0	0	0
John Carter	Boston	8	0	1	1	3	0	0	0	0
Bill Ranford	Boston	41	0	1	1	0	8	0	0	0
Cleon Daskalakis	Boston	2	0	0	0	0	0	0	0	0
Alain Cote	Boston	3	0	0	0	1−	0	0	0	0
Roberto Romano	Pittsburgh	25	0	0	0	0	0	0	0	0
	Boston	1	0	0	0	0	0	0	0	0
	Total	26	0	0	0	0	0	0	0	0
Dave Andreychuk	Buffalo	77	25	48	73	2	46	13	0	2
Phil Housley	Buffalo	78	21	46	67	2−	57	8	1	2
Christian Ruuttu	Buffalo	76	22	43	65	9	62	3	1	1
Mike Foligno	Buffalo	75	30	29	59	13	176	11	1	5
John Tucker	Buffalo	54	17	34	51	3−	21	4	0	0
Adam Creighton	Buffalo	56	18	22	40	4	26	6	0	3
Doug Smith	Buffalo	62	16	24	40	20−	106	7	0	2
Mike Ramsey	Buffalo	80	8	31	39	1	109	2	1	0
Wilf Paiement	Buffalo	56	20	17	37	2	108	2	0	3
Mark Napier	Edmonton	62	8	13	21	3	2	0	1	0
	Buffalo	15	5	5	10	5−	0	1	0	0
	Total	77	13	18	31	2−	2	1	1	0
Paul Cyr	Buffalo	73	11	16	27	16−	122	0	0	1
Clark Gillies	Buffalo	61	10	17	27	0	81	1	0	2
Scott Arniel	Buffalo	63	11	14	25	1−	59	0	0	3
Tom Kurvers	Montreal	1	0	0	0	1	0	0	0	0
	Buffalo	55	6	17	23	10−	24	1	0	1
	Total	56	6	17	23	9−	24	1	0	1
Lindy Ruff	Buffalo	50	6	14	20	12−	74	0	1	1
Ken Priestlay	Buffalo	34	11	6	17	3	8	3	0	0
Gilbert Perreault	Buffalo	20	9	7	16	2−	6	1	0	1
Jim Korn	Buffalo	51	4	10	14	3−	158	0	0	0
Shawn Anderson	Buffalo	41	2	11	13	0	23	0	0	0
Bob Logan	Buffalo	22	7	3	10	5	0	1	0	0
Gates Orlando	Buffalo	27	2	8	10	6−	16	0	0	0
Joe Reekie	Buffalo	56	1	8	9	6	82	0	0	0
Jeff Parker	Buffalo	15	3	3	6	1	7	0	0	0
Mike Hartman	Buffalo	17	3	3	6	2	69	0	0	0
Lee Fogolin	Edmonton	35	1	3	4	2−	17	0	0	0
	Buffalo	9	0	2	2	2−	8	0	0	0
	Total	44	1	5	6	4−	25	0	0	0
Don Lever	Buffalo	10	3	2	5	3−	4	3	0	1
Uwe Krupp	Buffalo	26	1	4	5	9−	23	0	0	0
Paul Brydges	Buffalo	15	2	2	4	4	6	0	0	0
Mark Ferner	Buffalo	13	0	3	3	2	9	0	0	0
Mikael Andersson	Buffalo	16	0	3	3	2→	0	0	0	0
Bob Halkidis	Buffalo	6	1	1	2	3	19	0	0	0
Phil Russell	Buffalo	6	0	2	2	0	12	0	0	0

PLAYER	TEAM	GP	G	A	PTS	+/−	PIM	PP	SH	GW
Bill Hajt	Buffalo	23	0	2	2	0	4	0	0	0
Jacques Cloutier	Buffalo	40	0	2	2	0	10	0	0	0
Dave Fenyves	Buffalo	7	1	0	1	3−	0	0	0	0
Richie Dunn	Buffalo	2	0	1	1	2	2	0	0	0
Steve Dykstra	Buffalo	37	0	1	1	7−	179	0	0	0
Tom Barrasso	Buffalo	46	0	1	1	0	22	0	0	0
Richard Hajdu	Buffalo	2	0	0	0	1	0	0	0	0
Doug Trapp	Buffalo	2	0	0	0	0	0	0	0	0
Daren Puppa	Buffalo	3	0	0	0	0	2	0	0	0
Jim Hofford	Buffalo	12	0	0	0	1−	40	0	0	0
Joe Mullen	Calgary	79	47	40	87	18	14	15	0	12
Al Macinnis	Calgary	79	20	56	76	20	97	7	0	2
Paul Reinhart	Calgary	76	15	54	69	7	22	7	0	2
Mike Bullard	Pittsburgh	14	2	10	12	1−	17	1	0	0
	Calgary	57	28	26	54	10	34	10	0	3
	Total	71	30	36	66	9	51	11	0	3
Carey Wilson	Calgary	80	20	36	56	2−	42	3	1	2
John Tonelli	Calgary	78	20	31	51	2−	72	10	0	3
Joel Otto	Calgary	68	19	31	50	8	185	5	0	1
Jim Peplinski	Calgary	80	18	32	50	13	185	0	2	3
Gary Suter	Calgary	68	9	40	49	10−	70	4	0	0
Hakan Loob	Calgary	68	18	26	44	13−	26	7	0	1
Jamie Macoun	Calgary	79	7	33	40	33	111	1	0	0
Steve Bozek	Calgary	71	17	18	35	3	22	2	2	4
Brian Bradley	Calgary	40	10	18	28	6	16	2	0	2
Colin Patterson	Calgary	68	13	14	27	7	41	0	1	3
Lanny McDonald	Calgary	58	14	12	26	3−	54	4	0	3
Tim Hunter	Calgary	73	6	15	21	1−	357	0	0	1
Gary Roberts	Calgary	32	5	9	14	6	85	0	0	0
Dale Degray	Calgary	27	6	7	13	3−	29	0	0	1
Neil Sheehy	Calgary	54	4	6	10	11	151	0	0	0
Perry Berezan	Calgary	24	5	3	8	4	24	0	1	0
Nick Fotiu	Calgary	42	5	3	8	3−	145	0	0	1
Kari Eloranta	Calgary	13	1	6	7	3	9	0	0	0
Joe Nieuwendyk	Calgary	9	5	1	6	0	0	2	0	1
Doug Risenbrough	Calgary	22	2	3	5	2−	66	0	0	0
Kevan Guy	Calgary	24	0	4	4	8	19	0	0	0
Brian Engblom	Calgary	32	0	4	4	7−	28	0	0	0
Paul Baxter	Calgary	18	0	2	2	5−	66	0	0	0
Mike Vernon	Calgary	54	0	2	2	0	14	0	0	0
Brett Hull	Calgary	5	1	0	1	1−	0	0	0	1
Doug Dadswell	Calgary	2	0	0	0	0	0	0	0	0
Rejean Lemelin	Calgary	34	0	0	0	0	20	0	0	0
Denis Savard	Chicago	70	40	50	90	15	108	7	0	7
Steve Larmer	Chicago	80	28	56	84	20	22	10	0	4
Troy Murray	Chicago	77	28	43	71	14	59	4	2	3
Wayne Presley	Chicago	80	32	29	61	18−	114	7	0	4
Al Secord	Chicago	77	29	29	58	20−	196	5	0	3
Ed Olczyk	Chicago	79	16	35	51	4−	119	2	1	2
Curt Fraser	Chicago	75	25	25	50	5	182	3	0	2
Doug Wilson	Chicago	69	16	32	48	15	36	7	1	1

PLAYER	TEAM	GP	G	A	PTS	+/−	PIM	PP	SH	GW
Bob Murray	Chicago	79	6	38	44	9−	80	4	0	1
Bill Watson	Chicago	51	13	19	32	19	6	0	0	0
Gary Nylund	Chicago	80	7	20	27	9−	190	2	0	0
Keith Brown	Chicago	73	4	23	27	5	86	2	0	0
Mark Lavarre	Chicago	58	8	15	23	11	33	0	0	0
Dave Donnelly	Chicago	71	6	12	18	7−	81	0	0	0
Rich Preston	Chicago	73	8	9	17	8−	19	0	0	1
Steve Ludzik	Chicago	52	5	12	17	3−	34	0	0	1
Darryl Sutter	Chicago	44	8	6	14	3−	16	1	0	0
Marc Bergevin	Chicago	66	4	10	14	4	66	0	0	0
Jack O'Callahan	Chicago	48	1	13	14	10	59	1	0	0
Mike Stapleton	Chicago	39	3	6	9	9−	6	0	0	0
Dave Manson	Chicago	63	1	8	9	2−	146	0	0	0
Everett Sanipass	Chicago	7	1	3	4	3	2	0	0	0
Bob Sauve	Chicago	46	0	4	4	0	6	0	0	0
Rick Paterson	Chicago	22	1	2	3	1	6	0	1	0
Murray Bannerman	Chicago	39	0	1	1	0	4	0	0	0
Darin Sceviour	Chicago	1	0	0	0	0	0	0	0	0
Jim Camazzola	Chicago	2	0	0	0	0	0	0	0	0
Bruce Cassidy	Chicago	2	0	0	0	1−	0	0	0	0
Warren Skorodenski	Chicago	3	0	0	0	0	0	0	0	0
Steve Yzerman	Detroit	80	31	59	90	1−	43	9	1	2
Brent Ashton	Quebec	46	25	19	44	12−	17	12	2	1
	Detroit	35	15	16	31	3−	22	3	1	3
	Total	81	40	35	75	15−	39	15	3	4
Gerard Gallant	Detroit	80	38	34	72	5−	216	17	0	4
Darren Veitch	Detroit	77	13	45	58	14	52	7	1	2
Petr Klima	Detroit	77	30	23	53	9−	42	6	0	5
Shawn Burr	Detroit	80	22	25	47	2	107	1	2	1
Adam Oates	Detroit	76	15	32	47	0	21	4	0	1
Mel Bridgman	New Jersey	51	8	31	39	8−	80	1	1	1
	Detroit	13	2	2	4	1	19	0	1	1
	Total	64	10	33	43	7−	99	1	2	2
Dave Barr	St Louis	2	0	0	0	1	0	0	0	0
	Hartford	30	2	4	6	1−	19	0	1	0
	Detroit	37	13	13	26	7	49	4	0	5
	Total	69	15	17	32	7	68	4	1	5
Mike O'Connell	Det	77	5	26	31	25−	70	3	1	0
Lee Norwood	Detroit	57	6	21	27	31	25−	70	3	1
Tim Higgins	Detroit	77	12	14	26	2−	124	0	1	1
Bob Probert	Detroit	63	13	11	24	6−	221	2	0	0
Joey Kocur	Detroit	77	9	9	18	10−	276	2	0	2
Harold Snepsts	Detroit	54	1	13	14	7	129	0	0	0
Ric Seiling	Detroit	74	3	8	11	4−	49	0	0	0
Mark Kumpel	Quebec	40	1	8	9	12−	16	0	0	0
	Detroit	5	0	1	1	2	0	0	0	0
	Total	45	1	9	10	10−	16	0	0	0
Gilbert Delorme	Quebec	19	2	0	2	1−	14	0	0	0
	Detroit	24	2	3	5	1−	33	0	0	0
	Total	43	4	3	7	2−	47	0	0	0
Dave Lewis	Detroit	58	2	5	7	12	66	0	0	0

PLAYER	TEAM	GP	G	A	PTS	+/-	PIM	PP	SH	GW
Doug Halward	Vancouver	10	0	3	3	8−	34	0	0	0
	Detroit	11	0	3	3	4	19	0	0	0
	Total	21	0	6	6	4−	53	0	0	0
Rick Zombo.	Detroit	44	1	4	5	6−	59	0	0	0
Steve Chiasson	Detroit	45	1	4	5	7−	73	0	0	0
Greg Stefan	Detroit	43	0	4	4	0	24	0	0	0
Mark Lamb	Detroit	22	2	1	3	0	8	0	0	0
Billy Carroll	Detroit	31	1	2	3	9−	6	0	0	1
Jeff Sharples	Detroit	3	0	1	1	0	2	0	0	0
Mark Laforest	Detroit	5	0	1	1	0	7	0	0	0
Joe Murphy.	Detroit	5	0	1	1	0	2	0	0	0
Chris Cichocki	Detroit	2	0	0	0	2−	2	0	0	0
Ed Johnstone	Detroit	6	0	0	0	1	0	0	0	0
Sam St. Laurent	Detroit	6	0	0	0	0	0	0	0	0
Dale Krentz	Detroit	8	0	0	0	2−	0	0	0	0
Glen Hanlon	Detroit	36	0	0	0	0	20	0	0	0
Wayne Gretszky.	Edmonton	79	62	121	183	70	28	13	7	4
Jari Kurri.	Edmonton	79	54	54	108	35	41	12	5	10
Mark Messier	Edmonton	77	37	70	107	21	73	7	4	5
Esa Tikkanen	Edmonton	76	34	44	78	44	120	6	0	5
Glenn Anderson	Edmonton	70	35	38	73	27	65	7	1	6
Paul Coffey	Edmonton	59	17	50	67	12	49	10	2	3
Kent Nilsson	Minnesota	44	13	33	46	2	12	8	0	1
	Edmonton	17	5	12	17	10	4	1	0	0
	Total	61	18	45	63	12	16	9	0	1
Mike Krushelnyski	Edmonton	80	16	35	51	26	67	4	1	2
Craig MacTavish	Edmonton	79	20	19	39	9	55	1	4	2
Kevin Lowe	Edmonton	77	8	29	37	41	95	2	2	1
Moe Lemay	Vancouver	52	9	17	26	2−	128	2	0	0
	Edmonton	10	1	2	3	2	36	0	0	0
	Total	62	10	19	29	0	164	2	0	0
Craig Muni	Edmonton	79	7	22	29	45	85	0	0	2
Kevin McClelland.	Edmonton	72	12	13	25	4−	238	0	0	1
Randy Gregg	Edmonton	52	8	16	24	36	42	0	0	2
Steve Smith.	Edmonton	62	7	15	22	11	165	2	0	1
Charlie Huddy	Edmonton	58	4	15	19	27	35	0	0	0
Dave Hunter	Edmonton	77	6	9	15	1	75	0	0	1
Reijo Ruotsalainen	Edmonton	16	5	8	13	8	6	3	0	1
Normand Lacombe	Buffalo	39	4	7	11	9−	8	1	0	0
	Edmonton	1	0	0	0	1−	2	0	0	0
	Total	40	4	7	11	10−	10	1	0	0
Jeff Beukeboom	Edmonton	44	3	8	11	7	124	1	0	1
Marty McSorley.	Edmonton	41	2	4	6	4−	159	0	0	0
Jaroslav Pouzar.	Edmonton	12	2	3	5	3	6	0	0	0
Danny Gare	Edmonton	18	1	3	4	2	6	0	0	0
Mike Moller.	Edmonton	6	2	1	3	2	0	0	0	0
Steve Graves.	Edmonton	12	2	0	2	2−	0	0	0	1
Grant Fuhr.	Edmonton	44	0	2	2	0	6	0	0	0
Andy Moog	Edmonton	46	0	2	2	0	8	0	0	0
Dave Lumley	Edmonton	1	0	0	0	0	0	0	0	0
Wayne Van Dorp	Edmonton	3	0	0	0	1−	25	0	0	0

PLAYER	TEAM	GP	G	A	PTS	+/−	PIM	PP	SH	GW
Ron Francis	Hartford	75	30	63	93	10	45	7	0	7
Kevin Dineen	Hartford	78	40	39	79	7	110	11	0	7
John Anderson	Hartford	76	31	44	75	11	19	7	0	5
Ray Ferraro	Hartford	80	27	32	59	9 −	42	14	0	2
Dean Evason	Hartford	80	22	37	59	5	67	7	2	2
Paul Lawless	Hartford	60	22	32	54	24	14	4	0	2
Steward Gavin	Hartford	79	20	21	41	10	28	3	2	4
Dave Babych	Hartford	66	8	33	41	18 −	44	7	0	1
Sylvain Turgeon	Hartford	41	23	13	36	3 −	45	6	0	4
Ulf Samuelsson	Hartford	78	2	31	33	29	162	0	0	0
Dave Tippet	Hartford	80	9	22	31	0	42	0	3	2
Dana Murzyn	Hartford	74	9	19	28	17	95	1	0	0
Doug Jarvis	Hartford	80	9	22	31	0	42	0	3	2
Paul MacDermid	Hartford	72	7	11	18	3	202	0	0	1
Mike McEwen	Hartford	48	8	8	16	9 −	32	5	0	2
Randy Ladouceur	Detroit	34	3	6	9	4 −	70	1	0	1
	Hartford	36	2	3	5	6	51	0	0	0
	Total	70	5	9	14	2	121	1	0	1
Dave Semenko	Edmonton	5	0	0	0	0	0	0	0	0
	Hartford	51	4	8	12	7 −	87	0	0	0
	Total	56	4	8	12	7 −	87	0	0	0
Scot Kleinendorst	Hartford	66	3	9	12	4	130	0	0	0
Joel Quenneville	Hartford	37	3	7	10	7	24	0	1	1
Sylvain Cote	Hartford	67	2	8	10	11	20	0	0	0
Pat Hughes	St. Louis	43	1	5	6	6 −	26	0	0	0
	Hartford	2	0	0	0	1 −	2	0	0	0
	Total	45	1	5	6	7 −	28	0	0	0
Mike Millar	Hartford	10	2	2	4	3	0	1	0	0
Mike Liut	Hartford	59	0	2	2	0	4	0	0	0
Torrie Robertson	Hartford	20	1	0	1	6 −	98	0	0	1
Bill Gardner	Hartford	8	0	1	1	2 −	0	0	0	0
Shane Churla	Hartford	20	0	1	1	1 −	78	0	0	0
Greg Britz	Hartford	1	0	0	0	0	0	0	0	0
Brad Shaw	Hartford	2	0	0	0	0	0	0	0	0
Wayne Babych	Hartford	4	0	0	0	5 −	4	0	0	0
Yves Courteau	Hartford	4	0	0	0	6 −	0	0	0	0
Gord Sherven	Hartford	7	0	0	0	6 −	0	0	0	0
Steve Weeks	Hartford	25	0	0	0	0	0	0	0	0
Luc Robitaille	Los Angeles	79	45	39	84	18 −	28	18	0	3
Bernie Nicholls	Los Angeles	80	33	48	81	16 −	101	10	1	2
Jimmy Carson	Los Angeles	80	37	42	79	5 −	22	18	0	2
Dave Taylor	Los Angeles	67	18	44	62	0	84	9	1	3
Jim Fox	Los Angeles	67	19	42	61	10 −	48	4	0	2
Bryan Erickson	Los Angeles	68	20	30	50	12 −	26	6	2	2
Steve Duchesne	Los Angeles	75	13	25	38	8	74	5	0	2
Grant Ledyard	Los Angeles	67	14	23	37	40 −	93	5	0	1
Jay Wells	Los Angeles	77	7	29	36	19 −	155	6	0	2
Morris Lukowich	Los Angeles	60	14	21	35	6	64	4	0	2
Dave Williams	Los Angeles	76	16	18	34	1 −	358	1	0	3
Sean McKenna	Los Angeles	69	14	19	33	11	10	0	1	0
Mark Hardy	Los Angeles	73	3	27	30	16	120	0	0	0

PLAYER	TEAM	GP	G	A	PTS	+/−	PIM	PP	SH	GW
Bob Carpenter	Washington	22	5	7	12	7−	21	4	0	0
	NY Rangers	28	2	8	10	12−	20	1	0	0
	Los Angeles	10	2	3	5	8−	6	0	0	0
	Total	60	9	18	27	27−	47	5	0	0
Bob Bourne	Los Angeles	78	13	9	22	13−	35	0	3	0
Phil Sykes	Los Angeles	58	6	15	21	10	133	0	1	0
Dean Kennedy	Los Angeles	66	6	14	20	9	91	0	0	1
Tom Laidlaw	NY Rangers	63	1	10	11	18−	65	1	0	1
	Los Angeles	11	0	3	3	1	4	0	0	0
	Total	74	1	13	14	17−	69	1	0	1
Larry Playfair	Los Angeles	37	2	7	9	1−	181	0	0	0
Craig Redmond	Los Angeles	16	1	7	8	1−	8	0	0	0
Paul Guay	Los Angeles	35	2	5	7	14−	16	0	0	0
Roland Melanson	Los Angeles	46	0	6	6	0	22	0	0	0
Joe Paterson	Los Angeles	45	2	1	3	15−	158	0	0	1
Lyle Phair	Los Angeles	5	2	0	2	1−	11	0	0	0
Ken Hammond	Los Angeles	10	0	2	2	2	11	0	0	0
Peter Kineen	Los Angeles	11	0	2	2	9−	8	0	0	0
Al Jensen	Washington	6	0	0	0	0	0	0	0	0
	Los Angeles	5	0	1	1	0	0	0	0	0
	Total	11	0	1	1	0	0	0	0	0
Darren Eliot	Los Angeles	24	0	1	1	0	18	0	0	0
Brian Wilks	Los Angeles	1	0	0	0	2−	0	0	0	0
Craig Duncanson	Los Angeles	2	0	0	0	0	24	0	0	0
Bob Janecyk	Los Angeles	7	0	0	0	0	2	0	0	0
Dino Ciccarelli	Minnesota	80	52	51	103	10	92	22	0	5
Brian MacLellan	Minnesota	76	32	31	63	12−	69	13	0	5
Craig Hartsburg	Minnesota	73	11	50	61	2−	93	4	0	1
Dirk Graham	Minnesota	76	25	29	54	2−	142	6	5	2
Brian Bellows	Minnesota	65	26	27	53	13−	34	8	1	2
Neal Broten	Minnesota	46	18	35	53	12	35	5	1	4
Dennis Maruk	Minnesota	67	16	30	46	5	50	4	0	0
Keith Acton	Minnesota	78	16	29	45	15−	56	1	1	3
Brian Lawton	Minnesota	66	21	23	44	20	86	2	0	2
Ron Wilson	Minnesota	65	12	29	41	9−	36	6	0	2
Bob Brooke	NY Rangers	15	3	5	8	3−	20	0	0	0
	Minnesota	65	10	18	28	6−	78	1	1	0
	Total	80	13	23	36	9−	98	1	0	0
Brad Maxwell	Vancouver	30	1	7	8	9−	28	1	1	0
	NY Rangers	9	0	4	4	1−	6	0	0	0
	Minnesota	17	2	7	9	3	31	0	0	1
	Total	56	3	18	21	7−	65	1	0	1
Paul Boutilier	Boston	52	5	9	14	2−	84	1	1	0
	Minnesota	10	2	4	6	1	8	0	0	0
	Total	62	7	13	20	1−	92	1	1	0
Larry DePalma	Minnesota	56	9	6	15	7−	219	2	0	0
Scott Bjugstad	Minnesota	39	4	9	13	6−	43	0	0	0
Gordie Roberts	Minnesota	67	3	10	13	7−	68	0	0	1
Bob Rouse	Minnesota	72	2	10	12	6	179	0	0	0
Willi Plett	Minnesota	67	6	5	11	1	263	0	0	1
Frantisek Musil	Minnesota	72	2	9	11	0	148	0	0	0
Mark Pavelich	Minnesota	12	4	6	10	7	10	0	0	0
Steve Payne	Minnesota	48	4	6	10	12−	19	0	0	0

PLAYER	TEAM	GP	G	A	PTS	+/-	PIM	PP	SH	GW
Raimo Helminen	NY Rangers	21	2	4	6	8 -	2	1	0	0
	Minnesota	6	0	1	1	3 -	0	0	0	0
	Total	27	2	5	7	11 -	2	1	0	0
Jari Gronstrand	Minnesota	47	1	6	7	4	27	0	0	0
Chris Pryor	Minnesota	50	1	3	4	6 -	49	0	0	0
Marc Habscheid	Minnesota	15	2	0	2	6 -	2	1	0	0
Paul Houck	Minnesota	12	0	2	2	2 -	2	0	0	0
Emanuel Viveiros	Minnesota	1	0	1	1	0	0	0	0	0
Jim Archibald	Minnesota	1	0	0	0	1 -	2	0	0	0
Colin Chisholm	Minnesota	1	0	0	0	0	0	0	0	0
Sean Toomey	Minnesota	1	0	0	0	1 -	0	0	0	0
Randy Smith	Minnesota	2	0	0	0	2 -	0	0	0	0
Mike Sands	Minnesota	3	0	0	0	0	0	0	0	0
Mats Hallin	Minnesota	6	0	0	0	3 -	4	0	0	0
Jack Carlson	Minnesota	8	0	0	0	0	13	0	0	0
Kari Takko	Minnesota	38	0	0	0	0	14	0	0	0
Don Beaupre	Minnesota	47	0	0	0	0	16	0	0	0
Mats Naslund	Montreal	79	25	55	80	3 -	16	10	0	3
Bobby Smith	Montreal	80	28	47	75	6	72	11	0	7
Claude Lemieux	Montreal	76	27	26	53	0	156	5	0	1
Larry Robinson	Montreal	70	13	37	50	24	44	6	0	3
Ryan Walter	Montreal	76	23	23	46	6 -	34	11	0	4
Guy Carbonneau	Montreal	79	18	27	45	9	68	0	0	2
Gaston Gingras	Montreal	66	11	34	45	2 -	21	7	0	2
Chris Chelios	Montreal	71	11	33	44	5 -	124	6	0	2
Stephane Richer	Montreal	57	20	19	39	11	80	4	0	3
Mike McPhee	Montreal	79	18	21	39	7	58	0	2	2
Sergio Momesso	Montreal	59	14	17	31	0	96	3	0	4
Brian Skrudland	Montreal	79	11	17	28	18	107	0	1	0
Shayne Corson	Montreal	55	12	11	23	10	144	0	1	3
Petr Svoboda	Montreal	70	5	17	22	14	63	1	0	1
Kjell Dahlin	Montreal	41	12	8	20	3 -	0	3	1	0
Chris Nilan	Montreal	44	4	16	20	2	266	0	0	1
David Maley	Montreal	48	6	12	18	1 -	55	0	0	0
Bob Gainey	Montreal	47	8	8	16	0	19	0	1	3
Craig Ludwig	Montreal	75	4	12	16	3	105	0	0	0
Rick Green	Montreal	72	1	9	10	1 -	10	0	0	0
Mike Lalor	Montreal	57	0	10	10	5	47	0	0	0
John Korkic	Montreal	44	5	3	8	7 -	151	0	0	0
Gilles Thibaudeau	Montreal	9	1	3	4	5	0	0	0	0
Brian Hayward	Montreal	37	0	2	2	0	2	0	0	0
Patrick Roy	Montreal	46	0	1	1	0	8	0	0	0
Serge Boisvert	Montreal	1	0	0	0	0	0	0	0	0
Scott Sandelin	Montreal	1	0	0	0	1	0	0	0	0
Aaron Broten	New Jersey	80	26	53	79	5	36	6	0	3
Kirk Muller	New Jersey	79	26	50	76	7 -	75	10	1	4
John MacLean	New Jersey	80	31	36	67	23 -	120	9	0	4
Pat Verbeek	New Jersey	74	35	24	59	23 -	120	17	0	5
Doug Sulliman	New Jersey	78	27	26	53	17 -	14	4	1	4
Mark Johnson	New Jersey	68	25	26	51	21 -	22	11	2	0
Greg Adams	New Jersey	72	20	27	47	16 -	19	6	0	1

PLAYER	TEAM	GP	G	A	PTS	+/−	PIM	PP	SH	GW
Claude Loiselle	New Jersey	75	16	24	40	7 −	137	2	1	3
Bruce Driver	New Jersey	74	6	28	34	26 −	36	0	0	0
Joe Cirella	New Jersey	65	9	22	31	0 −	111	6	0	0
Andy Brickley	New Jersey	51	11	12	23	15 −	8	1	3	0
Peter McNab	New Jersey	46	8	12	20	14 −	8	2	0	2
Uli Heimer	New Jersey	40	6	14	20	6 −	45	2	0	1
Anders Carlsson	New Jersey	48	2	18	20	11 −	14	0	0	0
Perry Anderson	New Jersey	57	10	9	19	13 −	105	2	0	1
Randy Velischek	New Jersey	64	2	16	18	12 −	54	0	0	0
Jan Ludvig	New Jersey	47	7	9	16	5 −	98	1	0	0
Ken Daneyko	New Jersey	79	2	12	14	13 −	183	0	0	0
Rich Chernomaz	New Jersey	25	6	4	10	11 −	8	2	0	0
Craig Wolanin	New Jersey	68	4	6	10	31 −	109	0	0	0
Gordon Mark	New Jersey	36	3	5	8	4 −	82	0	0	0
Steve Richmond	New Jersey	44	1	7	8	12 −	143	0	0	0
Tim Lenardon	New Jersey	7	1	1	2	2 −	0	0	0	0
Timo Blomqvist	New Jersey	20	0	2	2	3 −	29	0	0	0
Allan Stewart	New Jersey	7	1	0	1	4 −	26	0	0	0
Douglas Brown	New Jersey	4	0	1	1	4 −	0	0	0	0
Karl Freisen	New Jersey	4	0	1	1	0	0	0	0	0
Murray Brumwell	New Jersey	1	0	0	0	1	2	0	0	0
Kirk McLean	New Jersey	4	0	0	0	0	0	0	0	0
Chris Terreri	New Jersey	7	0	0	0	0	0	0	0	0
Craig Billington	New Jersey	22	0	0	0	0	12	0	0	0
Alain Chevrier	New Jersey	58	0	0	0	0	17	0	0	0
Bryan Trottier	NY Islanders	80	23	64	87	2	50	13	0	1
Mike Bossy	NY Islanders	63	38	37	75	8 −	33	8	1	5
Pat LaFontaine	NY Islanders	80	38	32	70	10 −	70	19	1	6
Brent Sutter	NY Islanders	69	27	36	63	23	73	6	3	8
Mikko Makela	NY Islanders	80	24	33	57	3	24	11	0	3
Patrick Flatley	NY Islanders	63	16	35	51	17	81	6	0	4
Denis Potvin	NY Islanders	58	12	30	42	6 −	70	8	0	1
Duane Sutter	NY Islanders	80	14	17	31	1	169	1	0	1
Tomas Jonsson	NY Islanders	47	6	25	31	8 −	36	1	1	0
Rich Kromm	NY Islanders	70	12	17	29	2	20	0	0	0
Ken Leiter	NY Islanders	74	9	20	29	1	30	4	0	0
Randy Boyd	NY Islanders	30	7	17	24	0	37	3	1	0
Brad Lauer	NY Islanders	61	7	14	21	0	65	1	0	1
Steve Konroyd	NY Islanders	72	5	16	21	5 −	70	3	0	0
Alan Kerr	NY Islanders	72	7	10	17	10 −	175	0	1	1
Bob Bassen	NY Islanders	77	7	10	17	17 −	89	0	0	1
Gord Dineen	NY Islanders	71	4	10	14	8 −	110	0	0	0
Greg Gilbert	NY Islanders	51	6	7	13	12 −	26	0	0	0
Ken Morrow	NY Islanders	64	3	8	11	7	32	0	0	0
Ari Haanpaa	NY Islanders	41	6	4	10	8	17	0	0	3
Brian Curran	NY Islanders	68	0	10	10	3	356	0	0	0
Dale Henry	NY Islanders	19	3	3	6	2	46	0	0	0
Gerald Diduck	NY Islanders	30	2	3	5	3 −	67	0	0	0
Neal Coulter	NY Islanders	9	2	1	3	2 −	7	0	0	0
Billy Smith	NY Islanders	40	0	2	2	0	37	0	0	0
Randy Wood	NY Islanders	6	1	0	1	1 −	4	0	0	0
Mark Hamway	NY Islanders	2	0	1	1	1 −	0	0	0	0

PLAYER	TEAM	GP	G	A	PTS	+/−	PIM	PP	SH	GW
Kelly Hrudey	NY Islanders	46	0	1	1	0	37	0	0	0
Derek King	NY Islanders	2	0	0	0	0	0	0	0	0
Walt Poddubny	NY Rangers	75	40	47	87	16	49	11	0	5
Marcel Dionne	Los Angeles	67	24	50	74	8−	54	9	0	2
	NY Rangers	14	4	6	10	8−	6	1	0	0
	Total	81	28	56	84	16−	60	10	0	2
Tomas Sandstrom	NY Rangers	64	40	34	74	8	60	13	0	5
Kelly Kisio	NY Rangers	70	24	40	64	5−	73	4	2	1
Pierre Larouche	NY Rangers	73	28	35	63	7−	12	8	0	3
Don Maloney	NY Rangers	72	19	38	57	7	117	3	3	0
James Patrick	NY Rangers	78	10	45	55	13	62	5	0	0
Tony McKegney	Minnesota	11	2	3	5	2	16	0	0	0
	NY Rangers	64	29	17	46	1−	56	7	2	6
	Total	75	31	20	51	1	72	7	2	6
Ron Greschner	NY Rangers	61	6	34	40	6−	62	1	1	1
Ron Duguay	Pittsburgh	40	5	13	18	8−	30	0	0	0
	NY Rangers	34	9	12	21	8−	9	2	1	0
	Total	74	14	25	39	16−	39	2	1	0
Willie Huber	NY Rangers	66	8	22	30	13−	70	3	1	0
Jan Erixon	NY Rangers	68	8	18	26	3	24	0	1	1
Curt Giles	Minnesota	11	0	3	3	2	4	0	0	0
	NY Rangers	61	2	17	19	3	50	0	0	0
	Total	72	2	20	22	5	54	0	0	0
Jeff Jackson	Toronto	55	8	7	15	11−	64	0	0	0
	NY Rangers	9	5	1	6	3−	15	2	0	1
	Total	64	13	8	21	14−	79	2	0	1
Larry Melnyk	NY Rangers	73	3	12	15	13−	182	0	0	1
Terry Carkner	NY Rangers	52	2	13	15	1−	120	0	0	0
Chris Jensen	NY Rangers	37	6	7	13	1−	21	0	1	2
Lucien Deblois	NY Rangers	40	3	8	11	7−	27	1	0	0
George McPhee	NY Rangers	21	4	4	8	2−	34	0	0	2
Pat Price	Quebec	47	0	6	6	7−	81	0	0	0
	NY Rangers	13	0	2	2	8−	49	0	0	0
	Total	60	0	8	8	15−	130	0	0	0
Stu Kulak	Vancouver	28	1	1	2	11−	37	1	0	1
	Edmonton	23	3	1	4	3	41	0	0	1
	NY Rangers	3	0	0	0	1−	0	0	0	0
	Total	54	4	2	6	9−	78	1	0	2
Dave Gagner	NY Rangers	10	1	4	5	1−	12	0	0	0
Jay Caufield	NY Rangers	13	2	1	3	2−	45	0	0	0
Mike Donnelly	NY Rangers	5	1	1	2	0	0	0	0	0
Bob Froese	Philadelphia	3	0	0	0	0	0	0	0	0
	NY Rangers	28	0	2	2	0	56	0	0	0
	Total	31	0	2	2	0	56	0	0	0
Gord Walker	NY Rangers	1	1	0	1	2	2	0	0	0
Don Jackson	NY Rangers	22	1	0	1	1−	91	0	0	0
Norm Maciver	NY Rangers	3	0	1	1	5−	0	0	0	0
Jim Leavins	NY Rangers	4	0	1	1	0	4	0	0	0
John Vanbiesbrouck	NY Rangers	50	0	1	1	0	18	0	0	0
Ron Scott	NY Rangers	1	0	0	0	0	0	0	0	0
Mike Siltala	NY Rangers	1	0	0	0	1	0	0	0	0
Ron Talakoski	NY Rangers	3	0	0	0	1	21	0	0	0

PLAYER	TEAM	GP	G	A	PTS	+/-	PIM	PP	SH	GW
Paul Fenton	NY Rangers	8	0	0	0	5-	2	0	0	0
Doug Soetaert	NY Rangers	13	0	0	0	0	14	0	0	0
Tim Kerr	Philadelphia	75	58	37	95	38	57	26	0	10
Peter Zezel	Philadelphia	71	33	39	72	21	71	6	2	7
Dave Poulin	Philadelphia	75	25	45	70	47	53	1	3	5
Brian Propp	Philadelphia	53	31	36	67	39	45	8	5	5
Mark Howe	Philadelphia	69	15	43	58	57	37	2	4	0
Per-Erik Eklund	Philadelphia	72	14	41	55	2-	2	5	0	0
Murray Craven	Philadelphia	77	19	30	49	1	38	5	3	2
Rick Tocchet	Philadelphia	69	21	26	47	16	296	1	1	5
Doug Crossman	Philadelphia	78	9	31	40	18	29	7	0	1
Brad McCrimmon	Philadelphia	71	10	29	39	45	52	3	2	4
Scott Mellanby	Philadelphia	71	11	21	32	8	94	1	0	0
Derrick Smith	Philadelphia	71	11	21	32	4-	34	0	0	0
Ilkka Sinisalo	Philadelphia	42	10	21	31	14	8	3	1	1
Ron Sutter	Philadelphia	39	10	17	27	10	69	0	0	0
Lindsay Carson	Philadelphia	71	11	15	26	2-	141	0	1	2
J.J. Daigneault	Philadelphia	88	6	16	22	12	56	0	0	1
Kjell Samuelsson	NY Rangers	30	2	6	8	2-	50	0	0	0
	Philadelphia	46	1	6	7	9-	86	0	0	0
	Total	76	3	12	15	11-	136	0	0	0
Brad Marsh	Philadelphia	77	2	9	11	9	124	0	0	1
Dave Brown	Philadelphia	62	7	3	10	7-	274	0	0	0
Ron Hextall	Philadelphia	66	0	6	6	0	104	0	0	0
Glen Seabrooke	Philadelphia	10	1	4	5	2	2	0	0	0
Ed Hospodar	Philadelphia	45	2	2	4	8-	136	0	0	1
Brian Dobbin	Philadelphia	12	2	1	3	2	14	0	0	0
Darryl Stanley	Philadelphia	33	1	2	3	6	76	0	0	1
John Stevens	Philadelphia	6	0	2	2	0	14	0	0	0
Al Hill	Philadelphia	7	0	2	2	1	4	0	0	0
Don Nachbaur	Philadelphia	23	0	2	2	1	89	0	0	0
Mark Freer	Philadelphia	1	0	1	1	1	0	0	0	0
Jeff Chychrun	Philadelphia	1	0	0	0	0	4	0	0	0
Jere Gillis	Philadelphia	1	0	0	0	0	0	0	0	0
Greg Smyth	Philadelphia	1	0	0	0	2-	0	0	0	0
Ray Allison	Philadelphia	2	0	0	0	2-	0	0	0	0
Kevin McCarthy	Philadelphia	2	0	0	0	1-	0	0	0	0
Steve Smith	Philadelphia	2	0	0	0	0	6	0	0	0
Mike Stothers	Philadelphia	2	0	0	0	0	4	0	0	0
Tim Tookey	Philadelphia	2	0	0	0	0	0	0	0	0
Craig Berube	Philadelphia	7	0	0	0	2	57	0	0	0
Kerry Huffman	Philadelphia	9	0	0	0	5	2	0	0	0
Glenn Resch	Philadelphia	17	0	0	0	0	0	0	0	0
Mario Lemieux	Pittsburgh	63	54	53	107	13	57	19	0	4
Dan Quinn	Calgary	16	3	6	9	6-	14	1	0	0
	Pittsburgh	64	28	43	71	14	40	10	3	4
	Total	80	31	49	80	8	54	11	3	4
Randy Cunneyworth	Pittsburgh	79	26	27	53	14	142	3	2	5
Craig Simpson	Pittsburgh	72	26	25	51	11	57	7	0	3
Terry Ruskowski	Pittsburgh	70	14	37	51	9	147	5	0	2
Doug Bodger	Pittsburgh	76	11	38	49	6	52	5	0	1

PLAYER	TEAM	GP	G	A	PTS	+/−	PIM	PP	SH	GW
Moe Mantha	Pittsburgh	62	9	31	40	6−	44	8	0	0
John Chabot	Pittsburgh	72	14	22	36	7−	8	0	0	1
Bob Errey	Pittsburgh	72	16	18	34	5−	46	2	1	1
Jim Johnson	Pittsburgh	80	5	25	30	6−	116	0	0	1
Dan Frawley	Pittsburgh	78	14	14	28	10−	218	0	0	1
Kevin Lavallee	Pittsburgh	33	8	20	28	2−	4	5	0	0
Dave Hannan	Pittsburgh	58	10	15	25	2−	56	0	1	2
Willy Lindstrom	Pittsburgh	60	10	13	23	9	6	1	0	1
Ville Siren	Pittsburgh	69	5	17	22	8	50	1	0	0
Warren Young	Pittsburgh	50	8	13	21	5−	103	3	0	1
Rod Buskas	Pittsburgh	68	3	15	18	2	123	1	0	0
Chris Kontos	Pittsburgh	31	8	9	17	6−	6	1	0	1
Troy Loney	Pittsburgh	23	8	7	15	0	22	1	0	1
Randy Hillier	Pittsburgh	55	4	8	12	12	97	0	0	0
Dwight Schofield	Pittsburgh	25	1	6	7	4	59	0	0	0
Norm Schmidt	Pittsburgh	20	1	5	6	8−	4	1	0	0
Phil Bourque	Pittsburgh	22	2	3	5	2−	32	0	0	1
Jim McGeough	Pittsburgh	11	1	4	5	5−	8	0	0	0
Mitch Wilson	Pittsburgh	17	2	1	3	3−	83	0	0	0
Lee Giffin	Pittsburgh	8	1	1	2	2	0	0	0	0
Mike Blaisdell	Pittsburgh	10	1	1	2	2	2	0	0	0
Neil Belland	Pittsburgh	3	0	1	1	0	0	0	0	0
Dwight Mathiasen	Pittsburgh	6	0	1	1	1−	2	0	0	0
Chris Dahlquist	Pittsburgh	19	0	1	1	2−	20	0	0	0
Pat Riggin	Boston	10	0	0	0	0	0	0	0	0
	Pittsburgh	17	0	1	1	0	2	0	0	0
	Total	27	0	1	1	0	2	0	0	0
Gilles Meloche	Pittsburgh	43	0	1	1	0	20	0	0	0
Todd Charlesworth	Pittsburgh	1	0	0	0	0	0	0	0	0
Alain Lemieux	Pittsburgh	1	0	0	0	1−	0	0	0	0
Steve Guenette	Pittsburgh	2	0	0	0	0	0	0	0	0
Mike Rowe	Pittsburgh	2	0	0	0	2−	0	0	0	0
Carl Mokosak	Pittsburgh	3	0	0	0	4−	4	0	0	0
Michel Goulet	Quebec	75	49	47	96	12−	61	17	0	6
Peter Stastny	Quebec	64	24	52	76	21−	43	12	0	4
John Ogrodnick	Detroit	39	12	28	40	2−	6	4	1	1
	Quebec	32	11	16	27	6−	4	2	0	1
	Total	71	23	44	67	8−	10	6	1	2
Anton Stastny	Quebec	77	27	35	62	3	8	6	0	5
Paul Gillis	Quebec	76	13	26	39	5−	267	0	0	3
Dale Hunter	Quebec	46	10	29	39	4	135	0	0	0
Risto Siltanen	Quebec	66	10	29	39	2−	32	8	0	0
Alain Cote	Quebec	80	12	24	36	4−	38	0	2	1
Mike Eagles	Quebec	73	13	19	32	15−	55	0	2	2
Jeff Brown	Quebec	44	7	22	29	11	16	3	0	0
Jason Lafreniere	Quebec	56	13	15	28	3−	8	7	0	0
Robert Picard	Quebec	78	8	20	28	17−	71	1	1	3
Doug Shedden	Detroit	33	6	12	18	3	6	1	0	1
	Quebec	16	0	2	2	5−	8	0	0	0
	Total	49	6	14	20	2−	14	1	0	1
David Shaw	Quebec	75	0	19	19	35−	69	0	0	0

PLAYER	TEAM	GP	G	A	PTS	+/–	PIM	PP	SH	GW
Basil McRae	Detroit	36	2	2	4	3-	193	1	0	1
	Quebec	33	9	5	14	1	149	3	0	1
	Total	69	11	7	18	2-	342	4	0	2
Bill Derlago	Winnipeg	30	3	6	9	3-	12	1	0	1
	Quebec	19	3	5	8	4-	6	0	0	0
	Total	48	6	11	17	7-	18	1	0	1
Lane Lambert	NY Rangers	18	2	2	4	2	33	0	0	1
	Quebec	15	5	6	11	1-	18	0	0	0
	Total	33	7	8	15	1	51	0	0	1
Normand Rochefort.	Quebec	70	6	9	15	2	46	0	0	0
Mike Hough.	Quebec	56	6	8	14	8-	79	1	1	0
Randy Moller.	Quebec	71	5	9	14	11-	144	1	0	1
Ken Quinney	Quebec	25	2	7	9	2	16	1	0	0
Steven Finn	Quebec	36	2	5	7	8-	40	0	0	0
Jean F. Sauve	Quebec	14	2	3	5	4-	4	2	0	0
Max Middendorf	Quebec	6	1	4	5	2-	4	0	0	0
Mario Gosselin	Quebec	30	0	3	3	2	20	0	0	0
Richard Zemlak	Quebec	20	0	2	2	0	47	0	0	0
Gord Donnelly	Quebec	38	0	2	2	3-	143	0	0	0
Clint Malarchuk	Quebec	54	0	2	2	0	37	0	0	0
Trevor Stienberg	Quebec	6	1	0	1	0	12	0	0	1
Greg Malone	Quebec	6	0	1	1	0	0	0	0	0
Yves Heroux	Quebec	1	0	0	0	0	0	0	0	0
Scott Shaunessy	Quebec	3	0	0	0	1-	7	0	0	0
Richard Sevigny	Quebec	4	0	0	0	0	14	0	0	0
Daniel Poudrier	Quebec	6	0	0	0	2-	0	0	0	0
Doug Gilmour	St Louis	80	42	63	105	2-	58	17	1	2
Bernie Federko	St Louis	64	20	52	72	25-	32	9	0	3
Mark Hunter	St Louis	74	36	33	69	19-	169	12	0	4
Greg Paslawski	St Louis	76	29	35	64	1	27	5	1	7
Brian Benning	St Louis	78	13	36	49	2	110	7	0	2
Gino Cavallini	St Louis	80	18	26	44	4	54	4	0	2
Rick Meagher	St Louis	80	18	21	39	9-	54	2	2	1
Rob Ramage	St Louis	59	11	28	39	12-	106	6	0	3
Ron Flockhart	St Louis	60	16	19	35	9-	12	2	0	2
Doug Wickenheiser	St Louis	80	13	15	28	22-	37	5	2	1
Ric Nattress	St Louis	73	6	22	28	34-	24	2	0	0
Cliff Ronning	St Louis	42	11	14	25	1-	6	2	0	2
Mark Reeds.	St Louis	68	9	16	25	20-	16	1	0	0
Tim Bothwell	Hartford	4	1	0	1	5-	0	0	0	0
	St Louis	72	5	16	21	14-	46	0	0	1
	Total	76	6	16	22	19-	46	0	0	1
Jocelyn Lemieux	St Louis	53	10	8	18	1	94	1	0	0
Herb Raglan	St Louis	62	6	10	16	6	159	0	0	0
Bruce Bell	St Louis	45	3	13	16	3	18	1	0	0
Doug Evans	St Louis	53	3	13	16	2	91	0	0	0
Charles Bourgeois	St Louis	66	2	12	14	16	164	0	0	1
Jim Pavese	St Louis	69	2	9	11	21-	129	0	0	0
Brian Sutter.	St Louis	14	3	3	6	5-	18	3	0	0
Michael Dark.	St Louis	13	2	0	2	0	2	0	0	0
Todd Ewen	St Louis	23	2	0	2	1-	84	0	0	0
Greg Millen	St Louis	42	0	2	2	0	12	0	0	0
Mike Posavad	St Louis	2	0	0	0	1	0	0	0	0

PLAYER	TEAM	GP	G	A	PTS	+/-	PIM	PP	SH	GW
Larry Trader	St Louis	5	0	0	0	5-	8	0	0	0
Rick Wamsley	St Louis	41	0	0	0	0	10	0	0	0
Russ Courtnall	Toronto	79	29	44	73	20-	90	3	6	3
Rick Vaive	Toronto	73	32	34	66	12	61	8	1	6
Steve Thomas	Toronto	78	35	27	62	3-	114	3	0	7
Wendel Clark	Toronto	80	37	23	60	23-	271	15	0	1
Gary Leeman	Toronto	80	21	31	52	26-	66	4	3	2
Tom Fergus	Toronto	58	21	28	49	1	57	2	1	2
Mark Osborne	NY Rangers	58	17	15	32	15-	101	5	0	2
	Toronto	16	5	10	15	1-	12	1	0	0
	Total	74	22	25	47	16-	113	6	0	2
Vincent Damphousse	Toronto	80	21	25	46	6-	26	4	0	1
Peter Ihnacak	Toronto	58	12	27	39	5	16	4	0	1
Todd Gill	Toronto	61	4	27	31	3-	92	1	0	0
Al Iafrate	Toronto	80	9	21	30	18-	55	0	0	3
Rick Lanz	Vancouver	17	1	6	7	13-	10	1	0	0
	Toronto	44	2	19	21	4	32	1	0	0
	Total	61	3	25	28	9-	42	2	0	0
Mike Allison	Toronto	71	7	16	23	1	66	1	3	2
Borje Salming	Toronto	56	4	16	20	17	42	0	1	1
Miroslav Frycer	Toronto	29	7	8	15	15-	28	3	0	0
Greg Terrion	Toronto	67	7	8	15	5-	6	0	2	0
Brad Smith	Toronto	47	5	7	12	15-	174	0	0	2
Chris Kotsopoulos	Toronto	43	2	10	12	8	75	0	0	0
Miroslav Ihnacak	Toronto	34	6	5	11	3	12	0	0	0
Ken Yaremchuk	Toronto	20	3	8	11	0	16	0	0	0
Dan Daoust	Toronto	33	4	3	7	0	35	0	0	1
Bill Root	Toronto	34	3	3	6	9-	37	1	0	0
Bob McGill	Toronto	56	1	4	5	2-	103	0	0	0
Ken Wregget	Toronto	56	0	4	4	0	20	0	0	0
Daryl Evans	Toronto	2	1	0	1	2-	0	1	0	0
Ted Fauss	Toronto	15	0	1	1	4	11	0	0	0
Terry Johnson	Toronto	48	0	1	1	5-	104	0	0	0
Tim Bernhardt	Toronto	1	0	0	0	0	0	0	0	0
Derek Laxdal	Toronto	2	0	0	0	1-	7	0	0	0
Val James	Toronto	4	0	0	0	0	14	0	0	0
Jerome Dupont	Toronto	13	0	0	0	5-	23	0	0	0
Kevin Maguire	Toronto	17	0	0	0	6-	74	0	0	0
Allan Bester	Toronto	36	0	0	0	0	8	0	0	0
Tony Tanti	Vancouver	77	41	38	79	5	84	15	0	7
Barry Pederson	Vancouver	79	24	52	76	13-	50	6	0	3
Petri Skriko	Vancouver	76	33	41	74	4-	44	10	6	4
Patrik Sundstrom	Vancouver	72	29	42	71	9	40	12	1	0
Doug Lidster	Vancouver	80	12	51	63	35-	40	3	0	0
Stan Smyl	Vancouver	66	20	23	43	20-	84	5	2	0
Rich Sutter	Vancouver	74	20	22	42	17-	113	3	0	2
Steve Tambellini	Vancouver	72	16	20	36	22-	14	9	0	0
Jim Sandlak	Vancouver	78	15	21	36	4-	66	2	0	3
Raimo Summanen	Edmonton	48	10	7	17	1-	15	0	0	0
	Vancouver	10	4	4	8	1-	0	1	0	0
	Total	58	14	11	25	2-	15	1	0	0

PLAYER	TEAM	GP	G	A	PTS	+/-	PIM	PP	SH	GW
Michel Petit	Vancouver	69	12	13	25	5-	131	4	0	1
Dan Hodgson	Vancouver	43	9	13	22	9-	25	4	0	0
Brent Peterson	Vancouver	69	7	15	22	14-	77	2	1	2
Garth Butcher	Vancouver	70	5	15	20	12-	207	0	0	0
Dave Lowry	Vancouver	70	8	10	18	23-	176	0	0	1
Dave Richter	Vancouver	78	2	15	17	2-	172	0	0	0
David Bruce	Vancouver	50	9	7	16	2	109	0	0	2
Jim Benning	Toronto	5	0	0	0	0	4	0	0	0
	Vancouver	54	2	11	13	9	40	0	0	1
	Total	59	2	11	13	9	44	0	0	1
Marc Crawford	Vancouver	21	0	3	3	8-	67	0	0	0
John Leblanc	Vancouver	2	1	0	1	1	0	0	0	0
Craig Coxe	Vancouver	15	1	0	1	3-	31	1	0	0
Wendell Young	Vancouver	8	0	1	1	0	0	0	0	0
Craig Levie	Vancouver	9	0	1	1	3	13	0	0	0
Robin Bartel	Vancouver	40	0	1	1	2	14	0	0	0
Troy Gamble	Vancouver	1	0	0	0	0	0	0	0	0
Jim Agnew	Vancouver	4	0	0	0	0	0	0	0	0
Taylor Hall	Vancouver	4	0	0	0	2-	0	0	0	0
Glen Cochrane	Vancouver	14	0	0	0	0	52	0	0	0
Frank Caprice	Vancouver	25	0	0	0	0	9	0	0	0
Richard Brodeur	Vancouver	53	0	0	0	0	2	0	0	0
Larry Murphy	Washington	80	23	58	81	25	39	8	0	4
Mike Gartner	Washington	78	41	32	73	1	61	5	6	10
Mike Ridley	NY Rangers	38	16	20	36	10-	20	4	0	1
	Washington	40	15	19	34	1-	20	6	0	3
	Total	78	31	39	70	11-	40	10	0	4
Scott Stevens	Washington	77	10	51	61	13	285	2	0	0
Craig Laughlin	Washington	80	22	30	52	3-	67	11	0	5
Gaetan Duchesne	Washington	74	17	35	52	18	53	0	1	4
Dave Christian	Washington	76	23	27	50	5-	8	5	0	2
Bob Gould	Washington	78	23	27	50	18	74	1	1	2
Greg Adams	Washington	67	14	30	44	9	184	2	0	0
Michal Pivonka	Washington	73	18	25	43	19-	41	4	0	2
Kelly Miller	NY Rangers	38	6	14	20	5-	22	2	0	1
	Washington	39	10	12	22	10	26	3	1	0
	Total	77	16	26	42	5	48	5	1	1
Alan Haworth	Washington	50	25	16	41	3	43	9	0	2
Garry Galley	Los Angeles	30	5	11	16	9-	57	2	0	1
	Washington	18	1	10	11	3	10	1	0	0
	Total	48	6	21	27	6-	67	3	0	1
Rod Langway	Washington	78	2	25	27	11	53	0	0	1
Kevin Hatcher	Washington	78	8	16	24	29-	144	1	0	2
Lou Franceschetti	Washington	75	12	9	21	9-	127	0	0	1
Dave Jensen	Washington	46	8	8	16	10-	12	2	0	0
John Blum	Washington	66	2	8	10	1	133	0	0	0
Greg Smith	Washington	45	0	9	9	6-	31	0	0	0
John Barrett	Washington	55	2	2	4	16-	43	0	0	0
Pete Peeters	Washington	37	0	4	4	0	16	0	0	0
Gary Sampson	Washington	25	1	2	3	9-	4	0	0	0
Jeff Greenlaw	Washington	22	0	3	3	2	44	0	0	0
Yvon Corriveau	Washington	17	1	1	2	4-	24	0	0	0
Ed Kastelic	Washington	23	1	1	2	3-	83	1	0	0

PLAYER	TEAM	GP	G	A	PTS	+/-	PIM	PP	SH	GW
Paul Cavallini..........	Washington	6	0	2	2	4-	8	0	0	0
Stephen Leach	Washington	15	1	0	1	4-	6	0	0	0
Yves Beaudoin	Washington	6	0	0	0	4-	5	0	0	0
Grant Martin	Washington	9	0	0	0	1-	4	0	0	0
Jim Thomson	Washington	10	0	0	0	2-	35	0	0	0
Bob Crawford	NY Rangers	3	0	0	0	1-	2	0	0	0
	Washington	12	0	0	0	0	0	0	0	0
	Total	15	0	0	0	1-	2	0	0	0
Bob Mason	Washington	45	0	0	0	0	0	0	0	0
Dale Hawerchuk	Winnipeg	80	47	53	100	3	54	10	0	4
Paul MacLean	Winnipeg	72	32	42	74	12	75	10	0	6
Brian Mullen	Winnipeg	69	19	32	51	2-	20	7	0	4
Thomas Steen	Winnipeg	75	17	33	50	7	59	3	3	1
Gilles Hamel	Winnipeg	79	27	21	48	3	24	1	1	4
Dave Ellett.............	Winnipeg	78	13	31	44	19	53	5	0	2
Mario Marois...........	Winnipeg	79	4	40	44	1-	106	1	0	0
Doug Smail	Winnipeg	78	25	18	43	18	36	0	2	4
Randy Carlyle	Winnipeg	71	16	26	42	6-	93	5	0	4
Laurie Boschman	Winnipeg	80	17	24	41	17-	152	1	1	2
Ray Neufeld	Winnipeg	80	18	18	36	13-	105	5	0	2
Fredrick Olausson	Winnipeg	72	7	29	36	3-	24	1	0	2
Andrew McBain........	Winnipeg	71	11	21	32	6	106	1	1	0
Tim Watters............	Winnipeg	63	3	13	16	5	119	0	0	0
Ron Wilson	Winnipeg	80	3	13	16	10	13	0	0	0
Jim Kyte	Winnipeg	72	5	5	10	4	162	0	0	1
Brad Berry.............	Winnipeg	52	2	8	10	6	60	0	0	0
Hannu Jarvenpaa........	Winnipeg	20	1	8	9	4-	8	0	0	0
Jim Nill	Winnipeg	36	3	4	7	1	52	1	0	2
Perry Turnbull	Winnipeg	26	1	5	6	2-	44	0	0	0
Steve Rooney	Montreal	2	0	0	0	0	22	0	0	0
	Winnipeg	30	2	3	5	4-	57	0	0	1
	Total	32	2	3	5	4-	79	0	0	1
Iain Duncan............	Winnipeg	6	1	2	3	1	0	0	0	0
Brad Jones	Winnipeg	4	1	0	1	2	0	0	0	0
Tom Martin	Winnipeg	11	1	0	1	1	49	0	0	0
Craig Endean...........	Winnipeg	2	0	1	1	1	0	0	0	0
Joel Baillargeon........	Winnipeg	11	0	1	1	3-	15	0	0	0
Randy Gilhen...........	Winnipeg	2	0	0	0	2-	0	0	0	0
Peter Taglianetti........	Winnipeg	3	0	0	0	4-	12	0	0	0
Peter Douris	Winnipeg	6	0	0	0	1-	0	0	0	0
Steve Penney	Winnipeg	7	0	0	0	0	7	0	0	0
Daniel Berthiaume.......	Winnipeg	31	0	0	0	0	2	0	0	0
Eldon Reddick..........	Winnipeg	48	0	0	0	0	8	0	0	0

GOALTENDERS' RECORDS

ALL GOALS AGAINST A TEAM IN ANY GAME ARE CHARGED TO THE INDIVIDUAL GOAL-TENDER OF THAT GAME FOR PURPOSES OF AWARDING THE BILL JENNINGS TROPHY

WON-LOST-TIED RECORD IS BASED ON WHICH GOALTENDER WAS PLAYING WHEN WINNING OR TYING GOAL WAS SCORED.

CODE: GPI—GAMES PLAYED IN. MINS—MINUTES PLAYED. AVG—60-MINUTE AVERAGE. EN—EMPTY-NET GOALS (NOT COUNTED IN PERSONAL AVERAGES BUT INCLUDED IN TEAM TOTALS). SO—SHUTOUTS. GA—GOALS AGAINST. SA—SHOTS AGAINST.

GOALTENDERS	TEAM	GPI	MINS	AVG	W	L	T	EN	SO	GA	SA
Brian Hayward	Montreal	37	2178	2.81	19	13	4	2	1	102	959
Patrick Roy	Montreal	46	2686	2.93	22	16	6	6	1	131	1210
Montreal	**Totals**	80	4864	2.97	41	29	10		2	241	2169
Bob Froese	Philadelphia	3	180	2.67	3	0	0	0	0	8	88
Glenn Resch	Philadelphia	17	867	2.91	6	5	2	1	0	42	436
Ron Hextall	Philadelphia	66	3799	3.00	37	21	6	4	1	190	1933
Philadelphia	**Totals**	80	4846	3.03	46	26	8		1	245	2457
Mike Liut	Hartford	59	3476	3.23	31	22	5	3	4	187	1625
Steve Weeks	Hartford	25	1367	3.42	12	8	2	2	1	78	615
Hartford	**Totals**	80	4843	3.35	43	30	7		5	270	2240
Daniel Berthiaume	Winnipeg	31	1758	3.17	18	7	3	1	1	93	810
Eldon Reddick	Winnipeg	48	2762	3.24	21	21	4	2	0	149	1256
Steve Penney	Winnepeg	7	327	4.59	1	4	1	1	0	25	134
Winnipeg	**Totals**	80	4847	3.35	40	32	8		2	271	2200

Berthiaume and Reddick shared shutout, Jan. 9)

GOALTENDERS	TEAM	GPI	MINS	AVG	W	L	T	EN	SO	GA	SA
Sam St. Laurent	Detroit	6	342	2,81	1	2	2	0	0	16	135
Glen Hanlon	Detroit	36	1963	3.18	11	16	5	3	1	104	976
Mark Laforest	Detroit	5	219	3.29	2	1	0	0	0	12	111
Greg Stefan	Detroit	43	2351	3.45	20	17	3	4	1	135	1082
Detroit	**Totals**	80	4875	3.37	34	36	10		2	274	2304
Mario Gosselin	Quebec	30	1625	3.18	13	11	1	3	0	86	758
Clint Malarchuk	Quebec	54	3092	3.40	18	26	9	1	1	175	1512
Richard Sevigny	Quebec	4	144	4.58	0	2	0	0	0	11	56
Quebec	**Totals**	80	4861	3.41	31	39	10		1	276	2326
Bill Ranford	Boston	41	2234	3.33	16	20	2	1	3	124	1137
Doug Keans	Boston	36	1942	3.34	18	8	4	1	0	108	909
Pat Riggin	Boston	10	513	3.39	3	5	1	0	0	29	236
Cleon Daskalakis	Boston	2	97	4.33	2	0	0	0	0	7	51
Roberto Romano	Boston	1	60	6.00	0	1	0	0	0	6	34
Boston	**Totals**	80	4846	3.42	39	34	7		3	276	2367
Pete Peeters	Washington	37	2002	3.21	17	11	4	3	0	107	931
Bob Mason	Washington	45	2536	3.24	20	18	5	3	0	137	1247
Al Jensen	Washington	6	328	4.94	1	3	1	1	0	27	184
Washington	**Totals**	80	4866	3.43	38	32	10		0	278	2362

GOALTENDERS	TEAM	GPI	MINS	AVG	W	L	T	EN	SO	GA	SA
Kelly Hrudey	NY Islanders	46	2634	3.30	21	15	7	1	0	145	1219
Bill Smith..........	NY Islanders	40	2252	3.52	14	18	5	3	1	132	1007
NY Islanders	**Totals**	86	4886	3.41	35	33	12		1	277	2226
Rejean Lemelin	Calgary	34	1735	3.25	16	9	1	4	2	94	825
Mike Vernon........	Calgary	54	2957	3.61	30	21	1	2	1	178	1528
Doug Dadswell......	Calgary	2	125	4.80	0	1	1	1	0	10	73
Calgary	**Totals**	80	4817	3.60	46	31	3		3	289	2426
Tom Barrasso.......	Buffalo	46	2501	3.65	17	23	2	4	2	152	1202
Jacques Cloutier	Buffalo	40	2167	3.79	11	19	5	1	0	137	1035
Daren Puppa	Buffalo	3	185	4.22	0	2	1	1	0	13	80
Buffalo...........	**Totals**	80	4853	3.81	28	44	8		2	308	2317
Warren Skorodenski..	Chicago	3	155	2.71	1	0	1	0	0	7	90
Bob Sauve	Chicago	46	2660	3.59	19	19	5	0	1	159	1497
Murray Bannerman ..	Chicago	39	2059	4.14	9	18	8	2	0	142	1122
Chicago...........	**Totals**	80	4874	3.82	29	37	14		1	310	2709
Kari Takko	Minnesota	38	2075	3.44	13	18	4	4	0	119	1061
Don Beaupre	Minnesota	47	2622	3.98	17	20	6	4	1	174	1439
Mike Sands	Minnesota	3	163	4.42	0	2	0	1	0	12	104
Minnesota	**Totals**	80	4860	3.88	30	40	10		1	314	2604
Richard Brodeur.....	Vancouver	53	2972	3.59	20	25	5	3	1	178	1391
Frank Caprice.......	Vancouver	25	1390	3.84	8	11	2	2	0	89	643
Troy Gamble........	Vancouver	1	60	4.00	0	1	0	1	0	4	23
Wendell Young	Vancouver	8	420	5.00	1	6	1	2	0	35	224
Vancouver	**Totals**	80	4842	3.89	29	43	8		1	314	2281
Allan Bester	Toronto	36	1808	3.65	10	14	3	3	2	110	991
Ken Wregget	Toronto	56	3026	3.97	22	28	3	3	0	200	1598
Tim Bernhardt	Toronto	1	20	9.00	0	0	0	0	0	3	7
Toronto	**Totals**	80	4854	3.94	32	42	6		2	319	2596
John Vanbiesbrouck..	NY Rangers	50	2656	3.64	18	20	5	6	0	161	1369
Bob Froese.........	NY Rangers	28	1474	3.74	14	11	0	1	0	92	784
Ron Scott..........	NY Rangers	1	65	4.62	0	0	1	0	0	5	35
Doug Soetaert	NY Rangers	13	675	5.16	2	7	2	1	0	58	368
NY Rangers	**Totals**	80	4870	3.99	34	38	8		0	324	2556
Roland Melanson	Los Angeles	46	2734	3.69	18	21	6	3	1	168	1420
Darren Eliot	Los Angeles	24	1404	4.40	8	13	2	5	1	103	692
Bob Janecyk	Los Angeles	7	420	4.86	4	3	0	0	0	34	222
Al Jensen	Los Angeles	5	300	5.40	1	4	0	1	0	27	154
Los Angeles	**Totals**	80	4858	4.21	31	41	8		2	341	2488
Kirk McLean........	New Jersey	4	160	3.75	1	1	0	1	0	10	73
Alain Chevrier.......	New Jersey	58	3153	4.32	24	26	2	3	0	227	1793
Chris Terreri........	New Jersey	7	286	4.41	0	3	1	1	0	21	173
Craig Billington	New Jersey	22	1114	4.79	4	13	2	0	0	89	569
Karl Friesen	New Jersey	4	130	7.38	0	2	1	0	0	16	80
New Jersey	**Totals**	80	4843	4.56	29	45	6		0	368	2688

All-Time NHL Records

Game

MOST GOALS: 7, Joe Malone, Quebec Bulldogs, Jan. 31, 1920 vs. Toronto St. Pats; (Modern) 6, Syd Howe, Detroit Red Wings, Feb. 3, 1944 vs. New York Rangers; 6, Red Berenson, St. Louis Blues, Nov. 7, 1968 vs. Philadelphia Flyers; 6, Darryl Sittler, Toronto Maple Leafs, Feb. 7, 1976 vs. Boston Bruins

MOST ASSISTS: 7, Bill Taylor, Detroit Red Wings, Mar. 16, 1947 vs. Chicago Black Hawks; Wayne Gretzky, Edmonton, Feb. 15, 1980 vs. Washington Capitals

MOST POINTS: 10, Darryl Sittler, Toronto Maple Leafs, Feb. 7, 1976 vs. Boston Bruins (six goals, four assists)

MOST PENALTY MINUTES: 67, Randy Holt, Los Angeles Kings, Mar. 11, 1979 vs. Philadelphia Flyers

Season

MOST GOALS: 92, Wayne Gretzky, Edmonton Oilers, 1981-82

MOST ASSISTS: 163, Wayne Gretzky, Edmonton Oilers, 1985-86

MOST POINTS: 215, Wayne Gretzky, Edmonton Oilers, 1985-86

MOST SHUTOUTS: 22, George Hainsworth, Montreal Canadiens, 1928-29; (Modern) 15, Tony Esposito, Chicago Black Hawks, 1969-70

MOST PENALTY MINUTES: 472, Dave Schultz, Philadelphia Flyers, 1974-75

MOST POINTS BY A ROOKIE: 109, Peter Stastny, Quebec, 1980-81

MOST ASSISTS BY A GOALIE: 8, Mike Palmateer, Washington Capitals, 1980-81

Career

MOST SEASONS: 26, Gordie Howe, Detroit Red Wings, Hartford Whalers, 1946-47 to 1970-71, 1979-80

MOST GAMES: 1,767, Gordie Howe, Detroit Red Wings, Hartford Whalers

MOST GOALS: 801, Gordie Howe, Detroit Red Wings, Hartford Whalers

MOST POINTS: 1,850, Gordie Howe, Detroit Red Wings, Hartford Whalers

MOST PENALTY MINUTES: 3,873, Dave Williams, Toronto, Vancouver, Los Angeles, 1974-87

MOST SHUTOUTS: 103, Terry Sawchuk, Detroit, Boston, Toronto, Los Angeles, New York Rangers

NHL Trophy Winners

HART MEMORIAL TROPHY

Awarded to the league's Most Valuable Player. Selected in a vote of hockey writers and broadcasters in each of the 21 NHL cities. The award was presented by the National Hockey League in 1960 after the original Hart Trophy was retired to the Hockey Hall of Fame. The original Hart Trophy was donated in 1923 by Dr. David A. Hart, father of Cecil Hart, former manager-coach of the Montreal Canadiens

1923-24 Frank Nighbor, Ottawa
1924-25 Billy Burch, Hamilton
1925-26 Nels Stewart, Montreal M.
1926-27 Herb Gardiner, Montreal C.
1927-28 Howie Morenz, Montreal C.
1928-29 Roy Worters, New York A.
1929-30 Nels Stewart, Montreal M.
1930-31 Howie Morenz, Montreal C.
1931-32 Howie Morenz, Montreal C.
1932-33 Eddie Shore, Boston
1933-34 Aurel Joliat, Montreal C.
1934-35 Eddie Shore, Boston
1935-36 Eddie Shore, Boston
1936-37 Babe Siebert, Montreal C.
1937-38 Eddie Shore, Boston
1938-39 Toe Blake, Montreal C.
1939-40 Eddie Goodfellow, Detroit
1940-41 Bill Cowley, Boston
1941-42 Tommy Anderson, New York A.
1942-43 Bill Cowley, Boston
1943-44 Babe Pratt, Toronto
1944-45 Elmer Lach, Montreal C.
1945-46 Max Bentley, Chicago
1946-47 Maurice Richard, Montreal
1947-48 Buddy O'Conner, New York R.
1948-49 Sid Abel, Detroit
1949-50 Charlie Rayner, New York R.
1950-51 Milt Schmidt, Boston
1951-52 Gordie Howe, Detroit
1952-53 Gordie Howe, Detroit
1953-54 Al Rollins, Chicago
1954-55 Ted Kennedy, Toronto

1955-56 Jean Beliveau, Montreal
1956-57 Gordie Howe, Detroit
1957-58 Gordie Howe, Detroit
1958-59 Andy Bathgate, New York R.
1959-60 Gordie Howe, Detroit
1960-61 Bernie Geoffrion, Montreal
1961-62 Jacques Plante, Montreal
1962-63 Gordie Howe, Detroit
1963-64 Jean Beliveau, Montreal
1964-65 Bobby Hull, Chicago
1965-66 Bobby Hull, Chicago
1966-67 Stan Mikita, Chicago
1967-68 Stan Mikita, Chicago
1968-69 Phil Esposito, Boston
1969-70 Bobby Orr, Boston
1970-71 Bobby Orr, Boston
1971-72 Bobby Orr, Boston
1972-73 Bobby Clarke, Philadelphia
1973-74 Phil Esposito, Boston
1974-75 Bobby Clarke, Philadelphia
1975-76 Bobby Clarke, Philadelphia
1976-77 Guy Lafleur, Montreal
1977-78 Guy Lafleur, Montreal
1978-79 Bryan Trottier, New York I.
1979-80 Wayne Gretzky, Edmonton
1980-81 Wayne Gretzky, Edmonton
1981-82 Wayne Gretzky, Edmonton
1982-83 Wayne Gretzky, Edmonton
1983-84 Wayne Gretzky, Edmonton
1984-85 Wayne Gretzky, Edmonton
1985-86 Wayne Gretzky, Edmonton
1986-87 Wayne Gretzky, Edmonton

VEZINA TROPHY

Awarded to the goalie voted most valuable by the Professional Hockey Writers' Association. Up until the 1981-82 season, the trophy was awarded to the goalie or goalies for the team which gives up the fewest goals during the regular season.

The trophy was presented to the NHL in 1926-27 by the owners of the Montreal Canadiens in memory of Georges Vezina, former Canadien goalie.

1926-27 George Hainsworth, Montreal C.	1964-65 Terry Sawchuk, Toronto
1927-28 George Hainsworth, Montreal C.	Johnny Bower, Toronto
1928-29 George Hainsworth, Montreal C.	1965-66 Lorne Worsley, Montreal
1929-30 Tiny Thompson, Boston	Charlie Hodge, Montreal
1930-31 Roy Worters, New York A.	1966-67 Glenn Hall, Chicago
1931-32 Charlie Gardiner, Chicago	Denis DeJordy, Chicago
1932-33 Tiny Thompson, Boston	1967-68 Lorne Worsley, Montreal
1933-34 Charlie Gardiner, Chicago	Rogatien Vachon, Montreal
1934-35 Lorne Chabot, Chicago	1968-69 Glenn Hall, St. Louis
1935-36 Tiny Thompson, Boston	Jacques Plante, St. Louis
1936-37 Normie Smith, Detroit	1969-70 Tony Esposito, Chicago
1937-38 Tiny Thompson, Boston	1970-71 Ed Giacomin, New York R.
1938-39 Frank Brimsek, Boston	Gilles Villemure, New York R.
1939-40 Davey Kerr, New York R.	1971-72 Tony Esposito, Chicago
1940-41 Turk Broda, Toronto	Gary Smith, Chicago
1941-42 Frank Brimsek, Boston	1972-73 Ken Dryden, Montreal
1942-43 Johnny Mowers, Detroit	1973-74 Bernie Parent, Philadelphia
1943-44 Bill Durnan, Montreal	Tony Esposito, Chicago
1944-45 Bill Durnan, Montreal	1974-75 Bernie Parent, Philadelphia
1945-46 Bill Durnan, Montreal	1975-76 Ken Dryden, Montreal
1946-47 Bill Durnan, Montreal	1976-77 Ken Dryden, Montreal
1947-48 Turk Broda, Toronto	Michel Larocque, Montreal
1948-49 Bill Durnan, Montreal	1977-78 Ken Dryden, Montreal
1949-50 Bill Durnan, Montreal	Michel Larocque, Montreal
1950-51 Al Rollins, Toronto	1978-79 Ken Dryden, Montreal
1951-52 Terry Sawchuk, Detroit	Michel Larocque, Montreal
1952-53 Terry Sawchuk, Detroit	1979-80 Bob Sauve, Buffalo
1953-54 Harry Lumley, Toronto	Don Edwards, Buffalo
1954-55 Terry Sawchuk, Detroit	1980-81 Richard Sevigny, Montreal
1955-56 Jacques Plante, Montreal	Denis Herron, Montreal
1956-57 Jacques Plante, Montreal	Michel Larocque, Montreal
1957-58 Jacques Plante, Montreal	1981-82 Billy Smith, New York I.
1958-59 Jacques Plante, Montreal	1982-83 Pete Peeters, Boston
1959-60 Jacques Plante, Montreal	1983-84 Tom Barrasso, Buffalo
1960-61 Johnny Bower, Toronto	1984-85 Pelle Lindbergh, Philadelphia
1961-62 Jacques Plante, Montreal	1985-86 John Vanbiesbrouck, NYR
1962-63 Glenn Hall, Chicago	1986-87 Ron Hextall, Philadelphia
1963-64 Charlie Hodge, Montreal	

ART ROSS TROPHY

Awarded to the player who compiles the highest number of scoring points during the regular season.

If players are tied for the lead, the trophy is awarded to the one with the most goals. If still tied, it is given to the player with the fewer number of games played. If these do not break the deadlock, the trophy is presented to the player who scored his first goal of the season at the earliest date.

The trophy was presented by Art Ross, the former manager-coach of the Boston Bruins, to the NHL in 1947.

Season	Player and Clubs	Games Played	Goals	Assists	Points
1917-18	Joe Malone, Mtl. Canadiens	20	44	–	44
1918-19	Newsy Lalonde, Mtl. Canadiens	17	23	9	32
1919-20	Joe Malone, Quebec	24	39	9	48
1920-21	Newsy Lalonde, Mtl. Canadiens	24	33	8	41
1921-22	Punch Broadbent, Ottawa	24	32	14	46
1922-23	Babe Dye, Toronto	22	26	11	37
1923-24	Cy Denneny, Ottawa	21	22	1	23
1924-25	Babe Dye, Toronto	29	38	6	44
1925-26	Nels Stewart, Montreal	36	34	8	42
1926-27	Bill Cook, N.Y. Rangers	44	33	4	37
1927-28	Howie Morenz, Mtl. Canadiens	43	33	18	51
1928-29	Ace Bailey, Toronto	44	22	10	32
1929-30	Cooney Weiland, Boston	44	43	30	73
1930-31	Howie Morenz, Mtl. Canadiens	39	28	23	51
1931-32	Harvey Jackson, Toronto	48	28	25	53
1932-33	Bill Cook, N.Y. Rangers	48	28	22	50
1933-34	Charlie Conacher, Toronto	42	32	20	52
1934-35	Charlie Conacher, Toronto	48	36	21	57
1935-36	Dave Schriner, N.Y. Americans	48	19	26	45
1936-37	Dave Schriner, N.Y. Americans	48	21	25	46
1937-38	Gordie Drillon, Toronto	48	26	26	52
1938-39	Toe Blake, Mtl. Canadiens	48	24	23	47
1939-40	Milt Schmidt, Boston	48	22	30	52
1940-41	Bill Cowley, Boston	46	17	45	62
1941-42	Bryan Hextall, N.Y. Rangers	48	24	32	56
1942-43	Doug Bentley, Chicago	50	33	40	73
1943-44	Herbie Cain, Boston	48	36	46	82
1944-45	Elmer Lach, Montreal	50	26	54	80
1945-46	Max Bentley, Chicago	47	31	30	61
1946-47	Max Bentley, Chicago	60	29	43	72
1947-48	Elmer Lach, Montreal	60	30	31	61
1948-49	Roy Conacher, Chicago	60	26	42	68
1949-50	Ted Lindsay, Detroit	69	23	55	78
1950-51	Gordie Howe, Detroit	70	43	43	86
1951-52	Gordie Howe, Detroit	70	47	39	86
1952-53	Gordie Howe, Detroit	70	49	46	95
1953-54	Gordie Howe, Detroit	70	33	48	81

Season	Player and Clubs	Games Played	Goals	Assists	Points
1954-55	Bernie Geoffrion, Montreal	70	38	37	75
1955-56	Jean Beliveau, Montreal	70	47	41	88
1956-57	Gordie Howe, Detroit	70	44	45	89
1957-58	Dickie Moore, Montreal	70	36	48	84
1958-59	Dickie Moore, Montreal	70	41	55	96
1959-60	Bobby Hull, Chicago	70	39	42	81
1960-61	Bernie Geoffrion, Montreal	64	50	45	95
1961-62	Bobby Hull, Chicago	70	50	34	84
1962-63	Gordie Howe, Detroit	70	38	48	86
1963-64	Stan Mikita, Chicago	70	39	50	89
1964-65	Stan Mikita, Chicago	70	28	59	87
1965-66	Bobby Hull, Chicago	65	54	43	97
1966-67	Stan Mikita, Chicago	70	35	62	97
1967-68	Stan Mikita, Chicago	72	40	47	87
1968-69	Phil Esposito, Boston	74	49	77	126
1969-70	Bobby Orr, Boston	76	33	87	120
1970-71	Phil Esposito, Boston	76	76	76	152
1971-72	Phil Esposito, Boston	76	66	67	133
1972-73	Phil Esposito, Boston	78	55	75	130
1973-74	Phil Esposito, Boston	78	68	77	145
1974-75	Bobby Orr, Boston	80	46	89	135
1975-76	Guy Lafleur, Montreal	80	56	69	125
1976-77	Guy Lafleur, Montreal	80	56	80	136
1977-78	Guy Lafleur, Montreal	78	60	72	132
1978-79	Bryan Trottier, New York I.	76	47	87	134
1979-80	Marcel Dionne, Los Angeles	80	53	84	137
1980-81	Wayne Gretzky, Edmonton	80	55	109	164
1981-82	Wayne Gretzky, Edmonton	80	92	120	212
1982-83	Wayne Gretzky, Edmonton	80	71	125	196
1983-84	Wayne Gretzky, Edmonton	74	87	118	205
1984-85	Wayne Gretzky, Edmonton	80	73	135	208
1985-86	Wayne Gretzky, Edmonton	80	52	163	215
1986-87	Wayne Gretzky, Edmonton	79	62	121	183

JACK ADAMS AWARD

Awarded by the National Hockey League Broadcasters' Association to the "NHL coach adjudged to have contributed the most to his team's success." It is presented in the memory of the late Jack Adams, longtime coach and general manager of the Detroit Red Wings.

1973-74 Fred Shero, Philadelphia
1974-75 Bob Pulford, Los Angeles
1975-76 Don Cherry, Boston
1976-77 Scotty Bowman, Montreal
1977-78 Bobby Kromm, Detroit
1978-79 Al Arbour, New York I.
1979-80 Pat Quinn, Philadelphia

1980-81 Red Berenson, St. Louis
1981-82 Tom Watt, Winnipeg
1982-83 Orval Tessier, Chicago
1983-84 Bryan Murray, Washington
1984-85 Mike Keenan, Philadelphia
1985-86 Glen Sather, Edmonton
1986-87 Jacques Demers, Detroit

FRANK J. SELKE TROPHY

Awarded to the forward "who best excels in the defensive aspects of the game."

The trophy was presented to the NHL in 1977 by the Board of Governors in honor of Frank J. Selke, a "Builder" member of the Hall of Fame who spent more than 60 years in the game as coach, manager and front-office executive.

1977-78 Bob Gainey, Montreal	1982-83 Bobby Clarke, Philadelphia
1978-79 Bob Gainey, Montreal	1983-84 Doug Jarvis, Washington
1979-80 Bob Gainey, Montreal	1984-85 Craig Ramsey, Buffalo
1980-81 Bob Gainey, Montreal	1985-86 Troy Murray, Chicago
1981-82 Steve Kasper, Boston	1986-87 Dave Poulin, Philadelphia

WILLIAM M. JENNINGS AWARD

Awarded to the goalie or goalies for the team which gives up the fewest goals during the regular season. To be eligible, a goalie must play at least 25 games.

The trophy was presented to the NHL in 1982 in memory of William M. Jennings, an architect of the league's expansion from six teams to the present 21.

1981-82 Denis Herron, Montreal	1984-85 Tom Barrasso, Buffalo
Rick Wamsley, Montreal	Bob Sauve, Buffalo
1982-83 Billy Smith, New York I.	1985-86 Bob Froese, Philadelphia
Roland Melanson, New York I.	Darren Jensen, Philadelphia
1983-84 Al Jensen, Washington	1986-87 Bryan Hayward, Montreal
Pat Riggin, Washington	Patrick Roy, Montreal

BILL MASTERTON TROPHY

Awarded by the Professional Hockey Writers' Association to "the NHL player who exemplifies the qualities of preseverance, sportsmanship and dedication to hockey." Named for the late Minnesota North Star player.

1967-68 Claude Provost, Montreal	1977-78 Butch Goring, Los Angeles
1968-69 Ted Hampson, Oakland	1978-79 Serge Savard, Montreal
1969-70 Pit Martin, Chicago	1979-80 Al MacAdam, Minnesota
1970-71 Jean Ratelle, New York R.	1980-81 Blake Dunlop, St. Louis
1971-72 Bobby Clarke, Philadelphia	1981-82 Glenn Resch, Colorado
1972-73 Lowell MacDonald, Pittsburgh	1982-83 Lanny McDonald, Calgary
1973-74 Henri Richard, Montreal	1983-84 Brad Park, Detroit
1974-75 Don Luce, Buffalo	1984-85 Anders Hedberg, New York R.
1975-76 Rod Gilbert, New York R.	1985-86 Charlie Simmer, Boston
1976-77 Ed Westfall, New York I.	1986-87 Doug Jarvis, Hartford

CONN SMYTHE TROPHY

Awarded to the Most Valuable Player in the Stanley Cup playoffs. Selected in a vote of the League Governors.

The trophy was presented by Maple Leaf Gardens Ltd. in 1964 to honor the former coach, manager, president and owner of the Toronto Maple Leafs.

1953-54 Red Kelly, Detroit	1970-71 Bobby Orr, Boston
1954-55 Doug Harvey, Montreal	1971-72 Bobby Orr, Boston
1955-56 Doug Harvey, Montreal	1972-73 Bobby Orr, Boston
1956-57 Doug Harvey, Montreal	1973-74 Bobby Orr, Boston
1957-58 Doug Harvey, Montreal	1974-75 Bobby Orr, Boston
1958-59 Tom Johnson, Montreal	1975-76 Denis Potvin, New York I.
1959-60 Doug Harvey, Montreal	1976-77 Larry Robinson, Montreal
1960-61 Doug Harvey, Montreal	1977-78 Denis Potvin, New York I.
1961-62 Doug Harvey, New York R.	1978-79 Denis Potvin, New York I.
1962-63 Pierre Pilote, Chicago	1979-80 Larry Robinson, Montreal
1963-64 Pierre Pilote, Chicago	1980-81 Randy Carlyle, Pittsburgh
1964-65 Pierre Pilote, Chicago	1981-82 Doug Wilson, Chicago
1965-66 Jacques Laperriere, Montreal	1982-83 Rod Langway, Washington
1966-67 Harry Howell, New York R.	1983-84 Rod Langway, Washington
1967-68 Bobby Orr, Boston	1984-85 Paul Coffey, Edmonton
1968-69 Bobby Orr, Boston	1985-86 Paul Coffey, Edmonton
1969-70 Bobby Orr, Boston	1986-87 Ray Bourque, Boston

CONN SMYTHE TROPHY

Awarded to the Most Valuable Player in the Stanley Cup playoffs. Selected in a vote of the League Governors.

The rophy was presented by Maple Leaf Gardens Ltd. in 1964 to honor the former coach, manager, president and owner of the Toronto Maple Leafs.

1964-65 Jean Beliveau, Montreal	1976-77 Guy Lafleur, Montreal
1965-66 Roger Crozier, Detroit	1977-78 Larry Robinson, Montreal
1966-67 Dave Keon, Toronto	1978-79 Bob Gainey, Montreal
1967-68 Glenn Hall, St. Louis	1979-80 Bryan Trottier, New York I.
1968-69 Serge Savard, Montreal	1980-81 Butch Goring, New York I.
1969-70 Bobby Orr, Boston	1981-82 Mike Bossy, New York I.
1970-71 Ken Dryden, Montreal	1982-83 Billy Smith, New York I.
1971-72 Bobby Orr, Boston	1983-84 Mark Messier, Edmonton
1972-73 Yvan Cournoyer, Montreal	1984-85 Wayne Gretzky, Edmonton
1973-74 Bernie Parent, Philadelphia	1985-86 Patrick Roy, Montreal
1974-75 Bernie Parent, Philadelphia	1986-87 Ron Hextall, Philadelphia
1975-76 Reggie Leach, Philadelphia	

CALDER MEMORIAL TROPHY

Awarded to the league's outstanding rookie. Selected by a vote of hockey writers and broadcasters in each of the 21 NHL cities. It was originated in 1937 by Frank Calder, first president of the NHL. After his death in 1943, the league presented the Calder Memorial Trophy in his memory.

To be eligible to receive the trophy, a player cannot have participated in more than 20 games in any preceding season or in six or more games in each of any two preceding seasons.

Prior to 1936-37, top rookies were named but there was no trophy.

1932-33 Carl Voss, Detroit
1933-34 Russ Blinco, Montreal M.
1934-35 Dave Schriner, New York A.
1935-36 Mike Karakas, Chicago
1936-37 Syl Apps, Toronto
1937-38 Cully Dahlstrom, Chicago
1938-39 Frank Brimsek, Boston
1939-40 Kilby MacDonald, New York R.
1940-41 Johnny Quilty, Montreal C.
1941-42 Grant Warwick, New York R.
1942-43 Gaye Stewart, Toronto
1943-44 Gus Bodnar, Toronto
1944-45 Frank McCool, Toronto
1945-46 Edgar Laprade, New York R.
1946-47 Howie Meeker, Toronto
1947-48 Jim McFadden, Detroit
1948-49 Pentti Lund, New York R.
1949-50 Jack Gelineau, Boston
1950-51 Terry Sawchuk, Detroit
1951-52 Bernie Geoffrion, Montreal
1952-53 Lorne Worsley, New York R.
1953-54 Camille Henry, New York R.
1954-55 Ed Litzenberger, Chicago
1955-56 Glenn Hall, Detroit
1956-57 Larry Regan, Boston
1957-58 Frank Mahovlich, Toronto
1958-59 Ralph Backstrom, Montreal
1959-60 Bill Hay, Chicago

1960-61 Dave Keon, Toronto
1961-62 Bobby Rousseau, Montreal
1962-63 Kent Douglas, Toronto
1963-64 Jacques Laperriere, Montreal
1964-65 Roger Crozier, Detroit
1965-66 Brit Selby, Toronto
1966-67 Bobby Orr, Boston
1967-68 Derek Sanderson, Boston
1968-69 Danny Grant, Minnesota
1969-70 Tony Esposito, Chicago
1970-71 Gil Perreault, Buffalo
1971-72 Ken Dryden, Montreal
1972-73 Steve Vickers, New York R.
1973-74 Denis Potvin, New York I.
1974-75 Eric Vail, Atlanta
1975-76 Bryan Trottier, New York I.
1976-77 Willi Plett, Atlanta
1977-78 Mike Bossy, New York I.
1978-79 Bobby Smith, Minnesota
1979-80 Ray Bourque, Boston
1980-81 Peter Stastny, Quebec
1981-82 Dale Hawerchuk, Winnipeg
1982-83 Steve Larmer, Chicago
1983-84 Tom Barrasso, Buffalo
1984-85 Mario Lemieux, Pittsburgh
1985-86 Gary Suter, Calgary
1986-87 Luc Robitaille, Los Angeles

LADY BYNG TROPHY

Awarded to the player combining the highest type of sportsmanship and gentlemanly conduct plus a high standard of playing ability. Selected by a vote of hockey writers and broadcasters in the 21 NHL cities.

Lady Byng, the wife of the Governor-General of Canada in 1925, presented the trophy to the NHL during that year.

1924-25 Frank Nighbor, Ottawa	1956-57 Andy Hebenton, New York R.
1925-26 Frank Nighbor, Ottawa	1957-58 Camille Henry, New YorkR.
1926-27 Billy Burch, New York A.	1958-59 Alex Delvecchio, Detroit
1927-28 Frank Boucher, New York R.	1959-60 Don McKenney, Boston
1928-29 Frank Boucher, New York R.	1960-61 Red Kelly, Toronto
1929-30 Frank Boucher, New York R.	1961-62 Dave Keon, Toronto
1930-31 Frank Boucher, New York R.	1962-63 Dave Keon, Toronto
1931-32 Joe Primeau, Toronto	1963-64 Ken Wharram, Chicago
1932-33 Frank Boucher, New York R.	1964-65 Bobby Hull, Chicago
1933-34 Frank Boucher, New York R.	1965-66 Alex Delvecchio, Detroit
1934-35 Frank Boucher, New York R.	1966-67 Stan Mikita, Chicago
1935-36 Doc Romnes, Chicago	1967-68 Stan Mikita, Chicago
1936-37 Marty Barry, Detroit	1968-69 Alex Delvecchio, Detroit
1937-38 Gordie Drillon, Toronto	1969-70 Phil Goyette, St. Louis
1938-39 Clint Smith, New York R.	1970-71 Johnny Bucyk, Boston
1939-40 Bobby Bauer, Boston	1971-72 Jean Ratelle, New York R.
1940-41 Bobby Bauer, Boston	1972-73 Gil Perreault, Buffalo
1941-42 Syl Apps, Toronto	1973-74 John Bucyk, Boston
1942-43 Max Bentley, Chicago	1974-75 Marcel Dionne, Detroit
1943-44 Clint Smith, Chicago	1975-76 Jean Ratelle, New York R.
1944-45 Bill Mosienko, Chicago	1976-77 Marcel Dionne, Los Angeles
1945-46 Toe Blake, Montreal	1977-78 Butch Goring, Los Angeles
1946-47 Bobby Bauer, Boston	1978-79 Bob MacMillan, Atlanta
1947-48 Buddy O'Connor, New York R.	1979-80 Wayne Gretzky, Edmonton
1948-49 Bill Quackenbush, Detroit	1980-81 Rick Kehoe, Pittsburgh
1949-50 Edgar Laprade, New York R.	1981-82 Rick Middleton, Boston
1950-51 Red Kelly, Detroit	1982-83 Mike Bossy, New York I.
1951-52 Sid Smith, Toronto	1983-84 Mike Bossy, New York I.
1952-53 Red Kelly, Detroit	1984-85 Jari Kurri, Edmonton
1953-54 Red Kelly, Detroit	1985-86 Mike Bossy, New York I.
1954-55 Sid Smith, Toronto	1986-87 Joe Mullen, Calgary
1955-56 Earl Reibel, Detroit	

STANLEY CUP WINNERS

Season	Champions	Coach
1892-93	Montreal A.A.A.	
1894-95	Montreal Victorias	Mike Grant*
1895-96	Winnipeg Victorias	

* In the early years the teams were frequently run by the captain.
** Victoria defeated Quebec in challenge series. No official recognition.
*** In the spring of 1919 the Montreal Canadiens traveled to Seattle to meet Seattle, PCHL champions. After five games had been played—teams were tied at 2 wins each and 1 tie—the series was called off by the local Department of Health because of the influenza epidemic and the death from influenza of Joe Hall.

Season	Champions	Coach
1896-97	Montreal Victorias	Mike Grant*
1897-98	Montreal Victorias	F. Richardson
1898-99	Montreal Shamrocks	H. J. Trihey*
1899-00	Montreal Shamrocks	H. J. Trihey*
1900-01	Winnipeg Victorias	
1901-02	Montreal A.A.A.	R. R. Boon*
1902-03	Ottawa Silver Seven	A. T. Smith
1903-04	Ottawa Silver Seven	A. T. Smith
1904-05	Ottawa Silver Seven	A. T. Smith
1905-06	Montreal Wanderers	
1906-07	Kenora Thistles (January)	Tommy Phillips*
1906-07	Montreal Wanderers (March)	Cecil Blachford
1907-08	Montreal Wanderers	Cecil Blachford
1908-09	Ottawa Senators	Bruce Stuart*
1909-10	Montreal Wanderers	Pud Glass*
1910-11	Ottawa Senators	Bruce Stuart*
1911-12	Quebec Bulldogs	C. Nolan
**1912-13	Quebec Bulldogs	Joe Marlowe*
1913-14	Toronto Blue Shirts	Scotty Davidson*
1914-15	Vancouver Millionaires	Frank Patrick
1915-16	Montreal Canadiens	George Kennedy
1916-17	Seattle Metropolitans	Pete Muldoon
1917-18	Toronto Arenas	Dick Carroll
***1918-19	No decision.	
1919-20	Ottawa Senators	Pete Green
1920-21	Ottawa Senators	Pete Green
1921-22	Toronto St. Pats	Eddie Powers
1922-23	Ottawa Senators	Pete Green
1923-24	Montreal Canadiens	Leo Dandurand
1924-25	Victoria Cougars	Lester Patrick
1925-26	Montreal Maroons	Eddie Gerard
1926-27	Ottawa Senators	Dave Gill
1927-28	New York Rangers	Lester Patrick
1928-29	Boston Bruins	Cy Denneny
1929-30	Montreal Canadiens	Cecil Hart
1930-31	Montreal Canadiens	Cecil Hart
1931-32	Toronto Maple Leafs	Dick Irvin
1932-33	New York Rangers	Lester Patrick
1933-34	Chicago Black Hawks	Tommy Gorman
1934-35	Montreal Maroons	Tommy Gorman
1935-36	Detroit Red Wings	Jack Adams
1936-37	Detroit Red Wings	Jack Adams
1937-38	Chicago Black Hawks	Bill Stewart
1930-39	Boston Bruins	Art Ross
1939-40	New York Rangers	Frank Boucher
1940-41	Boston Bruins	Coon Weiland
1941-42	Toronto Maple Leafs	Hap Day
1942-43	Detroit Red Wings	Jack Adams
1943-44	Montreal Canadiens	Dick Irvin

Season	Champions	Coach
1944-45	Toronto Maple Leafs	Hap Day
1945-46	Montreal Canadiens	Dick Irvin
1946-47	Toronto Maple Leafs	Hap Day
1947-48	Toronto Maple Leafs	Hap Day
1949-50	Detroit Red Wings	Tommy Ivan
1950-51	Toronto Maple Leafs	Joe Primeau
1951-52	Detroit Red Wings	Tommy Ivan
1952-53	Montreal Canadiens	Dick Irvin
1953-54	Detroit Red Wings	Tommy Ivan
1954-55	Detroit Red Wings	Jimmy Skinner
1955-56	Montreal Canadiens	Toe Blake
1956-57	Montreal Canadiens	Toe Blake
1957-58	Montreal Canadiens	Toe Blake
1958-59	Montreal Canadiens	Toe Blake
1959-60	Montreal Canadiens	Toe Blake
1960-61	Chicago Black Hawks	Rudy Pilous
1961-62	Toronto Maple Leafs	Punch Imlach
1962-63	Toronto Maple Leafs	Punch Imlach
1963-64	Toronto Maple Leafs	Punch Imlach
1964-65	Montreal Canadiens	Toe Blake
1965-66	Montreal Canadiens	Toe Blake
1966-67	Toronto Maple Leafs	Punch Imlach
1967-68	Montreal Canadiens	Toe Blake
1968-69	Montreal Canadiens	Claude Ruel
1969-70	Boston Bruins	Harry Sinden
1970-71	Montreal Canadiens	Al MacNeil
1971-72	Boston Bruins	Tom Johnson
1972-73	Montreal Canadiens	Scotty Bowman
1973-74	Philadelphia Flyers	Fred Shero
1974-75	Philadelphia Flyers	Fred Shero
1975-76	Montreal Canadiens	Scotty Bowman
1976-77	Montreal Canadiens	Scotty Bowman
1977-78	Montreal Canadiens	Scotty Bowman
1978-79	Montreal Canadiens	Scotty Bowman
1979-80	New York Islanders	Al Arbour
1980-81	New York Islanders	Al Arbour
1981-82	New York Islanders	Al Arbour
1982-83	New York Islanders	Al Arbour
1983-84	Edmonton Oilers	Glen Sather
1984-85	Edmonton Oilers	Glen Sather
1985-86	Montreal Canadiens	Jean Perron
1986-87	Edmonton Oilers	Glen Sather

Official 1987-88 NHL Schedule

*Afternoon Game

Thur Oct 8
Wash at Bos
Que at Hart
Minn at Buff
Mont at Phil
NYI at LA
Pitt at NYR
Tor at Chi
Det at Calg
StL at Van

Fri Oct 9
Pitt at NJ
Det at Edm

Sat Oct 10
Bos at Que
NYR at Hart
Buff at Mont
NYI at Van
NJ at Tor
Phil at Minn
Chi at Wash
StL at LA
Winn at Calg

Sun Oct 11
Hart at Bos
Wash at Buff
Phil at Chi
Edm at LA

Mon Oct 12
Que at Mont
Minn at NYR
Det at Van
Calg at Winn

Tues Oct 13
Buff at Pitt

Wed Oct 14
Hart at NJ
Tor at Minn
StL at Chi
Calg at Edm

Thur Oct 15
Bos at LA
NYI at Phil
NYR at Pitt

Fri Oct 16
Hart at Wash
Que at Buff
Mont at NJ
Tor at Det
Edm at Calg

Sat Oct 17
Bos at Edm
NJ at Hart
Buff at Que
Pitt at Mont
Phil at NYI
NYR at Wash
Det at Tor
Chi at StL
Winn at Minn

Sun Oct 18
Bos at Calg
Pitt at Phil
Winn at Chi
Van at LA

Mon Oct 19
Minn at Mont
Wash at NYR

Tues Oct 20
Calg at NYI
Winn at StL

Wed Oct 21
Bos at Van
Hart at Buff
Mont at Tor
Calg at NYR
NJ at Pitt
Chi at Det
LA at Edm

Thur Oct 22
Minn at Que
Wash at Phil

Fri Oct 23
Mont at Buff
NYI at NJ
Chi at NYR
Pitt at Det
LA at Winn
Edm at Van

Sat Oct 24
Bos at StL
Chi at Hart
Buff at Pitt
Mont at Wash
Calg at Que
NJ at NYI
NYR at Phil
Minn at Tor
Van at Edm

Sun Oct 25
LA at Winn

Mon Oct 26
Calg at Mont
Phil at NYR

Tues Oct 27
Edm at Que
Chi at NYI
Phil at NJ
LA at Pitt
Wash at Van
Minn at StL

Wed Oct 28
Buff at Hart
Edm at Mont
NYI at Tor
LA at NYR
Det at Winn

Thur Oct 29
Que at Bos
Tor at Pitt
StL at Minn

Fri Oct 30
LA at Buff
Mont at Det
Wash at Winn
Calg at Van

Sat Oct 31
Bos at Mont
Phil at Hart
Pitt at Que
NYR at NYI
Edm at NJ
Wash at Minn
Chi at Tor
Det at StL

Sun Nov 1
NYI at Bos
Hart at Que
Chi at Buff
Edm at NYR
LA at Phil
Van at Winn

Mon Nov 2
StL at Mont

Tues Nov 3
StL at Que
NJ at NYI

**NYR at Calg
Phil at Pitt
Van at Wash
Minn at Det**

Wed Nov 4
Bos at Hart
Buff at LA
Mont at Chi
NYR at Edm
Winn at Tor
Det at Minn

Thur Nov 5
Tor at Bos
Pitt at NYI
StL at NJ
Van at Phil
Edm at Calg

Fri Nov 6
Hart at Det
Que at Wash
Chi at Winn

Sat Nov 7
Pitt at Bos
Que at Hart
Buff at Edm
Phil at Mont
Det at NYI
NYR at LA
Wash at NJ
StL at Tor
Van at Minn

Sun Nov 8
Buff at Calg
NJ at Phil
Minn at Chi
Van at Winn
Mon Nov 9
Bos at Que
Tor at Mont

Tues Nov 10
Wash at NYI
NJ at NYR
Phil at StL
Cal at Winn
Edm at LA

Wed Nov 11
Bos at Tor
Mont at Hart
Buff at Van
Wash at Pitt
Det at Chi
Calg at Minn

Thur Nov 12
Mont at Bos
NYI at Edm
Winn at NJ
Pitt at Phil

Fri Nov 13
Minn at Buff
Que at Van
LA at Calg

Sat Nov 14
Hart at Bos
Chi at Mont
Que at LA
Winn at NYI
NYR at Pitt
*Det at NJ
*Tor at Phil
Minn at Wash
Edm at StL

Sun Nov 15
Tor at Buff
Winn at NYR
Edm at Chi
Van at Calg

Mon Nov 16
Hart at Mont

Tues Nov 17
Bos at Calg
LA at NYI
Pitt at Van
Det at Wash

Wed Nov 18
Bos at Winn
Buff at Hart
NYI at Mont
Que at Edm
Phil at NJ
StL at Tor
Minn at Chi

Thur Nov 19
Que at Calg
NYR at Minn
LA at Phil
Tor at StL
Van at Det

Fri Nov 20
Wash at Buff
NYR at Winn
Chi at NJ
Pitt at Edm

Sat Nov 21
Bos at Minn
Wash at Hart
NJ at Mont
NYI at Phil
Pitt at Calg
LA at Tor
Van at StL

Sun Nov 22
Bos at Det
LA at Buff
Van at Chi
Edm at Winn

Mon Nov 23
Mont at Que
NJ at Calg

Tues Nov 24
Tor at NYI

Wed Nov 25
Bos at Wash
Mont at Hart
Buff at Phil
Que at Pitt
Tor at NYR
NJ at Edm
Winn at Det
Chi at LA
StL at Minn
Calg at Van

Thur Nov 26
Winn at Bos

Fri Nov 27
Hart at Buff
Mont at Minn
NJ at Van
Pitt at Wash
StL at Det
Chi at Edm

Sat Nov 28
Det at Bos
Hart at Tor
Mont at Winn
Phil at Que
NYR at NYI
Wash at Pitt
Minn at StL
Calg at LA

Sun Nov 29
Edm at Buff
NYI at NYR
NJ at LA

Mon Nov 30
Bos at Mont
Chi at Calg

Tues Dec 1
Van at Que
Edm at Wash

Sat Nov 21 (cont.)
Tor at Minn
Winn at LA

Wed Dec 2
Bos at Hart
Van at Mont
NYI at Pitt
Edm at Det
Chi at StL

Thur Dec 3
NYR at Bos
Hart at Phil
Que at Buff
StL at NJ
Tor at Calg
Winn at LA

Fri Dec 4
NYI at Wash
Chi at Det

Sat Dec 5
Chi at Bos
Buff at Hart
LA at Mont
NJ at Que
NYR at StL
Van at Phil
Tor at Edm
Minn at Calg

Sun Dec 6
Van at Buff
NJ at Phil
LA at Wash
Minn at Edm

Mon Dec 7
Det at Tor

Tues Dec 8
Bos at Phil
Hart at Que
Mont at NYI
Calg at Wash
Minn at Van

Wed Dec 9
Wash at Hart
Buff at Chi
Mont at NYR
LA at NJ
Calg at Pitt
StL at Det
Winn at Edm

Thur Dec 10
LA at Bos
NYR at Phil
StL at Minn

Fri Dec 11
Que at Winn
NYI at Pitt
Calg at NJ
Phil at Det
Van at Edm

Sat Dec 12
Buff at Bos
LA at Hart
Det at Mont
Que at Min
NJ at NYI
NYR at Tor
Pitt at StL
Chi at Wash
Edm at Van

Sun Dec 13
Calg at Buff
Phil at Winn
Tor at Chi

Mon Dec 14
Det at NYR

Tues Dec 15
Van at Hart
StL at NYI
Phil at Pitt
Wash at Tor

Wed Dec 16
Que at Mont
NJ at NYR
Wash at Det
Chi at Minn
Winn at Calg
Edm at LA

Thur Dec 17
Van at Bos
StL at Hart
NYI at Phil
Pitt at NJ

Fri Dec 18
Mont at Buff
Tor at Wash
Minn at Det
Winn at Edm

Sat Dec 19
*StL at Bos
Hart at Edm
Buff at Mont
Phil at NYI
NYR at Pitt
NJ at Minn
Chi at Tor
Calg at LA

Sun Dec 20
Bos at Chi
Hart at Van
*Det at Que
Pitt at NYR
NJ at Winn
*StL at Wash
LA at Calg

Mon Dec 21
Minn at Tor

Tues Dec 22
Buff at Bos

Sat Dec 12 (cont.)
Hart at Calg
Wash at Que
NYI at Winn
Phil at NYR
LA at Edm

Wed Dec 23
Buff at Det
Wash at Mont
NYI at Chi
NJ at Pltt
Minn at Phil
Tor at StL
LA at Van

Sat Dec 26
Bos at NYI
Que at Hart
Mont at Tor
*NYR at NJ
Phil at Wash
Det at Pitt
StL at Chi
Minn at Winn
Edm at Calg
Van at LA

Sun Dec 27
Bos at NYR
*Hart at Que
Pitt at Buff
Det at Minn
Chi at StL

Mon Dec 28
Mont at Calg
NYI at NJ
Wash at Tor
Winn at LA
Van at Edm

Tues Dec 29
Bos at Pitt
Buff at Que
Mont at Van
NYR at NYI

Wed Dec 30
Tor at Hart
Wash at NJ
Phil at Edm
Det at StL
Minn at Chi
Winn at LA

Thur Dec 31
Bos at Buff
Que at NYR
Phil at Calg
StL at Det
Chi at Minn
Winn at Van

Fri Jan 1
*Pitt at Wash

Sat Jan 2
*Que at Bos

Sat Dec 26 (cont.)
NJ at Hart
Buff at Tor
Mont at LA
Pitt at NYI
NYR at Minn
Phil at Van
*Edm at Wash
Calg at StL

Sun Jan 3
Que at Buff
Det at Winn
Calg at Chi

Mon Jan 4
Edm at Bos
StL at NYR
LA at NJ
Van at Tor

Tues Jan 5
Minn at NYI
Wash at Phil
LA at Pitt

Wed Jan 6
Edm at Hart
Buff at Mont
Que at Chi
Van at NYR
Minn at Tor
StL at Det
Winn at Calg

Thur Jan 7
Bos at Pitt
Van at NJ
StL at Phil

Fri Jan 8
Hart at Buff
NYI at Calg
NYR at Wash
Tor at Chi
LA at Det
Edm at Winn

Sat Jan 9
Bos at StL
Pitt at Hart
Phil at Mont
Van at Que
NYI at Edm
NJ at Minn

Sun Jan 10
NYR at Buff
NJ at Phil
Pitt at Det
Wash at Calg
Tor at Winn
LA at Chi

Mon Jan 11
Hart at Bos
Chi at NYR
Wash at Edm
LA at Minn

Tues Jan 12
Buff at StL
NYI at Pitt
Winn at Van

Wed Jan 13
Bos at Mont
Hart at Chi
Que at NJ
Det at NYR
Wash at LA
Tor at Minn
Winn at Van
Calg at Edm

Thur Jan 14
Mon at Bos
Hart at StL
Buff at Phil
Que at NYI

Fri Jan 15
Tor at NJ
Phil at Pitt
Minn at Det
Winn at Edm
Calg at Van

Sat Jan 16
*Buff at Bos
Hart at LA
NYR at Mont
Chi at Que
NJ at NYI
Pitt at Tor
Wash at StL
Det at Minn

Sun Jan 17
NYI at Buff
Phil at NYR
Wash at Chi
Van at Winn

Mon Jan 18
Edm at Mont
Tor at Det

Tues Jan 19
Hart at Minn
Edm at Que
Pitt at NYI
NYR at LA
NJ at Wash
StL at Winn
Van at Calg

Wed Jan 20
Bos at Buff
Pitt at Chi

Thur Jan 21
Minn at Bos
NYI at Hart
StL at Mont
Que at Tor
Det at NJ
Edm at Phil
LA at Calg

Fri Jan 22
NJ at Buff
NYR at Van
LA at Winn

Sat Jan 23
*Phil at Bos
Minn at Hart
Buff at Wash
Pitt at Mont
StL at Que
Edm at NYI
Chi at Tor
*Calg at Det

Sun Jan 24
Det at Hart
Mont at Que
Minn at Phil
Van at Chi
*LA at Winn

Mon Jan 25
Buff at NJ
Edm at Pitt
Calg at Tor

Tues Jan 26
LA at Que
Winn at Wash
Chi at Det
Van at StL

Wed Jan 27
Hart at Calg
Mont at Buff
NYI at Minn
Winn at Pitt
LA at Tor

Thur Jan 28
Que at Bos
NYR at Phil
Pitt at NJ
Minn at StL

Fri Jan 29
Hart at Van
NYI at Buff
Mont at Wash
Chi at NJ
Tor at Det
Calg at Edm

Sat Jan 30
*NYR at Bos
Hart at Edm
Mont at NYI
Que at StL
*Winn at Phil
Chi at Pitt
Det at Tor
Minn at LA
Van at Calg

Sun Jan 31
*Winn at Buff
*Phil at Wash

Mon Feb 1
Bos at Chi
Hart at Mont
NJ at Calg
StL at Tor

Tues Feb 2
Buff at Que
NYR at NYI
Wash at Pitt
LA at Van

Wed Feb 3
Mont at Hart
NJ at Edm
Det at Chi
StL at Minn
Calg at Winn
Van at LA

Thur Feb 4
Mont at Bos
NYR at Que
Tor at Phil
Minn at Pitt

Fri Feb 5
Tor at Buff
NYI at Wash
NJ at Van
Calg at Det
Chi at Winn

Sat Feb 6
*Bos at Que
Hart at Pitt
Buff at NYI
Det at Mont
NYR at Wash
Phil at StL
Winn at Minn
Edm at LA

Sun Feb 7
*NJ at Bos
Tor at Hart
*Chi at Que
*Pitt at NYR
Calg at LA

Tues Feb 9
All-Star Game
at StL

Thur Feb 11
Mont at NJ
Que at LA
NYI at Tor
Wash at NYR
Edm at Van

Fri Feb 12
Bos at Edm
Buff at Winn
NYI at Wash
NJ at Det
Calg at Phil
StL at Chi

Sat Feb 13
Bos at Van
Hart at Mont
Que at Minn
Phil at Tor
Pitt at LA
Det at StL

Sun Feb 14
*Buff at Chi
Que at Winn
*NYI at NYR
NJ at Tor
*Calg at Wash
Van at Edm

Mon Feb 15
*Hart at Phil
*Mont at NYR
*Det at LA

Tues Feb 16
Buff at StL
Winn at Que
Calg at NYI

Wed Feb 17
Bos at Mont
Winn at Hart
Calg at NYR
Wash at NJ
Pitt at Van
Tor at Edm
Det at Chi
LA at Minn

Thur Feb 18
NYI at Phil
LA at StL

Fri Feb 19
Phil at Buff
NYR at NJ
Pitt at Edm
Wash at Winn
Tor at Van

Sat Feb 20
Hart at NYI
Que at Mont
Wash at Minn
Tor at LA
*Chi at Det
Calg at StL

Sun Feb 21
*Bos at NJ
NYI at Hart
Que at Buff
Van at NYR
*Det at Phil
StL at Pitt
Calg at Chi
*Edm at Winn

Mon Feb 22
Tor at Minn

Tues Feb 23
Bos at Hart
Mont at Que
Van at NYI
Phil at Det
Winn at Pitt
Edm at StL

Wed Feb 24
Van at Mont
Winn at NJ
Wash at LA
Minn at Tor
Edm at Chi

Thur Feb 25
Hart at Bos
StL at Buff
Chi at NYI
Pitt at NYR

Fri Feb 26
Que at Det
NYR at NJ
Calg at Van

Sat Feb 27
*Minn at Bos
Buff at Hart
Winn at Mont
Det at Que
Wash at NYI
Phil at LA
StL at Tor

Sun Feb 28
Winn at Buff
*Minn at NJ
*Pitt at Chi
Calg at Edm
LA at Van

Mon Feb 29
Mont at Que
StL at NYR

Tues Mar 1
Hart at Winn
Buff at Det
StL at NYI
NJ at Wash
Phil at Van
Minn at Pitt
LA at Edm

Wed Mar 2
Hart at Chi
Que at Tor
NYI at NYR
Wash at NJ

Thur Mar 3
Tor at Bos
Mont at StL
Phil at Calg
Minn at Det
Van at Winn

Fri Mar 4
NYR at Buff
Que at Wash
Phil at Edm

Sat Mar 5
*NJ at Bos
NYR at Hart
Mont at LA
*NYI at Pitt
Winn at Tor
Det at StL
Chi at Minn
Edm at Calg

Sun Mar 6
Bos at Buff
*NYI at Que
*Phil at NJ
*Van at Wash
Det at Chi

Mon Mar 7
Pitt at Calg
Edm at Winn

Tues Mar 8
Bos at Det
Hart at Que
Van at NYI
NJ at NYR
Tor at StL

Wed Mar 9
LA at Hart
Buff at Minn
Mont at Edm
Tor at Chi
Calg at Winn

Thur Mar 10
LA at Bos
Que at NYI
Wash at Phil
Pitt at StL
Van at Det
Winn at Calg

Sat Mar 12
Bos at Que
Hart at Mont
Buff at Calg
Det at NYI
NYR at Wash
*NJ at Phil
*Pitt at Minn
Chi at Tor
Edm at Van

Sun Mar 13
Wash at Bos
Que at Hart
Buff at Van
NYI at Det
Phil at Chi
*Pitt at Winn
StL at LA

Mon Mar 14
Mont at Minn

Tues Mar 15
Calg at Hart
Buff at Edm
Tor at Que
Phil at NYR
Chi at StL

Wed Mar 16
Mont at Winn
Wash at NYR
Tor at Pitt
Det at Minn
Van at LA

Thur Mar 17
Calg at Bos
Que at NJ
Chi at Phil
Minn at StL

Fri Mar 18
NYI at Wash
Winn at Edm
LA at Van

Sat Mar 19
*Buff at Bos
Hart at StL
Chi at Mont
Calg at Que
NYR at Tor
Phil at Pitt
Det at LA

Sun Mar 20
Bos at Buff
Hart at NYR
*NYI at Winn
*NJ at Wash
Pitt at Phil
StL at Chi
Edm at Minn

Mon Mar 21
Calg at Mont
NYI at Minn

Tues Mar 22
Bos at Phil
Winn at Hart
Buff at NYR
StL at Wash
Tor at Van
Edm at Det

Wed Mar 23
Que at Mont
NYI at LA
Wash at Pitt
Minn at Chi

Thur Mar 24
Winn at Bos
Hart at Det

Fri Mar 25
NJ at Buff
Mon at Pitt
Phil at Wash
Chi at Van

Sat Mar 26
*Que at Bos
Minn at Hart
Edm at NYI
*NYR at Det
Winn at Phil
Tor at StL
Chi at LA
Van at Calg

Sun Mar 27
Mont at Hart
Det at Buff
*Pitt at Que
*NYR at NJ

Mon Mar 28
Edm at Tor
Chi at Minn
StL at Calg

Tues Mar 29
Buff at Que
Phil at NYI
Pitt at NJ
Det at Wash
Winn at Van

Wed Mar 30
NYR at Chi
Minn at Edm
Calg at LA

Thur Mar 31
Mont at Bos
Hart at Buff
Que at Phil
Wash at NYI
NJ at Pitt

Fri Apr 1
NYR at Winn
Tor at Det
StL at Edm
Minn at Van
LA at Calg

Sat Apr 2
Bos at Hart
Buff at Mont
Phil at Que
*NYI at NJ
Pitt at Wash
Det at Tor

Sun Apr 3
NYI at Bos
Hart at Pitt

Mont at Buff
Que at NYR
NJ at Chi
Wash at Phil
*StL at Winn
*Minn at Calg
LA at Edm

Revised and updated with over 75 all
new sports records and photographs!

THE ILLUSTRATED
SPORTS RECORD BOOK
Zander Hollander and David Schulz

Here in a single book are more than 350
all-time sports records with stories and
photos so vivid it's like "being there." All the
sports classics are here: Babe Ruth, Wilt
Chamberlain, Muhammad Ali . . . plus the
stories of such active stars as Dwight Gooden
and Wayne Gretzky. This is the authoritative
book on what the great records are, and
who set them—an engrossing, fun-filled
reference guide filled with anecdotes of
hundreds of renowned athletes whose
remarkable records remain as fresh as when
they were set.